FORSYTH LIBRARY
2 1765 0056 4808 7

James G. Birney.

JAMES G. BIRNEY AND HIS TIMES

THE GENESIS OF THE REPUBLICAN PARTY
WITH SOME ACCOUNT OF
ABOLITION MOVEMENTS IN THE SOUTH BEFORE 1828

BY

WILLIAM BIRNEY

EX-BREVET MAJOR-GENERAL, UNITED STATES VOLUNTEERS

The abolition of slavery in the United States was neither an accident nor a miracle; it was a result of evolution.

NEGRO UNIVERSITIES PRESS
NEW YORK

Originally published in 1890
by D. Appleton and Company

Reprinted 1969 by
Negro Universities Press
A Division of Greenwood Publishing Corp.
New York

SBN 8371-1313-X

PRINTED IN UNITED STATES OF AMERICA

TO

THE STUDENTS OF AMERICAN HISTORY

THIS CONTRIBUTION TO ITS MATERIAL

IS RESPECTFULLY DEDICATED.

PREFACE.

SLAVERY agitation in the United States may be considered in two great periods. The first begins with the judicial abolition of slavery in Massachusetts in 1783, and the anti-slavery Ordinance of 1787 for the government of the Territory northwest of the Ohio River, and ends with the abolition of slavery in New York on the 4th of July, 1827. In its course the number of free States increased from one to twelve, and the number of freedmen nearly three hundred fold. It may be called the *abolition era.* It was a part of the larger movement which began in 1794 with the abolition of slavery in the French West Indies, extinguished it in numerous European colonies and several South American republics, and ended with its abolition in Mexico in 1829, and in the British West Indies in 1833 by act of Parliament.

The second period begins with the accession of General Jackson to the presidency in 1829, and ends with the abolition of slavery in the War of the Rebellion.

In the first period freedom was the assailant of slavery, seeking to extinguish it by moral and religious influences. In the second, the slave-power was the assailant, seeking to overthrow the freedom of speech, of the press, and of the mails, the right of trial by jury, the right of petition, and every other bulwark of civil liberty to extend slavery over the Territories of the United States and gain undisputed political supremacy in the nation.

It was JAMES G. BIRNEY who first called abolitionists away from obsolete issues to the true one. In the summer of 1835 he abandoned his Southern home and removed to Ohio, declaring that the slavery of the blacks had ceased to be the question before the country, and that the liberties of all American citizens and the safety of the republic were in danger. During the following ten years he was recognized by the opponents of the slave-power as their leader. In 1840, and again in 1844, he was made their candidate for the presidency by unanimous national conventions. No other name seems to have been thought of in connection with the nomination. His cordial admirer, ex-Representative George W. Julian, of Indiana, writes of him and his co-workers:

> Abolitionism, as a working force in our politics, had to have a beginning, and no man who cherishes the memory of the old Free-Soil party, and of the larger one to which it gave birth, will withhold the meed of his praise from the heroic little band of sappers and miners who blazed the way for the armies which were to follow, and whose voices, though but faintly heard in the whirlwind of 1840, were made distinctly audible in 1844. . . . Their political creed was substantially that of the Free-Soilers of 1848 and the Republicans of 1856 and 1860. They were anything but political fanatics, and history will record that their sole offense was the espousal of the truth in advance of the multitude, which slowly and finally followed in their footsteps.

James G. Birney was respected even by the enemies of his cause. He was universally regarded as without fear and without stain. The only charge ever made against him by any reputable person was of faithlessness to Henry Clay, in the campaign of 1844; and that was made by Horace Greeley in the white heat of his disappointment at the failure of the Whig campaign. Mr. Greeley afterward retracted it. Mr. Julian says of those who voted for Mr. Birney:

Now, in the clear perspective of history, they stand vindicated against their Whig assailants, whose fevered brains and party intolerance blinded their eyes to the truth ("Political Recollections," 1884, p. 43).

Hon. Carl Schurz is eminently fair in his treatment of this subject. He says, in his admirable biography of Henry Clay:

The Liberty party consisted of earnest anti-slavery men who pursued their objects by political action. They were not in sympathy with those abolitionists who lost themselves in "no-government" theories, who denounced the Union and the Constitution as a "covenant with death and agreement with hell," and who abhorred the exercise of the suffrage under the Constitution as a participation in sin. In the language of Birney, they "regarded the national Constitution with unabated affection" (vol. ii, page 253).

And again:

Birney, its candidate for the presidency, was a native of Kentucky. A slaveholder by inheritance, he liberated his slaves and provided generously for them. He was a lawyer of ability, a gentleman of culture, and a vigorous and graceful speaker. Obeying a high sense of duty, he sacrificed the comforts of wealth, home, and position to the cause of universal freedom—not as a wild enthusiast or unreasoning fanatic, but as a calm thinker, temperate in language, and firm in maintaining his conclusions. His principal conclusion was that *slavery and free institutions could not exist together.* He has been charged with committing an act of personal faithlessness in opposing Clay in 1844. This charge was utterly unjust. He had never given Clay or Clay's friends any promise of support. It is true, Clay and Birney had maintained a friendly intercourse until 1834; but in June of that year they had a conference on the subject of slavery which produced upon Birney a discouraging effect. From that time their friendly intercourse ceased, and Clay found in Birney only a severe critic (Schurz's "Henry Clay," vol. ii, page 254).

And again:

> The object of Henry Clay's highest ambition escaped him because, at the decisive moment, he was untrue to himself (ib., page 265).

For forty years after the sudden close of his political career the fame of James G. Birney escaped detraction. Numerous biographical sketches of him were published in magazines, cyclopædias, and newspapers; and to the tone of none of them could the most sensitive of his friends take exception. The unfriendly feeling of Mr. Garrison toward him was no secret in the anti-slavery world; but the most devoted of Mr. Garrison's friends did not appear to share it. No praise of Mr. Birney was more cordial or appreciative than that bestowed on him by Samuel J. May, Oliver Johnson, and Parker Pillsbury. The first devotes to eulogistic narrative of him more than eight pages of his "Recollections of the Anti-Slavery Conflict" (pages 203–211); the second indorses Mr. May's most eulogistic language, and adds that he was "a calm, dignified, and cultured gentleman and Christian"; and the third, in his curious volume, "Acts of the Anti-Slavery Apostles," mentions him many times and always in the most kindly temper. With such a consensus of favorable appreciation, there seemed to be no special need of a biography of James G. Birney. It transpired, however, about 1883, that the sons of Mr. Garrison were preparing an ample memoir of their father—a work which, from a filial standpoint, involved the reproduction and expression of Mr. Garrison's theories and prejudices. The first two volumes of the memoir appeared in 1885. They were noticed as follows by Hon. A. G. Riddle, of Ohio, ex-Representative in Congress, in his book "The Life of Benjamin F. Wade," ex-United States Senator, published at Cleveland in 1886:

To claim the arousing and marshaling of the force of the mind and conscience of the men of the North against slavery, as pre-eminently the work of one man, is a totally unwarranted assumption. There is a way of writing history lately attempted which, if accepted without protest, would for the time seem to accomplish this thing. The writers of the biography of the late W. L. Garrison rely quite extensively upon his "Liberator" for authority, and, thus sustained, there really was but one champion of God and freedom in the North. Should the sons of the late J. G. Birney accept the challenge, work as largely and as narrowly, drawing their authority from a similar source, they would for him make a case every whit as strong. Neither work would be accepted finally as history ; both would be great contributions to it, of value beyond estimation. This last work should be at once set about. It would have this unequaled advantage—slavery was overthrown *by political means*. Mr. Garrison refused their use, opposed with the might of his trenchant pen and resounding voice their employment and the men who used them.

Mr. Birney was among the first to see that the most effective single thing was the employment of political power, backed of course by all the moral forces. *He was the first to employ it.* He, too, was a candidate for the presidency in 1840.

He was hewn from the mountains, rejected of politicians, to become— But I am not to anticipate. He was placed in the field largely by the clear-seeing Myron Holley, . . . and received but 7,059 votes, provoking gibes and sneers from the Whigs, derision and sarcasm from Garrison. They were allies against Birney ("Life of Wade," page 158).

The "Life of William Lloyd Garrison" by his sons is in four large octavo volumes, the last two having been published in October last. They are the product of the labor of years, and, in the numerous notes and painfully minute references to authorities, most of them to the "Liberator," indicate that they were intended for students of history in public libraries rather than for the general reader. They may be regarded as in the nature of a legal brief, filed for posterity, in behalf of William Lloyd Garrison, against the American people, the South, the West, the Union, the Church, the clergy, the press, Benjamin Lundy, James G. Birney, and all other political abolitionists.

As the sons of Mr. Garrison have unequaled facilities for "sifting" their theories and filial claims into the public mind, being literary men by profession and connected as editors, contributors, readers, and managers, with publishing houses, magazines, and metropolitan newspapers, surviving political abolitionists can not afford to let their brief go without answer or protest. In the present volume, written in moments taken from the cares of an exacting profession, the writer has sought to correct their mistakes and errors, and to substitute a true for a false theory of the anti-slavery and slavery movements. Upon the issues made he invokes the impartial judgment of the men who write American history. If he shall not have the good fortune to win their attention and verdict, he trusts that the general reader will rise from the perusal of this book with clearer views of the strong currents of political opinion that preceded the Great Rebellion, and with increased respect and admiration for the men who dared for the liberties of this people to begin the battle with the Slave-Power, but who died before the victory was won.

Speak, History, who are Life's victors? Unroll thy long annals and say—
Are they those whom the world called the victors—who won the success of a day?
The martyrs or Nero? The Spartans who fell at Thermopylæ's tryst,
Or the Persians and Xerxes? His judges or Socrates? Pilate or Christ?

WASHINGTON, D. C., *December 15, 1889.*

CONTENTS.

JAMES G. BIRNEY AND HIS TIMES.

CHAPTER I.

THE ANCESTORS.

THE subject of this sketch was of pure Protestant Scotch-Irish descent. His ancestors on both sides belonged to that distinct type of mankind created by two centuries of civil wars and exclusive intermarriages out of the native Irishmen who had followed Henry VIII into the Church of England and the Scotch colonists of James I, with some intermixture of Englishmen and Huguenot exiles. It was confined to the nine counties in the north-eastern part of Ireland which are known as the province of Ulster; and, by its intelligence, thrift, industry, and inventive talent, has made that province one of the great manufacturing centers of the world. It has furnished to the United States many of the strong men who have helped to shape republican institutions. Among these may be named Andrew Jackson, John C. Calhoun, the Shelbys, the Logans, the McDowells, A. T. Stewart, and Horace Greeley—all distinguished for ability, energy, moral courage, and tenacity of purpose. With the aid of O'Hart's elaborate work on Irish pedigrees, the author might trace the genealogy of James Gillespie Birney to a remote period, finding some historical characters among his progenitors; but the facts, even if established, possess no anthropological value. Although it is true that each man is the result of converging hereditary forces, these are too numerous for examination, the ancestors within ten generations exceeding two thousand. It will be enough for the purposes of this book to give a few authentic data respecting the grandparents and parents.

The paternal grandfather owned the old family homestead near Cootehill, County Cavan. He was a prosperous farmer and miller, a church vestryman, a magistrate, and influential in local affairs. His wife was a member of the Church of England, and a woman of strongly marked character. There were several children.

The maternal grandfather was John Read, a native of Londonderry. Inheriting wealth and high social position, he had been liberally educated, and had traveled in foreign countries. His tall and graceful person, handsome features, ruddy complexion, blond hair, culture, and courtly manners made him a remarkable individual. For his grandson James he always had a strong affection, and, for several years, he made the boy his companion and pupil. His migration to the United States was a consequence of the discovery of some political intrigue of his against the British Government. He was in Kentucky as early as 1779. In that year he built a fort, about two miles from Danville, and a mansion which remains to this day. He married Lettice Wilcox. Their youngest son, Thomas B. Read, was, in 1826, United States Senator from Missisipi. Their daughters were carefully educated; they were all well married, and among their descendants are found many of the distinguished men of Kentucky, including Judge John Green, Judge Thomas Green, Rev. Lewis W. Green, D. D., Dr. Willis G. Craig, Dr. Edwards, of St. Louis, and General Humphrey Marshall. Mr. Read was remarkable for conversational talent, and some of the most able men of Kentucky were often his guests. It was in his parlors that his grandson received much of the kind of education given to youth by the conversation of the wise.

CHAPTER II.

THE FATHER.

James Gillespie Birney was an only son. When he was three years old his mother died, leaving him and an infant sister to the care of the father. The surviving parent did all a strong and rugged man could do to supply the place of maternal tenderness. The bright and sturdy boy awakened a strong paternal pride; and before he had learned his letters the father had marked out for him a course of training and studies with a well-formed intention to make of him a lawyer and statesman; and this course, with unimportant modifications, was afterwards persistently adhered to. This singular devotion was an important factor in the formation of the character of the son, and justifies an account of the father which in most biographies would be too minute.

In September, 1783, an adventurous Irish lad of sixteen, whose imagination was aglow with the glories of the young American republic, left secretly his father's comfortable home in the County Cavan, and embarked at Dublin for Philadelphia. He had little baggage and less money, but he was broad-shouldered and active, with a manly bearing and pleasing address. On the day of his arrival in Philadelphia, with no recommendation except intelligence and a clerkly handwriting, he obtained employment in a wholesale and retail dry-goods' house. There he remained until he was twenty-one years of age, working his way up until he was the leading employé of the firm.

Choosing the frontier settlement of Kentucky as his future home, he obtained a stock of goods in Philadelphia on credit, and, in the autumn of 1788, opened a store at Danville, which was then the leading town in Kentucky trade, politics, religion, and social life. Each year thereafter, until the Pennsylvania Canal was ready for use and steamboat navigation on the Ohio had facilitated the transportation of merchandise from the East to Kentucky, the young merchant traversed the great wilderness with an armed party, camping out at night and sleeping on his rifle, purchased his stock in Philadelphia, and conveyed it to Danville, using for part of the route covered wagons drawn by Conestoga horses, but for the roadless mountains and forests pack-horses and mules. The difficulties and dangers of this mode of transportation at that time required courage and energy on the part of the frontier merchant. As he prospered he established a branch store at Stamford and a bagging factory, with ropewalk, at Danville. He organized and became president of the local bank, and conducted it successfully for a great many years, turning it over to his successor in thrifty and sound condition. During the War of 1812 he was a contractor on a large scale for furnishing supplies to the Western army. All his business engagements were promptly met. A note with his name on it was never protested. His business enterprises were uniformly successful. For many years he was reputed to be the richest man in Kentucky, and one of the most cordial in his hospitality. His estate of Woodlawn, the front gate of which was but a short half-mile from Danville, was as beautiful as blue-grass slopes, noble forest trees, and good taste in landscape could make it. The view from the house was through the glades and avenues of a noble park. In the march of improvement railroads have so intersected this property, and houses have been so built upon it, that the original landmarks have disappeared. His winter residence was a large brick mansion in Danville.

In his day, James Birney was one of the noted men of Kentucky. From one end of the State to the other his name was familiar in every household. His sayings were quoted where he was not personally known. His character was strongly marked. Any old citizen of that State will remember him as a very positive man. He had no quality of a trimmer. One knew always where to find him. No one ever doubted that he would be true to his friends, or imagined that he would give back a hair's-breadth before his enemies. His courage, both moral and physical, had been proved in the numerous emergencies of frontier life. He was full of generous impulses; easily excited by meanness or disingenuousness; strong in his personal attachments; quick in his resentments; and frank, bold, and vehement in asserting a right or declaring an opinion. He took great interest in studying theories of government and the causes of the rise and fall of nations. The "Federalist" was his favorite book, and next to it, Gibbon's "Rome." In politics he was a Conservative, with Federalist tendencies. Washington was his *beau ideal* of a patriot and statesman, and Chief Justice Marshall of a judge. He dissected Jefferson and his opinions with a rough-edged scalpel. He believed cordially in a protective tariff, and cherished the warmest friendship, political and personal, for its advocate, "Harry Clay," receiving him as an honored guest on his frequent visits to Danville, and reading all his speeches, or, worse still (*horresco referens*), making the writer of this sketch read them to him. He admired Calhoun for his intellect, but detested his theories. For General Jackson he cherished an antipathy that amounted to rancor, and the feeling prepossessed him against the general's personal and political friends.

Into the shaping and direction of local affairs, including politics, he threw himself with ardor, firmly refusing, however, to seek or hold office. He was the mainstay of the Clay party in Mercer County up to about 1828, when his active business life was suddenly interrupted. The rustling of a dry corn-blade in a puff of wind caused a spirited horse to spring from him as he was mounting; the fall fractured his thigh-bone, and condemned him to his bed for a year and to crutches for life.

In religion he was a zealous rather than orthodox Episcopalian. The support of that Church was with him a matter of traditional family honor, and when his son joined the Presbyterians his pride was deeply wounded. This always remained a tender spot with him. To his efforts and liberality were chiefly due the erection of the Danville Episcopal Church building, about 1828, and the maintenance of a regular ministry. Every Sunday morning he occupied his large front pew at the left of the chancel and joined in the responses; and, generally, he had the minister home with him to a good dinner with friends. All this did not prevent his discussing Church history with striking disrespect for priestly rule and handling some of the Old Testament worthies without gloves. He was the first man the writer ever heard descant upon certain weaknesses in the characters of David and Solomon. It was a pleasure to him to engage theological students or ministers in controversy upon points of ecclesiastical history or doctrinal differences, and puzzle them with his irony, raillery, and thorough acquaintance with the authorities. His reading had been extensive—chiefly in politics, biography, history, and travels—and he used his knowledge with shrewd common sense, expressing himself with spirit, force, and often with wit. He knew little Latin and no Greek, but his conversation was bright enough to interest men of learning. Students, tutors, and professors from Center College were his frequent visitors, and few intelligent travelers passed through Danville without calling on the invalid. He received all with a bountiful hospitality that characterized Kentucky in the first half of the century. Though his sarcasm and frankness made him a terror to hypocrites and time-servers, he was respectful to the sincere and civil to strangers. To women he was gentle as summer, and to children, tender and indulgent. To his poor neighbors he was kind; of poor tenants he exacted no rent; and though one or two students were always members of his family, they were such on the footing of friends only. He invited those he liked and admired. In money matters he was liberal, refusing, however, to indorse notes for any except a few intimate friends. Woodlawn was the home of twenty-odd slaves. These were never punished or sold, being regarded as held for their protection as well as his convenience. All the harsh features of slavery were toned down. The overseer was obliged to manage without the whip, and got along peacefully with the slaves if not profitably for the owner. Most of the negroes had been born on the estate, and they looked upon their master with mingled fear and affection. It must be admitted, however, that they took the farming and rope-spinning life easily; they were almost as lazy as the fifteen to twenty pure-bred mares and colts that roamed through the rich pastures, costly pets of the owner.

It was the custom among the farmers in the neighborhood of Danville to visit town every Saturday. That was the great day for seeing each other on business, pleasure, or politics. Early in the morning of that day, during the years after his accident, when the weather permitted, James Birney was driven to town. His usual seat was in the store belonging to David Bell, his former clerk, his successor and life-long friend, and there he held a grand levee until late in the afternoon. It seemed to the writer, who was often his grandfather's attendant on such occasions, that hardly any tradesman, professional man, or farmer failed to pay his respects to the venerable cripple. He had a kind word or inquiry or jest for each one, and his chair was often surrounded by a group amused at his repartees, wit, and rollicking humor; in all which, however, he maintained a certain personal dignity, never uttering a coarse word. The man who forgot himself so far as to utter one in his presence never escaped without an effective rebuke.

About two years after James Birney opened his store at Danville he married Miss Read, one of the daughters of the political exile mentioned in the first chapter. Tradition makes her beautiful and intellectual. Her parents did not think the handsome and energetic young merchant a suitable mate for her, and the young people were obliged to make a Gretna Green affair of the marriage. Her home was a happy one, but she died in 1795, leaving a son and infant daughter, James Gillespie and Anna Maria. The latter married John J. Marshall, well known in Kentucky annals as a law reporter and judge. She was the mother of James Birney Marshall, who earned distinction as an editor, and of Humphrey Marshall, who was successively Representative in Congress, Minister to China, and Confederate major-general. For many years she was a leader in society at Frankfort, the State capital. Her reputation for conversational talent and general ability is one of the social traditions of Kentucky.

CHAPTER III.

INFANCY AND YOUTH.

1792–1808.

JAMES GILLESPIE BIRNEY was born, February 4, 1792, at Danville. After the death of his mother, he and his sister were placed under the care of Mrs. Doyle, the oldest sister of his father. She was a widow and childless, and, at the request of her brother, came from Ireland to take charge of his two children and preside over his household—duties for which an affectionate nature, sound sense, good education, agreeable manners, and fervent piety peculiarly qualified her. She continued to perform them until the children were grown and until the second marriage of her brother. His house was her home until her decease, about the year 1834. Her nephew could not have been dearer to her if he had been her own son; and he returned her affection. Whenever he was at Woodlawn, he passed much of his time with her. During his residence in Alabama he wrote to her regularly and frequently; and when the writer was sent, in 1828, to Woodlawn on a long visit it was strictly enjoined on him to do all in his power to amuse and make her happy. Dear old lady! how vividly I remember her venerable figure, with the shawl, spectacles, knitting, and prayer-book!

The boy grew up among numerous relatives and connections. His father's married sisters, Mrs. Gillespie and

Mrs. Whelan, with their husbands and children, migrated from Ireland and settled near Danville, about 1795. These families were intelligent and in good circumstances. Mr. Gillespie bought a valuable farm about a mile from Danville, and Mr. Whelan another, four miles distant, and extending to the precipitous bluffs and romantic scenery of Dick's River.

The relatives on the mother's side greatly exceeded in numbers those on the father's. There were two uncles and five aunts, all of whom had married, and, up to 1808, had their homes in Mercer County. There was no lack of cousins; the motherless child had many companions and playmates among them. The attachments formed then were generally strong enough to survive the political differences of mature years.

The boy was not timid, shy, or dreamy; he was sturdy, self-possessed, and gifted with strong common sense. He had inherited a healthful and robust constitution. He was not only vigorous, but active and bright. He took pleasure in athletic exercises; at an early age he learned to ride, shoot, swim, skate, and dance. He was fond of the companionship of girls. His father was proud of his beauty and promise. In his treatment of him the father was governed by the maxim of the ancient sage, "Respect youth." The intercourse between father and son was marked during their lives by affection, confidence, and the deferential manner of the old school. It is needless to say that the rod was not used. The father's pride and the aunt's gentleness alike forbade it. The boy grew up frank, truthful, manly, self-respecting, and courageous. In those days brutality was tolerated in schools; the teacher was called the "master," and the emblem of his authority, the rod, lay on his desk. James did not escape discipline; when he had committed a fault he scorned to shelter himself by evasion, but most of his troubles at school were due to the fact that he was always ready with his fists to aid a comrade against heavy odds.

At eleven years of age he was sent to Transylvania University, at Lexington. His companions were a son of ex-Governor Isaac Shelby and George Robertson, who afterward became a famous judge and was honored by having a Kentucky county named after him. He remained at that institution, vacations excepted, until the New Year's holidays of 1805–'6, when he returned home to enter a "seminary" which had been opened at Danville by Dr. Priestly. During his summer-vacation visit, when he was thirteen, there occurred an incident that illustrates his character. He went with two other boys, one a cousin, to a piece of deep water, to swim. He was a good swimmer, his cousin a beginner. At a distance from the shore a rail was driven into the bottom of the pond. Its place was marked by a float. On its top, a foot or two below the surface, one might pause and rest. On this James stood and encouraged his cousin to swim out to him. The attempt was a failure. The boy sank. James swam to him, and was trying to help him when he was clasped and pulled under the water; but he extricated himself and succeeded in placing the boy upon the rail. He then swam ashore, rested, and returning brought his comrade out in safety. While the danger was at its greatest, the companion, who was on the shore, shouted to James to save himself. Referring to this just after his escape, he said, quietly, "It never entered my mind to leave him." Many anecdotes of his unselfishness and courage were current among his relatives in the days of my boyhood. I give this one because I heard it from the cousin. It is given in Green's "Life of Birney," published in 1844.

The next two years were spent in studies preparatory to an intended course in the College of New Jersey. What these studies were and what his teacher thought of his character at the close of this period, and what, nearly a half-century later, he thought of his teacher may be gathered from the following documents :

On the first page of a large scrap-book made up by James G. Birney is this entry in his own handwriting, in 1856 :

February 4th.—For my grandson and namesake (James G. Birney, Jr., oldest son of James Birney) at Cincinnati:

This book, unlike most other things, will be more valuable as it advances in age. When you come to be a half-century old, or as old as I am, it will be to you a remembrancer of old times. I also send you with it a letter which you can keep. You will see it was written by a preceptor of mine who, I need hardly tell after such evidence as his letter affords, was a learned man. He was considerably advanced in age, and had had great experience in teaching. He had married, some twenty or five and twenty years before, a Miss McBride, whose family lived in or near Harrodsburg, and about that time had taught a school, I think, in Bairdstown, which was attended by many young men who afterward became distinguished in Kentucky—Felix Grundy, John Rowan, John Pope, and, I believe, Joseph V. Davis were among them. He then removed, if I mistake not, to Baltimore, where he had a school. Then he returned to Kentucky and settled at Danville. He was probably fickle and unsteady as to his residence; for, although he had a numerous school when I left it to go to Princeton, he had gone away before my return in about two years and a half. I have never heard of him since. He was a member, though by no means an active one, of the Presbyterian Church, and doubtless quite a learned man of those times.

Letter from James Priestly to James Birney, Esq., father of James G. Birney.

DANVILLE, *March, 30, 1808*

DEAR SIR: As you have determined rightly, I think, in the present state of the Western country, to send your son to a distant seat of learning, I will recount to you before he goes, as far as I can recollect, the studies he has pursued and the text-books he has used under my direction for the last two years. He gave but little of his time to the learned languages and none to geography, as I understood he had studied these as far as is common before he came to me. Part of Euclid, too, he had learned before. With me he studied the fifth and sixth books of Euclid, Simson's "Plane Trigonometry," the greater part of common arithmetic and algebra, as far as the solution of simple equations, Murray's "Grammar" without the exercises, Watts's "Logic" and "Improvement of the Mind," Ferguson's "Lectures" and "Astronomy," Blair's "Lectures," Adams and Kennet's "Roman Antiquities," Paley's "Moral Philosophy" and "Natural Theology," Blackstone's "Commentaries," and part of St. Pierre's "Studies of Nature." In the second year, a little time was employed in classical learning, and he read three comedies of Terence, one book of Tacitus's "Annals," and went hastily over the critical epistles of Horace, and three books of his odes, and read a book or two of Homer. A number of these studies have not been reviewed, as I entertained for a while the hope of resuming them in a course of lectures, of adding the many important ones that have not been touched, of referring to the best authors on each subject, and thoroughly investigating the whole. But this I found to be, in my situation, impossible. One person is not equal to the task of preparing good lectures on every subject; nor, if he even adopts the matured works of the best professors, can he study them all and make a proper use of them while he must at the same time superintend the conduct of all the classes in a seminary from the lowest to the highest, and instruct them all.

It is proper, therefore, that James should reside some years at a college, where there are many professors, with a good library and apparatus. If the rules of the place will allow him to live in a private house and to attend the lectures of several professors with different classes, as in the universities of Britain, he may pass those years with great profit. What he has already done will render some studies lighter and more pleasant, and leave him time and spirits for others that will be quite new to him, so that he may keep way with more than one class. I profited most when I began again with those who had never studied the same things before.

I mention a private family, because I think he does not need the discipline of academic rules to keep him to proper hours and from bad company; and because it would keep him from those intrusions which can not be avoided if he lodges in a college.

As far as I have had an opportunity of observing, his conduct has been perfectly correct, and has appeared to proceed from right disposition; so that I have reason to hope he will derive from an advantageous situation all the benefit it is capable of yielding to the most prudent.

With the best wishes for his good and your satisfaction,

I am sir, your obedient humble servant,

JAMES PRIESTLY.

JAMES BIRNEY, Esq.

The character of this youth, who was held in such high respect by his instructor, had been molded under uncommon influences. The follies, errors, and bad habits so often found in only sons of rich parents had been in great part prevented by the strong common sense of his father, the watchful love of his pious aunt, the constant moral pressure of a respectable family connection, and, better than all, by his well-balanced faculties and fortunate temperament. The social life about him was not that of an ordinary frontier settlement. Danville was in the very heart of that marvelously fertile region known to Americans generally as the "blue-grass country," and to Kentuckians as the "garden of the world." Its soil, constantly renewed by the decay of the abundant limestone ingredients, is inexhaustible; even the Shenandoah Valley of Virginia does not reward so richly the labor of the farmer. And its pasturage has given to Kentucky acknowledged pre-eminence for race-horses and fine beeves. To this land of milk and honey the intelligent and adventurous classes of Virginia, North Carolina, and Maryland began to migrate about the close of the Revolutionary War. Many of the immigrants had been officers in the army. Some of them were men of means and substance. Not a few had held civil office and took a live interest in public affairs. They were hardy and courageous men, able to bear the severe trials of life in the forest, and to measure strength and cunning with the Indian foe. Their descendants inherit from them thews, sinews, tall stature, and fighting qualities. At an early day the control of the site of Danville and its vicinity fell into the hands of men of means, who took pains to attract to it a good class of settlers. Among them were Isaac Shelby, the hero of King's Mountain, afterward governor of the State and secretary of war; Benjamin Sebastian, long a judge of the Court of Appeals; and many others who became prominent in national or State affairs, including Joshua Barbee and the members of the political debating club of which an account is given in the next chapter. Some of these men were members of the learned professions; all of them had been educated by the sharp experiences of frontier life. They were men of thought and action, qualified to lay the foundations of a State.

For a great many years Danville was the thought center of Kentucky. The numerous constitutional conventions were held there, also the synods. It was the permanent headquarters of Kentucky Presbyterianism. In 1808 it had only begun to feel the competition for leadership by Lexington and Louisville.

The social tone of Danville was not favorable to the ordinary vices of frontier life. Theology and politics were more in favor than the race-course and gaming-table.

CHAPTER IV.

ANTI-SLAVERY INFLUENCES IN YOUTH.

WHEN James G. Birney left home for college he was in his seventeenth year. Every advantage that wealth and a father's love could procure had been his; his literary and scientific education had been the best to be had in Kentucky, and his social opportunities and immediate surroundings left little to be desired. There are no indications that he had been spoiled; he appears to have been a robust, intelligent, and ambitious youth of good habits.

As the interest of his countrymen in his biography is due chiefly to his subsequent anti-slavery career, it is important to note the influences in which this had its origin. The foundations of his abolitionism were doubtless laid in his early youth.

Though his grandfather Read and his father had become slaveholders, they always professed a willingness to emancipate, if Kentucky could be made a free State. In 1792 they had taken an active part in promoting the election of the Rev. David Rice, a noted abolitionist, to the Constitutional Convention, and in 1799 they voted for delegates to a similar convention, who were pledged to support a constitutional provision in favor of abolition. The pious aunt who reared him had always refused, on religious principles, to own slaves or to accept their personal services without compensation.

The home influences were powerfully re-enforced and directed by the Rev. David Rice. He was pastor of the Danville Presbyterian church for many years during the youth of James G. Birney, and there being no Episcopalian services in the town, the boy and his aunt generally attended that church. Mr. Rice was a friend and a frequent guest of the family, and paid much attention to the son, who conceived an affection for him, and in after life gratefully remembered and spoke of him. In the State Constitutional Convention of 1792 Mr. Rice was the leader of the members who favored immediate abolition. His speech was clear and able, his conclusion being in the following words: "Therefore, I give it as my opinion that the FIRST thing to be done is to resolve UNCONDITIONALLY to put an end to slavery in this State."

The speech was reprinted many times. I have before me a copy of an edition published in New York in 1812. It makes an octavo pamphlet, large size, twelve pages, in small type, and double columns. Its reasoning throughout classes Mr. Rice with the uncompromising immediate abolitionists of his day, and refutes the charge of gradualism brought against him by Mr. Davidson, the historian of Kentucky Presbyterianism. Mr. Rice was an earnest man of definite convictions and an eloquent speaker, and he frequently preached against the sin of slavery, thus sowing the seed which was to yield a harvest many years after.

The Rev. David Barrow, of Mount Sterling, preached before 1808 several anti-slavery sermons at Danville, which were always favorably remembered by my father. He was the author of a widely distributed pamphlet, entitled "Involuntary, Unmerited, Perpetual, Absolute, Hereditary Slavery examined on the Principles of Nature, Reason, Justice, Policy, and Scripture," which advocated immediate abolition; and in 1808 he was generally regarded as the most influential and able leader of the anti-slavery Baptists in Kentucky.

The Baptist Church was the first one organized in the State; it dates from 1781. From that year until the War of 1812 it was the most numerous and powerful religious organization in Kentucky. About 1787 Joshua Carman, a Baptist elder from Virginia, began a movement for the abolition of slavery, which for many years agitated both the Church and State. It was doubtless the leading cause of the political excitements of 1792 and 1799.

In 1787 Elder Carman was organizing church societies in Kentucky, chiefly in Hardin, La Rue, and Nelson Counties. Between that year and 1801, when he emigrated to Ohio, he was pastor of several leading Baptist churches. For fourteen years he preached immediate abolition and no Christian fellowship with slave-holders. In 1789 his church sent up to Salem Association the query: "Is it lawful in the sight of God for a member of Christ's Church to keep his fellow-creatures in perpetual slavery?" In 1797 he was present at the General Conference in Ohio, at which the Miami Association was organized, "with a view," Dunlevy says in his history of that association (page 133), "to prevent the newly organized body from holding any correspondence with slave-holders"; and he succeeded in his object.

Elder Carman was an able man and "an easy, fluent, and pleasant speaker," and he made numerous converts to abolitionism among the most zealous and efficient preachers of his denomination. The first was Josiah Dodge; and the movement started by Carman spread until, before 1808, the following leading Baptist preachers were among its adherents: Carter Tarrant, John Sutton, Donald Holmes, Jacob Gregg, George Smith, George Stokes Smith, Cornelius Duese, John H. Owen, Thomas Whitman, John Murphy, Elijah Davidson, William Buckley, David Barrow, William Hickman, James Garrard, and Ambrose Dudley. All of these, except the last three, maintained the high standard of immediatism during their continuance in the pulpit. Collins, in his "History of Kentucky" (page 419), states their position as follows: They "declared for the abolition of slavery, alleging that no friendship should be extended to slave-holders, as slavery in every branch of it, both in principle and practice, was a sinful and abominable system, fraught with peculiar evils and miseries, which every good man ought to abandon and bear testimony against."

It does not enter into the plan of this work to describe the schisms in the Baptist Church of Kentucky caused by dissensions in regard to the course to be pursued in the treatment of slavery. This was acknowledged to be a sin, but the majority of church-members were unwilling to make it a cause of exclusion from the Church. In the evasive language of a church body in 1789: "The association judge it improper to enter into so important and critical matter at present." The Baptists were divided into "regulars" and "separatists." An "Emancipation Association" was formed in Nelson County, and the "Licking Locust Association," abolitionist, contained a large number of churches. For details the reader is referred to Spencer's "History of the Kentucky Baptists," to the histories of Kentucky by Collins and by Shaler, and to Benedict's "History of the Baptists." "Biographical Sketches of the Kentucky Emancipationists" were published by the Rev. Carter Tarrant, and short ones may be found in the works above referred to.

The popular sentiment at Danville had been decidedly anti-slavery from the first. For many years the town, to use Shaler's expression (page 121), "was the center of the State life." From 1786 to 1790 a political club existed there which "was composed of about thirty of the brightest spirits of the time who were resident in and about this little town. On its roll we find the names of many of those who had already or were afterward to lead the State in the paths of peace and war" (Shaler, page 113). Among its members were William McDowell (lawyer and afterward judge of the United States District Court), Samuel McDowell (who presided at eight State constitutional conventions), Henry Innes, Christopher Greenup, Robert Craddock, Thomas Todd, George Mutor, Peyton Short, James Speed, Abe Buford, Benjamin Sebastian, Willis Green, and William McClung, whose names are identified with the history of Kentucky. The record of the club shows that their debates were confined to great questions of polity. They discussed the proposed Constitution of the United States, article by article, and voted to strike out the clause prohibiting Congress from preventing the importation of slaves until 1808. It was probably owing to the influence of the members of this club that the Rev. David Rice was elected delegate to the Constitutional Convention of 1792. The question whether Kentucky should be a free State does not appear to have been made a distinct issue in the election. For several years the people had been greatly disturbed by questions of independence growing out of the strong opposition made to their separation from Virginia. There were not more than fifteen thousand slaves in Kentucky, and the settlers did not appreciate the paramount importance of the slavery question. George Nicholas, an able lawyer and politician from Virginia and a slave-holder, was the controlling spirit of the convention and drafted the Constitution. This instrument forbade the importation of slaves into the State for sale, or of any imported into America since 1789, and empowered the Legislature to enact laws permitting emancipation.

The Constitution of 1792 was not submitted to the

people. It had hardly gone into operation when a strong free-State sentiment declared itself. This was general among the Baptists, and also among the Presbyterians, the next sect in numerical force and influence. It was shared by many of the leading men in and about Danville. Patrick Brown and his brother William, of Nelson County, were especially active in extending it. The Constitution had provided that the people might vote for or against a convention to revise that instrument. A first vote was to be taken in May, 1797, and a second in May, 1798. If both these should be in favor of a convention, the Legislature meeting in the winter of 1798–'99 was to order an election of delegates to be held in May, 1799; and the convention was to meet within three months thereafter (see Article XI of Constitution of 1792). The Constitution needed amendment in several particulars; but the abolition of slavery was undoubtedly the dominant issue at the polls in 1797 and 1798. The vote in the latter year stood 8,804 for the convention, 3,049 against. The issue had been fairly made up; the State had been thoroughly canvassed; and the result showed that the free-State party had a majority of nearly three to one. If the convention could have been held in May, 1798, immediately after the election, Kentucky would have been made a free State and the causes of the civil war destroyed in the germ.

On the 25th of June, 1798, the Alien and Sedition Law was passed by Congress. The wave of instantaneous reaction against it became a tidal one in Kentucky. George Nicholas and John Breckenridge, the defeated leaders of the pro-slavery faction, promptly availed themselves of the excitement to recover their control of affairs. Public meetings were called to denounce the Federalists. At these, Henry Clay, then a few months over twenty-one years of age, was first revealed as a popular orator. In

November, when the Legislature met, John Breckenridge offered what history knows as "the Kentucky resolutions of 1798." They were passed by both Houses, approved on the 16th of the month, and forwarded to Congress and the Legislatures of other States. A hot answer was returned by Massachusetts. Before the election in May, 1799, Kentucky was ablaze with political excitement against the Alien and Sedition Law, and John Breckenridge, Benjamin Logan, John Rowan, Felix Grundy, and other pro-slavery men who were advocates of the Kentucky resolutions, were elected delegates to the convention called to revise the Constitution. The all-important measure of making Kentucky a free State had been blown out of sight by a gusty side-wind.

As Henry Clay and his relation to slavery will necessarily be adverted to more than once in subsequent pages, it may be well to ascertain here the extent of his co-operation in the political movement beginning in 1796 to make Kentucky a free State. Mr. Clay arrived in Lexington in November, 1797 (Collins's "History"), about six months after the first victory of the free-State party at the polls. He was admitted to the bar in April, 1798, a few days after he became of age. The second victory of the free-State party was in the May following. Between the date of his arrival and the vote in May, 1798, a period of six months, Mr. Clay had, from time to time, co-operated with the free-State party by advocating its objects in a debating society of which he was a member, and by writing some favorable articles for a local newspaper. There is no proof that he made any "stump speech" on the subject, and it is improbable that he did so. In the early summer of 1798 he was conspicuous as a speaker at the large field meetings held near Lexington to denounce the alien and sedition laws, working side by side with John Breckenridge and George Nicholas, the leaders of the pro-slavery faction.

On one occasion of this kind, he and Nicholas "were put in a carriage and drawn by the people through the streets of the town amid great shouting and huzzaing" (Schurtz, "Life of Clay"). During the Legislative excitements of the ensuing winter, and for many years thereafter, he continued to be identified with the Jefferson party. In April, 1799, he married Miss Hart, the daughter of a wealthy slave-holder, and became the owner of several slaves. The election for delegates to the Constitutional Convention took place in the following May and there is no reason to doubt that Mr. Clay voted the pro-slavery ticket headed by his friend John Breckenridge, the pro-slavery leader, or that he was from that time identified politically with the anti-free-State men, and owed his rapid success to their friendship. He had become a slave-owner, and found an easy road to success through the excitement caused by the passage of the Alien and Sedition Law. In his famous Frankfort speech in 1829, intended to open his campaign for the presidency, Mr. Clay conciliated Northern sentiment by an apology for his course in 1799, which, with studied euphemism, he described as submitting with grace to the decision of the majority. But if during the thirty years preceding this apology Mr. Clay did an act evidencing his desire for a practical effort to make Kentucky a free State, no biographer has found it.

The free-State sentiment in Kentucky did not die out after 1799. Agitation continued. In 1807, a Baptist association that refused Christian fellowship to slave-holders numbered twelve churches (I, Spencer, 186). Manumissions for religious reasons became frequent. In the decade ending with 1810, as compared with the one preceding it, the increase in the number of freedmen in Kentucky was one hundred and fifty per cent. In September, 1807, a State convention was held in Woodford County to form the "Kentucky Abolition Society"; a committee was appointed to draft a constitution,* and the society was formed and constitution adopted in a similar convention, held September 27, 1808, at the same place. The members pledged themselves: "First, to pursue such measures as may tend to the abolition of slavery in a way which will consist with the Constitution and laws of the Commonwealth."

This society existed many years, and may appear again in this narrative.

The facts already given will suffice to show that the boyhood of James G. Birney was passed under influences which were distinctly anti-slavery. In his after life, he was accustomed to say he could not remember a time when he believed slavery to be right. It is not improbable that he had never heard, before he went to Princeton, such a belief expressed by any respectable person. He may not have heard it at Princeton, for the time had not then come when slavery was defended on its merits or on Biblical ground.

---

* The entire constitution of the "Kentucky Abolition Society" was republished October 9, 1822, in the "Abolition Intelligencer," a monthly paper, published at Shelbyville, Ky., by the Rev. John Finley Crowe, under the auspices of the society.

CHAPTER V.

LIFE AT PRINCETON.

1808.

JAMES G. BIRNEY entered the sophomore class in the College of New Jersey, in April, 1808, and was graduated, in due course, September 26, 1810. At the time of his admission the class numbered eighteen; in the junior year, forty; and at graduation, twenty-five. Several of his classmates became famous in after life as lawyers and statesmen: among them were Richard Stockton, of Mississippi, Oliver S. Halstead, of New Jersey, Kensey Johns, of Delaware, A. De Witt Bruyn, of New York, Joseph Cabell Breckenridge, of Kentucky, and George M. Dallas, of Pennsylvania. His room-mate at Nassau Hall was young Breckenridge, and the intimacy thus formed ripened into a life-long friendship. His pleasant relations with Dallas led to his studying law in the office of Alexander J. Dallas, the father, and to a correspondence which extended over many years. He was popular with his classmates and fellow-students. Some of these expressed their indignation when it was announced that the first honor of the class had been given to another, but he calmed them by his declaration that the faculty had decided fairly, because he had always been inferior in mathematics to his successful competitor. For the abstractions of science he had no taste and a talent not more than respectable, but he greatly excelled in history, moral and political philosophy, general literature, and the classics. He was especially proficient in Latin, and read it easily without a dictionary—a practice he kept up during life. Much of his time in college was given to preparation for debates and to his studies in logic and moral and political philosophy, pursued under the direction and instruction of Samuel Stanhope Smith, Doctor of Laws, Doctor of Divinity, and president of the college. Dr. Smith was a man of strong character, extensive learning, and captivating eloquence; he was an expert logician and a most plausible casuist. His qualities gave him great influence over his pupil, an influence perceptible for many years in the latter's course in life. The doctor was a Princeton graduate; he had been president of a Virginia college four years, had returned to Princeton in 1779 as professor, and had been made president in 1795. He took a deep interest in all questions touching slavery and the African race. In 1787 he published an elaborate work, "An Essay on the Causes of the Variety of Complexion and Figure in the Human Species," etc. In 1810 he published, at New Brunswick, a second and enlarged edition of this work, with an appendix. It is remarkable for the ingenuity and varied learning displayed by the author in defense of his theory of the unity of the race; and it is still an interesting book for the general reader. During the stay of James G. Birney at the college, Dr. Smith was preparing for the press the great work of his life, "Lectures on Moral and Political Philosophy." They were published in 1812, at Trenton, in two volumes. Both the "Essay" and the "Lectures" formed part of my father's library in Alabama, being kept on the same shelf with "An Essay on the Treatment and Conversion of African Slaves in the British Sugar Colonies," by the Rev. James Ramsay, M. A. (London, 1784); "The History of the Rise, Progress, and Accomplishment of the Abolition of the African Slave Trade by the British Parliament," by Thomas Clarkson, M. A. (2 vols., first American edition, Philadelphia, 1808). The "Lectures" were mementos, and the other works relics of his college life.

Dr. Smith taught his pupils that men are of one blood, and that slavery is wrong morally and an evil politically; but that there is no remedy except in voluntary manumission by masters; that citizens acquire slave property under the sanction of the laws, and can not equitably be compelled to sacrifice it; that property rights of all kinds should be held sacred, etc. "What free people," he asks, in his "Lectures," "would allow their legislature to dispose in the same manner of any other portion of their property?" This sophistry appears to the modern reader wretchedly bald; but it had its effect in 1810. Imagine a youth saturated with it for two years and a half by a venerated preceptor!

During his college life the discussion of slavery in the country went on without intermission. In 1804 the State of New Jersey had passed a gradual emancipation act, following the example set by New York three years before and by Pennsylvania at an earlier date. In those three States slavery was in process of extinction under a settled policy. The institution had been condemned by public opinion. In 1808, after several years of exciting debates, Congress had prohibited the importation of African slaves and declared it piracy, and the year before it had refused to consider the suspension for ten years of the free-soil clause in the ordinance of 1787, for the purpose of legalizing the temporary introduction of slaves into the territory northwest of the Ohio. The subject of slavery was the frequent topic of debate in the college literary societies. It was in the political atmosphere and was daily suggested by the presence of the slaves who swept the corridors of the dormitories. Professor MacLean was an outspoken friend of abolition, and some of the leaders of the free-soil movement in the State resided at Princeton. Many of the students were from the Southern States, and it may be supposed that the slavery discussions were spirited. What part was taken in them by James G. Birney is not known. That he did not defend slavery we know by his repeated statements in his manhood that he had never done so; but as to the remedy for it, his judgment may have been warped and his generous ardor chilled by the plausible fallacies of President Smith.

In his college career there was little to interest the general reader. His few breaches of discipline were not serious, and he was in good standing with the faculty. With the Rev. Philip Lindsley, tutor in languages, he contracted a friendship which continued through life. Dr. Lindsley became afterward president of the University of Tennessee, at Nashville, and was my father's guest on several visits to Huntsville, Alabama.

CHAPTER VI.

BETWEEN COLLEGE AND THE BAR.

1810–1814.

RETURNING to Kentucky immediately after taking his diploma, he passed a few days at home, and then joined the party of Mr. Clay's friends who were escorting him during his canvass of the district for a seat in Congress. On this excursion, which lasted about a month, he became acquainted with many of the men who were prominent in Kentucky politics. His heart was quite won by the tact and kindness of Mr. Clay, and he remained for many years thereafter an admirer and friend of that eminent orator and statesman. He had expected to study law at Danville, but had hardly read a chapter in Blackstone before his father made the necessary arrangements for him to become a student in the office of Alexander J. Dallas, then a celebrated lawyer and the United States District Attorney at Philadelphia. The next three years and a half were spent in that city, except the time taken for a tour through New England, two visits to Washington city, and a yearly visit home.

Mr. Dallas was an able, but not an attentive instructor, his time being much absorbed by his professional duties; but there were in the office several well-educated and zealous fellow-students, with whom legal doctrines and cases were discussed; and Mr. Dallas was ever ready to answer questions and solve difficulties. Attendance on interesting trials and hearings was required, with a full report on the points involved. The office library was large and the books well chosen. Mr. Birney made good use of his opportunities, and was admitted to the Philadelphia bar, passing a creditable examination.

The social advantages he enjoyed during his long residence in Philadelphia were very great. His purse was liberally supplied by a generous father, who insisted that he should live in all respects as a man of fashion. His dress was costly, and he drove tandem a pair of blooded bays sent him from the Woodlawn pastures. After the fashion of the day, he wore high, fair-topped, tasseled boots when he drove. He had no vices or habits of dissipation, but he cultivated æsthetic tastes, and was accustomed to making liberal expenditures to gratify them. During life he was noted for his rich and tasteful garb, love of fine furniture, beautiful table services, and good horses. He frequented the society of people of culture, finding them both among the Quakers and the fashionables. He made numerous acquaintances among men eminent for talent. It was then his life-long friendship with Abraham L. Pennock, the Quaker merchant, was formed, and that he made the acquaintance of Mr. Forten, the colored sail-maker. For this excellent man he conceived a high regard, showing it by calling on him in after years whenever he visited Philadelphia. Mr. Forten was intelligent, thoughtful, and full of sympathy for his race, and was just the man to discuss slavery with his young Kentucky friend. We have no proof that he did so, or that during the residence of James G. Birney in Pennsylvania his attention was especially attracted to the institution of slavery, then dying out in that State. In May, 1814, he returned to Danville and began the practice of law.

CHAPTER VII.

HIS LIFE IN KENTUCKY.

1814–1818.

He did not have to wait long for business. The Danville Bank made him its regular attorney, and his popular manners, thorough preparation, carefulness in details, diligence, and energy soon secured for him a good clientage. He traveled the circuit, which included several counties, and practiced in both civil and criminal cases, gaining a valuable professional experience. The condition of affairs in the State, however, prevented his court practice from being lucrative. The war had unsettled trade. The suspension of the exportation of products by the Mississippi River had been calamitous; money was scarce; the Bank of Kentucky was discredited, and its paper was refused in payment of debts. "Relief laws," staying executions on judgments, were passed in aid of the debtor class; and they were in force from January, 1816, to February, 1818. The young lawyer derived his chief income from the amicable adjustment of claims.

He identified himself with the community in which he lived. Soon after his return to Danville he was made a Freemason in the local lodge—Franklin, No. 28—his father, a passed master of that order, performing the ceremonies of the initiation. At the fall elections in 1814 he was elected to the town council, and as a member of that body was active in founding the Danville Academy. He mixed freely in social life, attending balls and parties and renewing the acquaintanceships of his youth.

Among the girls he had known from childhood was Agatha, the fifth daughter of William McDowell, United States District Judge, and niece of George Madison, Governor of Kentucky, and of Bishop Madison, of Virginia. The admiration he had felt for the pretty and vivacious school-girl was changed into love for the accomplished, intelligent, and charming woman. His wooing was successful. Relatives and friends were all pleased. The groom's father quite forgot that the lady belonged to a family noted for its stanch Presbyterianism. The marriage took place on the 1st of February, 1816. It proved to be a happy one until the decease of the wife in 1838. The husband was always loving, considerate, and respectful; and the wife was happy in her husband, her children, and her home, over which she presided with the love of a mother, the grace of a tactful hostess, and the skill of a model housewife. She clung to her husband with unwavering faith through his varying fortunes. In the last years of her life, while suffering from infirm health, she felt keenly the alienation of her kindred and former friends from her husband. The plan of this sketch does not permit more than the above brief mention of the domestic life of its subject.

Among his wedding gifts were several household slaves, presented by his father and father-in-law. His acceptance of them is logically inconsistent with the anti-slavery principles and opinions attributed to him in the previous chapters of this narrative. It may be palliated, however, by the fact that in his day such inconsistency was common. Patrick Henry said of slave-holders: "Every thinking honest man rejects it in speculation, but how few in practice from conscientious motives! Would any one believe that I am master of slaves of my own purchase? I am drawn along by the general inconvenience of living without them. I will not, can not, justify it."

Washington did not free his slaves except by will; and the Rev. Stanhope Smith, logician, had persuaded himself that, though slavery was wrong in principle, it was right in practice. It must be admitted that in the James G. Birney of 1816 there was no outward indication of the future aggressive abolitionist; but the principles were latent in him, and were to be made visible in the fierce political heats of the future. In the summer and autumn of 1815 he took an active part in the political campaign, making stump speeches in favor of Henry Clay for Congress, and of George Madison for Governor. Both of these candidates were elected.

In August, 1816, at the first election after he became twenty-four years of age, and thus eligible under the Constitution, he was elected member of the Lower House of the General Assembly of Kentucky, virtually without opposition. He took his seat on the second day of the following December. There were one hundred and fifty-one statutes passed at the session, and in shaping them he rendered valuable service. Standing committees were not then known in the legislative practice of the State, but he was appointed on several special committees to which important bills were referred, and repeatedly on privileges and elections. He procured the enactment of a law to incorporate the Danville Academy and to appropriate the proceeds of certain lands for its endowment; and of another to prohibit the circulation of private notes as currency. He voted for Martin D. Hardin and John Adair for the United States Senate; but Mr. Adair was defeated by John J. Crittenden. He supported a joint resolution "commemorating" Jackson's victory at New Orleans; and another relating to the free navigation of the river Mississippi, protesting against the seizure by the Louisiana authorities of the "steamboat Enterprise," under "the pretended authority of a law enacted by the Legislature of the late Territory of New Orleans," declaring that Kentucky will maintain inviolate, by all legitimate means, the right of her citizens to navigate said river and its tributary streams, and requesting the co-operation of Pennsylvania, Virginia, Ohio, Indiana, and Louisiana.

It was at this session he gave the first sign, so far as known, of his unwillingness to be used as a tool by the slave-holding interest. The Senate had passed without opposition a joint resolution requesting the acting Governor to open a correspondence with the Governors of Indiana and Ohio, respectively, with a view to procure in each of those States the enactment of laws for the recaption and delivery of fugitive slaves. In demanding this measure, the slave-holders stood upon their alleged legal rights as embodied in the United States fugitive slave act of 1793. When it came to the House it was vigorously opposed by James G. Birney, and defeated. "What!" he asked, "shall the State of Kentucky do what no gentleman would—turn slave-catcher?" After the vote the pro-slavery men rallied, and, under the able leadership of Judge Rowan, succeeded in passing a substitute, which omitted the most objectionable language and softened the tone of the original resolution. Mr. Birney did not vote for the substitute. About twenty years later, he said he did not believe his opposition to the measure would have cost him a single vote in Mercer County, that cotton was not king in 1817, and he was not aware that any unfavorable comment on his course had been made by the press. In fact, he attached no special importance to it at the time.

He was already sighing for a wider sphere for his ambition. The Kentucky paths to high political place were already crowded by distinguished and able aspirants. Clay, Crittenden, Adair, Hardin, and others of the generation before him would be his competitors for many years to come, with fearful odds in their favor. A Mr. Love, a friend and fellow-member of the Legislature, was intending to go to Alabama after the adjournment of the session, and pressed him to visit that Territory with him. He did so, and was so much pleased with its fertile soil and the political and professional prospects open to him in the embryo State, that he decided to close up his affairs in Kentucky and make his future home in Alabama. His plan was to practice law in the Huntsville circuit, and reside on a plantation near that growing town. At that day, in the far South every lawyer was a politician, and, if he was rich enough, a planter. Clement C. Clay, Arthur F. Hopkins, and Reuben Chapman, all of Huntsville, followed the three occupations. James G. Birney bought a plantation in Madison County, near Triana and the Tennessee River, and within two hours' ride of Huntsville. To this place he removed with his family in February, 1818.

CHAPTER VIII.

LAWYER—PLANTER—POLITICIAN.

1818–1823.

In 1818 the roads between Danville and Huntsville were such as are commonly found in new and heavily wooded countries. Railroads and even turnpikes were then unknown in Kentucky and Tennessee. Rough passage-ways were chopped through the forests by the pioneers. The small trees were cut away; stumps and large trees were left, and about these the wagon-tracks wound in the most convenient curves. There were no ditches, no grading the roads on higher levels; the drainage was as Nature made it. The favorite tool of the pioneers was the axe, not the spade. There were long stretches of flat lands, where the water lay a foot deep several months in the year. These were made passable by "corduroy causeways," constructed of small logs, cut into twelve-foot lengths and covered with small branches, the leaves still on. Rude bridges of heavy timbers were thrown over narrow creeks which were too deep to be forded. The broader streams were crossed on flat-boats, pulled over by means of strong ropes which were stretched from one bank to the other and fastened at each end. The transportation of goods was effected in covered wagons, each drawn by four or six mules or horses. For mutual aid of drivers in case of miring, these wagons were driven in trains. When they met each other on a causeway, one train was driven as close as practicable to the left side of the road and halted, allowing scant room for the other to pass. When the drivers met citizens in vehicles, they would often refuse to give room, compelling them to turn, drive back, sometimes for miles, and leave the road until the wagon teams had passed by. When a citizen in a light vehicle caught up on a causeway with a wagon-train, it was a delicious practical joke for the wagoners to keep him from passing them. The roads from Kentucky to Alabama were crowded with immigrants in February, 1818.

James G. Birney accomplished safely the removal of his family and property, and at once threw himself with energy into his new duties. The plantation was in good order, and most of the fields intended for crops had been plowed; but there were many cares to absorb his attention. Plantation duties did not prevent him from cultivating social relations with the planters of the county, the lawyers at Huntsville, and the leaders in State poli-itics. The Territorial Legislature in 1818 was a small body. The Senate consisted of a single member, who united in himself all its offices. His name was Titus, and it was his humor to go punctiliously through all the forms of legislation, discussing bills sent up from the House, putting them to vote, signing them as Speaker, countersigning them as clerk, and forwarding them with due formality to the Governor. The Legislature met at St. Stephens, a town on the Tombigbee River, about eighty miles from Mobile. It was regarded by the leading men in north Alabama as important that the Constitutional Convention should be held at Huntsville, and this place was designated in the "Enabling Act," passed by Congress in March, 1819, partly through the intervention of James G. Birney with John J. Crittenden, United States Senator, and Henry Clay, then Speaker of the House of Representatives. In Madison County two tickets were elected—one of members of the Convention; the other of members of the first General Assembly. Clement C. Clay headed the first; James G. Birney, the second.* The Convention was in session from the 5th of July to the 2d of August, 1819, during which time James G. Birney was present almost as regularly as if he had been a member. That he was a valuable aid, both because of his literary training (which was uncommon at that time in Alabama) and his sound sense and knowledge of the law, is certain. His liberality and humanity, too, have left their traces in the sections of the Constitution which relate to slavery. In the Mississippi Constitution of 1817 the model had been the one framed for Kentucky in 1799; but the sections relating to slavery had been made more harsh. The Kentucky model empowered the Legislature to emancipate slaves, with or without consent of owners, on making previous compensation, and secured an impartial trial by petit jury to any slave charged with felony. The Mississippi copy limited the legislative power of emancipation without consent of owners to cases in which the slaves had rendered distinguished services to the State, in which cases full compensation was to be made; and it secured an impartial trial by petit jury to slaves in *capital cases* only. On the first point the Alabama Constitution, which in most parts was copied from that of Mississippi, rejected the harsh and narrow Mississippi provision, and empowered the Legislature to abolish slavery on making compensation to owners, as in Kentucky; and on the second it was more liberal than either the Kentucky or Mississippi instrument, as it secured to slaves the petit-jury trial in all prosecutions for crimes above the grade of petty larceny. It adopted from Kentucky the clause so ominous of future emancipation: "So long as any person of the same age or description shall be continued in slavery by the laws of

* See Pickett's "History of Alabama."

this State." And it added the following section which, it is believed, was the first of the kind ever inserted in the constitution of a slave State:

SECTION 3. Any person who shall maliciously dismember or deprive a slave of life shall suffer such punishment as would be inflicted in case the like offense had been committed on a free white person, and on the like proof; except in case of insurrection of said slave.

It is true that these words are found in the Georgia Constitution of 1798; but they are rendered nugatory by the addition of a second exception: "And unless such death should happen by accident in giving such slave moderate correction." Such deaths were not uncommon in Georgia; but, as no master was ever tried, convicted, and hanged for the murder of his slave, all the deaths, to use the constitutional phrase, must have "happened by accident."

It may be well to note here that the General Assembly of Alabama for many years exercised its power to emancipate slaves. The statute books of the State show the number freed at each session for the first eleven years of its existence to have been as follows:

Session.	Slaves freed.
1819	16
1820	4
1821	13
1822	21
1823	11
1824	18
1825	6
1826	12
1827	10
1828	37
1829	55
Total	203

or, an average of more than eighteen for each year.

In October, 1819, James G. Birney took his seat as a representative in the first General Assembly of Alabama, and devoted several months to the task of legislation. Of the large number of organic acts passed at this session, we know that he aided in the preparation of the elaborate "act to regulate the proceedings in courts of law and equity"; and that he was the author of the "act concerning the trial of slaves," which allowed paid counsel to all slaves tried by jury, and which excluded from the jury both the master and the prosecuting witness and the relatives of both. This law made effective the constitutional provision on the subject; it was the outcome of a sentiment of justice and humanity toward a class that had few friends.

At this session circumstances occurred which closed the promising political career of James G. Birney.

The fall races took place in November on the Huntsville course; and under the pretext of attending them with several fine horses, General Andrew Jackson remained two or three weeks in the town, becoming meanwhile intimate with many of the members of the Assembly. After his victory at New Orleans he had been generally regarded at the Southwest as a future President. In November, 1815, Aaron Burr had suggested him as an available candidate; and in 1819 the idea had assumed a certain force in politics. In January and February of that year General Jackson had passed several weeks at Washington; in February he had accepted public receptions at New York, Philadelphia, and Baltimore; and in March his journey from Knoxville to Nashville, on his return home, was a continuous and magnificent ovation, military and civil. Though he denied it on several occasions, the presidential bee was already buzzing in his bonnet.

In Alabama the enthusiasm for Jackson was probably greater than in any other State of the Union; he had fought battles and won victories on its soil, he had protected the men, women, and children of the State from massacre by the Indians, and he was the hero of New Orleans! He was almost a fellow-citizen, too, for he owned a farm near Tuscumbia, on the Alabama bend of the Tennessee River. In the midst of the festivities incidental to Jackson's visit, a Colonel Rose, of Autauga County, a member of the Assembly, offered for adoption a joint resolution of the most complimentary character to the general, and indorsing him as a nominee for the presidency. Mr. Birney had no personal hostility to the general. For a resolution of compliment to Jackson as a military chieftain he would probably have voted—he had done as much in the Kentucky Legislature—but his deepest convictions made it impossible for him to pledge himself to Jackson's political fortunes. To him the general appeared a contemner of the law, a headstrong and violent man, who, in hanging Arbuthnot and shooting Ambrister, in April, 1818, had disregarded evidence and crowned the long series of brutal deeds which proved his unfitness to wield power. He not only voted against Colonel Rose's resolution, but gave his reasons in a calm and forcible speech. From that date his election to political office in Alabama was impossible, and he did not again become a candidate. In the August following, and at several annual elections thereafter, there was no opposition in Madison County to the ticket nominated by Jackson's friends.

During the years 1820, 1821, and 1822, Mr. Birney became embarrassed in his financial affairs. Owing to his frequent absences from home, the inexperience of his slaves in the methods of cotton culture, and his repugnance to severities in plantation management, his cotton crops had not proved profitable. Cotton culture requires skilled labor unceasingly applied in some form for at least eleven months in the year. It admits of no awkwardness in the use of the hoe, no negligence in keeping the weeds from the plants, no clumsiness in picking, no ignorance of the processes of ginning and baling. Kentucky farm-hands who had never seen a cotton field could not at once be made profitable operatives in one.

The idea of buying a few slaves thoroughly trained in cotton culture, and using them to train those he had brought from Kentucky farms, does not appear to have occurred to him during the five years of his experience as a planter. It may be stated here that, although James G. Birney was a slave-holder for sixteen years in Alabama, he never bought a slave in the market. Those taken with him from Kentucky had all been obtained from near relatives of himself or wife—most of them by gift. Before 1832 he had no thought of interfering with slavery further than to restrain importation of slaves into the State, to make public slave-markets illegal, and to punish masters for cruelties inflicted. These measures were the natural result of his early impressions, patriotism, training for public life, and generosity of temperament; and in none of them did he go beyond what was approved by the leaders of public sentiment of that day in Alabama. This is proved by the adoption of his measures by the Constitutional Convention and the Legislature of the State. In 1822 his feelings in regard to buying slaves of a professional slave-trader were such that if it had been proposed to him he would have answered, "Is thy servant a dog, that he should do this thing?"

His manner of living at this time was not economical. He did not deny himself the luxuries to which he had been accustomed from his youth. A carriage, fine driving and saddle horses, expensive furniture, and a lavish hospitality, he regarded as indispensable. In Kentucky he had fallen into the fashion, universal in those days among Southern gentlemen, of playing for stakes and laying wagers on horse-races.

Henry Clay and Daniel Webster were noted examples of devotion to the gaming-table, and they did not differ in this respect from other public men of their day, especially of the South, who were not members of the Church. This fashion is still prevalent in some parts of the South among gentlemen. That it is not yet looked on in Arkansas as a vice may be inferred from the testimony recently volunteered by Attorney-General Garland, before a congressional committee, that he had always "lost at poker." For several years Mr. Birney had been so fortunate as neither to lose nor to win; but a man of his generous disposition could not escape the common fate of all who tempt chance. Several heavy losses in the period now under review, added to his failures as a planter, compelled him to borrow money on mortgage security given upon his plantation and slaves. His slaves had all been reared in either his own or his wife's family; and it would have cut him to the heart to see them sold separately under the hammer to such masters as chance might provide. He made then two resolves: One, never to bet again, which was sacredly kept; the other, to pay off the mortgage upon his property by the more active practice of the law. To carry out the latter, he determined to remove to Huntsville, leaving in charge of an overseer until better times his plantation and slaves, with the exception of Michael, Michael's wife, and three children, whom he would take with him as house-servants.

In January, 1823, he had taken up his residence at Huntsville.

CHAPTER IX.

LIFE AT HUNTSVILLE.

1823–1826.

MADISON COUNTY, Alabama, bounded on the north by Tennessee and on the south by the Tennessee River, is remarkable for the depth and fertility of its soil. Its climate is genial and healthful, being redeemed from the sultriness and blazing heats of the "cotton belt" to the southward, by heavily wooded spurs from the mountain-ranges of the Alleghanies. Cheap transportation for heavy products to New Orleans is afforded by the Tennessee and Mississippi Rivers. The access to it is easy from Tennessee, Virginia, and North Georgia. Owing to these favoring causes, the stream of immigrants, chiefly from the last-mentioned States, began to set into it as early in the century as the county was comparatively safe from the murderous incursions of the Indians. In 1822, Madison was the most thickly populated county in Alabama.

Huntsville, the county-seat, was one of the prettiest towns in the Southern country. Within two or three miles to the south and east a mountainous range, dark with cedars, hickories, walnuts, oaks, and other forest trees of large growth, ran up into a lofty peak, which attracted visitors by its picturesque ruggedness and sandy sea-beaches, shells, and other signs of ancient deluge; and at its northern extremity, flattened into a broad forest-covered plateau, which ended in an abrupt precipice several hundred feet in height. This plateau, shady, cool, and commanding a view of the distant hills of Tennessee, was the summer retreat of the wealthy citizens of Huntsville; it was called Montesano. The site chosen for Huntsville was on high and rolling ground, easily drained. It was a high bluff, from the base of which burst one of the wonderful springs of the world. At its very source, the volume of water was enough to float a vessel of four feet draught in a channel forty feet in width; it was transparent as crystal, cool, and pure. On rolling hills, falling by gentle slopes to the fertile plains of the neighborhood, the town was laid out. The streets were parallel and cross; and the public square, for the court-house and county offices, was in the center. The sides of the public square were built up in stores and shops. The beauty and healthfulness of Huntsville had attracted a number of men of fortune and leisure. General Walker lived in a house resembling the Parthenon; it looked down on the town from a height on the east. Ex-Governor Bibb and other planters occupied costly mansions. In January, 1823, the population exceeded two thousand and was increasing rapidly.

The sudden growth and many advantages of north Alabama had attracted to Huntsville a large number of lawyers. Among them were John McKinley, afterward Representative in Congress, United States Senator, and Justice of the Supreme Court of the United States; Clement C. Clay, Sr., afterward United States Senator; Arthur F. Hopkins, William Kelly, Harry I. Thornton, James McClung, Jeremiah Clements, and Caswell R. Clifton, all of whom became distinguished in public life. The bar was both brilliant and able. It gave a warm welcome to James G. Birney, who had already gained a high standing as a lawyer by his occasional practice on the circuit.

McKinley, a Virginian, who had practiced law at Louisville and known Mr. Birney at Frankfort, and the genial Thornton, a Kentuckian, started a movement which resulted in the almost unanimous election of Mr. Birney by the two Houses of the Alabama General Assembly as solicitor for the Fifth Circuit. This embraced five of the most populous counties in the State. The solicitor prosecuted all criminal cases, and acted as attorney or counsel for the State in all civil cases to which it was a party. For each service rendered a fee was paid from the State treasury. In the hands of an energetic lawyer the office was lucrative. It led, too, to practice in other cases.

When it is remembered that Mr. Birney was then known throughout the State as an Anti-Jackson man, that every member of the Assembly was a Jackson Democrat, and that every member of the Huntsville bar, except one, belonged to the same party, the compliment of Mr. Birney's election will be appreciated. He accepted the position, and entered at once upon the performance of its duties.

At the end of the first year of his residence in Huntsville Mr. Birney concluded not to continue his ownership of a plantation which he had learned by experience he could not in person conduct with profit.

As to employing again an overseer, he would not do that, for during the year of his absence he had been unable to prevent the exercise of brutalities toward the slaves, the overseer insisting that he could not manage without using the lash. The complaints of these poor creatures when he visited the plantation and their appeals to him affected him deeply. Mentioning his difficulties to his friend and neighbor, Mr. William Love, the Kentuckian who had served with him in the Kentucky Legislature and migrated with him to Alabama, that gentleman offered to buy from him all the slaves, at a low price, to be paid one fourth in cash and the rest in installments at long date.

Mr. Love was known as a kind-hearted man and humane master who did his own management. The slaves were satisfied with the change, and rejoiced that they were not to be separated. The arrangement was carried into effect at once, the mortgagee accepting part in cash and Mr. Love's notes in satisfaction of the balance. A subsequent sale of the plantation enabled Mr. Birney to satisfy the claim secured upon it, and left him free from debts and in easy circumstances. About the same time he bought a valuable half-acre corner lot in Huntsville, two squares from the head of the Big Spring.

In 1824 and 1825 Mr. Birney had become so prosperous in worldly affairs that he erected a large brick house as a family residence. With successive additions and improvements it became one of the handsomest and most convenient dwellings in Huntsville. It was on the corner of two streets. A broad, paved sidewalk, bordered with China trees, extended along the street sides of the property, and a high wall sheltered from view a beautiful garden. This was both ornamental and useful, and was kept in excellent order under the supervision of the master and mistress, both of whom had a decided taste for horticulture.

It was his custom to spend about half an hour after tea on spring and summer evenings among the roses, vines, and vegetables, giving a touch here and there with the hoe or pruning-knife, tying up vines, and trimming the young trees. This was his favorite recreation, though once in a great while he went out fishing or hunting.

He and his wife were both fond of social life. Friendly relations were cultivated with the best families in the town and country. Calls were returned, and dinners and parties given. The large double parlors of the house were frequently filled with company. Members of the bar from abroad were hospitably entertained. At the evening parties there were often music and dancing. It was the fashion in those days for very nice people, even clergymen, to drink in moderation; at dinner parties cut-glass decanters glittered on the sideboard, and wine-glasses of varied hue and thickness were placed near the plate of each guest. James G. Birney followed the fashion in this respect. He no longer followed it in having card-tables. These were not to be seen in his house; and, as time rolled on, his social circle gradually assumed a more grave and quiet tone.

His professional practice rapidly increased. He had the qualities which attract clients. He was always in condition for business, and always prepared on his case. He was methodical. Letters received were promptly answered, indorsed, and filed. Papers in the same case were kept together in properly marked jackets; he neither lost nor mislaid them. He knew how to use files, drawers, and pigeon-holes, and could lay his hand without hesitation on any paper in the office. His memorandum-book was kept and consulted; he forgot nothing. If he rejected business, he did so plainly; if he accepted it, he attended to it and thoroughly. He studied each case until he had mastered both the facts and the law, and he never, probably, continued one because he was not ready. He was courteous to other attorneys and to witnesses; he never browbeat, but his cross-examinations brought out the truth, or exposed the equivocations or perjury of the witness. He excelled in the statement of his case and in arguments addressed to the court. In addressing juries he was unaffected and simple, rising to eloquence in none but extraordinary cases. But no man at the bar won cases more surely. This was partly because he never knowingly took an unjust one. A son who wished to sue his father for a board bill was ordered out of Mr. Birney's office. Men went to him with good cases, or with those that were marked with strong equities. He compromised often, and it was generally understood that a case could be settled with him on its merits.

As a public prosecutor he was fearless, but he would not knowingly convict an innocent man. He would not sacrifice an accused party to professional vanity. He neither overstated nor misrepresented the testimony. He represented public justice, and not private passions. When the proof was clear that the accused was guilty, he rarely escaped, for juries came to believe that James G. Birney would not ask a conviction if it were not due.

In such cases his eloquence rose to the occasion, and he was a match for the best counsel. It is probable, however, that his remarkable success at the bar was chiefly due to his well-established reputation for moral courage, integrity, justness, and moderation of thought, candor, and perfect truthfulness. He became the most successful practitioner in North Alabama, with the largest professional income. As early as 1825, his practice had become so large that Arthur F. Hopkins, an able lawyer and eloquent speaker, and greatly respected in the State, returned to Huntsville from Autauga County to accept the position of his junior partner. In 1826 he resigned the office of solicitor for the purpose of devoting his attention exclusively to civil business.

In a book published long after Mr. Birney's death, Henry S. Foote, ex-United States Senator, who visited Huntsville in 1825, testified as follows:

> The famous James G. Birney was also, at the time mentioned (1825), a member of the Huntsville Bar, where he was exceedingly loved and respected. When he afterward became the zealous advocate of African emancipation, though his friends in Alabama could not approve this part of his public career, he still retained much of their respect and kindness, and his integrity as a man was never called in question by them ; nor were

his learning and eloquence as a forensic advocate. Mr. Birney was a singularly fluent and polished speaker, and was known to have given much more attention to the niceties of orthoëpy than was then customary among the lawyers of this newly settled region. (See "Bench and Bar of the Southwest," by H. S. Foote, of Mississippi.)

His practice in the local and appellate courts of Alabama and Tennessee continued to grow until the date in 1831, when he began to reduce it, with a view of removing to Illinois. As his professional career is of minor interest only in this biography, it may be dismissed with the following extract from pages 7 and 8 of the sketch of his life by the Rev. Beriah Green, and a fact stated by a townsman:

A single fact from the history of Mr. Birney's professional career in Alabama, illustrating his integrity, courage, magnanimity, and generosity, may be as acceptable to our readers as it is refreshing to us. The following statement, from authority on which the fullest reliance may be placed, we give in the language, slightly altered, of our informant. Jackson County lay in his circuit. Three years' practice there as solicitor had made him acquainted with nearly all the people of the county. He was personally popular, though as prosecutor he had acted rigorously. The making of counterfeit coin had become quite a business in that county, after he had resigned his office as solicitor. One day a young man of very humble and rough appearance applied to him at Huntsville, where his office was, to bring a suit for him against some of the most respectable men in the county, for having lynched him on suspicion of his having aided his father, who *was* a notorious coiner, and who as such had also been lynched. Between eight and nine hundred of the people of the county, embracing most of the influential men, had associated together as a lynch club; and such was their power, that they inflicted punishments openly—knowing that no verdict could be had against them in Jackson County, where they would be sure to get some of their own friends upon the jury, if they failed to intimidate those whom they had injured. It was hinted to him that unless his cause was just and himself free from the stains of a bad character, it must be far from desirable to engage for him in a struggle with such an influential corps. Satisfied in this respect, Mr. Birney undertook for him, and issued his writs against the wealthiest and most responsible men in the band, all of whom were personally his friends. It had been his custom, in order to avoid traveling on Sunday to the court-house, as was the custom of his brother lawyers, to go to the village where the court was held the *Saturday* before. He had, of course, to travel alone. It was given out that he durst not go to the court-house—that he would be lynched, and so on. He proceeded, however, as if nothing unusual had happened. Within a few miles of the village he met a man who was very anxious that he should return and stay with him till Monday, when the judge and the officers of the court would be in the village. His exposure, then, would be less fearful. He went on, however, and put up at the tavern where he usually boarded. On the Sabbath he was at church, and on Monday went about his business as usual, saluted even those whom he had sued, quietly and in full self-possession, as if nothing had happened. Each wondered that all except himself did not insult him. But they were confident that no jury could be found in that county from which he could obtain a verdict. This he understood as well as they. He had, therefore, made provision through which the cause was to be tried in due season at Huntsville, the place of his residence. *Before he left, however, he brought the defendants to terms agreeable to his client; pecuniary remuneration was made for the trespass, and an agreement was entered into by them never more to molest him. The lynching business was broken up for that time,* AND THE ASSOCIATION DISSOLVED.

Rev. William T. Allen, who was brought up at Huntsville, mentions the following fact in "Slavery as it is" (1838): "While I lived in Huntsville, a slave was killed in the mountain near by. The circumstances were these: A white man, James Helton, hunting in the woods came upon a black man and commanded him to stop. The slave kept on running; Helton fired his rifle, and the negro was killed" (page 46).

Mr. Birney, then prosecuting attorney, drew up an indictment and procured the finding of a true bill against Helton. The murderer escaped and fled the State.

In the newly populated State of Alabama, as in the young States of the West and Southwest, the moral and physical courage of every prominent man was put to frequent severe tests. Until communities became settled and regular, what is called in the Far West "sand" is a prime requisite of character. On many occasions of danger occuring during the first six years of his Alabama residence he met every requirement in this respect. So well was his reputation for coolness and nerve established that the inhabitants of Huntsville, a year after he became a resident of the town, elected him mayor for the purpose of securing the suppression of the bloody brawls and affrays which had become of almost daily occurrence in the streets and public square. Stabbing and shooting affairs were making the name of Huntsville a by-word in the South The officers of the law were helpless and discouraged. The new mayor reorganized the force, headed it when necessary, making some arrests of disorderly persons with his own hands, and succeeded in establishing the supremacy of the law. He served two years as mayor, refusing the salary attached to the office.

James G. Birney was not of a nature to allow his professional pursuits to engross his attention to the injury of the interests of the community in which he lived. What concerned the public, concerned him. From the time he began practice in Kentucky as a lawyer, he had shown the liveliest sympathy with educational movements. He had aided in founding and endowing the Danville Academy. He had become so identified with this kind of public service that, in 1819, he had been appointed one of the trustees of Centre College, at Danville, the new institution which was expected to grow into the leading university of the West; and each year afterward he timed his visits to Kentucky so as to attend the meetings of the trustees. Soon after his removal to Alabama he had been appointed trustee of Greene Academy, a classical school at Huntsville, and he performed the duties of that position through the entire period of his residence in the State. In 1823, one of his first acts after his removal to town was to organize the Huntsville Library Company. In December, he procured a charter in which he was named corporator with Dr. Thomas Fearn, Samuel Hazard, John Boardman, Miles S. Watkins, and other leading citizens. He joined cordially in movements for the improvement of the city. Among these were throwing a strong dam across the head of the Big Spring; creating a water-power and erecting works which forced the water through wooden pipes for the supply of each building with pure water for drinking and all domestic purposes; and digging a canal from the Big Spring, a distance of eleven miles, to the Tennessee River, for the transportation of cotton and other heavy products.

As he grew older, Mr. Birney lost all interest in frivolities, and was gradually becoming disinclined to the amusements common in the South. His relinquishment of play had separated him from many former companions. He had never been a profane man or joined in drinking-bouts. His views of life were becoming more serious, more earnest. In 1825 his children were five in number. Under the responsibilities of domestic, social, and professional life, he had grown into the conservative citizen and exemplary head of a family. His wife was a faithful member of the Presbyterian Church, and for three years he had been her companion at the Sunday services. The two oldest children sat in the pew with their parents. They attended the Sunday-school, and the father sometimes went with them. Under the quiet influence of the mother, social ties had been formed with many church-members; also, with the pastor, Dr. Allen, who was an able, learned man, and a gentleman who recommended religion in his conduct. From his youth up, James G. Birney had reverenced religion; he had never been a skeptic, and he felt a profound respect for the Church and the duties of its ministers. His deep and sincere nature and love of truth predisposed him to the acceptance of religious principle as the guide of his life, and his heart had been won by the beauty of piety as exemplified in his beloved wife. If she had been an Episcopalian, he might have been better content; but it probably never occurred to him to prefer the Church of his fathers to hers. His nature was too broad for sectarianism. For two or three years his tendencies to a religious life had been so marked that when, in the spring of 1826, he made a public profession and connected himself with Dr. Allen's church his friends and the public were not surprised.

From that event dates his new and better life, his performance of duty as he saw it, his increasingly intelligent conscience. From that time he began that slow moral and intellectual growth which, in a few years, brought him to the full stature of a philanthropist and statesman. In future chapters will be traced the almost imperceptible degrees by which he rose from measures designed to benefit his locality to those for the good of his State, the South, and, finally, the country. His growth was organic, not spasmodic. In all he did he was clearly the product of the best elements of Southern society, and his movements in advance were on the prolongation of the lines on which he started.

CHAPTER X.

LIFE AT HUNTSVILLE.

1826, 1827.

One of the first effects of his conversion to the doctrine of doing as you would be done by was the revocation of his refusal, made in 1824, to act as attorney or legal protector of the Cherokee nation, which occupied the northeastern corner of the State. The position was not desirable, popular prejudice running high against the Indians and manifesting itself in frequent depredations, outrages, and crimes against their property and persons. To protect them in their legal rights was not easy; and it exposed the protector to the hatred of ruffians. Mr. Birney had refused to act in this capacity, but the reasons he had offered did not satisfy his sense of duty, and he notified the chiefs that he would accept, if they had made no other arrangement. They closed joyfully with his offer. The plan of this volume will not permit me to recount his acts in behalf of this harrassed and oppressed people in the six years beginning with 1826. He caused missionaries to be sent and schools to be established among them; he encouraged them to cultivate farms, build houses, and open roads; he aided an educated Indian, who had invented an alphabet for the language, to start a Cherokee paper; he defended them in their property rights, and brought to punishment some of the authors of the outrages upon their persons; he counseled them to peace and good behavior; and, most surprising of all, he succeeded in introducing, quietly and without opposition, several Indian girls as pupils into the Huntsville Female Seminary. It was said they were daughters of chiefs. They attended the Presbyterian Church, and were reputed to be wards of Mr. Birney. Two of them I remember as beautiful. The Indians visited Huntsville from time to time for the sale of pelts, nuts, blow-guns, bows and arrows, and game, and they never failed to pass by my father's house, and leave for him some token of their gratitude.

Early in 1826 he began to take an interest in the American Colonization Society, which he regarded "as a scheme of benevolence to the whole colored population, and as a germ of effort capable of expansion adequate to the largest necessities in the extermination of slavery." (See his letter on colonization, 1834.) He aided in getting up a contribution to the funds of the society. This is the first indication in his career of sympathy with the slave, and a consciousness of his personal duty in regard to the evil of slavery. Every year thereafter he and some of his neighbors united in making a similar contribution.

In December, 1826, when he went to the Capitol of Alabama to attend the session of the Supreme Court, he took with him the rough draught of a bill "to prohibit the importation of slaves into this State for sale or hire." This was intended to give effect to a clause in the Constitution of 1819, which gave power to the General Assembly "to prevent slaves from being brought into this State as merchandise"—a clause which had remained a dead letter. The bill was passed, with little opposition, January 12, 1827. The prohibition was to take effect on the first day of the following August. The penalty was—

To forfeit and pay the sum of one thousand dollars for each negro so brought in—one half thereof to the person suing for the same, and the other half to the use of the State. . . . And, moreover, any person thus offending shall be subject to indictment, and, on conviction, shall be liable to be fined in a sum not exceeding five hundred dollars for each offense, and shall be imprisoned not exceeding three months, at the discretion of the jury trying said offense. (Alabama Statutes, 1826–'27.)

This law was not favored by some of the large planters, who desired unlimited facilities for buying field hands; but it pleased those who desired to limit the introduction of slaves into the State, and those who despised slave-traders. That this last class was numerous at the South is testified to by Henry Clay in his compromise speech in January, 1850, as follows: "Sir, it is a great mistake at the North, if they suppose that gentlemen living in the slave States look upon one who is a regular trader in slaves with any particular favor or kindness."

In February, 1827, Mr. Birney revisited Danville, Ky., and spent two weeks with his father and friends. He attended the regular meeting of his Masonic lodge —Franklin, No. 28—and met the brethren in a social reunion. We may fairly attribute to his efforts the remarkable resolution and circular adopted by that lodge, and sent to the Masonic lodges in Kentucky. The resolution was:

FRANKLIN LODGE, No. 28,
DANVILLE, *March 3, 1827.*

Whereas the commerce in slaves carried on by importation to this State from the other slave-holding States conflicts with those feelings of benevolence and philanthropy which it is the duty of every Mason to cherish and inculcate, and is also in direct violation of the laws of the State in which we live, which every worthy Mason is bound to respect and obey;

Therefore, *Resolved*, as the opinion of this lodge, that said commerce is inconsistent with the principles of Free and Accepted Ancient York Masonry and ought to be discountenanced by every member of the fraternity.

The circular was temperate and forcible. It closed with these words:

> We feel it to be the duty of the craft to warn its members from, and to mark with pointed reprobation, all participation in that commerce which, under the influence of a degraded cupidity, imports from other States hundreds of slaves every year to be sold as merchandise in this country, in violation of an express law of the land and the best feelings of our nature, and, as we believe, against the permanent interest of our country.
>
> By order, respectfully and fraternally, your brother,
>
> D. G. COWAN, *Master*.

This document is the companion-piece of the Alabama law passed in the preceding January, and is evidently from the same hand. It was first published, and with praise, in the "Western Luminary" (Lexington, Ky.,) and may be found in full in Lundy's "Genius," etc. (Baltimore, Md.,), of November 24, 1827. For many years James G. Birney entertained the idea of getting slavery into a manageable condition in each State by stopping the interstate slave trade. As in 1827 the slave population was less than one hundred thousand in Alabama and about one hundred and fifty thousand in Kentucky, the idea was not, at the first blush, a chimerical one.

It was during this February visit to Kentucky that the first alienation of any of James G. Birney's relatives or connections from him took place. He was now thirty-five years of age, and had enjoyed their love and friendship without interruption; but in one or more of his conversations on slavery—perhaps among the Masons—he had commented with severity, it was alleged, on the conduct of a cousin by marriage, Ninian Edwards, then Governor of Illinois, contrasting him, much to his disadvantage, with ex-Governor Coles, of the same State. Edwards was born in Maryland, but moved to Kentucky about 1793, before he was of age; he was a lawyer, judge, and finally Chief Justice of the State, when, in 1809, he was appointed Governor of the new Territory of Illinois. In 1792 he had been a zealous advocate of a free constitution for the State of Kentucky; and from 1809 to 1818, the whole term of his service as Territorial Governor, he had resisted the introduction into Illinois of slaves as property, and recommended a free constitution for the future State; but when that constitution was adopted and he was made United States Senator, he voted for the admission of Missouri as a slave State, and the consequent extension of slavery—being one of the renegades among Senators from the Northern States. In the struggle in Illinois, between 1822 and 1824, to prevent the establishment of slavery in that State, Senator Edwards had stood aloof, not appearing to care whether freedom or slavery should triumph. And when a majority of the population, being immigrants from slave States, had voted that Illinois should remain a free State, Edwards had maintained silence and indifference.

On the other hand, Edward Coles, a Virginian, heir to several hundred slaves, a man of education and talent, who had been for six years private secretary to President Madison, had taken his slaves from Virginia, where he could not free them, to Illinois, given them deeds of emancipation, bought lands and built cabins for them, given them stock and farming-tools, and watched over their interests until the freedmen were able to take care of themselves without aid. In each deed of emancipation Mr. Coles had said:

> *And whereas I do not believe that man can have a right of property in his fellow-man, . . . I do, therefore, . . . restore to the said . . . that inalienable liberty of which they have been deprived.* (Deed of July 19, 1819.)

From that time Edward Coles* had thrown himself,

* See E. B. Washburne's "Sketch of Governor Coles," p. 202.

with all his weight, into the work of defeating the schemes of certain Southern politicians to make Illinois a slave State, and in August, 1824, had won victory at the polls.*

Mr. Birney censured Ninian Edwards as a renegade to his own principles, and eulogized Edward Coles as a patriot and statesman. His remarks gave great offense to some of the connections common to him and Governor Edwards, and the rupture was never wholly healed. The incident is important in this biography, as, in the absence of contemporaneous proofs, it shows conclusively that his sympathies had been with the free-soil men in the Missouri controversy.

In 1827, two of his Democratic friends in Madison County, Robert Chambers and Jeremiah Clemens, both lawyers and planters and men of wealth, died, the former leaving him co-guardian of an only son and executor of his estate, and the latter leaving him sole executor of his estate and guardian of his two sons and daughter. These sacred trusts were faithfully performed. One of the sons of Mr. Clemens, Jeremiah, was elected United States Senator in 1849. He wrote several novels of some merit. During his life he cherished a warm regard for his former guardian, never failing to call on him when in the same city. He did what he could to keep Alabama and Tennessee from going out of the Union, but finally adhered to the Confederate Government.

In 1827 Mr. Birney joined, with his usual vigor, in the project to establish in Huntsville a free school on the Lancastrian plan, then in great vogue; but protested against raising the necessary funds by lottery—a plan authorized by the Legislature in January, 1828.

In the same year he sold his handsome residence to A. F. Hopkins, Esq., his partner, and bought, in the northeast

* See Brown's "Early Movements in Illinois for the Legalization of Slavery."

part of the city, a handsome lot of more than two acres in area, with good but not fine buildings. On the opposite side of the street he bought a ten-acre grass lot. Here his taste for building, beautifying, and gardening had full scope. He drained, leveled, graded, planted shade trees, sowed grass seed, built additions, laid out walks, introduced new varieties of grapes, plums, damsons, figs, pears, peaches, melons, etc., made fences, both for fancy and utility, painted and arranged, until the place was as beautiful and attractive as good soil, a genial climate, a southern sun, æsthetic taste, and liberal expenditure of money could make it. In the broad, smooth walks and vine-covered arbors of the garden, the young people of Huntsville found pleasant promenades in the long evenings of summer.

At a later period he bought between three and four hundred acres of fertile land on the Flint River, about ten miles east of Huntsville. It was a romantic spot, on the road to Bellefonte, and he had often passed it on his way to court. A sugar-loaf mountain, with clear springs near its base, the stream from which rippled across the road, and rich bottom-land stretching to the small forest-shaded river half a mile away. Intending it for a stock-farm, he built cabins near the springs, and placed on it a manager and a few hired hands. To this place it was his pleasure to retire when he needed recuperation from professional work. He would join in the labor of clearing up the new fields, burning brush and logs, building fences, and putting in crops. His muscular power was greater than that of ordinary men, and the exercise improved his health; but his highest gratification in farming was in bringing order and beauty out of chaos and ugliness. He was an artist in making homes.

The manager of this farm chafed a good deal under the prohibition of the use of the lash on the servants. On one occasion he sent by the writer, who had been at the farm hunting ducks and squirrels, which were numerous, a note stating that Jack, a negro, must be whipped. My father was much troubled by this note, but sent me back to tell the manager that if Jack would not behave himself he should send him at once to his master. In speaking with me about the matter, he said: "It is hard to tell what one's duty is toward these poor creatures; but I have made up my mind to one thing—I will not allow them to be treated brutally."

CHAPTER XI.

THE POLITICAL CAMPAIGN.

1828.

FROM the date of his anti-Jackson speech in the Alabama Legislature of 1819, Mr. Birney had been identified with the national party that favored a protective tariff, internal improvements, and a liberal construction generally of the Constitution. His high reputation, socially and professionally, gave him influence and prominence in the party councils, and in 1828 he was nominated as one of the electors on the Adams and Rush ticket for Alabama. He immediately took the field, and spoke during the summer and autumn at numerous political meetings held in the chief towns of the State, eulogizing the Conservatism of Adams and attacking the politics of Jackson and Calhoun as fatally dangerous to the maintenance of the Union.

To understand his course and motives, the reader must comprehend the then existing condition of Southern politics and sentiment in relation to slavery and its extension. The truth on this subject has seldom, if at all, been fairly and fully stated.

The friends of Crawford, Jackson, and Calhoun are unwilling to admit inferences unfavorable to them in the present state of public opinion; writers with pro-slavery sympathies reject the idea that there were Union men and abolitionists at the South; and anti-slavery authors, especially most of the Massachusetts ones, concur in this rejection, their bias being to exaggerate the importance of the Northern movement against slavery. The average belief at the North, owing to these errors of superficial or biased writers, is that, after the Missouri struggle of 1820–'21, the nation went fast asleep on the slavery question; that the subject was not discussed at the South because of danger to life, or at the North because of apathy; that the Southern politicians who had achieved the admission of Missouri had at once abandoned their schemes to extend the area of slavery; in short, that, for a decade of years, "thick darkness" and ignorance and acquiescence in wrong enveloped the nation. This erroneous belief, which has become general, has amazing vitality and persistency; I can hardly expect to shake it, but I must do so or fail to make intelligible the public career of James G. Birney, which began to move on well-defined lines in his anti-Jackson campaign in 1828. The reader will indulge me, therefore, in a statement of facts that reflects light on the Southern politics and sentiment of that period.

The "Solid South" took its definite form for the first time in the Missouri struggle. As John Quincy Adams says (diary, March 3, 1820): "In this instance the slave States have clung together in one unbroken phalanx, and have been victorious by means of accomplices and deserters from the ranks of freedom."

The admission of Missouri as a slave State was but a small part of the plan of the slavery extensionists, of whom Crawford was the most able and intriguing. Another part was the restoration of slavery in Illinois, Indiana, and Ohio. John Q. Adams (diary, March 3, 1820) says: "I have had information from the Governor of the State of Indiana that there is in that State a party countenanced and supported by Crawford, whose purpose it is to introduce slavery into that State; and there is reason to believe that the same project exists in Ohio and Illinois." This project had been on foot for many years in the three States above named.

The close of the Missouri controversy was the signal for renewing with energy the struggle to establish slavery in Illinois. A large majority of the voters in the State were immigrants from the South, and the pro-slavery men expected an easy victory. The contest awakened a national interest. Money was contributed freely by Southern slave-holders to one party, and by Philadelphia Quakers to the other. Pamphlets, some of which were written in other States, were circulated broadcast and newspapers were established to discuss slavery. In his interesting "Sketch of Governor Coles," E. B. Washburne has traced this battle from its open beginning to its close. On page 191, he says: "It was on the first Monday of August, 1824, that the election was to take place. The hand-to-hand struggle had continued eighteen months, and superhuman exertions had been made on both sides. Both parties welcomed the arrival of the moment that was finally to end a struggle that had evoked so much feeling and passion, involved so much labor, and absorbed such intense interest."

The friends of slavery were defeated by a large majority. The vote was a deliberate verdict against the institution by men who knew all about it. Even "Egypt" decided against it. This disaster greatly perplexed the leaders of the political South, coming as it did in the midst of a campaign for the presidency. The "Southron" and the "Telescope," two South Carolina papers of the fire-eating class, advised the immediate calling of a convention of the planting States, under pretext of opposition to the moderate tariff law, which had been passed on the preceding 16th of April. But the wiser heads counseled delay and the election in November of a slave-holder to the presidency.

The unexpected defeat of Jackson and election of John Quincy Adams by the House of Representatives caused an immediate change in slave-holding tactics.

Previous to that event, four favorite sons of the South, Clay, Calhoun, Crawford, and Jackson, had disputed for her favor. Clay was popular among Northern manufacturers and in Virginia and Kentucky; and, to capture Southern support, he could refer to his early championship of the Kentucky and Virginia resolutions of 1798; to his advocacy, in 1820, of setting aside the Florida treaty and seizing Texas by force of arms; and to his successful efforts to effect the admission of Missouri into the Union as a slave State.

Calhoun, by his free-trade, pro-slavery, and ultra State-rights doctrines, had alienated the support of the North for the presidency. His tendencies were generally believed to be toward separation of the South from the North. With professions of personal preference for the Union, he generally coupled declarations of his belief that the South would be forced out of the Union and compelled to form an alliance with Great Britain (Adams's diary, February 24, 1820). Any refusal to let the South have its way in anything was, in his eyes, an application of force to that section. All his subtly conceived but illogical theories were based upon the right of each State to nullify the laws of the nation; but, with diplomatic caution, he expressed the hope that no occasion might be presented for the exercise of this right. He was earnestly in favor of the acquisition of Texas and the extension of slavery westward, and is generally credited with being the first to suggest the brilliant scheme afterward incorporated in the creed of the "Knights of the Golden Circle"—the creation of a slave-holding empire, including the Southern States, Texas, Mexico, and Central America.

Crawford had been for a long time Secretary of the Treasury, and had great capacity for intrigue. He was a strict constructionist, and could rely upon the support of Virginia and Georgia, and of Jeffersonian Democrats generally. His devotion to slavery extension was undoubted.

Jackson was not identified with any theory of politics; he was a man of the people, and had received a majority of the popular vote at the election of 1824. Besides, he was an illustrious general, and had gained the most brilliant victory in the annals of his country. While his devotion to the extension of slavery was undoubted and unquestionable, he was opposed to nullification, believing that the slave States should remain in the Union and rule it.

Immediately after the election of Adams a coalition appears to have been formed by the Southern friends of Crawford, Calhoun, and Jackson. The general, as the most available candidate, was to be made President in 1828; Calhoun was to be Vice-President; and Crawford, who was in ill-health, was to be suitably provided for in case of success of the coalition. Adams appears to have been aware of this scheme soon after it was formed. January 27, 1825, he enters in his diary that Calhoun said "his personal wish was for my election. This contrasts singularly with the conduct of all his electioneering partisans." And February 11th, of the same year, he mentions Calhoun's plan "to bring in General Jackson as the next President."

On Clay's confirmation as Secretary of State, fourteen Senators, most of them Southern, including one from Virginia, and all from North Carolina and Georgia, voted in the negative, which votes, Mr. Adams thought, indicated "the rallying of the Southern interests and prejudices to the men of the South."

Another indication of the coalition is thus noted by Mr. Adams: "Thomas H. Benton, who, from being a furious personal and political enemy of General Jackson, became, about the time of the recommendation, a furious partisan in his favor" (diary, March 5th).

It was in the same year (1825) that Mr. Calhoun said to Nathan Sargent that it (the Adams administration) "must be defeated at all hazards, regardless of its measures." (See Van Holst's "Life of Calhoun," page 65.)

From the election of Adams to that of his successor, in 1828, all means were employed "to fire the Southern heart." Public meetings were held in every part of the Carolinas and the Gulf States, and inflammatory harangues were made, until the South was ablaze with excitement. The tariff of 1824 was the pretext until the passage of the Tariff Act of April, 1828; and this was denounced as an aggravation of the evils of the first. It was assumed by the free-trade orators that manufacturing industries were impossible at the South, which could be only agricultural; that Europe was the only market for cotton; and that the tariff was a Northern measure, calculated to impose upon the cotton-planters the whole burden of the expenditures of the National Government. The citizens of Columbia and Richland, in a memorial to the South Carolina Legislature, said, "The Northern and Middle States are to be enriched by the plunder of the South."

In an address to the people of South Carolina, the citizens of Colleton District said of the tariff: "It lifts them" (the North and West) "to prosperity, while it sinks us into ruin. We have done by words all that words can do. To talk more must be a dastard's refuge."

They advised "an attitude of open resistance to the laws of the Union."

It was recommended in a South Carolina paper that the Southern States should prohibit the introduction into them from the Northern States of horses, mules, hogs, beef, cattle, bacon, bagging, and other products; and should impose a municipal tax, large enough to be prohibitory, on all goods, wares, and merchandise, the produce of those States.

A Georgia paper addressed to the North the words of Abraham to Lot: "Separate thyself, I pray thee, from me," etc.

A congress was suggested to devise means of protection "from the operation of the tariff bill, and prevent the introduction and use of the tariffed articles in their respective States." (See Young's "American Statesman.")

At a meeting in Columbia, S. C., in 1827, Dr. Thomas Cooper, president of the State college, made a speech which contained the following passages: "A drilled and managed majority has determined at all hazards to support the claims of the Northern manufacturers and to offer up the planting interest on the altar of monopoly." Protection—"a system by which the earnings of the South are to be transferred to the North. . . . We of the South hold our plantations under this system as the serfs and operatives of the North." "Is it worth our while to continue this union of States, where the North demands to be our masters and we are required to be their tributaries?"

At a grand tariff banquet in Richmond, Va., in 1827, William B. Giles, a free-trade leader, proposed and the guests drank a toast "to the Tariff Schemer! The South will not long pay tribute." (See Logan's "Great Conspiracy.")

January 15, 1828, the Legislature of Alabama passed "A joint remonstrance to the Congress of the United States against the power assumed to protect certain branches of industry," and denounced the proposed woolen bill "as a species of aggression little less than legalized pillage on her property, to which she can never submit until the constitutional means of resistance shall be exhausted."

The enactment in April, 1828, of another tariff, enabled the political leaders at the South to heap fresh fuel on the fire. Soon after this a public meeting, held at Walterborough, S. C., issued an address calling upon the people "to resist," repeating in different paragraphs "We must resist," and ending with: "Does timidity ask when? We answer, now!"

About the same time the anonymous nullification pamphlet of fifty-six pages, known in political history as "The South Carolina Exposition," was printed. Before the end of summer it was in the hands of all the prominent pro-slavery politicians of the South. It was a manual of the arguments for nullification, presented with all the ability of its author, John C. Calhoun; and its influence in shaping pro-slavery policy was very great. This candidate for the Vice-Presidency, on the Jackson ticket, was actively and secretly engaged in undermining the Union!

The outcry against the tariff had its minor-key accompaniment in charges against President Adams of hostility to the South. He was not a slave-holder, refused to employ slaves at the White House, had appointed abolitionists to office, had recommended sending delegates to the Panama Congress, and was opposed to the acquisition of Texas and to the extension of slavery.

Henry Clay did what he could to allay apprehensions of danger from Adams, and to dissuade the political South from forming a pro-slavery party. In his speech at Lewisburg, Va., August 30, 1826 (see page 380, volume of his speeches, published in 1827), he said:

There are persons who would impress on the Southern States the belief that they have just cause of apprehending danger to a certain portion of their property from the present Administration. It is not difficult to comprehend the object and the motive of these idle alarms. Suppose an object of these alarmists were accomplished, and the slave-holding States were united in the sentiment that the policy of this Government, in all time to come, should be regulated on the basis of the fact of slavery, would not union on the one side lead to union on the other. The slave-holding States can not forget that they are now in a minority, which is in a constant relative diminution, and should certainly not be the first to put forth a principle of action *by which they would be the greatest losers.*

There were not wanting eminent and able men at the South who advocated the tariff. Among these were James Madison, of Virginia. His two tariff letters to Joseph C. Cabell, printed in 1828, still hold an honorable place in political literature. James G. Birney went further—he not only advocated the tariff, but took issue with the South Carolina nullifiers and the slavery extensionists. In numerous speeches delivered in different parts of the State, he exposed the sophistries of the resolutions of 1798, pointed out the dangers of attempting to control national politics in the interest of a single pecuniary interest, and warned the slave-holders not to invite a national discussion of slavery by attempting to extend it over new States in Texas, thus destroying the balance of power between the North and the South. He appealed to them not to repeat the agitations of the Missouri controversy; not to awaken the sleeping lion; and he developed and illustrated the suggestions made by Henry Clay in his Lewisburg speech, in 1826.

If the reader believes in the prevalent error, that, in the decade ending with 1830, any and every discussion at the South of slavery or its extension, was promptly punished with death at the hands of a mob, he will be incredulous in regard to the character of Mr. Birney's speeches in 1828. To remove skepticism on this subject, I propose to devote the twelfth chapter to stating a few of the many facts tending to prove that freedom of speech was not unknown at the South during and before the period in question. It is believed that careful historical research will establish the truth of the following propositions in regard to the mobbing of abolitionists in the South:

1. In the border slave States, with the exception of Missouri, during the agitations of 1820–'21, it had been almost unknown before the election of General Jackson to the presidency; and in the Gulf States, it was local, occasional, and rare before that event.

2. After the election of Jackson the toleration of slavery discussion was rapidly narrowed in its limits; and the prejudice against Yankees led to an increase in the number of cases of mob violence.

3. The horrible slave insurrection of August, 1831, at Southampton, Va., caused a panic that resulted in mobs and the expulsion from the South of a number of persons suspected of tampering with the slaves, and in the general strengthening of "the patrol system," organized under law to keep the slaves in subjection.

4. The defeat of the nullifiers, in the winter of 1832–'33, turned all their activities into the agitation of slavery, for the purpose of creating a sectional feeling as a basis for a future separation of the States. Hostility to Northerners was fomented, and vigilance committees were formed, the chief duty of which was "to hang abolitionists" on short shrift. In this work the Jackson and Clay men vied with the nullifiers; and before the end of 1835 the South was terrorized into silence, and thoroughly organized to support the claims of the slave power.

That this was the view taken by Thomas H. Benton

may be inferred from the following passage from the second volume of his "Thirty Years in the Senate":

> Mr. Calhoun, when he went home from Congress in the spring of that year (1833), told his friends that "The South could never be united against the North on the tariff question—that the sugar interests of Louisiana would keep her out, and that the basis of the Southern union must be shifted to the slave question." Then all the papers in his interest, and especially the one at Washington, published by Mr. Duff Green, dropped tariff agitation and commenced upon slavery, and in two years had the agitation ripe for inauguration upon the slavery question.

CHAPTER XII.

ABOLITION IN THE SOUTH BEFORE 1828.

THERE were many portions of the South which were not under the control of any one of the three schools of slavery extensionists. In East Tennessee, before 1828, the stream of anti-slavery opinion was full and strong. It was formed of two confluents—the Presbyterian and the Quaker—both from North Carolina.

The most prominent Presbyterian abolitionist in that region between 1800 and 1830 was the Rev. Samuel Doak, D. D. He was born and brought up in Virginia. His parents being unable to bear the expense of giving him a liberal education, he built for himself a cabin near the college at Lexington, Va., supported himself as a student by working and teaching, graduated with honor, went to Princeton, and took his theological degree in 1775; taught as tutor in Hampden Sydney College for two years; was licensed as preacher, and migrated in 1777 to the Holston Valley, in Tennessee. He fought the Indians, taking his rifle and leading his congregation; was member of the Constitutional Convention held in 1784; established an academy which grew into Washington College, and was president of it from 1795 to 1818. He then resigned in favor of his son, the Rev. John M. Doak, D. D., and established the "Tusculum Academy" at Bethel, Tenn., which also developed into a college, in the presidency of which he was succeeded by another son, the

Rev. Samuel W. Doak, D. D. During his whole career he taught theology and prepared a large number of students for the ministry. He died in 1830. (See Sprague's "Annals," page 303.)

He was a large and strong man, healthy, and both able and willing to do a great amount of work. His striking characteristics were manly good sense, calm dignity, indomitable firmness, and powerful intellect; and his moral influence over those brought in contact with him, especially the young, was very great. He was commonly called the Presbyterian bishop. Though he had been for many years opposed to slavery, he did not take the step of emancipating his own slaves until about 1818. Eleven of his freedmen removed to Brown County, Ohio, and their descendants are there at present. From about that time he inculcated upon all his students, theological and literary, the principles of immediate abolition. It was probably due to his teachings that the noted Sam Houston, one of his pupils, gave his vote many years later against the Kansas-Nebraska bill, and vetoed the Texas ordinance of secession; and that his step-son, Robert McEwen, kept the national flag flying over his house at Nashville during the whole course of the rebellion. It was through his influence chiefly that the Presbyterians of his own and the neighboring county bought two promising young men of color, John Gloucester and George Erskine, freed and educated them for the ministry of their Church, and that the Union Presbytery of East Tennessee licensed and ordained them. They were eloquent preachers. Gloucester became pastor of a colored congregation in Philadelphia, and Erskine had charge for a time of a white congregation. (See A. T. Rankin's "Truth Vindicated," page 5.)

The presbytery just named was formed in part of ministers whose ethics had been fashioned in their youth by the strong hands of the venerable Dr. Doak, and it was always distinguished by liberality on the slavery question. Some of his graduates were members of the Abingdon Presbytery. The famous abolitionist Rev. John Rankin was his pupil for three years (1813–1816). The Rev. Jesse Lockhart, who from about 1820 preached immediate abolition, and lectured on it in southern Ohio, was taught by him.

For half a century Dr. Doak was recognized as the principal column on which rested the Presbyterian Church of East Tennessee, and as his influence was always thrown against slavery, public opinion was liberal on that subject.

It was principally under Quaker influence that the Manumission Society of Tennessee was formed in 1814. Membership was not limited, however, to that sect. Charles Osborn, Quaker, sat in it side by side with John Rankin and Jesse Lockhart, Presbyterians. The State legislation urged for compulsory emancipation was that a day should be fixed, on and after which every child born in the State should be free. Most of the members believed in preparing the slaves for liberty; some, among whom were Charles Osborn, John Rankin, and Jesse Lockhart, believed in immediate abolition. This society held annual conventions and issued annual addresses to the people with great regularity; and several times before 1829 was represented in the American Convention to promote the Abolition of Slavery. The minutes of its eleventh annual convention, held August 15, 1825 (see Lundy's "Genius" for September of that year), show an attendance of delegates from twelve auxiliary societies with a membership of five hundred and seventy persons, three of which societies were county organizations, and that ten auxiliaries were not represented. It was resolved by that body to establish at Greenville a quarterly paper to be entitled "The Manumission Journal."

In 1820, at Jonesborough, Tenn., Elihu Embree, a

Friend, had established an octavo monthly paper called "The Emancipator," probably the first newspaper in the United States whose avowed object was the abolition of slavery. Mr. Embree was a manufacturer on a large scale, belonged to a numerous family, and was a man of influence in his county. He died a few months after starting his journal, and Benjamin Lundy, of Mount Pleasant, Ohio, who had already published at that place eight numbers of the "Genius of Universal Emancipation," removed to Tennessee and continued its publication, first at Jonesborough and afterward at Greenville, in the adjoining county, until October, 1824, when it was issued at Baltimore. (Appendix B.)

A Greene County, Tenn., correspondent of the "Genius" (No. 9, October 16, 1829) announces the re-election in that county of John Magaughy to the Assembly, and adds: "Mr. Magaughy did more in the last Assembly on the subject of slavery, in behalf of the Manumission Society, than any one ever did at any previous session."

The fertile flat breadths of land in West Tennessee were favorable to large plantations and working numerous gangs of slaves; but the American sentiment of inalienable and equal rights found advocates there also. In December, 1824, a number of persons convened at Columbia, Maury County, and formed "The Moral, Religious Manumission Society of West Tennessee." The preamble to the constitution* declares that slavery "exceeds any other crime in magnitude"; that instrument declares it "the greatest act of practical infidelity," and that "the Gospel of Christ, if believed, would remove personal slavery at once by destroying the will in the tyrant to enslave," and prescribes as follows:

ART. 8. None that own or hold slaves can be admitted as members of this society.

---

* Published in full in the "Genius" of February, 1825.

That the movement in Tennessee was not an isolated one will be demonstrated by a few facts taken almost at random from those occurring in other slave States.*

The Manumission Society of North Carolina was formed in 1816. Ten years later, the number of its auxiliaries was forty-five, and its cause was advocated by the "Patriot," a newspaper edited with marked ability. The most active men in the membership were probably the Mendenhalls, the Coffins, and the Swains—William and Moses. There were several auxiliary societies of ladies not counted in the number above given.

In the proceedings of this State Society, there is one document which establishes conclusively the existence in North Carolina of many "immediate abolitionists" in 1825. It is printed at length in the number of the "Genius" for September, 1825. The heading is as follows: "Queries proposed by the Board of Managers of the Manumission Society of North Carolina, to be answered separately by the branches, and forwarded to the next meeting of the General Association."

This "next meeting" was held September 9, 1825. It is presumed the answers were all in. A committee was appointed to collate them and "prepare general answers." The fifth query was in these words:

5th. Is a majority of the citizens of North Carolina opposed to slavery?

The general answer to this was as follows:

5th. We suppose the popular sentiment of North Carolina may be estimated according to the following view, viz., *one thirtieth of the people are crying out for immediate emancipation among us;* one twentieth are for gradual emancipation; one fifteenth are supporting schemes of emigration and colonization; three

* The "Abolition Intelligencer" was published in 1822 and 1823 by the Rev. John Finley Crowe, D.D., of Shelbyville, Kentucky.

fifths are ready to support emancipation by paying their money and otherwise, provided masters would cheerfully give up their slaves and Government would undertake the work on a plan that would operate with justice, and insure the safety of all parties; one twentieth have never thought of the subject, and neither know nor care anything about it; three twentieths are moderately opposed to emancipation, merely because they think it impracticable; and one twentieth are bitterly opposed to it in almost every shape, not because they expect to sustain a material loss in property by the emancipation of slaves, but because they are ignorant enough to think that heaping senseless execrations on manumission societies, etc., is an excellent way of flattering the rich or avaricious. According to this view, it appears that three fifths of the people, or sixty in every hundred, are favorably disposed toward the principle of emancipation, but are sitting at ease, waiting for some exciting cause to shake off the prevailing apathy and give impulse to that course of policy which they know already is just and expedient. We believe about three twentieths, or fifteen in every hundred, are at this time active supporters of universal emancipation in some way or other.

This is the whole answer to the query. In its estimate of the proportion of "immediate abolitionists" it must be taken to be impartial; for in the answer to the sixth query the opinion of the society as to the best means of abolishing slavery is in effect formulated thus: 1. Non-importation of slaves into the State; 2. Prohibition of all sales of slaves; 3. Freedom of all born after a fixed date; and 4. Emigration and colonization of the blacks. The queries and answers were signed by Richard Mendenhall, President, and Aaron Coffin, Secretary, and were forwarded by order of the society to Benjamin Lundy for publication.

As the above is the only deliberate census of Southern opinions on slavery, taken in forty-five different localities in a State, made and published before 1828, and as it was sanctioned by intelligent and conscientious men, citizens and knowing the facts, it may be safely taken as a sure guide to public sentiment at its date, not only in North Carolina, but in Tennessee and Virginia. The proportion of abolitionists, immediate and gradual, in Maryland and Kentucky was, for obvious reasons, much larger. With the mention of the single fact that in the years 1824, 1825, and 1826, about two thousand slaves were freed in North Carolina, and 726 in one body were removed from the State as required by law, by the Society of Friends, we will pass to the State of Maryland.

At the time (October, 1824) Benjamin Lundy began the publication, at Baltimore, of the fourth volume of his paper,* it was generally expected that Maryland would soon take her place among the free States. Only four years had elapsed since the people of the city of Baltimore, at a public meeting, the mayor, Edward Johnson, presiding, had denounced the admission of Missouri into the Union as a slave State, and two thousand of her citizens had signed a petition to Congress to the same effect; and only eight months since Elisha Tyson, the philanthropist and emancipator, had fallen at the ripe age of seventy-five, after a life whose deeds of heroism entitle him to rank among the great souls of our race. He was born of a family of Philadelphia Quakers, but removed to Harford County, and afterward to Baltimore, in early manhood. When he witnessed the sufferings of the enslaved and persecuted Africans, his soul was seized with a mighty love and pity for those wretched people, and he consecrated the best energies of his life to their service. If any one was illegally held in slavery, he hunted up the proofs and appealed to the courts. To this class belonged all those brought into the State. Some were freedmen who had lost their papers; others were descended from Indians or other free persons; some had mothers who were freed-

* "Life of Tyson," p. 103.

women. He was indefatigable in bringing these cases before the judge of the county court, who, to his honor be it said, enforced the law. From his biography, published by Lundy in 1825, and written by John S. Tyson, his nephew, I extract the following passage:

> The labors of Mr. Tyson were not confined to a single district, they extended over the whole of Maryland. There is not a county in it which has not felt his influence, or a court of justice whose records do not bear proud testimonials of his triumphs over tyranny. Throwing out of calculation the many liberations *indirectly* resulting from his efforts, we speak more than barely within bounds when we say that he has been the means, under Providence, of rescuing at least two thousand human beings from this galling yoke of a slavery which, but for him, would have been perpetual.

He exerted himself to put down the traders in slaves and turned the business into disgrace. His biographer says:

> The traffic in human flesh, once so common, and carried on by persons looked upon as respectable, came to be of very limited extent, and conducted by the lowest and basest of mankind. Dungeons for the reception of slaves about to be exported dwindled down to two or three. . . . All this happy revolution was the work of one man . . . (p. 12).

He procured the passage of several laws ameliorating the condition of the slaves and facilitating emancipation, persuaded many masters to give deeds of manumission, and aided in the erection of churches and schools for the freedmen.

Mr. Tyson's whole life proves that he regarded slavery as a sin, to be repented of and abandoned instantly by the slave-holder. It is probable, however, that when there was question of general abolition by compulsory statutes, he thought it wiser to follow the example of the States which had become free. It must be borne in mind that, in 1824, New York was still a slave State, and there were slaves held in Pennsylvania, New Jersey, and Illinois.

Another efficient anti-slavery worker in Maryland was Daniel Raymond, a lawyer of high standing and a member of the Baltimore bar. Of liberal education, he had devoted much time to the study of political economy. In 1820 he published the first, and in 1823 the second edition of an elaborate work on that subject in two octavo volumes containing eight hundred and fifty-six pages. All the implications of the work are against systems of forced labor, and he devotes the thirteenth chapter of the second volume to the discussion of "The Influence of Slavery on National Wealth." A few extracts will show its character:

> The mass of human suffering which has been already caused by negro slavery. . . . The most ardent philanthropists and the most splendid talents have, during the last thirty years, been employed in portraying the horrors of slavery. . . . The man who should now justify the slave-trade would be looked upon as a monster of human depravity. . . . It behooves a Christian people to use all diligence in purifying itself from this abomination. . . . The current of popular opinion is against slavery. . . . Slavery, a hackneyed, worn-out subject. . . . A very little reflection, however, will satisfy any man that the scheme [colonization] is utterly hopeless, so far as it proposes to rid our country of the black population or abolish slavery. . . . If the Gordian knot of slavery is not untied within a century from this day it will be *cut*. . . . They are here, and have as much right to remain here as the whites. . . . There are people enough who would set their slaves free provided the law allowed it.

Comparing slavery to a noose about the neck of the slave States, he says:

> The only way of getting out of the noose is by forcing the slave-owners to let go their hold upon the slaves and set them free. . . . *Diffusion* [through new slave States] is about as effect-

ual a remedy for slavery as it would be for the small-pox or the plague. . . . By procrastinating the day of manumission we increase the difficulty of manumitting. . . . All that is required is a general permission in all the States for masters to manumit their slaves whenever they see fit. Such a law would promote manumission fast enough for the present . . . no great and sudden changes would be produced in society.

Mr. Raymond had been a colaborer with Elisha Tyson, and he gave a cordial welcome to Benjamin Lundy. On the formation of the Maryland Anti-Slavery Society, August 25, 1825, he was elected its president. He was three times the candidate nominated by that society on the abolition platform for the House of Delegates of Maryland. In 1825 he received six hundred and twenty-four votes. In 1826 he was again brought forward. On the 2d of September the officers of the State Anti-Slavery Society published an address "to the independent voters of the city of Baltimore (see "Genius" of that date) recommending Daniel Raymond for their suffrages. It is four columns in length. The gist of it is in the following extracts:

A period must be fixed by law for the termination of slavery. . . . Nothing will be adequately effectual [against kidnapping] but the total abolition of slavery, nothing but the annihilation of the market for slaves.

The following is valuable historically:

In our sister State of North Carolina the advocates of general emancipation are increasing with a rapidity unparalleled in the annals of this nation. It is believed that nearly three thousand citizens of that State have enrolled themselves as members of anti-slavery societies within a period of two years. . . .

The Anti-Slavery Society of Maryland consists at this time of four respectable branches with several hundred members, although thirteen months have not yet elapsed since the first proposition was made for its organization.

In the States of Virginia and Delaware, societies for the abolition of slavery have also recently been formed, and many influential individuals therein are actively engaged in promoting the doctrines of universal emancipation.*

There were nine candidates. The result was as follows:

J. S. Tyson	3,898	*D. Raymond*	974
J. Stricker	2,507	C. R. Richardson	616
G. H. Steuart	2,420	C. S. Walsh	528
R. Purviance	1,319	M. A. Dysart	39
C. C. Harper	1,011		

The two gentlemen elected were on the National Republican or Adams ticket. The next two were Jackson Democrats.

Among other comments the "Genius" says:

Walsh, the most violent antagonist we had, was completely prostrated, receiving but about half the number of votes that he did last year. . . . It is admitted by many that Stricker owes his election entirely to the favorable views he took of the anti-slavery principle. And Tyson has always been known to be zealously opposed to the system of slavery, though he has never consented to pledge himself to advocate its abolition upon the plan of the Anti-Slavery Society.†

The abolition party was so encouraged by the result of the election that, two days afterward, October 4, 1826, it put Raymond in nomination for the next year's election, and issued an address to the voters of Baltimore. But, alas, for human expectations! Before the October elections of 1827 the storm blew fiercely for General Jackson, the military hero, who was secretly pledged to the

* "Genius," October 7, 1826.

† "Genius," October 13, 1827. This gentleman was the biographer of Elisha Tyson.

extension and national ascendancy of slavery; and Mr. Raymond was obliged to withdraw from the canvass.

Lundy wrote: "There are, it is true, a few advocates of emancipation in the Jackson party; but the number of substantial, reflecting men among them is small, compared with those favorable to the Administration."

The Jackson party elected its candidates in Baltimore, both city and county. Its victory, however, was a mortal blow to the Maryland Anti-Slavery party which languished from that time. It did not feel strong enough to nominate a candidate in 1828, but it brought forward Mr. Raymond again in 1829. He came in at the foot of the poll, receiving only one hundred and eighty-six votes. That was the last political effort of the abolition party in Maryland. After the inauguration of Jackson, blandishments, honors, and offices were used freely to win the State; and gradually a free press and anti-slavery men were put under the ban, disappearing almost altogether after the Southampton insurrection. It has been argued that if the Baltimore abolitionists had nominated and voted for their ticket in 1827, they would have increased their vote from year to year. But this argument leaves out of view the fact that the movement in Maryland was subject to the same general causes which impeded and finally arrested similar movements in all the more northern slave States. The retardation of anti-slavery efforts in the South kept even pace with the advance of the slaveholding Democracy. Abolitionism lost as Jacksonism gained.

One more fact must end this chapter. Between the close of the war in 1815 and the end of 1828 the following journals which avowed the extinction of slavery as one, if not the chief one, of their objects, were published in the Southern States:

1. "The Emancipator" (Tennessee), 1819.

2. "The Abolition Intelligencer" (Kentucky), 1822.

3. "The Genius of Universal Emancipation" (Tennessee and Maryland), 1821.

4. "The Liberalist" (Louisiana), 1828.

The "Genius," Lundy's paper, was the best of the four, and had the largest circulation. It was published more than twelve years in the South.

CHAPTER XIII.

LONG VISIT TO THE FREE STATES.

1830.

THE manner of conducting in the North the canvass of the Adams party in 1828 had not met the approval of Mr. Birney. During its progress, he had repeatedly written to the leading men and managers, urging that personalities against Jackson should be dropped and prominence given in the press and on the platform, to the real issues—"Texas annexation and nullification." For unexplained reasons his views did not prevail; Clay was irresponsive, and Adams stood coldly aloof. The contest was waged mainly on such immaterial issues as the alleged bargain for office between Clay and Adams, the degree of social polish and literary education of General Jackson, his marriage, his execution of Ambrister, Arbuthnot, and others, and his military qualifications, in all which the popular prejudices were against the Adams party. Coffin handbills increased the vote for Jackson. The people elected the military hero, without inquiring into, or knowing his probable policy in regard to the extension of slave territory, or his views touching the right of a State to nullify the laws of the Union.

At this result, Mr. Birney was surprised as well as grieved. He had expected better things from the Northern and Middle States. Having done his political duty with energy in a State in which his party was in a hopeless minority, he wasted no time in idle regrets. Resuming his practice in Alabama and Tennessee, he again devoted himself to his professional duties.

One of the first effects in Alabama of Jackson's election was the repeal, January 22, 1829, of the law of 1827, which prohibited the introduction of slaves into the State for sale or hire.

The inauguration was promptly followed by measures calculated to bring about the acquisition of Texas.

Soon after the close of the war with Great Britain (1815), the emigration of slave-holders to Texas had been encouraged by Southern politicians, with a view to the ultimate seizure of the country. In 1819, an armed invasion of Texas from the Southwest had been prevented by the United States Government. Between 1825 and 1829, five insurrections had been attempted by colonists, who were acting, the Mexican Government believed, with the connivance of Joel R. Poinsett, of South Carolina, the United States Minister to Mexico. After the accession of Jackson, the demonstrations of Mr. Poinsett became so marked that in August, Mexico demanded his recall because of his intermeddling with her internal affairs.

During the same period, it became generally accepted by intelligent men in Tennessee and North Alabama that the well-known Sam Houston, always a confidential friend and political *protégé* of General Jackson's, was actively employed in plans for another insurrection in Texas, though ostensibly acting as an Indian chief.

In the summer of 1829 a series of able essays, over the signature "Americanus," urging the immediate purchase of the province of Texas, were published in the "Richmond Enquirer," and copied into many of the other Democratic papers of the South. The author was understood to be Thomas H. Benton, who was then in the President's secret councils. (Lundy's "Genius," September 25, 1829.) It was claimed by him that "five or *six more slave-holding States may thus be added to the Union,*" which would give the South "a preponderating influence in the councils of the nation." The comment of the "Enquirer" was: "The statesmen who are at the head of our affairs are not the men we take them to be if they have not already pursued the proper steps for obtaining the cession of Texas, even before the able numbers of Americanus saw the light."

August 25, 1829, President Jackson, through the Secretary of State, authorized the United States Minister at Mexico to offer four million, and, if necessary, five million dollars for the purchase of Texas. One of the arguments to be used for the sale was the insurgent disposition of "the present inhabitants of Texas (not Spanish), which has," says Van Buren's letter, "in the short space of five years, displayed itself in not less than four revolts, one of them having for its avowed object the independence of the country." *

The offer to buy was indignantly refused by the Mexican Government, and for the purpose of preventing further efforts by President Jackson to extend slave territory by dismembering Mexico, a decree was published by President Guerrero in the September following abolishing slavery in that country. This was a heroic remedy for slaveholding encroachment. It had the effect of arresting for a time open measures by Jackson to effect annexation, but it stimulated emigration from the South to Texas. The emigrants went armed, and many of them took slaves with them in defiance of Mexican law. Another effect was greatly to strengthen the influence of the nullifiers or separatists over the cotton-planters of the South, always

---

* See correspondence in full in Dr. Mayo's "Eight Years in Washington."

eager to exchange worn-out fields for fertile ones farther west.

Mr. Birney regarded the political situation as growing worse instead of better, and frequently made it the topic of conversation with his visitors, especially with Nicholas Davis and Arthur F. Hopkins, who were Union men, and had been his coadjutors in the campaign of the preceding year.

In December, 1829, he received from Henry Clay a letter introducing Josiah F. Polk, Esq., an agent of the Colonization Society, and inclosing a copy of the very able colonization speech recently made by Mr. Clay in Kentucky.

Mr. Polk was a man of ability. He was Mr. Birney's guest for several days, and no doubt developed to him fully, as he understood them, the views of Mr. Clay. Up to this time Mr. Birney does not appear to have connected himself with any colonization society, but, in January, he aided Mr. Polk to form one at Huntsville (Dr. Watkins, president), and became a subscriber to the "African Repository," the monthly published by the national organization. Not long after he joined in the formation of the Madison County Colonization Society, of which he acted as treasurer for about two years.

In the same month, in the Senate of the United States, occurred the bitter attack upon the New England States by Colonel Hayne, of South Carolina, and the masterly answers by Daniel Webster. These speeches brought out strongly at the South the lines of demarkation between the Union and the secession elements. On which side the sympathies of James G. Birney lay was shown in the fact that he caused one of his sons to memorize and declaim at Greene Academy one of the finest passages in Webster's speech. At no time in his life did he ever admit the thought of disunion. In looking forward to the future he saw no divided country. In his patriotism he knew no North, no South, no East, no West. For the first time in the history of American oratory had the grand idea of "the nation" been adequately expressed. He looked upon Webster's speech as affording a basis for the organization of all good men, North and South, into a party for the defense of the Union and the prevention of slavery extension. He determined to visit the free States, confer with leading Union men, and judge for himself the condition of public opinion. It was only a few months before the opportunity to visit the North on a highly honorable mission was extended to him. In the summer of 1830 the board of trustees of the University of Alabama, having received a more liberal endowment, resolved to add to the faculty of the institution a president and four professors. They unanimously requested Mr. Birney to visit the Atlantic States on their behalf, make selections of such persons as he should think suitable, and recommend them for appointment. The request was communicated by Governor Moore with a private letter urging him to accept. Such a tribute from political opponents was grateful. He accepted. As soon as this was known his co-trustees of the Huntsville Female Seminary requested him to select three teachers for it. In the performance of this double duty he left home about the first of August and was absent until the end of October, visiting Virginia, Pennsylvania, New Jersey, New York, Connecticut, Massachusetts, and Ohio. He bore letters of introduction from Governor Moore, C. C. Clay, Henry Clay, and some other men of note, and appears to have visited many prominent educators and statesmen in the East. His daily memoranda from August 31st to October 1st have been preserved. They are very brief and were evidently intended simply to remind him of dates of visits:

August 31st.—Went this morning and delivered a note written by Mr. John Sergeant to his brother Thomas.

Delivered my letter from Governor Moore to the Hon. Mr. Hemphill. He received me very kindly.

Delivered my letter to Dr. Chapman. It was from Mr. H. Clay. Received very kindly. Soon felt as if I were conversing with an old acquaintance or confidential friend; and yet there is at first something very courtier-like in his address.

Delivered a letter of introduction from President Woods, of Lexington, to the Rev. W. T. B. . . . He conversed with great ease as a scholar of good taste.

In the afternoon Mr. Dallas (Geo. M.) went with me to the house of Joseph R. Ingersoll. . . . I felt much pleased at the frank and polite manners of Mr. Ingersoll.

Dr. McAuley, who, all men with whom I have conversed who know him say, is qualified in a remarkable manner for such a presidency, declines being considered as a candidate. He recommends Dr. Wisner, of Boston, or Mr. Spencer, of Northampton.

He went from Philadelphia to Princeton, and saw Drs. Miller and Alexander; then to New Brunswick, where he called on his old college friend, George Wood, "the most distinguished lawyer in the State," and made the acquaintance of the President and professors of Rutgers College; then to New York, where he saw Profs. Charles Anthon, Henry Vethake, Renwick, Griscom, and others; then to New Haven, where he saw President Day, Drs. Taylor and Fitch, Judge Daggett, Mr. Ingersoll, and others. There, and in the neighborhood, he made the acquaintance of Messrs. Andrews and Stoddart, afterward distinguished as authors of a Latin grammar.

In the afternoon, heard Mr. Bacon (Leonard G.), a Congregational preacher, a very superior man.

At Middletown he saw Wilbur Fisk, president of the Methodist college. At Hartford he called on Henry Hudson, whose wife—

a very sensible and polite woman, on my expressing a desire to see Miss Beecher (Catherine), accompanied me to her home and introduced me to her. She is good-looking—not handsome—good figure. I informed her of my wish to engage teachers for a female academy at Huntsville. She recommended three young ladies in her school, and desired until to-morrow to consult with them in relation to the matter. Before I left her lodgings she presented me with a copy of her work on education. Retired to my room and read it through before bedtime.

The result of several visits to Miss Beecher and the three young ladies was the employment of the latter to teach at Huntsville. They were Misses Brown, Southmayd, and Baldwin. They remained several years at Huntsville, and were eminently successful. Mr. Birney was so much pleased with Miss Emmons's infant school, a sort of "kindergarten" affair, that he induced her to go to Huntsville with the other ladies and establish her school there, guaranteeing a certain pecuniary success. Such a school was a novelty in Alabama, and, under the able management of Miss Emmons, flourished for many years.

Mr. Birney visited the famous Round Hill School, then kept by Mr. Cogswell and George Bancroft, now famous as a historian; and he recorded his pleasure in the conversation of Mr. Bancroft, who, among other things, "gave me some history of the management of German universities, showing a very excellent plan."

He reached Boston September 17th, the second centennial anniversary of that city. There he saw many eminent men. He notes Mr. Evarts as "one of the most unostentatious and sensible men I have met," and Dr. Wisner as "all he had been represented—fine appearance, easy and flowing in language," etc.

Went to deliver my letter from Dr. Chapman to Daniel Webster. Received me in his office very courteously. He concluded by referring me to Mr. Ticknor, a learned professor of Harvard, to whom he addressed a note, and sent a servant to show me the house.

He dined with Dr. Wisner. Among the guests invited to meet him was Dr. Bacon, of New Haven.

Sept. 19th.—Heard Dr. Channing in the morning. He fell below my expectations in everything but in the *finish* of his essay, for it could scarcely be called a sermon. Heard Dr. Beecher (Lyman) in the afternoon. His manner not good, though sometimes impressive.

Sept. 20th.—Went to Cambridge this morning and delivered my letter from Mr. Clay to President Quincy. . . . Went after dinner again to Charlestown to see Mr. Everett (Edward). Found him a most polite and affable gentleman, etc.

Sept. 21st.—Went in company with Mr. Evarts, Dr. Beecher, and others to Andover, this being the "commencement."

He revisited Middletown, Hartford, and New Haven, and entered into negotiations at New York with Theodore D. Woolsey, afterward professor and president at Yale.

After seeing hundreds of persons, including many public men, and finding that most of those he would have preferred as professors were unavailable, either because of previous engagements or disinclination to make homes in the South, he returned home by way of Ohio and Kentucky. One of the results of his Northern tour was the following recommendations to the trustees of the University of Alabama:

Rev. Alva Woods, D. D., President; Gordon Salstonstall and William W. Hudson, Professors of Mathematics, Natural Philosophy, and Astronomy; John F. Wallis, Professor of Chemistry, Mineralogy, and Geology; Henry Tutwiler, of the University of Virginia, Professor of Ancient Languages; and Rev. Henry W. Hilliard, of English Literature. All these entered upon the duties of their respective posts in 1831. The trustees of the university unanimously voted a letter of thanks to Mr. Birney for his services in the selection.

The most marked effect of his long visit to the North was to freshen and strengthen his convictions of the superiority of free over slave institutions. He started on his return journey, thinking seriously of the problem of adding Kentucky and Virginia to the list of free States, but greatly disappointed at the apparent unconsciousness among Northern public men of any imminent danger in the political situation. He returned through Ohio, in order to observe for himself the condition of a free State in the West.

CHAPTER XIV.

ABANDONS PARTY POLITICS—INTENDED REMOVAL TO ILLINOIS—VISIT OF T. D. WELD.

1830–1832.

BEFORE returning to Alabama Mr. Birney spent two weeks in Kentucky. The special purpose of this delay was to confer with Mr. Clay in relation to the movement in behalf of gradual emancipation which had been foreshadowed and outlined in the latter's speech of the previous December. Mr. Birney went to Lexington, and made several visits to Ashland. What passed between him and Mr. Clay was never stated by either of them. The result, however, was that the two never again traveled on the same political path. In October, 1830, James G. Birney's practical connection with the national Republican party ceased. He took no part either in the political preparations for the candidacy of Henry Clay in 1832, or in the campaign; and he did not vote at the election in that year. It may be added that when the Whig party was formed he did not join it, or act, or vote with it; *he never cast a Whig ballot.* The contrary has been so often asserted as to have become a conventional statement in sketches of his life written by Whigs; the only foundation for it being his political friendship for Henry Clay up to the month of October, 1830.

The personal friendship between them remained unbroken. Mr. Birney maintained ever afterward a guarded reticence in reference to Mr. Clay, and the latter, it is believed, never uttered an unkind or disrespectful word about his former friend, even under the provocations and mortification of his defeat in 1844—a defeat falsely attributed by many of his friends to Mr. Birney. In truth, they never saw each other again, except once in 1834; and the previous correspondence between them, in which Mr. Clay had repeatedly spoken of him as "one of his most esteemed friends," shrunk into a few letters on professional business written at long intervals. For several years immediately preceding these visits Mr. Birney had not seen Mr. Clay, and his idea of the man had been formed of youth's illusions crowned with a halo of Mr. Clay's fame as an orator and statesman. In these years Mr. Birney himself had greatly changed; his character had been purified and strengthened by his religious faith; his knowledge of men was without selfishness. The interviews at Ashland dispelled his illusions in regard to Mr. Clay; instead of a statesman, he found a rhetorician and politician. He left Ashland deeply disappointed, and, it may be added, perplexed and discouraged.

In October, 1830, the times were propitious for a political movement against the menaced annexation of Texas and consequent permanent domination of the slave-holding interest, and in favor of a reduction in the number of slave-holding States by emancipation in Kentucky and Virginia. In such a movement, alone, could the issues tendered by the Jackson Democrats be fairly met, or a successful appeal be made to that national sentiment which had united the North in 1820 against the admission of Missouri, excluded slavery from Illinois in 1824, and abolished it in New York in 1827. The North, which had never listened to the cry of oppressed humanity, might be depended upon to resist its own subjugation to the South. As to the two principal border States, an influential portion of the slave-holders themselves favored freedom. At its first annual meeting, held in 1830, the Kentucky Colonization Society had adopted the following statement in the manager's report: "The late disposition to voluntary emancipation is so increasing that no law is necessary to free us from slavery, provided there was an asylum accessible to all liberated. (See "African Repository," May, 1830.)

Such a movement was contemplated in 1821, under the leadership of Rufus King; but it was defeated by the non-concurrence of the friends of John Quincy Adams, who hoped to be made President in 1824, with a Southern man as Vice-President—General Jackson being the one considered as available.

Everything pointed to Henry Clay as the leader of such a movement in 1830. He was the favorite son of Kentucky, a popular man in his native State of Virginia, and the champion of the capitalists and manufacturers of the Northern and Eastern States. For his disastrous errors on the Arkansas and Missouri questions he had apologized in declarations, often repeated, against the "curse of slavery"; and, in his December speech in 1829, he had sketched a programme of operations for the final extinction of slavery which authorized all thinking men to believe him ready to join in them.

But Mr. Clay took a different view. For his expected candidacy in 1832 he was trimming his sails to catch the winds from both North and South, hoping to win General Jackson's friends, and work his way to the presidential chair by concessions to enemies, glittering but equivocal phrases, and waivers of his professed principles, which gained for him repeated defeats and the unenviable title of "the compromiser." He not only refused to participate personally in a gradual emancipation movement in Kentucky, but advised his friends not to do so; and it was chiefly through his influence that the efforts to set one on foot were chilled.

Before calling on Mr. Clay Mr. Birney had talked over the gradual emancipation project with the Rev. John C. Young, the eloquent President of Centre College; with Rev. J. D. Paxton, Judge John Green, Daniel Yeiser, P. G. Rice, Michael G. Yonce, and William Armstrong—all of Danville; with his wife's uncle James McDowell, and his long-time friends Thomas T. Skillman, bookseller and publisher, and the Rev. Robert J. Breckenridge—all of Lexington.

All these were ready to act, and thought many others would join them. The following paper was circulated for signatures. Fourteen respectable citizens subscribed their names. At this point effort ceased until, at the instance of Mr. Birney, who wrote from Alabama, Mr. Skillman, the proprietor of the "Western Luminary," of Lexington, published the paper in that journal.

GRADUAL AND SAFE EMANCIPATION.

We, the undersigned, slave-holders, under a full conviction that there are insurmountable obstacles to the general emancipation of the present generation of slaves, but equally convinced of the necessity and practicability of emancipating their future offspring, have determined to form ourselves into a society for the purpose of investigating and impressing these truths upon the public mind, as well by example as by precept ; by adopting among ourselves such a system for the gradual emancipation of our slaves as we would recommend to our fellow-citizens for their adoption as the law of the land ; and by dispersing such writings as may be likely to contribute to so good an end. The society will not be called together until fifty subscribers are obtained.

Wm. R. Hines, Bardstown; Samuel K. Snead, Jefferson Co.; J. M. C. Irvin, R. J. Breckenridge, of Fayette Co.; A. J. Alexander, Charles Alexander, J. R. Alexander, Woodford Co.; James McCall, Rockcastle Co.; John Wallace, Fayette Co.; Norman Porter, Thomas T. Skillman, Lexington; George Clarke, Fayette Co.; James Blythe, Lexington; George W. Anderson, Fayette Co.; James G. McKinney, Lexington; James H. Allen, James McDowell, Fayette Co.

These gentlemen were among the most respected citizens of Kentucky. Within a few weeks thirty-four more slave-holders sent in their names as members, and, as received, they were published in the "Luminary." They were as follows:

Fayette Co.: J. S. Berryman, Rowland Chambers, Geo. M. Chambers, John C. Richardson, Hugh Foster, J. C. Harrison, Rev. Robert Stuart, James C. Todd, and John H. Bell; Mercer Co.: Thomas Cleland, Michael G. Yonce, P. G. Rice, President John C. Young, William Armstrong, Rev. John D. Paxton, and Daniel Yeiser; Lincoln Co.: Judge John Green, John L. Yantis, and Samuel Warren; Woodford Co.: William E. Ashmore, Samuel Wingfield, Samuel V. Marshall, Robert Moffett, Dr. Louis Marshall, Colonel John Steele, and Dr. C. Wallace; Franklin Co.: C. P. Bacon and Rev. J. T. Edgar; Hardin Co.: David Weller; and Jefferson Co.: Warrick Miller.

Any native Kentuckian familiar with the old families of the State will recognize the above list as remarkable for the intelligence, wealth, and influence of the persons named in it. Most of them were Presbyterians, and at least six of them were Presbyterian preachers, three of these Reverends—Robert J. Breckenridge, John C. Young, and John D. Paxton—being men of national reputation. Mr. Birney, not being a resident of the State did not sign the paper; but he was alluded to as follows by his friend Mr. Skillman, of the "Luminary":

In reply to a correspondent in Illinois, who wishes to know what Presbyterians are doing in this cause, we remark that the first projector of this emancipation scheme, as published in several of our last numbers, is a Presbyterian; and that, so far as we are informed, Presbyterians generally have taken a prominent part in promoting these benevolent schemes, whose object is the amelioration of the condition of our colored population.

But this well-considered scheme came to naught, for want of a leader in Kentucky. Among its friends, this *rôle* might have been taken by Judge Green, R. J. Breckenridge, or John C. Young; but the Judge was absorbed in business, Mr. Breckenridge about that time quit law for theology and had his hands full of controversies, and Mr. Young was the president of a college. Mr. Clay's friends were begging for postponement, until after the next presidential election, of a movement likely to compromise him either with the South or the North; and they were full of promises. The opportune moment was lost, and the Gradual Emancipation Society was not organized when it might have accomplished something. It was postponed to a more convenient season.

Mr. Birney had now experienced three disappointments: The trade in slaves between Alabama and the slave-breeding States of Kentucky and Virginia had been again legalized; he had been forced to dismiss Henry Clay out of his life and hopes; and his native State appeared to be on the downward road to the abyss. His letters to his father in 1831 were decidedly pessimistic so far as the South was concerned, and that, with his estrangement from Clay, caused his father much concern. The writer was under his grandfather's care at the time, heard these letters read as they were received, and has never forgotten the impression made by them. The worst elements of Southern society seemed to Mr. Birney to be rapidly gaining the mastery; and neither the Church nor the state indicated any power of resistance. What distressed him more than anything else was that circumstances were forcing him to bring up his children amid the corrupting influences of slavery. He was apparently tied down to Alabama by his established profession, his friends, his home, his church, his large property, and his usefulness in the educational interests of the State. From all these he began to think of separating himself, in order to flee from the Sodom of slavery with his large family. It was not possible, without heavy pecuniary sacrifices. He had under advisement the project of closing up his business, selling out his property, and finding a home for his family in a free State, when the startling news of the Southampton, Va., insurrection, in August, 1831, burst upon the South, with its train of bloody horrors. It may have been this that turned the trembling balance in favor of removal. In the months of October and November following Mr. Birney visited Ohio, Indiana, and Illinois, with a view to the selection of a place in which to rear and educate his children. After seeing the principal cities and towns in those States, he made choice of Jacksonville, Ill. Aside from its beautiful site and the fertility of the adjacent country, the chief attraction was the intelligence of the population and the imminent establishment of a college, of which the Rev. Edward Beecher was to be the president. When he returned to Huntsville, it was with the definite intention to wind up his law business, sell his landed property, and make all other necessary adjustments of his affairs, so that he might remove his family, including his servants, to Jacksonville. This, he thought, would require from eighteen months to two years. He began at once, by declining new law business and making sale of half his largest piece of real estate in Huntsville.

On his journey homeward through Tennessee an incident occurred which illustrates his benevolence. After supper, one evening, he was sitting on the front porch of the tavern at which he was stopping for the night when he was startled by piercing shrieks and the sound of blows of a whip from an outhouse. The voice was that of a woman. Such sounds were not uncommon in the South, but Mr. Birney could not bear them; he interfered. The person wielding the cowhide was a large and powerful white woman; the victim was a negro woman about twenty-five years old, who was tied by her wrists to a joist of the upper floor in such a manner that she stood on tiptoe. Her clothing was stripped from her shoulders to the waist, and her bared back was interlaced with bluish welts, old and new. A mulatto girl child of about five years old cowered in a corner of the room, terrified and silent. The cause of the punishment was explained at once; the slave-woman was the mistress of the tavern-keeper; the child was theirs; and the wronged wife was wreaking her vengeance upon her rival. The voice of sympathy was to the poor slave as the voice of an angel of God. She watched her opportunity, found Mr. Birney alone, and implored him to save her and her child from the hell on earth in which they had lived for five years. In short, Mr. Birney bought the woman and child from his host, who, to do him justice, was glad to send them out of reach of his wife, put them into the stage-coach, and took them with him to Huntsville. The writer well remembers the wretched plight of the woman and child when they arrived, and that for a year or two afterward the child did not entirely lose the nervous, frightened look of a timid and hunted creature.

At the time of this purchase, Mr. Birney was not an abolitionist; no cavils as to the propriety of his action perplexed him. Indeed, after he became one, he was not given to those subtle quiddities of doctrine which prevented some abolitionists from contributing funds to buy the freedom of Frederick Douglass, because, forsooth, the purchase would be a recognition of the right of the master. He always, in proper cases, contributed his share of the ransom. Like the sisters Grimké, who also were Southern abolitionists,* Mr. Birney never reached that sublimation

---

* See "The Sisters Grimké," pages 41, 133, 233, 250, and 314.

of doctrine which made some turn away from the slave when he besought aid in the anguish of his soul.

Early in January, 1832, the news of a bloody slave insurrection in Jamaica, involving the burning of many sugar plantations and the loss of many lives, reached Tuscaloosa, where the Alabama General Assembly was in session. From day to day the wildest rumors spread through the State of arson and massacre; it was said that all the slaves of that island had revolted, and were devastating the country and massacring the women and children. The truth was that the whites were murdering the blacks, killing in January more than two thousand, and the blacks were making feeble defense and reprisals.

Occurring within a few months after the insurrection in Virginia, the event caused a general panic through the slave-holding States. At Tuscaloosa, the effect was a strong reaction in favor of re-enacting the law of 1827, which had been repealed in 1829. Mr. Birney was at Tuscaloosa in attendance on the courts. He and others prepared an elaborate bill in more than twenty sections, entitled "An Act to prevent the introduction of slaves into Alabama, and for other purposes"; and this, with a few amendments, was passed and approved by the Governor on the 16th of January, 1832. It was the expiring throb of the free-soil sentiment in Alabama, for the reaction died out within a few months, and the ten most important sections of the law were repealed by the next General Assembly on the 4th day of December, immediately after the beginning of the session. It is believed that no subsequent effort was made to check the importation of slaves into the State. Cotton was king, and ruled until its crown was torn off by the bloody hand of war.

Before Mr. Birney left Tucaloosa, he had informed Mr. Clay's friends of his intention to take no part in the pending presidential campaign; and during the year 1832 he was not present at any meeting held for political purposes, nor did he contribute to any party fund. He simply held himself aloof, and devoted his energies to closing up his business and making sale of his real estate, preparatory to removing to Illinois. This intention, however, was not yet publicly declared.

Since his early manhood, his liberalism in regard to slavery had been generally recognized; but during the five years preceding 1832 he had become widely known in Kentucky, Tennessee, and Alabama, as a friend of gradual emancipation. Among the Presbyterians his reputation in this respect was well established. His wife and older children were well aware of his intention to take his slaves to Illinois and free them there; and his sons had been carefully taught habits of self-reliance, and forbidden to avail themselves of the services of the slaves.

It is not strange, therefore, that when the famous platform orator, Theodore D. Weld, was making his arrangements in Ohio, in the spring of 1832, for a lecturing tour on temperance and manual-labor education through Kentucky, Tennessee, and Alabama, he heard of James G. Birney as a Union man and emancipationist, and obtained letters of introduction to him. The commendations bestowed on him by the writers of these letters inspired Mr. Weld with a strong desire to make his acquaintance. How he did so is best told by himself. In 1882 the author wrote Mr. Weld for the details of his conversation with Mr. Birney. Under date of September 10th of that year, Mr. Weld answered:

Your honored father's bearing and spirit in those conversations so strongly moved me that now that I write that aspect of serene right-mindedness is all undimmed, although I look at it through the mists of half a century. It seems just as fresh and vivid as when, in 1832, it first won my love and reverence at Huntsville, whither I went with a letter of introduction to him from

Prof. Larrabee, of Jackson College, Tennessee, afterward for some twenty-five years president of Middlebury College, Vermont. As Prof. Larrabee handed me the letter, he said: "Mr. Birney is one of the noblest men I've ever met. Though a slaveholder, he *has nothing of the slave-holding spirit.*" How true to the letter I found that testimony during the close intimacy of years that followed. When I called at his house to deliver the letter, he was away on his judicial circuit, and not to be at home for a week.*

Mr. Weld became the guest of Dr. Allen, the Presbyterian preacher. He says:

I found the doctor the holder of two families of slaves, fifteen in number—the oldest ones the marriage portion of his wife, the younger their children. He said that one of his slaves was a Baptist elder, and generally preached on Sunday to the slaves on the neighboring plantations. The doctor was quite free to talk of slavery.

Nothing could have suited Mr. Weld better. He had been an immediate abolitionist from early boyhood, was versed in the philosophy of human rights, familiar with all the aspects of slavery, was full of fire and eloquence, and a match for the doctor in argument, although the latter was distinguished for his ability. At that time the padlock had not become the normal attachment to the lips of men in the South. Mr. Weld says:

In previous years, while yet in my teens, and just out of them, say from eighteen to twenty-one, I had often talked with slaveholders about the system—when slavery was not a contraband topic. My travels and sojourn were mainly in Maryland, Delaware, Virginia, North Carolina, and District of Columbia, and those with whom my introductions brought me in contact, and who often made me their guest, talked about slavery with entire freedom, not only tolerating my dissent, but even encouraging it

* This fact fixes the date of this visit in June. During May the session of the court was in Huntsville.

by never showing irritation or impatience; and always (indeed, I can recall no exception) condemning it as a system, but generally were hopeless of deliverance; and here and there I found a slave-holder saying, "I agree with you," and one who pooh-poohed at the prophecy that if the slaves were emancipated they would cut their masters' throats. "Nonsense! they might do it to get their liberty, but *never because* they had it." But though I had thus much talk with slave-holders previously, Dr. Allen was the only one with whom I had in such length and minute detail discussed the question.

The discussion between Mr. Weld and Dr. Allen lasted a week, much of it turning on the nature of the right under which one man could claim another as a slave. When Mr. Birney returned, Dr. Allen invited him to meet Mr. Weld at dinner, advising him of the discussion on slavery, and informing him that he should now turn Mr. Weld over to him. Mr. Birney called in acknowledgment of the invitation. The impression he made is thus described by Mr. Weld:

At this first sight of him, that blended dignity, courtesy, and amenity, so characteristic of his uniform bearing, was its own interpretation.

The same day, when the three withdrew to the parlor after dinner, your father said in substance: "Gentlemen, I learn you have been having a week's discussion on slavery, and that I, being a slave-holder, am expected to take up the cudgel upon the side of slavery." He then said that, before declaring his side, he "must know how both sides stand in the discussion thus far; so I must depend upon you to tell me what points have been made, how supported, how refuted—in a word, the process you have gone through together and brought the question up to its present stage."

So it was agreed that Mr. Weld should restate the arguments; which he doubtless did in his own bright and interesting style. Before he had finished, the summons came to tea.

> Meanwhile [says Mr. Weld], the only part taken by your father during the afternoon was to ask a variety of questions touching different points made in the discussion. The manner and spirit in which these questions were put greatly attracted me. They bespoke the utmost candor, a simple, earnest intent in pursuit of truth, a quick conscience, perfect fairness—the traits of a mind that *could not be partisan.* Indeed, during the whole afternoon, as I went on in the rehearsal from one point to another, I felt assured that he was with me, head and heart, in the positions which I had taken throughout.

Mr. Weld judged rightly. He had given eloquent expression to the deepest convictions of his hearer. But Mr. Birney said nothing that evening. He excused himself from tea and retired, after inviting Mr. Weld to dine with him next day. At that time he fully indorsed all Mr. Weld had said, and declared that the legal right of the slave holder was a "monstrous moral wrong."

In a conversation with Mr. Weld a few days later he said to him: "I shall not live a legal slave-holder any longer than till I can devise the wisest and safest way of putting my slaves in legal possession of themselves, and making such provision for them in liberty as justice and benevolence require."

This is the testimony of the only surviving witness to these conversations. Taken in connection with the facts heretofore narrated it throws a flood of light upon the motives which had influenced Mr. Birney for several years. One other fact if it had been known to Mr. Weld at the time would have accounted for Mr. Birney's guarded language as to the time he would take to emancipate his slaves. Michael, the husband and father of the family legally owned by Mr. Birney and who had been brought up with him from boyhood, had been unable to conquer his appetite for strong liquors, and needed the constant watchful care of his master and friend. For some years the probability was that if free he would become a confirmed drunkard and beggar his family. The children were nearly grown, but had little mental capacity. For years Michael had understood that his freedom would be restored to him as soon as he could control his love of ardent spirits. My father's intention, well understood by his family, was to take Michael and his children to Illinois; but his habitual reticence did not permit him to speak of those matters to a stranger.

Henry Wilson, in his "Rise and Fall of the Slave Power in America," attributes to Mr. Weld the "conversion of James G. Birney to anti-slavery principles." This is flatly contradicted by Mr. Weld in a letter to the author, and is inconsistent with the facts of Mr. Birney's life. The error, however, has been repeated until it is accepted by many as the truth. The effect of the profound discussions by Mr. Weld was to give Mr. Birney a deeper interest in the subject of slavery and a conviction in regard to its removal. If he had not seen Mr. Weld, he would probably have removed to Illinois before the end of the year 1832. Having seen him, he was in a state of mind favorable to the acceptance of the mission offered him in July—to operate against slavery—and which will be the subject of our next chapter. Mr. Weld's visit was important in its collateral results, and as laying the foundation of a life-long friendship, but it "converted" Mr. Birney to nothing. His anti-slavery principles were the organic growth of a lifetime, not a sudden revelation.

A second accredited theory of this supposed "conversion," the conventional sudden change of heart being assumed as indispensable, is that Mr. Birney happened to read a stray copy of the "Liberator," and that the random shaft went home. With reference to this, the author inquired of Mr. Weld whether, in his conversations in Alabama with Mr. Birney, any allusion was made by either party to Mr. Garrison's paper. The following passage in Mr. Weld's letter quoted from above is, I presume, his answer to the inquiry: "The news of Mr. Garrison's "Liberator," though started some months before, had not yet reached Alabama. Indeed *I did not myself hear of it until my return to New York* some months later." *

While it is certain that Mr. Birney had never seen the little Boston paper, it is not at all improbable that he had seen the "Emancipator," published in 1820, at Jonesborough, Tenn., by Elihu Embree; the "Genius of Universal Emancipation," published from 1821 to 1824, at Greenville, Tenn., by Benjamin Lundy; and the "Abolition Intelligencer," published in 1822 and 1823. But his very accurate knowledge of slavery was the fruit of personal observation and experience; and his repugnance to it grew out of an enlightened conscience, early impressions, education in free States, a strong sentiment of justice, and his conviction that it was undermining the free institutions of the country and endangering the Union of the States.

---

* Seventeen months; the first number was issued January 1, 1831. Mr. Weld did not hear of the "Liberator" until it was nearly two years old.

CHAPTER XV.

EXPERIENCE AS AN AGENT OF THE COLONIZATION SOCIETY.

1832–1833.

If any reader has taken up this memoir with the idea that Mr. Birney's inspiration to work against slavery was instantaneous or even hurried, that he had the divine afflatus of one of the Hebrew prophets, or even imagined himself specially commissioned of God for any purpose, he has probably been stripped of his illusions by this narrative. Mr. Birney was a man of his time and place; not superior to the limitations that restrain men generally, susceptible to social influences, bound to the South by the ties of birth and kindred, and devoted to his native and adopted States. In his early liberalism on the subject of slavery he did not differ from very many of the leading men of Kentucky or from many of the most intelligent citizens of Alabama prior to the reign of Jackson. That he always desired the extinction of slavery is probable; that he did so in 1826 rests on his own testimony.*

It would be interesting to know the names of the Alabamians who shared his anti-slavery views and who cooperated with him in obtaining the restrictions on slavery enacted in 1819, 1827, and 1832; but, in the lapse of time, the materials for the statement of them have perished or

* See his letter on Colonization.

are inaccessible. Mr. Birney was a very practical man as well as a sincere Christian. He was prudent as well as bold, having regard to possibilities as well as to theories, and never forgetting common sense in favor of radical abstractions. At the time we have reached his abhorrence of slavery was banishing him from his native South, but he shuddered at the thought of the horrors he thought would follow the general immediate abolition of slavery. To him, as to most Southerners, it appeared to involve social convulsions, the overthrow of civilization in the South, and the substitution of immorality and barbarism. His sentiment on these subjects is the key to his course in 1832.

His preparations for removal to Illinois had occasioned very vigorous protests from his friends at Huntsville, which, however, did not cause him to hesitate. Early in July he was greatly surprised at receiving an appointment as an agent of the Colonization Society. His district was to include Tennessee, Alabama, Mississippi, Louisiana, and Arkansas. His acceptance was urged in a highly complimentary letter from Rev. R. R. Gurley, who, among other kind expressions, had termed him "one of the most distinguished lawyers in the South." Mr. Birney answered it in a long letter,* dated Huntsville, Ala., July 12, 1832. Some extracts will interest the reader:

> The call given by your society, to all appearance *providential*, added to the earnest resistance of my most esteemed religious friends to my project of removing from among them, has really staggered me not a little.

The above passage contains perhaps the only indication of a belief on Mr. Birney's part in the doctrine of special providences. Such an offer, coming unsolicited

---

* The originals of this, and several other letters from J. G. Birney to the Rev. Dr. Gurley, have been kindly placed in my hands.

and unexpected at the only time in his life when he would have considered it, would have shaken the unbelief of the most incredulous. He had delayed his answer several days, for two reasons: First, to receive a pamphlet which Mr. Gurley had promised to send—

the last annual report of the society, after the perusal of which I would be better informed as to its true condition and the possibility of my being able to render essential service as an agent.

He tells Mr. Gurley he has not yet decided to accept, and that there is one obstacle to his doing so—

which I fear will be almost insurmountable. I mean the necessity which will be imposed upon me as agent to be absent from home, and, of course, prevented from giving any attention to the education of my children for such long periods. I apprehend that if I neglect the duty of educating my children, . . . as I must necessarily do by annual absences from home of five or six consecutive months, the taking upon myself of the agency offered would no longer be a duty.

He writes of his having advertised his property for sale, "with a determination to leave the State," and gives the reason as follows:

I had become so fully convinced of the corrupting influences of slavery on the character of the *young* among us, especially those of our sex (and six of my seven children are boys), that although born in Kentucky and always commanding the services of slaves, I had visited Illinois and decided to remove there.

Of the salary offered him, he says:

The compensation proposed, though very far inferior to my professional gains, is liberal. No one who would in the present circumstances of the society ask more would be morally qualified for so great a work as would devolve upon your agent. His commanding motive must be to do good, because it is *the will of God*, or he will be comparatively unsuccessful.

As his acceptance will be a matter of great moment to

him and his family, he wishes to have a clear understanding of all that will be expected of him; and he, therefore, asks full answers to ten questions. Most of these are not now of interest. The first is as follows:

1. Say, I spend each year from three to four months continuously in the Southern and Southwestern portions of the district, attending Legislatures, conferences, synods, etc., of ecclesiastical bodies, the rest of the year in the northern part of the State and in the Tennessee Valley, *where I think much may be done;* and in the State of Tennessee, say within one hundred miles of this place, the excursions to be for ten, fifteen, and twenty days, with opportunities for frequently being at home for short periods—would this be a compliance, etc., with the society's rules respecting its agents?

The fifth is as follows:

5. How will the society expect its agents to travel? In the cheapest practicable manner, or by the ordinary modes of conveyance, such as steamboats, stages, etc.? My own opinion is that in the South he must travel as any gentleman in good circumstances would do not employed on an agency. He must not be placed in the attitude of one *rendering* thanks for what the community may do favorable to the society, but rather to *receive thanks* from the community.

He asks to have sent to him all the annual reports, the proposed history of the society, the names of its members, the opinions of distinguished men about it, some missing numbers of his set of the "African Depository," and other documents. He wants time at the next two or three terms of court to wind up such law business as he could not transfer; and time to study his subject fully. He wishes to make complete preparation, believing that an agent "should be possessed of all the material facts in relation to the whole scheme of colonization, and have them so authenticated as to place their genuineness beyond all manner of doubt in the minds of those upon whom he is to act."

He is evidently inclined to accept, but wishes to have all the light possible on the subject; and he reserves his decision. Toward the close he mentions difficulties, but adds, in his great-hearted sanguineness: "And yet I can not but believe that, with prudence and diligence, the public mind in the South may be awakened to some mighty effort."

He touches again upon the bright outlook in a part of the district:

> In the Valley of the Tennessee [he says] there is, among many professors of Christianity, no small feeling as to their duty to put their slaves in a way of final emancipation, with a view of sending them to Liberia. Their consciences are too much awakened again to sleep without some action.

On the 26th of July Mr. Gurley wrote to Mr. Birney an answer to his inquiries of the 12th, and inclosing a commission to him as agent of the American Colonization Society for the Southwestern District. This letter was held under advisement until the 23d of August, Mr. Birney wishing to consider "the matter calmly, dispassionately, and in all its aspects," before making a decision which would involve so great a change to himself and his large family. He then accepted. He writes:

> I am now engaged in preparing myself for active operations by a careful study of the whole subject. . . . Facts are the strong weapons, and they will, if properly presented, command success.... Fine speeches, embracing *generalities* only, may do well enough for an anniversary meeting, to attract admiration to the speaker, but, in my humble judgment, there must be facts, the whole in the cause, authenticated beyond all controversy, and exhibited in such a manner as to show the entire practicability of the scheme and its good effects upon all parties concerned, before men will be moved in *masses* to intelligent and persevering action in its favor.
>
> The first step that should be taken in this district, where

jealousy of the society exists, from an apprehension that its object is an interference with the rights of property, is to gain the good-will, at least, *of the Legislatures*. This being done, the agent will not be looked upon in the country as "raw head and bloody bones," and all undue fear of his influence upon the slaves will be removed.

It must be borne in mind that, although the Colonization Society had been welcomed by many of the leading men in the border slave States, it was viewed with suspicion and alarm by the planters in the "cotton belt," and had gained no substantial foothold in the States of the "far South." The letter continues:

I have sketched out for myself the following plan: Attend the meeting of the Legislature of Mississippi, at Jackson, early in November; thence to New Orleans, for the purpose of addressing the Legislature of Louisiana, . . . to superintend there the contemplated expedition to Liberia; thence to Tuscaloosa, to operate, if possible, upon the Legislature of this State.

I deem it altogether important that the subject be first fully discussed before these bodies before it is introduced elsewhere among the people, unless very peculiar and favorable circumstances should call for a different course. To make a favorable impression upon the Legislature of Louisiana and upon the population of New Orleans, in which I include the planters upon the coast of the Mississippi, I consider a matter of prime importance.

* * * * * *

The chief points in the lower part of this State are Tuscaloosa, Montgomery, Claiborne, and Mobile. The State society, established in 1829–'30 by Mr. Polk, has gone entirely to decay but I doubt not it can be revived. In the other places mentioned I shall endeavor to establish societies on my first visit. It is my intention, at present, to return to Huntsville, after visiting these several points in this State, and visit all the points on and near the Mississippi River, in January, February, and March. I will leave for summer operations East Tennessee and that portion of West Tennessee which can not be conveniently penetrated by steamboats. . . . The society in this place, considered by me one of the most important in the whole region, has been recently in rather a languid condition. . . . I received all the pamphlets you sent me, except Mr. Carey's; it had doubtless miscarried. . . . Is not Mr. Carey a Roman Catholic? also Mr. Walsh, of the "American Quarterly"? Tell me the names of any other distinguished Catholics who are friendly to the society. . . . Where will I find any approving resolutions of the Protestant Episcopal, of the Baptist, the Unitarian, the Roman Catholic Churches? I want, if there be any such, the time, place, and very words of them.

He asks for information about opinion in Charleston for the latest publications on the subject, and for facts with which to answer objections commonly made in the South.

The letter next in order of time which has been preserved bears date October 13, 1832. Mr. Birney had visited Tennessee and lectured in three different towns. The chief object of the letter appears to have been to ask an explanation of a discrepancy in the statements of an important fact. Mathew Carey, whose pamphlet, published by the society, he had just received, stated the number of colonists sent to Liberia as two thousand, and the manager, in a recent address to the people of the United States, had stated it at a much larger figure. He says:

Statements on important points varying so essentially and made in publications favorable to the society, produce much embarrassment in the mind of one desirous to impart precise information. In the estimates which I have made in some addresses which I have lately delivered, taking for their basis the documents above mentioned, the whole number of the colonists, inclusive of those sent out by the society, those restored to Africa by the Government, the natural increase, and those sent out in the expeditions since June, has been set down at three thousand. Is this within the bounds of the truth? If it be not, I desire to correct it, believing that our cause will, in the long run, be injured just in proportion as the statements made in its favor are unsupported by facts.

He remits moneys collected, states that the Colonization Society of Huntsville had appointed a committee to draught a memorial to our Legislature on the subject of the emancipation laws of the State, and adds:

> The weight of responsibility which the society at Washington, by leaving almost everything to my own discretion, has thrown upon me, I feel to be very great. . . . I will within this month visit the principal places in the Tennessee Valley.

The reader will have noticed that between the dates of his letters of August and October Mr. Birney has modified his plan of operations. He had intended to go southward in the first place, reserving Tennessee for his work during the next summer; but, on more full information, he has already lectured in several towns in Tennessee, and now proposes to visit the valley before any other part of his district. In the States north of Alabama a good reception had been generally given to the advocates of colonization; but sixteen years of effort had failed to remove the coldness or allay the irritable jealousy toward them in the States of the "Cotton Belt." To employ a native of the South, a man of good reputation and social standing to present the cause was the last, the only resort. If that failed the cause was desperate. To influence the South it was important to ship many emigrants from New Orleans in the spring expedition. Mr. Birney thought he could secure them in Tennessee.

The letters written by him from Tennessee on his visit to that State in the autumn of 1832 have not been preserved. That he was successful in securing a number of emigrants for the intended expedition from New Orleans in April will appear hereafter. From Tennessee he returned to Huntsville. Thence he went to Tuscaloosa and Montgomery. His letters from those places are missing, but from a statement in one of December

21st, from Mobile, we learn that at each of the three places he answered objections made to the society, particularly "the *Southern* objections, that the American Colonization Society is a Northern institution, set on foot by fanatics, etc.; that the subject ought not to be discussed in the slave States; and that it has a tendency to produce a restless and agitated state of feeling among the slaves, etc." But the subject was one the discussion of which was not favored by the public. He writes that at his first meeting, Mobile, December 18th: "Quite a small audience collected at the appointed time in one of the churches."

He was heard respectfully. At the close of the lecture some intelligent persons expressed their "great satisfaction at my manner of treating the subject." The subject itself, however, seemed to have no friends. A second meeting, appointed at the same place for the next evening, was attended by so very few that he did not speak. A third meeting was also a failure, and he abandoned his intention to take up a collection and form an auxiliary to the State society. In his letter he admits that "appearances here and all through the southern portions of this State are gloomy."

I shall leave this place to-day on my return to Tuscaloosa and Huntsville. I scarcely know what opinion I could give on the subject of keeping up an agency in this district, or of making *for the present* any additional effort. Should Virginia act with efficiency at the session of her Legislature now holding, it would be a fact strongly tending to excite this State to some similar course. There is, however, a deadness to the subject of African colonization in this portion of Alabama which is altogether discouraging. I think something beneficial may be done in Tennessee. . . . In counties where slave labor is valuable, it requires benevolence to keep up our cause—Christian benevolence, the stock of which is exceedingly small all through this region. It was my intention to be in New Orleans during the session of the

Louisiana Legislature this winter, but I am now doubtful whether such a visit would be useful.

The next letter is under date of "Huntsville, January, 24, 1833." He details the steps he has taken to have emigrants for Liberia aided to reach New Orleans in time for the April expedition; * and continues:

I have read with much satisfaction the article written by Mr. Harrison on the slavery question in Virginia. (See 3 Afric. Repos.,† 193.) It will, I apprehend, have a strong tendency to counteract the one-sided statements and the very unfair arguments of Mr. Dew. I am pleased to see the whole question concerning the black population of our country exciting so strong an interest and provoking such learned discussion. It will eventuate, I trust, in something favorable to the cause of humanity, and, of course, to the true honor and strength of our country.

He announces his intention to leave next week for New Orleans, taking steamboat at Florence, and going *via* the Tennessee, Ohio, and Mississippi Rivers. He expresses a wish to visit St. Louis, and Jacksonville, Illinois, stating that he has not abandoned his intention "to remove to Illinois, that I might rid myself and my posterity of the curse of slavery."

My mind is ill at ease on the subject of retaining my fellow-creatures in servitude. I can not, nor do I believe any honest mind, can reconcile the precept "Love thy neighbor as thyself"

---

* Before he left for New Orleans, he did propose to his slaves to send them with the expedition; but they all refused absolutely, being much frightened at the proposition.

† An able defense of the Colonization Society, delivered at Lynchburg, July, 1827. One passage is noteworthy:

"The scope of the society is large enough; but it is in no wise mingled or confounded with the broad, sweeping views of a few fanatics in America who would urge us on to the *sudden and total abolition of slavery*." This arrow is aimed at Osborn, Lundy, Duncan, Rankin, Bourne, *et al.*

with the purchase of the body of that neighbor and consigning him and his unoffending posterity to slavery, a perpetual bondage, degrading and debasing him in this world, and almost excluding him from the happiness of that which is to come. Should I remove from this State, I shall send all the slaves I own to Liberia.

He proceeds to suggest the discussion of the "duty of Christians in regard to slavery," before the ecclesiastical bodies of Kentucky and Tennessee. He says:

Could the Christian community, or even a respectable part of it, be aroused to what, I believe—nay, to what I *know*—to be their duty in this matter, one might almost say of this great work of humanity, "*It is finished.*"

He adds:

If I do [visit Illinois this spring] my object will be to make preparations for a removal—perhaps, within a year. . . . I am anxious to have an opportunity of discussing it [colonization] before the Legislature [of Louisiana].

His next letter is from New Orleans, under date of March 18, 1833. His proposition to call a public meeting was discouraged as injudicious by the president of the State Colonization Society, who represented the state of public sentiment as unfavorable. The society had held no meeting since its first organization, had appointed no executive committee, and collected no funds. He succeeded at length in holding a meeting, Sunday evening, in Mr. Clapp's church. A large congregation assembled, and listened in a respectful and attentive manner.

The blacks, both free and slave, were permitted to be present. But I could not rouse the society into action, although there seemed to be, without exception, *individual* approbation of what had been said. . . . The president of the society was present at neither of the addresses. . . . I am much afraid that our cause will languish unto death here. I know not what to do to revive it. . . . . They are most deplorably inert. . . . I shall leave to-morrow for Natchez, where also, I fear, things are in a languishing state, as I have been informed an unsuccessful attempt has been made to secure [a hall for] the regular annual meeting of the society at that place.

Of the prospect at New Orleans, he says: "It is gloomy enough, yet not so much so as to unnerve us altogether."

Under date of "New Orleans, April 8, 1833," he gives an account of his trip to Natchez and Port Gibson, and of his lectures at those places. The Natchez society was in good hands and prosperous; it had sixteen hundred dollars in its treasury. He spoke twice on Sunday—in the afternoon, in the Presbyterian church, to a good audience; and in the evening, in the Methodist church, to a very large one. The result was collections amounting to fourteen hundred dollars. The meeting at Port Gibson was not large, owing to heavy rains. The collections amounted to about sixty dollars. He then hastened to New Orleans, met there one hundred and forty-eight emigrants bound to Liberia, and chartered a vessel for their transportation. He writes: "I am making great exertions to attract public attention to the sailing of this expedition; but the apathy here upon the subject of colonization is almost discouraging."

In a long letter of April 13, 1833, full of suggestions and business details, he writes:

I have determined on returning to Huntsville immediately after dispatching the pending expedition, and on publishing in our "Gazette," in weekly numbers of a column or two thirds of a column each, the views I have generally presented in my public addresses. I trust that arrangements can be made for their republication throughout all my district.

These essays he expects to issue in pamphlet form for circulation among members of the different State Legislatures, "*bodies from which alone in the South any effectual aid can be expected.*"

It is evident he has already given up all hope of success from the action of societies formed at the South. Under date of April 15, 1833, he expresses the opinion—

> that the remarks contained in the latter part of Mr. Finley's address at the last anniversary will do injury to our cause at the South. . . . To call the slave-holders—even that class of them who are willing to perpetuate the odious relation which my soul hates—indeed, to call any description of persons who may be opposed to us *enemies*, to treat them as such by hard names, to push them into the ranks of an unrelenting opposition, is not, in my judgment, calculated to promote our success. Rather let us, as those are wont to do who are conscious of having a good cause, try to convince opposers by forbearance and kindness and sober argument that they are wrong, and thus persuade them to become our friends and co-operators.

April 20th.—The brig Ajax, with one hundred and fifty emigrants, dropped down the river. She sailed April 22d. On the day last named, Sunday, an afternoon meeting at Mr. Clapp's church, for which Mr. Birney had made all the necessary arrangements, gaining the promise of three distinguished gentlemen to speak, advertising it by placards and in the newspapers, "failed utterly." "The gentleman who was to submit the first resolution" was absent. "The other two who were to introduce the second and third resolutions declined going on with the addresses." He thinks that "but little must be asked in the way of personal effort" from professed colonizationists at New Orleans. There is no popularity to be obtained by openly espousing the cause of colonization." But "in the older parts of Mississippi there is a better spirit in all benevolent things than in this region."

The cholera broke out on the steamboat on which he took passage to the mouth of the Tennessee. "The boat," he says, "was like a hospital for cholera patients." Reaching Huntsville early in May, he began the preparation of his essays on colonization, intended for republication in the Southern newspapers. This work was interrupted by a trip to Kentucky between the 5th and 26th of June, intended to establish "entire co-operation" between the Kentucky Colonization Society and those of his district. All public meetings in that State were prevented by the sudden prevalence of cholera. Returning through Nashville, he took steps there to secure the circulation by all the colonization societies in Tennessee of petitions to the State Legislature for pecuniary aid, and engaged to attend the anniversary of the State society to be held in October at Nashville during the meeting of the Legislature. On this trip he made a short visit to his father, and for this reason declined to charge to the society any part of his traveling expenses.*

In a letter of June 29, 1833, he makes a suggestion for the consideration of the board of managers. The following extracts will show its character:

> *Proposition: Our great object is to call into effect the powers of the nation. How can this most surely be done?* We have been trying it since the first institution of the Colonization Society without success, by appealing directly to Congress. . . . We have always met with defeat, and we have always roused Southern prejudice. Shall we go on in the same way?

The chief cause of the defeat, he thinks, is that the method pursued has excited "jealousy and suspicions of a settled intention to force Congress to legislate upon a subject which the South has declared must remain untouched by national legislation." He advises ceasing the direct application to Congress:

* Though he passed through Lexington, his letters make no mention of any visit to Henry Clay.

We may then press upon the individual States to make appropriations. We may, when we have their full confidence, excite them to exertion singly ; and having their *good will*, if their own resources should be insufficient, they will be the very organs of carrying their and our wishes before Congress, and of pressing upon it for assistance to accomplish them. . . . I verily believe this is the speediest way of reaching Congress successfully, and the best for doing service to our country whose safety is now jeoparded, if I mistake not, by the indiscretion and fury of Northern abolitionists and the (plots) of *Southern nullifiers*. . . . I have been heretofore always in favor of applications to Congress ; I am now satisfied I was wrong. Sir, this *Union is precious to me.* If it be destroyed the world may mourn, for its liberty is lost.

On the 5th of August he writes to Mr. Gurley:

Yet sometimes I fear that the South will *do* nothing until it is too late, as it will be in ten years from this.

About the same date he began the publication in the "Huntsville Democrat" of a series of newspaper articles on colonization. The editor of that sheet said in introducing them: "We give place to the communications of our respected fellow-citizen James G. Birney, Esq., with great pleasure. It is a subject upon which it becomes every man to form an opinion, and the materials for forming a correct one can nowhere be found in a more agreeable form than they will be made to assume in the short essays of Mr. Birney."

The general drift of these essays is apparent in the following extracts:

They saw their country suffering under an evil proved by indisputable testimony coming from all parts of it to be great. . . . Our country, especially that portion known as the slave-holding States, is laboring under a "great and growing moral and political disease."

To the objection that the plan originated in the free States, he answers:

Shall prejudice so narrow as this persuade us to lay aside a scheme salutary and profitable in itself because its inventors have, by the providence of God, their places of residence in the North or East? Heretofore we have acted a wiser part; we did not say to Whitney, the ingenious inventor of the cotton-gin, "You are from the land of steady habits."

He admits that the abolitionists are "found almost exclusively in the free States," but claims that the leading ones are hostile to colonization. In proof he cites the charges made by Mr. Garrison against the society in his "Thoughts on Colonization," and quotes from the review of that pamphlet in the June number, 1832, of the quarterly "Christian Spectator."

In his fourth number he refers to "a more recent review" in the "Spectator" "of the rhapsodies of Mr. Garrison," etc., and makes a quotation from it.*

In his fifth he says:

If, on the other hand, to furnish the owner, in the good conduct of the slave, every motive to feel benevolently toward him,

---

*In the number for January, 1833, of the "African Repository," which paper Mr. Birney read, Rev. Mr. Gurley replies to an article in the "Liberator." We make a few extracts:

"He" (Mr. Garrison) "states that, in June last, in Philadelphia, he put a copy of his 'Thoughts' into my hand, and that 'a review of it was then promised—a triumphant, destructive review'—and exclaims: 'After six months, behold the result!' It is true that Mr. Garrison very obligingly presented me with his book; but in regard to the other part of the statement, I apprehend he has been indebted (as I fear he is in some other cases) to his imagination for his fact. . . . Mr. Garrison pronounces the charge that he vilifies the South totally false." Mr. Gurley says: "Having selected certain passages from the writings of such men as Messrs. Clay, Harper, Mercer, Harrison, of Virginia, Rev. Dr. Caldwell, of North Carolina, and others, he exclaims: 'Ye crafty calculators! Ye hard-hearted, incorrigible sinners! Ye greedy and relentless robbers! Ye contemners of justice and mercy! Ye trembling, pitiful, pale-faced usurpers, my soul spurns you with unspeakable disgust!'" ("Thoughts," p. 107.)

to treat him kindly, and at last to let him go free, bestowing upon him a share of that "wherewith the Lord his God has blessed" the master—if, I say, this be to favor emancipation, the society can offer no plea but that of "guilty" to the charge. So fully do I trust to the efficacy of this process in the States of Maryland, Virginia, Kentucky, and Tennessee that all that is wanting, in my judgment, to disburden them of slavery in a reasonable time, is means to defray the cost of a comfortable conveyance to a safe and pleasant home of all slaves who may be offered by their owners for removal. . . . I would not venture the opinion that there would, in this way, be any sudden extinguishment of slavery in those States, but it would not be hazarding my reputation for forecast to say that it would be continually approaching its termination.

He proceeds to combat the idea of trying the experiment of abolition before every other feasible plan is tried; and he lays down a general proposition, "that there is in society an inherent power for self-preservation, which it is authorized to use *for the removal of any evil* that in its nature tends to produce social dissolution, although it may be unavoidable that another evil be introduced, instead of the one removed, provided it be of less magnitude."

This was a two-edged sword, and it gave great offense, as asserting the legislative right to remove slavery.

In his seventh number he assents to the proposition that "the evil of a settled, self-perpetuating system, by which a large and increasing number of our race are, through all ages, to be debarred of rights declared to be indestructible is greater than any evil affecting the general welfare to be produced by their liberation among us"; thinks the South is in a situation "which it is desirable to change; and examines the duty of a slave-holder uneasy under the operation of conscientious scruples and desirous of releasing himself from the relation of master." He refers to slavery as "that hydra which, with bloody crest, has been well-nigh crushing to death, in its horrid folds, the ripening manhood of our country"; and expresses the opinion that "benevolence and wisdom, if properly led on, will, at length, enable every part of this enlightened land to see that to her greatest strength and highest happiness slavery must, in the nature of things, be ever opposed— and to throw off the foul clog by which she has been encumbered as the leader of the nations in their march to freedom."

It may be easily imagined what a stir and excitement these articles caused among Southern politicians. They were without precedent in the annals of the press of the Gulf States. Though opposed to instantaneous, they strongly advocated gradual abolition. And they were written by a native Southerner! A man of standing! The first two or three were copied from the Huntsville "Democrat" by a great many slave-State papers; but, as the series went on, the number of copying papers fell off; at the seventh number there were none; and the "Democrat" itself refused the eighth, for prudential reasons!! The Alabama press was closed to Mr. Birney. The Gulf States had refused to hear his appeal. He was forced to the conclusion that if he wished to pry up slavery from its deep foundations, he must seek farther north for a place to plant his lever.

In a letter to Mr. Gurley, under the date of September 14th, 1833, Mr. Birney writes:

How greatly shall I be pleased to see you personally, that I might communicate to you more fully than I can in a letter the results of my observations in the South. The *truth is appalling to every friend of the Union*. . . . Yet I fear I should have nothing to communicate that would encourage the friends of colonization and humanity. I have been greatly disappointed in the insensibility of the religious community on the subject of slavery. So far from sending their slaves to Liberia, the greater part are not slow to justify slavery in our circumstances. . . . I must give you my opinion candidly as to our prospects in the

South. I fear nothing effectual will be done here for getting rid of slavery until the evil shall cure itself. The only effectual way that seems open to my view is the *withdrawal of Virginia* (or Maryland or Kentucky) *from the slave States, by the adoption of some scheme of emancipation.* Should this be done, the whole system of slavery in the United States would, from the very pressure of public opinion, be brought—and that in a few years —in shivers to the ground. In proportion as the slave-holding territory is weakened in political influence, it will be weakened in the power of withstanding the force of public sentiment; and the last State in which slavery shall exist—although its slaves, as property, may be hedged around by laws and constitutions, and absolutely intangible—yet will it be perfectly odious. . . . I assure you, sir, I have no hope for the South. . . . There is no escape but in doing that which I am almost certain will not be done.

What I would now suggest would be, *to press with every energy upon Maryland, Virginia, and Kentucky for emancipation and colonization.* If one of those States be not detached from the number of slave-holding States, *the slave question must inevitably dissolve the Union,* and that before very long. Should Virginia (or Maryland or Kentucky) leave them, the Union will be safe, though the sufferings of the South will be almost unto death. Indeed, I am by no means certain but that Lower Mississippi and the country bordering on the Gulf of Mexico will ultimately be peopled almost entirely by blacks.

In the same letter he gives notice that the official connection between him and the Colonization Society will cease on the 15th of the following November.

On the 14th of the following October he was present at a meeting at Nashville of the Tennessee Colonization Society. He writes:

Many members of the Legislature, then in session, were present. The meeting was held in the Representatives' Hall, which was so crowded that many who came to hear were unable to get into the room. I spoke for about an hour and a half, and, going beyond what I had done or could with propriety do south of

Tennessee, I assumed the position that slavery must not be regarded as a permanent condition among us ; and I attempted to show that there are causes now in very active operation to bring it to a termination. . . . My propositions were so much bolder than they had ever been elsewhere that I was prepared to expect some complaint from the timid and indolent lovers of slavery. But there was none at all.

He spoke also to crowded houses at Gallatin, Franklin, and Elkton. He writes:

It is my sincere belief that the South, at least that part of it in which I have been operating, has within the last year become very manifestly more and more indurated on the subject of slavery. . . . They (the planters) are as blind to the natural rights of their slaves as the whites of the West Indies ever were.

With his Tennessee trip, and the promotion of petitions from all parts of his district to the State Legislatures for pecuniary aid to the Colonization Society, his official relations to it came to an end. In a letter written about this time to Mr. Gurley he says:

I am pleased to see *all engines at work for the extirpation of slavery* from our land. I believe the condition of slavery to be altogether unchristian, and that therefore its tendency is to our ruin as a people.

About the 15th of November, 1832, he removed from Alabama to his native county in Kentucky, and established his home a mile and a half from Danville, on a purchased farm of one hundred and thirty acres, immediately adjoining his father's.

CHAPTER XVI.

FROM COLONIZATION, THROUGH GRADUAL EMANCIPATION, TO IMMEDIATE ABOLITION.

HIS reasons for removing to Kentucky are best given in the following extract from a letter, dated November 27, 1833, to a friend, Gerrit Smith, of New York:

> Two years and a half ago, while residing in the State of Alabama, my mind became greatly aroused to the sin of slave-holding. This, aided by the malignant influence that I saw slavery exerting upon my children, determined me to visit Illinois for the purpose of removing thither, of there pursuing my profession, and of liberating the few slaves that I had. I authorized a friend of mine to purchase property for me in Jacksonville. The owner of it refused to sell. Mrs. Birney, whose health has always been delicate, was somewhat averse, after residing so long at the South, to try so high a latitude and to fall in with habits and modes of life so different from those to which she had been accustomed. My father, who is considerably advanced in age and a cripple, too, was anxious for me, his only son, to return to Kentucky and reside in this neighborhood near him. To all these considerations, which I will not say would have been insufficient in themselves, another was added of commanding importance—I looked upon it as the *best site in our whole country for taking a stand against slavery.*

He and his family were received with open arms by their numerous relatives and connections and the people of Mercer County. If he had desired preferment in the political world, he was at that time in a position to obtain it easily. He was in good circumstances, an only son, and the prospective heir to half of a large estate; his experience in public business and legal practice had been varied; he was always a good speaker, often an eloquent one; he was personally popular; he belonged to an influential family which ramified into all parts of Kentucky; and no act of public notoriety had as yet separated him from the dominant party in the State. His entry into politics would have much gratified his father.

Before he left Alabama he had written to the slave-holders in Kentucky, who in 1830–'31 had pledged themselves to gradual emancipation, urging them to issue a call for a convention at Lexington to form a State society. The call was issued. The time named was the 6th of December. Hardly had he reached his new home when he saw in person or wrote to every Kentucky slave-holder likely to join in the movement. At that time he was sanguine of success. The whole number of slaves of all ages in the State did not exceed one hundred and sixty-eight thousand. Under the unceasing agitation of abolition, since the formation, about 1807, of the Kentucky Abolition Society by Presbyterian and Baptist preachers—by James Duncan, John Rankin, John Finley Crowe, R. J. Breckenridge, and others; by the "Abolition Intelligencer," the "Western Luminary," and "Russellville Messenger"; and by the advocates of the convention to change the Constitution, the per cent of increase of slaves, which had been 99 between 1800 and 1810 and 57 in the next decade, had been lowered to 20⅓ in the decade ending with 1830; and forty-eight slave-holders of influence and standing had in 1831 publicly declared their intention to accomplish gradual emancipation in the State. The hour to strike the final blow at the decaying institution of slavery seemed to Mr. Birney to have arrived.

That the blow had been too long deferred soon became

evident to him. The answers by the reformers of 1831 to his letter were generally unsatisfactory. Some of these gentlemen avowed a change of opinion, and others declined to attend or had doubts or thought the convention ill timed. A few were willing to attend, but hoped the proceedings would be marked with great prudence. Only nine persons, all slave-holders, were present at the convention. A prolonged discussion elicited many facts which were new to Mr. Birney. It appeared that, within the two preceding years, a number of secret societies, composed of members of both political parties, had been formed in different parts of the State for the ostensible object of protecting the constitutional rights of the slave States from the encroachments of the North; that, in the newspapers and in debates and political speeches, the existence in the national Constitution of guarantees for slavery was widely asserted; that a jealous sectional feeling was in process of formation; that many persons were justifying slavery from the Bible as well as on political grounds; that the acquisition of Texas, "peaceably if we can, forcibly if we must," was gaining friends; and that, because of the closer organization and aggressive position of the large slave-holders, freedom of discussion and action in regard to slavery was greatly narrowed down everywhere in the State and that emancipationists were subjected to social ostracism more or less severe. The result of the deliberations was the formation of a society upon the principle of emancipating the future offspring of slaves at the age of twenty-one. This fell very far short of Mr. Birney's expectations; but he succeeded in obtaining the adoption of a clause admitting to membership non-slave-holders who would pledge themselves to promote gradual emancipation. The meetings of the convention were public, and were continued through two days without interference. The mob period had not then begun in

Kentucky. After its adjournment Mr. Birney devoted himself for a short time to obtaining members and organizing auxiliaries. Lectures, private correspondence, essays for several Kentucky newspapers whose columns were open to him, and reading the abundant literature of the subject, absorbed his attention and energies.

From the time of his removal from Alabama he entered upon the most thorough study of the history of slavery, of the institution as it existed in the West Indies and the United States, and of all the efforts to ameliorate or abolish it. For this purpose he obtained a large number of British, American, and French books and pamphlets on the subject, both anti-slavery and pro-slavery, both for and against gradualism. He gave special attention to the results of British legislation for the regulation of slavery in the West India islands, reading carefully not only the parliamentary debates and reports relating to them, but the essays, treatises, and books of travels by private persons who had visited the islands, and several volumes of the "Anti-Slavery Monthly Reporter," which he sent for to London. Among the works kept on his table were "Four Essays on Colonial Slavery," by John Jeremy, Esq.; "An Outline for Immediate Emancipation," by Charles Stuart; Clarkson's "Thoughts"; George Thompson's "Three Lectures on Colonial Slavery"; "Facts proving the Good Conduct and Prosperity of Emancipated Negroes"; "The Abolitionist's Catechism," abridged, published at Bristol, England, in 1830. Wilberforce's "Appeal," Clarkson's "History," and several others had been in his library many years. (See Appendix A.)

Though he had been prepossessed by the "rhapsodies of Garrison" against Northern abolitionism as unfair in argument and malevolent in feeling, he was too liberal and just not to hear that side. He accordingly subscribed for the "New York Evangelist," a Presbyterian or Congregationalist weekly, and, being pleased with its tone, temper, and ability, he added to it the "Emancipator" (New York), the organ of the American Anti-Slavery Society. It was not long before he subscribed to the different publications of that society, and learned to appreciate the moderation, candor, Christian spirit, liberality, firmness, and devotion to truth with which they were conducted. He received and read the poet Whittier's admirable tract entitled "Justice and Expediency; or Slavery considered with a View to its Rightful and Effectual Remedy, Abolition"; Elizur Wright's "Sin of Slavery and its Remedy"; Beriah Green's "Four Sermons," preached at Western Reserve College in 1832; and sundry other anti-slavery tracts of the day. Of American anti-slavery books, he procured those of Bourne (1816), Kenrick (1816), Torrey (1817), Duncan (1824), Rankin (1824), Stroud (1827), and Phelps (1833). For Whittier, as a man and reasoner, he conceived a high esteem, which ripened into friendship during their intimacy in later years; of Rankin, he always spoke with respect; and to the Rev. A. A. Phelps, pastor of the Pine Street Church, Boston, and author of "Lectures on Slavery and its Remedy," he gave the praise of having produced the most full and satisfactory argument contained in American works on the subject. A paper that had great weight with him was the one signed in 1833 by one hundred and twenty-four clergymen of different denominations, stating reasons for repudiating colonizationism, and indorsing immediate abolition; it was reprinted as a preface to Phelps's lectures. He made also an exhaustive study of legal decisions in England and the United States and of the national and State Constitutions on questions touching slavery, and framed his argument that freedom is national, and slavery local only.

In February, 1834, the famous debate at Lane Seminary on slavery began, having been suggested and promoted by Arthur Tappan, who was the most generous benefactor of the seminary, and who, in the preceding December, had become president of the newly organized American Anti-Slavery Society (Appendix C). It was continued through eighteen sittings, held at intervals, and closing in April. It was the most able and thorough discussion of the subject ever held in this country. The participants were eighty students of theology. In age they ranged from twenty-one to thirty-five. Some of them had been lecturers for religious and benevolent societies. A few were noted as platform-speakers. Of these, Henry B. Stanton was one of the best. The leader, however, was Theodore D. Weld. He had already gained a reputation throughout the West and Southwest for effective oratory. As a speaker on temperance and education, he had no equal. Profoundly religious in temperament, sympathetic with all human emotion, nobly simple in manner, free from thought of self, he touched the springs of the human heart with a sure hand. No revivalist—not even Finney or Moody—could bear his hearers to such heights of passion or through such a wide range of feeling. They wept or laughed with him, and did not suspect that they had listened to one of Nature's greatest orators until they remembered that no one had ever before so moved them, and felt a consciousness of living on a higher plane than before they had heard him. His diction was copious, and his language so apt that every thought found natural expression. Poetry, pathos, and humor gave variety to his eloquence, and purity and love were its atmosphere. He catered to no prurient taste; uttered no malice; sharpened no phrase so that its venomed point might rankle in another's breast. He was incapable of hate; his great soul was full of compassion for the oppressor and oppressed. Secretary Stanton and Wendell Phillips pronounced him the foremost orator of his time; they might have added, "and one of the greatest men." He had none of the vanity of leadership, no egotism, no pretentiousness. He had been an abolitionist from boyhood, had traveled through the South, and was well informed in regard to the nature and effects of slavery. His knowledge and pervasive influence informed the Lane Seminary debate, lifting it to the height of its subject. As it progressed, its results were published in the "Journal," a Cincinnati religious weekly, to which Mr. Birney was a subscriber. When in May the Lane Seminary students, burning with enthusiasm and well equipped with arguments, set out to abolitionize the Northwest, they carried with them the sympathies of the leading emancipationist in Kentucky.

It is impossible to trace with accuracy each step of the slow advance of Mr. Birney to immediatism. All the prejudices of his youth and early manhood, gained in New Jersey and Pennsylvania, were in favor of gradual emancipation, if effected by compulsory legislation. That method of reaching ultimate abolition had been successful in the Middle and Eastern States, and had seemed to him the most expedient one for the border slave States. Such a measure could be made effective by State legislation only; and he appears to have regarded it as a political result to be accomplished under a changed state of public opinion. After a public advocacy of gradualism extending through a few weeks only, he became convinced that the political classes were deaf to all appeals on the subject, and that the active men of both national parties were for the first time united in opposition to any discussion of it. Nor could he make any impression on slave-holders by arguments addressed to the selfish principle. In a letter of this date to Gerrit Smith, then a gradualist and colonizationist, he says:

We may take the Kentucky slave-holder, having, say, fifty slaves ; show him from the undisputed statistics of our country the advantages enjoyed by Ohio over his own State ; prove to him that it is owing to *free labor* and nothing else ; you may further, by comparing *his* number of slaves with their *aggregate* in the whole State, demonstrate to him what is his *individual loss;* and it will, I apprehend, all amount to nothing. He will admit all your facts, that your calculations are correct and your "answers" undeniable. Yet he will reply to you, "Sir, I am willing, for the sake of my ease and the indulgence of those habits in which I have been educated, to pay the sum that you have so satisfactorily shown I shall lose by remaining a slave-holder." With such a man, using such a weapon, you can not proceed a step further ; he fails you completely.

On more thorough study of the subject, he became convinced that a gradual emancipation law in Kentucky would result not in the increase of the number of freedmen, but in the sales to the cotton-raising States of nearly all the prospective freedmen; that immediate abolition would be less dangerous to society and the labor supply in the Gulf States than freeing the slaves in classes, say, of ten thousand each, and attempting to maintain the free and slave labor systems side by side; and, in short, that gradual emancipation would not work in practice as well as immediate abolition. To do justice was the highest expediency.

As his speeches were generally made in Presbyterian churches, they were naturally addressed rather to religious than political motives.

His arguments to public audiences became more and more based on the *sinfulness* of slavery. He was too clear a reasoner not to be conscious of the discrepancy between this premise and the conclusion that slavery might be continued. The more he thought and spoke on gradualism, the more sensible he became of his entanglement in what was not only bad logic, but false theology.

His powerful appeals led several slave-holders to give deeds of manumission to their slaves, and each act of this kind tended to convince him of the hollowness of gradualism, and to encourage him to have more faith in the might of the truth. In a letter to Gerrit Smith, written just after he had embraced immediatism, he says:

> The only means of succeeding at all is to apply the *whole truth* to the conscience. If less be done, it will be as inefficient as would be the preaching of *gradual* and *partial* repentance toward God. Let there be set up a principle false or unsound in any of its parts; under the false or unsound part slave-holders as well as sinners will take refuge. . . . If *gradual* emancipation be insisted on, the conscience of the slave-holder is left undisturbed, and you gain nothing.

About the first of June, having complied with the Kentucky law requiring a bond with sureties, to indemnify the State and county against bad conduct or pauperism on the part of persons manumitted, he gave a deed of emancipation to each of his six slaves. Each paper was witnessed by his two oldest sons, and delivered in the presence of the assembled family.

His freed people were strongly attached to him. They remained with him on wages until he left Kentucky. They were a family of five—Michael, his wife, son, and two daughters. Also a mulatto child of six years of age. The son he apprenticed to an Ohio blacksmith, and for one of the daughters he obtained the place of housemaid in a respectable family. The little mulatto girl was apprenticed to him until her majority. He took her, in 1835, with the family to Cincinnati, gave her a good common-school education, and had her taught to be a seamstress. All of them became respectable working people. To Michael he gave for his life work as a slave the wages of a free laborer, with interest on the amount for each year. With Michael's consent, this sum was invested for him in stocking a livery stable at Louisville. In this new business Michael was skillful, kept his temperance pledge faithfully, and prospered.

Two years after this act of justice he was cruelly slandered by W. L. Stone, Esq., editor of a New York paper. Mr. Stone had been, up to 1828, a prominent member of the Biennial Conventions to Promote the Abolition of Slavery. On the election of General Jackson, he abandoned that organization, and distinguished himself by his hostility to his former associates and their coadjutors. So long as he confined himself to general invective he was not noticed, but when he made a specific charge Mr. Birney wrote him a letter. Mr. Stone refused to publish it, and it appeared in the "Emancipator." It is reprinted here as the only authentic statement of the matter in question. (See Appendix D.)

At the time of his removal from Alabama he had lost all faith in colonization as a means for the extinction of slavery. He did not attend the anniversary meeting of the National Colonization Society or the annual meeting, in January, of the Kentucky auxiliary. In his absence he was elected one of the vice-presidents of the latter, an honor of which he was not officially notified. As he did not hesitate in his public addresses to allude to the inefficacy of colonizationism to meet the exigencies then pressing upon the State and country, the change in his opinions became noised abroad, and inspired no little anxiety among the friends of that cause. One of these, Mr. Peers, formerly president of Transylvania University, published early in 1834 a prospectus for a colonization paper to be issued at Lexington. Having relied in some degree on Mr. Birney's influence to support it, he was disturbed by the reports of his change of opinion, and went to Danville for the purpose of ascertaining the truth in a personal conference. He was treated with frankness and, being at heart opposed to slavery, was so shaken by Mr. Birney's arguments that on returning home he recalled his prospectus and abandoned his project. The reasons for his course becoming known, some of the Kentucky papers mentioned the fact that Mr. Birney was one of the vice-presidents of the Kentucky Colonization Society. To relieve himself from this false position, he wrote out, early in May, his resignation. As first written, it was expressed in about twenty lines. He had not mailed it when he received a letter from a friend at Paris, Ky., suggesting that a full statement of his reasons was due to his former associates. This was followed by a paragraph in the "Luminary," expressing the desire of many Presbyterians to know his objections to colonization; and this was copied and approved by several religious journals in the North. Yielding to these requests, he threw aside his first letter and wrote a second and longer one. This, too, was nothing but a resignation of office, with reasons assigned. It fell short of what was wanted, and went into the waste basket. As he wrote, the fire within him burned; and he took up his pen again and wrote the well-known pamphlet which, under the unpretending title of "Letter on Colonization," is a most touching, cogently reasoned, and powerful appeal to the American people for suffering millions and an imperiled Republic. It first appeared in the "Western Luminary," was copied into a large number of Northern journals, including all the larger anti-slavery papers proper, and was immediately republished in a large edition in pamphlet form by the American Anti-Slavery Society.*

It appeared July 15, 1834, in Lexington, Ky. The time was opportune. Public attention throughout the

* Many subsequent editions were issued in New York and elsewhere, and the pamphlet kept its place in anti-slavery bookstores up to 1861.

country had been drawn to the slavery question by the Lane Seminary debate and the subsequent lectures in the Western States by more than fifty of the students; by the imminence of the emancipation of 800,000 slaves in the West Indies (it was fixed by law for the 1st of August); by the riotous proceedings, July 4th, to prevent David Paul Brown from delivering an abolition speech in New York city; and by the Chatham Street riots, the sacking of Lewis Tappan's house, and the mobs against the colored people, all of which had kept New York City in turmoil from the 4th to the 12th of July. These mobs were fomented by politicians and led by slave-holders, and they had stirred the nation to its depths. The Tappans and their co-laborers at New York were in danger of their lives. They issued, July 17th, a circular, correcting the common misrepresentation of their principles; but their houses and persons were still under guard when the "Letter on Colonization" was republished in the Eastern cities, including New York. Its effect on public opinion was almost marvelous. To the Tappans, the calm, fearless voice from Kentucky was as welcome as the sound of the Scotch slogan in the distance was to the beleaguered garrison of Lucknow. It was an appeal by a Christian statesman; it was the first of the kind by a native Southerner! The enthusiasm it excited may be imagined, when a reverend doctor of divinity, Samuel H. Coxe, of Brooklyn, N. Y., could say of it: "A Birney has shaken the continent by putting down his foot; and his fame will be envied before his arguments are answered or their force forgotten." From this date James G. Birney had a national reputation, and was regarded as the leading representative of conservative anti-slavery statesmanship.

CHAPTER XVII.

ANTI-SLAVERY WORK IN KENTUCKY.

JULY, 1834, TO APRIL, 1835.

AT the time of writing the "Letter," Mr. Birney was not a member of any anti-slavery society or in correspondence with Northern abolitionists. It was not long, however, before they sought him out. The first to visit him was Henry B. Stanton, of Ohio. Then came Prof. Mahan from the same State; and, after him, Charles Stuart, of England. Each of these spent from one to three days under his roof. About the same time, he made a very short visit to Cincinnati, where he saw Weld, Wattles, Thome, Morgan, Robinson, and a few others of the Lane Seminary lecturers, encouraged them in their work, and exchanged views with them. Some of them urged him to take the platform in Ohio; but he declined, thinking his proper field of action was in Kentucky. One of the objects of his visit was to renew his personal friendship with Theodore D. Weld, whom he had learned in Alabama to admire and esteem. From the date of this reunion at Cincinnati, until his decease, these two men were united in an intimate friendship.

The following extracts from his letters to Mr. Weld will enable us to follow part of his course in Kentucky:

While I was in Cincinnati an attempt was made in our lyceum to have the "immediate abolition of slavery" discussed. It was voted out on the ground, as I understood, that it was improper to discuss it here. The evening before last I presided in the lyceum, when, altogether without my knowledge beforehand, the utility of colonization was proposed for the subject of discussion at our next meeting.

With a view to his permanent appointment as Professor of Ancient Languages, the trustees of Centre College had engaged him to fill the place of Prof. Breckenridge during a short absence. All parties were satisfied with his manner of filling the chair. The result, however, is thus noticed by him:

To make a short story of it, everything else was acceptable to the trustees *save my abolition views*. On this ground alone, as I was informed by President Young, they passed me by. . . . The result of this has added greatly to the pressure upon me at home; my nearest friends, though hating slavery in the abstract, and wishing there was none of it, think it very silly in me to run against the world *in a matter that can not in any way do me any good*. . . . I do not believe I can remain in Kentucky. . . . I shall (probably) be compelled to become a citizen of Illinois, scuffle along in my profession, and do what good I can, as occasions may arise. . . . I discover that my father would be much opposed to my removal; but how can I stay here at the cost of having fetters put upon every attempt that I make? . . . My nearest friends here are of the sort that are always crying out: "Take care of yourself—don't meddle with other people's affairs—do nothing, say nothing, get along quietly, make money." . . . I glanced over a pamphlet entitled; "Hints on Colonization and Abolition," ascribed to the Rev. R. J. Breckenridge. It is a farrago of incongruities. He thinks slavery a sin, but when it should cease is questionable. We want a paper in the West to dissect and hold up for public condemnation all such wretched conditions. . . .

[*July 26, 1834.*] What effect upon our cause will be produced by the New York riots? Good, I trust. They will not deter a single friend worth having; and, if I mistake not, they will alarm the considerate who have not been our friends, when they are thus brought to see in what danger the very principles of our Government stand, when brought into opposition with the principle of slavery, even at its present growth.

He discourages the discussion of the social equality of blacks and whites as ill timed, and expresses the opinion that the first thing to be looked to is the freedom of the slaves. Adverting to a suggestion in a former letter of his removal to Illinois, he says:

I might possibly do more good by remaining here some time, provided the state of public sentiment should justify it. This, I trust, I shall ascertain in a short time. Should a good effect be produced by my publication and any friends appear to be rising up, I have thought it would be well for me to visit all those who would be willing to come out openly, and such others of the same temper as I might hear of in my trip, and try to effect an embodying of ourselves for joint action. . . . To remove now would look like surrendering the cause in Kentucky without having made any effort for success and taking refuge, as it were, among strangers. I could see many of our friends before the meeting of the Kentucky Synod in October. I am now preparing an address to the ministers and elders in this synod on the subject of slavery. . . . I desire to publish this before I go out to see such as may be our friends. . . . Slavery, emancipation, etc., are more and more talked of here, and I am looked upon by many pretty much as a disturber of the peace. All begin to complain of their slaves that they are getting worse and worse.

August 19, 1834. He writes that he has finished his address to the "elders and ministers," and will publish it the next week in the Lexington "Luminary." He continues:

Immediately afterward I will go out in quest of abolitionists among the Presbyterians, to rally for the meeting of the synod on the 2nd Wednesday in October. . . . An onset must be made at that time with whatever numbers, few or many, can be brought up to the right point. I have no small hope in the course that will be taken by the remote and younger members of the synod. . . . [About August 7.] There was a discussion of abolition before the societies in the college. President Young and I were the principal debaters. At the conclusion of the argument. . . . the vote was *twenty* for and *twenty-two* against abolition. . . . I am much vilified and abused about Danville. I hear none of it myself. . . . Notwithstanding, I begin to think it not at all unlikely that I can sustain myself in Kentucky and even publish a paper here if the effort in the synod prove at all successful. . . . On my trip South, I found two abolitionists—preachers in our Church—one at Glasgow, the other at Greensburg, both highly respectable in every way. [They had been converted by his "Letter."]

A diary kept by Mr. Birney between September 1 and October 23, 1834, has been preserved. From it we glean a few facts and make a few extracts.

Sept. 1st.—A clergyman, from Talladega County, Alabama, owning four slaves, and greatly troubled about his duty to them, came to ask my advice, and decided to set them free. The clergyman's wife is opposed to slavery, yet she wishes—as I discover is the case with nearly all wives who are opposed to it—to escape from it by migrating to a free State.

Sept. 1st.—I started on my tour among the Presbyterian clergymen, visiting them at their homes. The first was —— ——, a doctor of divinity, a suitable person, if he were sound on the question of slavery, to introduce it in the synod. He claimed to have "always been opposed to slavery, so much so from early manhood that his father had left him by will no part of his slaves, but had left him in lieu other property." However, it had so turned out that he then owned two women and three children. He objected to synods declaring slavery a sin, "because there were many female members of the Church whose husbands were not members and who would still retain slaves; many persons who held them as guardians for minors, etc.; and that, as there could not be a uniform operation of a rule against slavery, it would, on the whole, be well enough to do nothing about it."

These objections were repeated by several other clergymen who were visited.

Sept. 13th.—Received a letter from Mr. Weld, accepting my invitation to meet me near Georgetown, Ky., and informing me that the "Address to the Kentucky Ministers and Elders" will be published entire in the Cincinnati "Journal."

Sept. 14th.—Conversed with Rev. Mr. Taylor. He has one slave according to law, though he has never so regarded her *in fact.* She came to him by his wife, and he agreed to receive her on condition that she should consider herself free. He has been in the habit of rewarding her for her services. Talked also with Rev. John Blackburn.* He did not *own* slaves; he *hired* them. Thought immediate emancipation of all slaves worse than a continuance of slavery. I had several conversations with Rev. Robert Davidson, of Lexington [afterward the historian of the Presbyterian Church in Kentucky], and found him greatly prejudiced against the Eastern abolitionists, and this, in no small degree, from the fact that they are the very newest of the "new school-men." (Meaning the Tappans, Beriah Green, Joshua Leavitt, etc.) He has never owned a slave, intends never to own one, though he has one *hired.* He has also two girls who are *free*, hired as servants. He will vote in the synod, I think, for a declaration that *slavery is sinful.*

Here I also saw Henry Thompson, lately a student of Lane Seminary, who turned abolitionist and manumitted his two slaves upon whose hire he was educating himself. He has been greatly tormented and persecuted in Jessamine County, where he lives.

From this time until his removal from Kentucky Mr. Birney had Mr. Thompson as an inmate of his family, while the latter pursued his studies under Dr. Young, of Centre College.

Sept. 15th.—Reached Lexington in the afternoon, wrote a note to Mr. Clay, requesting a short interview with him on the

---

* A relative of Rev. Gideon Blackburn, D. D., once president of Centre College, who had advised a dying and penitent slave-trader to make a will freeing all his slaves and giving all his blood-stained money to trustees to be used for benevolent purposes. The will was made. (See Davidson's "History of the Presbyterian Church in Kentucky.")

subject of slavery, etc. He did not come home until near sunset—too late for me to see him this evening; but he sent me a note inviting me to breakfast with him to-morrow morning.

Sept. 16th.—Breakfasted this morning with Mr. and Mrs. Clay and one of their sons. Afterward Mr. Clay invited me into the parlor, where we conversed, he being the chief speaker, for about an hour. He seems never to have gone beyond the outer bark of the subject; his views "vulgar," not "deep." He said that slavery in Kentucky was in so mitigated a form as not to deserve the consideration of a very great evil; that men's interest in *property* had been found an insurmountable barrier to gradual emancipation *then* (in 1799); that now they were more formidable. The case was hopeless by any direct effort, and was to be left to the influence of liberal principles, as they should pervade our land. He spoke of Mr. Robert J. Breckenridge having put himself down in popular estimation by his having advocated emancipation, and that he and Mr. John Green—two gentlemen of great worth—had disqualified themselves for political usefulness by the part they had taken in reference to slavery. He related to me two facts, that I have recorded elsewhere, to show that the opinion expressed in his speech before the Kentucky Colonization Society in 1829, *that the South* (Louisiana) *maintained her stock of slaves from their natural increase* was incorrect. He had become satisfied of his error. The impression made upon me by this interview was that Mr. Clay had no *conscience* about this matter, and therefore that he would swim with the popular current.

As this was the last personal interview that ever took place between Mr. Birney and Mr. Clay, the former's memorandum of the conversation, made on the same day, is given above *verbatim et literatim*. It will be remembered that in October, 1830, Mr. Birney had called on Mr. Clay to urge him to place himself at the head of a national free-soil, gradual emancipation movement, and had then, in consequence of what passed between them, lost confidence in Mr. Clay as a political leader. From September 16, 1834, Mr. Birney knew that Mr. Clay would antagonize his movements in Kentucky. From that date, though their personal relations remained on a friendly footing, they were foemen in political measures. Neither misunderstood the other on this point.

The entry for September 16th in the diary continues:

After this interview I proceeded to the place, twenty miles north of Georgetown, where I was to meet my dear friend Weld. We had appointed 3 o'clock P. M., and were not more than five minutes apart in arriving at the spot.

A quiet house of private entertainment was near at hand. Here we remained until four o'clock in the afternoon of the next day, talking over the whole matter, what course it would be best to pursue, etc. We parted, greatly refreshed, as I trust, on both sides. I have seen in no man such a rare combination of great intellectual powers with Christian simplicity. He must make a powerful impression on the public mind of this country if he lives ten years.*

Sept. 17th.—Saw the Rev. Simeon Salisbury, of Georgetown. He has never hired nor owned a slave. Is greatly in favor of the Church acting in condemnation of slavery.

Sept. 18th.—Saw Rev. John T. Johnson (Campbellite). Found him very favorably disposed, going so far as to say that he did not think the approaching winter would pass over without his having set his slaves, some eight or nine as I understood him, free.

Sept. 19th.—Dined at Lexington. In the evening called upon the Rev. Wm. W. Hall, who, I had understood, was very favorably disposed to the slaves of that city, teaching a negro Sunday-school and lecturing the blacks on religious truth. . . . Never have I seen one who seemed more willingly to open his heart to the truth. Mr. Hall took me to see Mr. James Weir, a Presbyterian, who had recently inherited eighty slaves. Mr. Weir had thought much about his religious duty to them. He said this

* In 1832, in the winter, Mr. Weld had been swept away in the icy current of Alum River in an attempt to cross, and had been taken out apparently drowned and frozen. His voice was never so strong afterward, and he could not use it freely for public speaking after 1836.

much: if he were satisfied it would benefit his slaves to manumit them he would not hesitate a moment to do so. I think he was sincere. Mrs. Weir is willing to give up slavery on condition of removing to a free State.

Sept. 21st.—Saw again the Rev. Mr. Taylor, who requested me to write for him a deed of manumission for his negro woman Pleasants, as he wished to be able unhesitatingly to say he was not a slave-holder.

Of another he writes:

The doctor proposes to send by the next Western expedition to Liberia a negro woman with five small children and having no husband. He thinks she can support them all there.

Sept. 25th.—Greatly to my mortification, my father, after having appeared enlightened on the Christian duty of emancipation, has promised to give a negro woman (Maria) and her four children (girls) to Mrs. Polk in Danville. I lament much that he has thought proper to leave such a memorial behind him.

Sept. 30th.—I this day wrote to my father [he had gone to reside with his daughter, the wife of Judge Marshali, at Louisville] requesting the privilege of paying out of my own means what he would say ought to satisfy Mrs. Polk instead of the negroes he promised to *give* her. . . . About the close of last session there were said to be in Centre College about fourteen young men who were firm abolitionists. Dr. Luke Munsell is so decidedly. . . . He is superintendent of the Deaf and Dumb Asylum.

. . . I have heard that old Mr. Humphrey Marshall is an abolitionist and that he has liberated all his slaves, hiring their services. Abram T. Skillman, bookseller at Lexington, is said to be an abolitionist.

Of the members of the synod he says:

The Rev. Messrs. Calvert, of Bowling Green, Woods, of Glasgow, Salisbury, of Georgetown, Sawtell, of Louisville, and Cole, of Augusta, are all that I know who are favorable to immediate and total emancipation. . . . There may be others of whom I am uninformed. And this is the whole number . . . to do this mighty work in which we have to meet the strongest interests and talents.

Oct. 1st.—A very prominent and wealthy citizen, a widower, called on Mr. Birney, told him his suit to a Philadelphia lady had been rejected, and, as he understood, because of his being a slave-holder, and requested Mr. Birney to write the lady and inform her she might manumit his slaves as fast as she pleased if she would marry him. As Mr. Birney was a kinsman of the suitor and a friend of the lady, he wrote the letter as desired.

Oct. 6th.—Had an interview with Dr. Munsell and disclosed to him my plan of operations prior to commencing a paper. Much approved by him.

Oct. 7th.—Attended as a spectator the Presbytery now sitting in Danville. Saw Professor Buchanan, who told me that the Rev. Mr. Shannon, of Shelbyville, had read my letter to the ministers and elders of the Presbyterian Church of Kentucky, and had determined to come up to the synod after having disentangled himself from slavery.

Oct. 8th.—Synod of Kentucky organized. I conversed with several members on the subject of slavery.

After a discussion of three days, a resolution was adopted declaring slavery a sin and to favor all proper measures for voluntary, gradual emancipation. The vote stood: Yeas, 56; nays, 8; *non-liquet*, 7. The year before a weaker resolution, substituting "moral evil" for "sin," had been postponed indefinitely by a vote of yeas, 41; nays, 36; *non-liquet*, 1. The evident advance in opinion was very encouraging to Mr. Birney, who on the evening of the 11th addressed the public, including many members of the synod, at the Danville Presbyterian Church in favor of abolition. Among the converts at this meeting was the Rev. Mr. Stamper, the local Methodist preacher, who recanted in 1836.

Oct. 23d.—Received a letter from T. D. Weld, informing me of his appointment as agent in Ohio.* He is a man of great

* The Pittsburg "Times," in noticing the rapidly increasing audiences flocking to hear a course of lectures by Mr. Weld in that city on free

mental powers and the most simple-hearted and earnest follower of Christ that I have known. . . . Prepared to-day to set off to Cincinnati in the morning to attend the anniversaries to be held there next week.

At Cincinnati he made many acquaintances among men prominent in the various benevolent movements of the day, and was much gratified by the numerous indications of the general and deep interest taken at the North in his movement against slavery in Kentucky. He then returned home to continue his work, and especially to prepare for the publication at Danville of an anti-slavery weekly paper.

J. G. Birney to Gerrit Smith.

Nov. 20, 1834.—. . . I do, indeed, thank God and take courage. Not that I approve of what the synod has done *in toto*, for it has declared the system to be sinful and the *continuance* of it not so, but because it has been moved at all toward the proper point. There is no room for despair, for if God continue so to prosper the cause of human liberty as he has done here during the last year, the next synod will witness, if not the absolute death of slavery, at least its convulsive and dying throes in the Church of which it has supervision. . . . Whatever may have been the errors of Northern abolitionists — and I do not say they have been exempt from them, though surely with liberal minds the persecution and abuse they have suffered furnish no small palliation—they have beyond all doubt the *right principle*, and, if I do not greatly mistake, they are now using it with much discretion and effect. Do you not think it probable that very

discussion and slavery, says "Mr. Weld is one of Nature's orators—not a declaimer, but a logician of great tact and power. His inexhaustible fund of anecdote and general information, with the power of being intensely pathetic, enables him to give the greatest imaginable interest to the subject. His powers of teaching are of the first order—that is, his facility for generalizing broadly and regularly, for passing into profound abstractions and bringing his wealth of ideas into beautiful light by clear, striking, and familiar illustrations."

gentle and calm measures would not have been sufficient to rouse up from its torpor the public sentiment of this nation?

. . . In the present state of things surely nothing more is wanting than the kindest and most Christian course. Why not, then, if we think so, act upon their *principle*—gently correct by our example their indiscretions whenever they may appear, and thus be instrumental in bringing patriots, philanthropists, and Christians into one noble and dignified and swelling stream of action for God and our country? . . . Should you desire, . . . I will present to you fully all my views. I have no secret as to my anti-slavery operations. There is no item in my contemplated action on the public mind that is concealed. I am at present identified with no free-State anti-slavery association. I think it probable that for some time to come I may remain so. My efforts are now directed to an organization for this State. I am not without hope that one may be gotten up by next spring. Should this turn out to be the case, the next movement will be to get up a paper that will in the main speak the sentiments of the society and serve as a point of concentration for all the immediate emancipation material lying scattered throughout the State.

Same to Same.

Danville, Ky., Dec. 30, 1834.—. . . I shall look with much interest for the essays about to be published (by G. S.) in the "Journal of Freedom"—the more because you say that on the "immediate emancipation" doctrine and on the subject of anti-slavery "there will in all probability be but little difference in our views." . . . There is an aspect in which colonization has been presented to my mind that I have never yet discussed, except in conversation. . . . It is this: The best way to promote the kind of colonization that will eventuate in Christianizing Africa—and, of course, in civilizing it—is to grant immediate emancipation here from *Christian* principle.

He develops the idea that intelligent converted negroes would go as missionaries:

Let colonization become strictly missionary in its character. . . . One thought more on this subject: Emancipation, to be blessed of God and *safe*, must proceed from love—love to God and man—and must be so conducted that it shall excite in the bosoms of the emancipated love for our principle and love for us.

To a request from Gerrit Smith for leave to publish one of his letters, he says:

Of the letter to you, I have no copy. I have so much writing to do that really I have not time, if I deemed it necessary, to copy my letters. Another reason why I do not: I express no opinion that I do not honestly entertain. If I have said anything that is erroneous, I am always willing, when convinced of the error, to retract it. The only doubt I have about the propriety of publishing it is that I wrote it without expectation of such a thing. . . .

There is yet among even some clever and firm abolitionists here a little fearfulness of what has been called "the fanaticism of Northern abolitionists." However, I think it will in no very long time disappear, and there will be a full fraternization. . . . I think it not improbable, my dear friend, that I may have the pleasure of seeing you in the city of New York next spring. . . . How heartily and thankfully would I enjoy the pleasure of a long, long conversation with you on the great subject to which God, I trust, has called us both! . . . Ah! if I were to quarrel with all who differ from me here on the subject that now so fully occupies my mind and interests my feelings, or were I to feel uncharitably toward them, I might always be unhappy and cheerless!

Of Mr. Smith's "Essays," he says:

I do not know of any paper in Kentucky that would publish them.

Jan. 31, 1835.—Of the sixty-four-page pamphlet, "Report of the Synod Committee on Slavery," written by President Young, and recommending a plan of gradual emancipation,* he writes to Gerrit Smith:

---

* For this plan, see Davidson's "History of the Kentucky Presbyterian Church," p. 339, and Stanton's "The Church and the Rebellion,"

I am now almost daily contemplating the injury it has done to the cause of emancipation in the Presbyterian Church. I know of several instances of brethren whose minds were earnestly inquiring for the truth in relation to the *sin* of slavery who have to all appearance sunk to sleep from the anodyne he has administered. Young showed me his manuscript before he sent it to Cincinnati to be published. I thought, as an argument, it was grossly sophistical and unworthy of his mind. I besought him, as a brother, to abstain from its publication. . . . I was anxious that he should not commit himself before the nation on the side of the slave-holder. He did refrain for a week. . . . I have just come from his house, after a conversation of an hour or two containing nothing encouraging as to his entertainment of more correct views. I do very much lament his course ; I wanted to see him eminently useful. . . .

While I was at Frankfort, Judge Underwood delivered the annual colonization address. It was intended as an answer to the abolitionist and to demonstrate the practicability of exterminating Kentucky slavery by African colonization. His knowledge of abolitionism was very crude. In a few instances he was illiberal ; in the main, he is a liberal man.

Underwood's plan was for Kentucky to expend one hundred and forty thousand dollars yearly in the transportation of four thousand negroes—girls and youths from seventeeen to twenty years of age. This, continued for fifty years, would rid the State of slaves. Mr. Birney asks:

Will the people of the State give up this year, for the purpose of colonization, four thousand slaves, at the ages when they are most valuable, when human flesh is selling in the Kentucky market for about four to five dollars a pound ? And will they

---

p. 423. The pamphlet was a powerful and faithful exposure of slavery, with the lame conclusion of gradualism. John C. Young, D. D., President of Centre College, was always acute, ingenious, and eloquent. His wife was the daughter of J. Cabell Breckenridge. That fact and his many amiable traits had endeared him greatly to Mr. Birney as a friend.

give from the State coffers one hundred and forty thousand dollars for their transportation to Africa? . . . It is by holding up such schemes as this, by exhibiting such arithmetical benevolence, that the Northern professed friends of freedom are beguiling the slave States from that repentance which would save them. . . . I do not think it probable that I shall *review* your essays. I read the first (published in the "Emancipator") with great pleasure. . . . Would that our excellent Brother Bacon [Dr. Leonard G. Bacon] could see his error! He does us great damage. The slave-holder lays hold of any doctrine that furnishes the least shadow of excuse, and holds to it with the tenacity of a drowning man. Notwithstanding the declaration and resolutions of the synod, which sat *here*, since that time slaves have been sold to the Southern slaver by a member of the Danville Church.

J. G. Birney to Lewis Tappan.

Danville, Feb. 3, 1835.—I returned a few days since from Frankfort. . . . I heard while there most of the debates on the "Convention Bill," into which the subject of slavery and emancipation always entered. I conversed on these subjects with many of the members of the Legislature as well as with other intelligent gentlemen from different parts of the State. The conclusion to which my mind has been brought is this, that emancipation in some form or another—in most instances, in the crudest form imaginable—occupies the mind of this community; and that the feeling in favor of it is growing. . . . I am not without hope that the subject of emancipation will be taken up in many parts of the State by the candidates for the next General Assembly. . . . With the *political action* of political men and the holy action of religious men there is no inconsistency that is irreconcilable. That the oppressor's reign should end from *any* principle should cause us to rejoice.

On the 19th of March, 1835, the Kentucky Anti-Slavery Society was organized at Danville. It numbered forty members, most of them intelligent men, and all respectable. Some of them had been slave-holders. Before May, the number was increased to forty-five. To effect this organization, Mr. Birney had devoted much time and energy.

J. G. Birney to Gerrit Smith.

Danville, March 21, 1835.—. . . I have been very much engaged for the last month, not only in preparing for the organization of our State Anti-Slavery Society, but in actually discussing publicly the merits of "immediate emancipation." Within that time, I have had two debates some distance from home, in which my chief adversary was a minister of the Gospel, an aged and influential minister. . . . Between two and three weeks since I undertook to review in our Danville Lyceum, in the way of lecture, the letter of President Young on slavery. I gave notice in the newspapers of the village, that all who felt an interest in the subject of it should read and understand the letter that they might come prepared to appreciate the arguments with which the principles would be met and to detect any fallacy or sophistry more easily, if any should be attempted by me. I was a long time in exposing, as I thought it was easy to do, the fallacies of his letter. He was present and so stung that he asked an adjournment of the lyceum till the next evening, when he would undertake to reply. He did so. I think his effort was not considered a successful one in vindication of his cause. . . . He greatly abused abolitionism, and, in speaking of Mr. Garrison, he *out-Garrisoned Garrison himself*. He went so far as to say he would not be an abolitionist because Mr. Garrison was one. . . .

Although I am in the midst of enemies (though I must say, not *personal*, unless they have transferred their malignant feelings from the cause of freedom to its advocate), and am often much perplexed, yet, altogether, I have never had so much peace. . . . The day before yesterday was organized the "Kentucky State Anti-Slavery Society, auxiliary to the American Anti-Slavery Society," with Prof. Buchanan,* of Centre College, as its president. Our proceedings were very harmonious among ourselves and uninterrupted † from without. The fifty dollars which

* He had just manumitted his three slaves.

† There would have been few mobs if it had not been for the wire-working of politicians.

you thought proper to confide to my discretion for the advancement of the cause of *immediate* emancipation, I have devoted to paying the expenses of printing and distributing our proceedings. . . . Immediate emancipation will have to be sustained here by the comparatively poor and humble. The aristocracy, created and sustained by slavery, will be ugly enemies—aye, and they will be so almost to our extermination. . . . I do not think there is good reason for your refusing to give your name and influence to the American Anti-Slavery Society.

He refers to his wife's bad health as making it doubtful whether he could attend the anti-slavery anniversary in New York, on May 12th, but "should her situation allow of my leaving her, it is my intention to be at Zanesville, Ohio, at a meeting of the convention" (April 22nd, to form a State anti-slavery society).

The state of public opinion in Kentucky in the spring of 1835 has some light thrown upon it by the following report, in the "New England Spectator," of statements by Mr. Birney, at Boston, in May:

Mr. Birney stated that he had recently received a letter from Kentucky, which stated that the subject of immediate emancipation is greatly talked about. A discussion of the subject has recently been had in the Young Men's Institute of Louisville. He (Mr. Birney) had been written to to take a part in the debate, it not being known that he had left [for the East]. Dr. Marshall, brother of the Chief Justice, stated that so strong is the impression against slavery in Louisville, that when a slave-holder recently wished to lay claim to a colored man in Louisville, the affair was so unpopular that he wished the privilege of prosecuting his claim in another place.

No hinderance whatever is thrown in the way of our meetings. The church in Danville was freely given to me for the convention (to form a State anti-slavery society). The pastor of the church, although opposed to me on this subject, yet gave notice of my lectures held in that place. No church in that State has ever been refused me. (Appendix to "American Report, 1835," of the American Anti-Slavery Society, p. 78.)

On the same occasion he said of the race prejudice against the negro:

> There is less *negro hatred* in the slave than in the free States. They are subject to more insult in the latter than in the former.*

* At that time a colored person could travel in the stage-coaches of the South, but was excluded from public conveyances in the North. As late as 1864, colored servants in attendance on ladies and carrying white children were driven from street-cars in Philadelphia—a brutality without example in the South.

CHAPTER XVIII.

A WIDER SPHERE OF ACTION.

APRIL, 1835.

EVENTS not foreseen by Mr. Birney attracted the attention of the whole country to him and his operations in Kentucky after the general publication of his letter on colonization, in July, 1834. The emancipation of eight hundred thousand slaves in the British West Indies, on the first of August in that year, had made the abolition of slavery the topic of universal discussion in the United States. That measure revived the memories of the emancipation of half a million in those islands by the first republic of France; of the abclition of slavery by Chili, in 1811; by Buenos Ayres, in 1813; by Columbia, in 1821; at the Cape of Good Hope, in 1823; by New York, in 1827; and by Mexico, in 1829. There were rumors of prospective abolition in Brazil and of the emancipation of the serfs in Russia. The outlook was that the states of this republic and the monarchy of Spain would be the last governments to maintain slavery. In the contemporaneous language of a frank South Carolina member of Congress, "The sentiment of the Christian world is against slavery." That the great majority of the American people shared this sentiment is also true. Every State Constitution contained bills of rights and guarantees of personal freedom. Every court administered justice generally on the principle of equality of rights before the law. The orator, the teacher, and the preacher insisted alike upon justice between individuals. Slavery was the one horrible exception to American law and the American sense of right.

This exception was maintained by a small minority of the people of the South. De Bow, a pro-slavery writer, makes the following admissions:

"I am satisfied that the non-slave-holders far outnumber the slave-holders perhaps by three to one." *

According to the same author, there were, in 1850, only 7,929 slave-holders owning each more than fifty slaves. In 1833 the whole number of slave-holders did not exceed two hundred and eighty thousand. But they possessed the rich lands and the wealth of the Southern States; and their intelligence, social position, and identity of interest enabled them when united to control nominations to office and the use of the political power of the South. The machinations of Calhoun and his friends, after the defeat of nullification, to bring slavery to the front as a political question, were powerfully aided by the emancipation legislation of Great Britain. The slave-holders drew together under this double pressure. Brave and self-reliant, they defied the moral power of Christendom; and, determined to present an unbroken front, they tolerated neither criticism nor debate nor the non-committalism of silence. Between 1833 and the summer of 1835, the ordinary lines of political parties were effaced in the South, so far as slavery was concerned; Whigs and Democrats vied with each other in professions of loyalty to the slave-power; and devotion to slavery became the test of Southern patriotism. The obliteration of all anti-slavery societies in the slave States, which had begun with

* 2 "Resources of the South and West," p. 106. See also Van Holst, "State Sovereignty," p. 342 and note.

the election of Jackson, became an accomplished fact. Free speech had perished at the South in 1835.

But there was one exception—Kentucky. Tongue and pen were still free in many parts of that State. Many of the churches were open to anti-slavery speakers; crowds listened to discussions of abolition; several newspapers admitted able anti-slavery essays to their columns. The synod of the Presbyterian Church had published the most eloquent arraignment of slavery ever issued by an ecclesiastical body and a recommendation of emancipation hardly falling short of immediate abolition; and forty respectable men, most of them ex-slave-holders, had formed a State society auxiliary to the American Anti-Slavery Society!!

This formidable movement, menacing the labor system of the South, had for its soul and leader a native Southerner, a man of conscience and courage, an ex-slave-holder, a lawyer, and statesman. In 1834–'35 the Mordecai in the king's gate for the slave power was James G. Birney.

For the Northern States, he was the observed of all observers. He was the only abolitionist who was grappling with slavery in a slave State; and the imagination of the masses attributed to him all the qualities of a heroic soul, while the intelligent admired his firmness, moderation, freedom from exaggeration, and thorough knowledge of his subject.

His famous "Letter" had brought him numerous messages and assurances of sympathy, encouragement, and admiration from all parts of the North. Friendly travelers had called on him at his home; several prominent abolitionists had visited him there, and he received from many residents of Northern cities invitations to speak on slavery in those places, with assurances of good halls and large audiences. Among these correspondents were Mr. Gazzam, of Pittsburg; David Paul Brown, of Philadelphia; Judge

William Jay, of New York; and William Ellery Channing, of Boston. The prominent abolitionists of Ohio were anxious that he should be present at the formation in April of the State Anti-Slavery Society; and the Tappans and Joshua Leavitt were urgent for his attendance at the May anniversary of the American Anti-Slavery Society, to which he had been appointed delegate from Kentucky.

Yielding to these requests, he left home for Cincinnati, reaching that city April 17, 1835, and taking lodgings at the Henry House, which was situated on Third near Main Street, in the central part of the city. His arrival was announced in the daily papers. He was met at the hotel by several prominent anti-slavery lecturers, and he remained there more than two days, during which time he received a large number of visitors, among whom were Salmon P. Chase and Dr. G. Bailey. His presence in the city excited curiosity and interest, but there was no indication of a mob spirit. He was pressed to lecture in one of the churches, but refused because of want of time to give the notices required; and then, in company with the Hamilton County delegation, he journeyed by stage-coach to Zanesville to aid in the formation of a State society which should be auxiliary to the American Anti-Slavery Society. The local societies in Ohio had generally been independent, each acting on its own plan.

The convention consisted of one hundred and ten delegates, representing Anti-Slavery societies in twenty-five counties. Among the societies not represented were some of the oldest in the State. They had been established without concert, at different times, under different names, and with constitutions framed on no common model; and never having affiliated with each other for concerted action, they were now reluctant to place themselves under the control of State and national societies of recent origin, a step that would apparently compel them to change their names and constitutions and take date from the change. This last concession was not made, even in subsequent years, by such old societies as the Mount Pleasant, the West Union, the Monroe County, or the Ripley, which was the oldest of all; and when these became auxiliary, they stood without date of origin on the records of the American Anti-Slavery Society. (See its "Annual Reports" for 1836–'38.) The date of the organization of the first abolition society at Bethel is unknown. It was not later than the Missouri Controversy. The town was laid out in 1797, by Obed Denham, from Kentucky, a Baptist abolitionist. In his deed of dedication and plat of the village (see Clermont County Records) occurs this sentence:

> I also give two in-lots, Nos. 80 and 108, for the use of the regular Baptist Church, who do not hold slaves, nor commune at the Lord's table with those that do practice such tyranny over their fellow-creatures.

The men who migrated from Kentucky with Obed Denham—the Becks, Frazees, Burkes, and others—were as stanch Baptists and abolitionists as he was; and their first preachers, the Rev. Moses Hutchins, and his successor, the Rev. Moses Edwards,* always kept the banners well advanced. When the Bethel Society was reorganized in 1836, James Denham, a grandson of Obed, was the secretary.

Lundy had organized the Mount Pleasant Society in 1815; and Rev. Dyer Burgess that of West Union about 1818. We do not know when the Aiding Abolition Society of Monroe County was formed; but, on the 24th of June, 1826, its chairman and secretary published in Lundy's paper a two-column "Memorial" beginning with these words:

---

* He officiated as clergyman at the marriage of Gen. Grant's father to Hannah Simpson, June 22, 1821.

"Convinced of the iniquity of slavery in all its bearings, as attached to the colored race, and having associated together for the purpose of aiding in the *immediate abolition* thereof" etc.

The Ripley Society, which had been formed early in the century, set the good example to the older societies of sending delegates.

The society at Zanesville had been formed in 1826 as the Emancipation Society, its expressed object being "the total *extinction* of slavery in the United States at the earliest practicable period" (MS.). It had been reformed July 4, 1833, as the United States Constitution Society.* with the expression of the object strengthened by substituting "*abolition*" for "extinction," and "*possible*" for "practicable." This society had called the convention.

The Columbiana Abolition Society had been organized January 6, 1827, and in the first three months numbered five hundred members. Its doctrine was *abolition, without condition or qualification.* (See "Genius" of April 14, 1827.) It sent delegates. When it became auxiliary to the American Society, it refused to take a date and stood on its old record. A few persons took seats, not as delegates, but as recognized abolitionists. Two of them were members of the Methodist Reformed Church, which, in 1826, had adopted the following rule:

> Article 8th. No person holding a slave shall be admitted into this society on any condition. Any member of the society buying a slave shall be immediately expelled from it. All persons receiving money as heirs, in consequence of the sale of slaves, shall be immediately expelled from the society.†

---

* In 1836 it became the Putnam Anti-Slavery Society, and dates from that year on the records of the American Society.

† "London Anti-Slavery, Reporter," for July, 1827, which copies it from Lundy's "Genius."

Three of them were members of the Associate Reformed Presbyterian Church, which, in 1831, had settled the form of its rule against slavery as follows:

> No member shall, from and after this date, be allowed to hold a human being in the character and condition of a slave. ("Life of Dr. Crothers," p. 181).

Of the veterans who had fought the battles of *immediate* abolition in Ohio for more than ten years, there were present one farmer, John B. Mahan, of Brown County; two business men, Col. Robert Stewart, of Ross County, and Col. William Keys, of Highland; and five clergymen, John Rankin, Samuel Crothers, William Dickey, James H. Dickey, and John Wallace, all members of the Chillicothe Presbytery,* and all immigrants from slave States. Levi Whipple, Horace Nye, and Henry C. Howell had been in the ranks more than five years. Elizur Wright had been publicly active in the cause since 1831. The Lane Seminary group present was composed of Theodore D. Weld, Henry B. Stanton, James A. Thome, Horace Bushnell, Augustus Wattles, and William T. Allan (Alabama). Morgan County sent Hiram Wilson, who was so widely known in after years as the devoted missionary to the colored refugees in Canada; and Cincinnati sent Augustus Wattles, who, as superintendent of the colored schools in that city, had, with his self-denying coadjutors, achieved a great work of elevation and reform for the negro population. John B. Mahan, a tall, muscular, raw-boned, stalwart, and swarthy man of middle age, had long been one of the most active friends of fugitive negroes. He was a farmer and local Methodist preacher. He had not been in a slave State since childhood; but, from about 1820, any man fleeing from bondage could rely upon his hospi-

* In 1826 this Presbytery issued a pamphlet on the evils of slavery and the duty of masters to free their slaves.

tality and protection. His strength and courage, tested in sundry conflicts with slave-catchers, had given them a salutary respect for him. He knew reliable friends in the counties adjoining his own to whom he could confide fugitives. In 1826 a close connection was formed by him and his associates with Levi Coffin (see "Coffin's Reminiscences," page 108) and other Quakers in Wayne County, Indiana. An earlier one had been established with Western New York in order to baffle the slave-catchers who were stationed at Detroit; and, after 1826, the recapture of a fugitive negro who could cross the Ohio River and get five miles north of it, was a rare occurrence. In emergencies the house of any Quaker was a refuge; no questions were asked, food and lodging were quietly given, and the traveler was speeded on his way in the safest manner. * Mahan was a taciturn man; he was no boaster, but his somber piety and bravery would have endeared him to Oliver Cromwell. Before the convention was over he was appreciated by his fellow-members. †

Rev. Samuel Crothers was a Presbyterian preacher. He had been brought up in Kentucky, and left that State in 1810, when he was twenty-eight years of age. For ten years he was a pastor in Ross County. In 1820 he took charge of the church at Greenfield, Highland County, and kept it for thirty-six years. His moral and political, as well as his religious influence was very great in that part of Ohio. From his entrance into the State (we have no

* Friend Butterworth, a Warren County Quaker, who had come with a covered wagon to Cincinnati, was asked in my hearing in 1838, "Can you take a poor man as passenger?" "Yea, I have room." The place was named for taking him. "I will call for him at eight." This was all. But it saved a man who was hard beset.

† September 17, 1838, he was kidnapped and taken to Kentucky to be tried on a charge of stealing slaves. Acquitted on the criminal charge, his friends paid the amount of the bond in a civil suit, rather than risk Kentucky justice.

record of his life in Kentucky) he was known as an *immediate abolitionist*, in full sympathy with Gilliland, Burgess, Rankin, and the Dickeys. His sermons on the subject have not been preserved, but we have from his pen fifteen letters published between 1827 and 1831 and republished in 1831, entitled "An Appeal to Patriots and Christians in Behalf of the Enslaved Africans." The sturdiness and thoroughness of his abolitionism is manifested in his striking answer to the apology, "It is necessary to keep the Africans in slavery to avoid the evils of emancipation." He tolerated no instant of sin. He likens it to the fabled apology of a certain Scotch clan for stealing: "We are an honest race of people; we never steal—except a little now and then, for a living." When President Young, of Centre College, published his plea for gradualism, Dr. Crothers answered in five letters, published early in 1835. Those letters were logical, witty, and sarcastic; they utterly riddled Dr. Young's house of cards. There was no speaker or writer in the anti-slavery ranks between 1825 and 1835 who dug down quicker or with surer stroke to the primal granite than Dr. Crothers.*

The most noted abolitionist in the convention was doubtless John Rankin. When Henry Ward Beecher was asked after the war, "Who abolished slavery?" he is said to have answered, "Rev. John Rankin and his sons did it."

The humor of the answer lies in its quaint exaggeration of the effects of the services rendered to the cause by Rankin. These were very great. Many Western men have called him "the father of abolitionism," and it was not an uncommon thing in the thirties to hear him called "the Martin Luther" of the cause. In 1827, the year in

* Ritchie's "Life of Dr. Crothers."

which New York abolished slavery within her limits, John Rankin was one of the five most prominent advocates in this country of *immediate abolition*. He was also one of the earliest. Charles Osborn and Rev. George Bourne date as abolitionists from 1814, John Rankin and Benjamin Lundy from 1815, and Rev. James Duncan from about 1820. Of the many thousands who joined the modern anti-slavery movement within the first twelve years after its revival at the close of the War of 1812, these five names have been most familiar to abolitionists, and the two brightest are those of Lundy and Rankin.

John Rankin, born Feb. 4, 1793; died March 18, 1886, a native of East Tennessee, was graduated at Washington College in 1816, and licensed to preach in 1817. Having become an immediate abolitionist in 1815, he persuaded Dr. Doak, whose daughter he married soon after, to manumit his slaves. In November, 1817, he left Tennessee, intending to go to Ohio, but, being unable to get farther than Carlisle, Nicholas County, Ky., he preached there during the winter and became pastor of the church in April, 1818.

In the next three years he organized at Carlisle and other places in Kentucky societies auxiliary to the "Kentucky Abolition Society,"* which had been established in 1807. In a speech at the anniversary meeting, May, 1839, of the American Anti-Slavery Society, Mr. Rankin said:

* R. M. Johnson, of Kentucky, afterward Vice-President, may have been a member. In his speech on the Missouri question, Feb. 1, 1820, reported in the "National Intelligencer" of April 29, 1820, he advises: "Encourage Sunday-schools, multiply Bible societies, increase missionary exertions, animate to deeds of benevolence *abolition societies*, . . . and you will perform the duties of Christians and patriots," etc.

In Lundy's "Genius," of October, 1822, is printed a circular "sent down by the Abolition Society of Kentucky at their late convention to the several branches." It is dated Maysville, Sept. 12, 1822, and signed by Hugh Wiley, President, and E. Duncan, Jr., Secretary.

"I rejoice in the triumph of the principles of immediate emancipation because," etc. . . . "I was a member of an anti-slavery society in Kentucky twenty years ago *on the same principle* as this. The doctrine of immediate emancipation is said to be new, but societies were formed all over the country twenty years ago, and *many members of these societies advocated this same doctrine.*" In January, 1822, Mr. Rankin became pastor of the Presbyterian Church at Ripley, Ohio, and held the place thirty-three years. Most of the members of his church in Kentucky removed before 1830 to Decatur County, Indiana, to escape the evil of slavery, and these formed a church of which one of his sons has been pastor for more than twenty-five years. Between 1822 and 1830 he preached and lectured against slavery. In 1823 he published a series of letters on slavery in the "Castigator," Ripley, Ohio. They were republished in book-form in 1824, and passed through many editions, several of which were issued by the American Anti-Slavery Society. In 1830 and several previous years, the abolition books of largest circulation in the United States were those by Rankin, Bourne, Duncan, and Stroud. During the year 1836 Mr. Rankin was a traveling lecturer in the employ of the national society, and at a later date he was made one of its managers for Ohio. His house at Ripley was situated near the town on a hill about three hundred feet high, and was visible at a great distance from the Kentucky side of the river, especially at night when lighted up. Many fugitives reached it, and not one was ever turned away. They were always conducted to friends by one or more of Mr. Rankin's seven sons. These young men all volunteered in the Union army and served through the war, thus demonstrating the soundness of their anti-slavery education. Mr. Rankin was a man of judgment, perseverance, piety, and strong character. His influence in

Ohio and Kentucky was powerful. Henry Ward Beecher knew him intimately, and both he and Mrs. Stowe visited him several times at his home and learned to respect him. Mr. Rankin would have disclaimed Mr. Beecher's compliment, for he was free from vanity and his modesty was equal to his great merit.

Our space will not permit us to sketch others of the noteworthy men present, though some of them—for instance, Elizur Wright, H. B. Stanton, and James A. Thome—afterward became men of national reputation. The impression made upon Mr. Birney by the men present was favorable. They were probably all members of the Church. They were temperate. The extremely small number of tobacco-chewers among them attracted his notice. The discussions were able, moderate in language, and to the point. At that stage of the cause speakers aiming at personal notoriety only had not sought in any large number the anti-slavery platform in Ohio. Sincerity and earnestness were in the atmosphere. The visitor from Kentucky was, of course, the central object of attention. He was invited to a seat as member, and to address the convention, and he was made chairman of the principal committee—the one charged with the duty of preparing and bringing forward business. To Mr. Birney the most significant part of the action of the convention was an amendment to his reported resolution against the "Black Laws." To a denunciation of them as "cruel, impious, and disgraceful to a Christian State" was added a pledge to vote for such candidates only for legislative office as were pledged to repeal them. The latter clause was stricken out—a change which appeared in the minutes as an adoption of the report "after being slightly amended." The "Declaration of Sentiment" was subjected to a similar emasculation; under the head of "Plan of Operations" the committee, among other things, had reported: "We shall absolve ourselves from the political responsibility of national slave-holding by petitioning Congress," etc., and had added a clause, equivalent to a pledge, to vote for such candidates as would grant the petitions. The clause was stricken out, leaving in the "declaration" the absurd proposition that a citizen could avoid responsibility for bad laws by *petitioning* for their repeal! As Mr. Birney expressed it, they had loaded with powder, but forgotten to ram down a bullet! He could not easily comprehend how men could have political principles and not vote on them. It was represented, on the other hand, that a pledge to vote would alienate a certain sect which regarded voting as a sin. The strongest reason probably was that the clergymen and religious men generally belonged to the class, then rapidly increasing in the country, of men who do not go to the polls. In his letter to Lewis Tappan of February 3d, he had claimed that the political action of political men and the holy action of religious men should be reconciled, and that the "elevated principles of holiness" should be brought to bear so as to effect legal abolition. He left the Ohio Convention content with the character of his coadjutors, but satisfied that a vast amount of work would be necessary to make them effective for the practical work of abolition by law.

The fifteen days following the adjournment of the convention were devoted to filling the engagements which had been made for him to speak at Columbus, Pittsburg, Harrisburg, and Philadelphia. At every one of these places he was welcomed by crowded and enthusiastic audiences, and the notices in the press were all favorable to him personally, and most of them to his cause. At Philadelphia he spoke three times. In none of the four cities were there indications of mob violence. His reception by the people was in the nature of an ovation, and he reached New York greatly encouraged.

The "anniversary week" of May, 1835, at New York, of the national benevolent and religious societies elicited unusual interest. Much of this was due to the peculiar circumstances in which the second anniversary of the American Anti-Slavery Society was to be held. The preceding year had been marked in New York city by mobs, which had destroyed the property and sought the lives of the Tappans, and it was probable that the assembly of anti-slavery men would be dispersed by a rabble, excited by inflammatory appeals of political newspapers, encouraged by the immunity promised by politicians, and led by custom-house officials, merchants' clerks, kidnappers, and slave-holders. It had been marked also by manifestations in every part of the North and in one part of the South of the national sentiment against slavery. The toleration in Kentucky of free discussion, the formation there of a State anti-slavery society, the prospect of the early establishment at Danville of an uncompromising immediate-abolition newspaper, had turned all eyes to that State and to the movements of James G. Birney. His speeches on his way eastward had been favorably reported by the press. His appearance on the New York platform was therefore eagerly awaited by friends, enemies, and the public generally. On the 9th of May, Mr. Garrison wrote from New York to the "Liberator": "Of course, Mr. Birney will be the observed of all observers."

When the anniversary meeting was called to order on the 12th, the large church was crowded even in the aisles and galleries. Elizur Wright, the secretary, read parts of the "Annual Report." One of the first passages was in the following words, and was received with applause:

Soon after the last anniversary the anti-slavery cause received efficient aid from the accession of Mr. Birney, of Kentucky. The The fact of his being a Southern man, a distinguished agent of the Colonization Society, and of his proving his sincerity by emancipating his own slaves, gave great weight to his letters, which of themselves were unanswerable arguments for the futility of colonization and the truth and efficiency of the doctrine of immediate emancipation. If he has not brought all good men openly to renounce colonization, he has at least placed the scheme in such a light that comparatively few such choose to defend it, and fewer still to give it practical support.

The president, Mr. Arthur Tappan, then introduced Mr. Birney to the audience.

A moment's silence as the speaker stepped forward on the platform, and then he was greeted with thunders of applause. A dignified, imposing presence, a noble countenance, self-possession, a handsome, strongly built, and graceful figure above middle height,* and the florid complexion of healthy middle age were the first impression. The second was of finely cut and regular features, soft, prematurely gray brown hair, blue eyes, broad and high forehead, and a mouth expressive of both gentleness and firmness. His manner conciliated opponents and awakened curiosity and interest to hear him. The first round of applause was followed by approving murmurs, and the managers felt that the meeting was in no danger of interruption by mob violence. Mr. Birney read the first resolution:

That, *for the permanent safety of the Union*, it is indispensable that the whole moral power of the free States should be concentrated and brought into action for the extermination of slavery among us.

No verbatim report of this speech was made; the only report was the imperfect one furnished to the "New York Observer" and the "New York Evangelist." This is to be regretted, for the speech struck the key-note of his future anti-slavery career. It was a well-considered argu-

* He was five feet nine inches in height.

ment and a patriotic appeal for the preservation of the Union—a demonstration that free discussion would not rend it, but that "slavery, if it continues many years longer, must itself dissolve the Union, and that *inevitably.*" He pointed to the tendency of slavery to create large landed estates; to drive the poorer whites, mechanics, and laborers to the North; to build up a class of non-resident proprietors and another of overseers managing the cotton and sugar plantations; to increase the demands of the South for protection by the United States through standing armies against slave insurrections; and to cause demands by the South for legal restrictions on the right of petition, the freedom of speech and of the press, leading to the destruction of all the safeguards of personal liberty in the free States. These demands can not and will not be conceded; hence strife and disunion. "If you wish to preserve the union of these States," said the orator, "slavery must go down!" He was faithful in portraying the gathering of the storm-clouds which, if not averted, "will burst over the land with tremendous and desolating violence." The remedy he proposed was that "the moral power of the free States should be concentrated and *brought into action*" for the abolition of slavery. It was not enough to "concentrate" it; the further step must be taken of bringing it into effective "*action.*" The political power of the free States should be exerted to put an end to slavery in the District of Columbia and the Territories and to the interstate slave-trade, legislation being the only method known in this republic of bringing *moral power* into *action.* In his view a principle held was a principle to be acted upon; an abolitionist who refused to vote on principle was not worthy of respect. From the first of his anti-slavery career to the last he regarded the non-voting abolitionists as tinkling cymbals. His nature was too sincere, practical, and logical to bear patiently such inconsistency between professions and practice. That he did not go into detail on this point was wise; a good deal of work was still to be done before many abolitionists could be converted to the doctrine of "political action" as laid down in the constitution of the National Society. In this speech Mr. Birney declared his fidelity to the national Constitution: "I trust in God that it may ever live!" At its close he was applauded, and the resolution was adopted "*unanimously*."

His stay in New York was prolonged about ten days. During this time he was the guest of the Tappans and of Judge William Jay, spending several evenings at the country residence of the latter. In the judge he found a congenial spirit, and for him he formed a friendship that was never clouded. Mr. Jay was a son of John Jay, former Chief Justice of the United States, and one of the most active promoters of abolition in New York. The son had been an immediate abolitionist from his youth up. At the request of the Tappans, Judge Jay had prepared and they had published his "Inquiry," a comparative view of the Anti-Slavery and Colonization Societies—an admirable work which held its place for many years. In the conversations between Mr. Birney and Judge Jay, the general plan was suggested of a book on the action of the National Government in behalf of slavery. The necessary investigations of the facts were subsequently made by the judge, and the book was finished and published in 1838, under the name of "Jay's View," etc. As a contribution to the political literature of the anti-slavery cause, it took the leading place. An edition of five thousand was exhausted in 1838, and a second was published in 1839. The book was a *vade mecum* of the lecturers appointed by the National Society, and contributed greatly to turn the current of anti-slavery thought to political action. It arrested the attention of many public men, and did much to give dignity and weight to the abolition movement as one touching practical statesmanship. Jay's writings on slavery continued until 1853 (he died in 1858, at the age of sixty-nine), and were always forcible as well as timely. They fill a closely printed octavo volume of six hundred and seventy pages, and will give him name and fame long after most of his anti-slavery coadjutors shall have been forgotten. He was founder of the Bible Society in 1815, and became a member, about that time, of the New York Manumission Society. As first judge of Westchester County (which office he held from 1820 to 1842, when he was superseded because of his anti-slavery writings), he charged the Grand Jury in 1835 that it would be the duty of every citizen to resist the enforcement of any statute that might be passed to restrict the free discussion of slavery. His manly stand, it is thought, prevented the passage of such a statute by the New York Legislature. He was a wise, conservative, and statesmanlike abolitionist. As a member of the Executive Committee of the American Anti-Slavery Society, and author of its constitution, his services were most valuable. He and Mr. Birney were not only personal friends, but stood shoulder to shoulder in all the exigencies of the anti-slavery movement. They had many qualities in common; Mr. Jay was at his best as counselor and essayist; Mr. Birney excelled also as a speaker and in the practical and executive management of the reform. It is safe to say, that after May, 1835, no important step was taken or important document issued by the Executive Committee, without the previous sanction of both of them. In the month last named, Mr. Birney was elected a vice-president, and Mr. Jay, foreign corresponding secretary for the society.

During the anniversary week, invitations to lecture in different parts of the North were showered upon Mr. Birney. He accepted enough to occupy his time for several weeks, and visited Connecticut, Rhode Island, Massachusetts, and New Hampshire. His reception everywhere was gratifying. His audiences were large and undisturbed, there being no little curiosity among the people to see him and hear his opinions. At Boston, Dr. Channing was one of his hearers. The impression he made was reflected in the press. One newspaper called him—

> One of the most candid, temperate, and urbane speakers that ever addressed a popular assembly.

Another said of him:

> Mr. Birney's manner of speaking is pleasant, his statements candid, his language persuasive. His mind is of a high order. . . . Such a man. . . in the cause he is engaged in will be the means of executing much good.

As a lecturer, Mr. Birney was not habitually emotional. By nature, he was intellectual and judicial; and, being free from affectation, he exhibited these qualities in his ordinary speeches. He was creative, but not imitative. To seekers after truth he was a safe guide, leading them on a path luminous with fact. He gained the implicit confidence of his hearers; and without any demonstrations of oratorical art he carried them, by faultless logic, with him to his conclusions. No one ever called him a "silver-tongued orator," but he made as many converts as any of his brother agitators. Lewis Tappan is reported to have said that no other reform movement or church could produce five platform orators equal in effectiveness to Birney, Weld, Stanton, Gerrit Smith, and Alvan Stewart, each differing from the others in method. As a speaker, Mr. Birney suggested great power in reserve. This he had. The passionate depths, the intense earnestness of his nature, were only revealed in the heat of debate or the pressure of some great exigency. The great speeches of his life were in defending a client indicted for murder; in debating the slavery question against President

John C. Young, before a Kentucky audience; in vindicating the anti-slavery character of the Constitution of Ohio, in the Matilda slave case, before the Common Pleas Criminal Court at Cincinnati; and in pleading for the right of free discussion before the mob assembled in mass meeting at the Cincinnati court-house, in 1836, with the intention to destroy his press and take his life. On those occasions his reticence and reserve were swept away; every mental faculty was alert; every nerve tense with life; and the audience was moved to tears and laughter and shame at the will of the speaker. No man who heard him on any of those occasions ever thought of him again except as a consummate orator. But he did not fire up Vesuvius to cook a dinner.

An episode in his Eastern tour was his offering a resolution at the New England Anti-Slavery Convention, at Boston, against the use of "personalities" by abolitionists. In that locality, and under all the circumstances, this was a noteworthy thing to do. It implied a censure of the violent language commonly used by the "Liberator," and was so understood generally, though H. C. Wright affected not to perceive its application. The convention passed the resolution.

But while he was lecturing to the New Englanders, a storm was brewing against him in Kentucky. Letters from Danville summoned him to return home to meet the machinations of emissaries who had come from other places and were busy in organizing a movement to prevent the publication of his paper, the "Philanthropist," which was announced for the 1st of August. With reluctance, he canceled appointments to speak in Albany, Utica, and other cities in Central New York, and relinquished the long-expected pleasure of visiting his friend Gerrit Smith at Peterboro. When he reached home, about the 10th of July, he found the county in commotion.

CHAPTER XIX.

HE IS OSTRACIZED IN KENTUCKY AND GOES TO OHIO.

1835.

DURING his absence from home, which had been prolonged nearly three months, nothing had been left undone to turn public sentiment against him in Mercer County. Several local meetings in different parts of the county were followed by a mass meeting at Danville. These were addressed in inflammatory speeches by orators from other parts of the State. Resolutions were passed pledging the citizens present to prevent the publication of the "Philanthropist," "*peaceably if we can, forcibly if we must.*" Threats of personal violence were made against any and all men who should countenance the paper or aid in its circulation. Rumors of intended slave insurrections were spread, and many women and some timid men were excited or frightened by them. The mass meeting at Danville was composed in large part of persons from other counties than Mercer. It appointed an executive committee of thirty-three persons to address to Mr. Birney a letter of remonstrance and "take such other steps as might be necessary."

From their letter, prepared by a Whig member of Congress from another district, we quote the most important passages:

We address you now in the calmness and candor that should characterize law-abiding men, as willing to avoid violence as they are determined to meet extremity, and advise you of the peril that must and inevitably will attend the execution of your purpose. We propose to you to postpone the setting up of your press and the publication of your paper until application can be had to the Legislature, who will by a positive law set rules for your observance, or, by a refusal to act, admonish us of our duty. We admonish you, sir, as citizens of the same neighborhood, as members of the same society in which you live and move, and for whose harmony and quiet we feel the most sincere solicitude, to beware how you make an experiment here which no American slave-holding community has found itself able to bear.

To this communication, dated July 12th and delivered in the evening of that day, Mr. Birney promptly answered, suggesting that it would have been more in the character of "law-abiding citizens, which they professed to be, had the signers abstained entirely from the threat that a resort might be had to violence to prevent the exercise of one of the most precious rights of an American—a right which can never for a moment be surrendered."

He concluded his answer with: "However desirous I may be of obliging you as citizens and neighbors, I can not accede to your proposition."

The gauntlet flung down by the committee of thirty-three had been lifted, and the next move, according to their programme, was to mob Mr. Birney when he should ride into town next morning as it was his habit to do. They were busily engaged in marshaling on the main street "lewd fellows of the baser sort," when a young Kentuckian mounted a store-box, and, reminding the crowd that he had opposed Mr. Birney's views, declared that he honored him for his sincerity and goodness, and no harm should be done him by one or many assailants unless they were numerous enough to march over the dead bodies of the speaker and many others. The brave orator now enjoys an honored old age. He is widely known as ex-chaplain of the United States Senate and Moderator of the last General Assembly of the Presbyterian Church, South, the Rev. Joseph J. Bullock, of Washington city. Friends of law and order rallied on his appeal, and when Mr. Birney, half an hour later, rode through the street and dismounted at the post-office, he was not molested.

The next day he wrote to Gerrit Smith:

> Circumstances have occurred since my return that lead me to fear that my projected newspaper will be forcibly suppressed and that all open discussion of the subject of slavery will be inhibited in Kentucky. . . . I am making preparation for the publication of the "Philanthropist," a notice of which you have doubtless seen. If I am permitted to go on with it I will send it to you. It will probably be out by the 15th of August.

Neither his fear nor his expectation was verified. Money effected more than threats. The committee quietly bought out the printer. Mr. Birney's arrangements for printing his paper had been made with one Dismukes, the owner of the "Olive Branch," the Danville weekly newspaper, and he had given him a bond of indemnity against all damages from mobs. Mr. Birney had seen Dismukes on the 14th of July and found him apparently resolute.

Next morning, about eleven, he rode into town. A group of people were gathered about the printing-office, waiting and curious. Dismukes, with his family, had disappeared about midnight. His office with all its materials was in the hands of another person, who showed a bill of sale in due form, and his dwelling with its furniture was held by the same party under a deed properly signed, attested, and acknowledged. Dismukes was said to have been bought out at a high price and to have gone to Missouri. The slave-holding party enjoyed its triumph without open exultation, publishing widely, however, the threat that any man who should attempt to print the "Philanthropist" at Danville would do so at the risk of his life.

For nearly two months he endeavored, through correspondence and personal visits to Lexington, Frankfort, and Louisville, to procure a practical printer to issue the proposed newspaper.

He did not extend his negotiations outside of Kentucky. A citizen of the State might join him without peril of life; no man from a free State could. Before the middle of September he relinquished the effort as useless. It had become manifest that an anti-slavery paper could not be published at Danville.

In July, 1835, Prentice, editor of the Louisville "Journal," published the following squib:

> Mr. James G. Birney has issued proposals for publishing a paper at Danville, in this State, to be called "The Investigator." His object is to effect the emancipation of the slave population. He is an enthusiastic, but, in our opinion, a visionary philanthropist, whose efforts, though well intended, are likely to be of no real service to the cause of humanity. He at least shows, however, that he has the courage to reside among the people whose institutions he assails. He is not like William Lloyd Garrison living in Massachusetts and opening the battery upon the States five hundred or a thousand miles off. He is not such a coward or fool as to think of cannonading the South and West from the steeple of a New England meeting-house.

During the excitement in July, wishing to speak to the people, he tried to rent for that purpose the old Presbyterian church, which was commonly used as a lecture hall and in which he had delivered many anti-slavery addresses, but it was refused him. Similar applications for halls and churches in other towns were also rejected. From the time of his return from the East he was unable to procure any public building in which to defend himself before the the people. Free speech was brought within very narrow limits in Kentucky.

In the last half of July the irregularity in the delivery of his mails led him to suspect that his letters were tampered with and his papers destroyed. The explanations of the postmaster were not satisfactory. Early in August Mr. Birney wrote Gerrit Smith: "I have just been informed that our Danville postmaster has determined to become my intellectual caterer! He is beginning to withhold my papers."

A sharp remonstrance elicited the answer that the postmaster would cheerfully obey any order that might be given on the subject by Postmaster-General Kendall, to whom Mr. Birney was referred for redress. Repeated letters to Mr. Kendall remained unanswered. On the 22d of August, however, Amos Kendall wrote as follows to the New York city postmaster, who had excluded anti-slavery papers from the mails, and reported the fact with a request for instructions as to his duty:

> I am deterred from giving an order to exclude the whole series of abolition publications from the Southern mails only by the want of legal power, and if I was situated as you are I would do as you have done.

This letter signed by the Postmaster-General was exhibited to Mr. Birney by the village postmaster as his authority for a course which personally he disapproved. The signal for a general refusal by Southern postmasters to deliver anti-slavery papers was given July 29, 1835, by the leading citizens of Charleston, S. C., who broke into the post-office of that city, seized all Northern papers suspected of anti-slavery leanings, and burned them on the public square. For some two months before his removal from Kentucky Mr. Birney did not receive any anti-slavery papers through the mails. Letters addressed to him were delivered.

He was sorely tried, too, by the estrangement of many of his friends and relatives and by the genuine grief of many who adhered to him socially. He felt that he was regarded by many as an enemy to the peace of the community and that he was the occasion of discord among kindred. The younger members of his family were exposed to rude speeches and unpleasant incidents. His usefulness and happiness in Kentucky were at an end.

On the 13th of September he wrote to Gerrit Smith a letter, from which we make a few extracts:

> I have determined to remove to Cincinnati. I am now making preparations for doing so, and expect to have my family there by the 10th of next month.

In this letter he speaks of "the exorbitant claims of the South on the *liberties of the free States*, demanding that everything that has been heretofore deemed precious to them shall be surrendered, in order that the slave-holder may be perfectly at his ease in his iniquity."

And he adds a passage which was widely published at the time, and was the forerunner of Seward's "irrepressible conflict" and Lincoln's "This country can not exist half free and half slave." It is as follows:

> The contest is becoming—has become—one not alone of freedom for the blacks, but of *freedom for the whites*. It has now become absolutely necessary that slavery shall cease, in order that freedom may be preserved to any portion of our land. The antagonist principles of liberty and slavery have been roused into action, and one or the other must be victorious. There will be no cessation of the strife until *slavery shall be exterminated* or *liberty destroyed*.

Several false reports have gained a certain credence in regard to the manner in which Mr. Birney left Kentucky.

One has it that he escaped at night, taking his family with him; another, that he fled for his life, leaving his family behind him; and the third, that he narrowly avoided falling into the hands of a mob. In fact, the removal involved no dramatic situations whatever. For about a month his preparations for changing his residence to Cincinnati were made without secrecy. He bought a dwelling-house in that city, sold his farm near Danville, wound up his affairs there, made and received parting calls from relatives, connections, and friends, a few of whom sought by courtesies to make amends for past estrangement, and, when everything was in readiness, accompanied on horseback the carriage that contained his family, passing through the main street of the town, and halting there to say "Good-by" to some friends who were awaiting him. It is true he was going into exile from his native State, but there were few respectable men in Danville who would not even then have stood between him and personal danger.

The feeling cherished toward James G. Birney by the best of his Kentucky townsmen is expressed by one of them, Hon. Thomas Green, of Maysville, in his "Sketch of the McDowells and their Connections: an Historical Family" (1879). He describes him as "a man of whom his relatives, *State, and country* have good reason to be proud."

The following passage is an extract from a speech made by Robert J. Breckenridge, of Kentucky, in his famous discussion, in June, 1836, in Glasgow, Scotland, with George Thompson, the English abolitionist:

> Nor can he who traduces my brethren, my kindred, my home —all that I most venerate and revere—honor me so much as by traducing me They had been told that Mr. J. G. Birney had fled from Kentucky, and left his wife and children behind him in great danger, he being obliged to flee for his life! It was

true, he believed, that Mr. Birney, excellent and beloved as he was, had found it best to emigrate from that State. But that he had *fled* rested, he believed, on Mr. Thompson's naked assertion. That he had left his wife and children behind, believing them to be in personal danger, was a thing *which it would require amazingly clear proof to establish against the gentleman in question* (page 107 of printed report).

Mr. Breckenridge had known Mr. Birney from boyhood.

CHAPTER XX.

THE GENESIS OF THE REPUBLICAN PARTY.

1835–1836.

THE bonfires of Northern newspapers, in the evening of July 29, 1835, on the public square of Charleston, S. C., were lighted by an orderly assemblage of gentlemen of both political parties, the postmaster being present and aiding. In the morning of that day he had written to Postmaster-General Kendall for his instructions; but he probably knew in advance what they would be, and that he risked nothing by prompt action. Mr. Kendall answered, August 4th:

. . . Upon a careful examination of the law, I am satisfied that the Postmaster-General has no legal authority to exclude newspapers from the mail nor prohibit their carriage or delivery on account of their character or tendency, real or supposed. . . . But I am not prepared to direct you to forward or deliver the papers of which you speak. The Post-Office Department was created to serve the people of *each* and *all* of the *United States*, and not to be used as the instrument of their destruction. None of the papers detained have been forwarded to me; . . . but you inform me they are in character "the most inflammatory and incendiary and insurrectionary in the highest degree."

By no act or direction of mine, official or private, could I be induced to aid knowingly in giving circulation to papers of this description, directly or indirectly. We owe an obligation to the laws, but a higher one to the communities in which we live;

and if the former be perverted to destroy the latter, it is patriotism to disregard them. Entertaining these views, I can not sanction and will not condemn the step you have taken. . . .

I am, etc., AMOS KENDALL.

This letter was generally published in the newspaper organs of the Administration. On the 20th of the same month the Postmaster-General published a second letter, which purported to be in answer to a request made by some citizens of Petersburg, Va., that he should adopt a department regulation to prevent the transmission by mail of anti-slavery papers and documents. In it he said it was not in his power to obviate the evil by regulation, but he regarded such transmission "from one State to another as a violation of the spirit, if not the letter, of the Federal compact, which would justify on the part of the injured States any measure necessary to effect their exclusion." For the present the only means of relief was in *responsibilities voluntarily assumed by the postmasters.* He hoped Congress would at the next session put a stop to the evil, and pledged his exertions to promote the adoption of a measure for that purpose.

On the 24th of the same month he wrote to the postmaster of New York city, advising him to detain anti-slavery papers, and making an argument for the propriety of such action.

If [wrote he] in time of war a postmaster should detect the letter of an enemy, a spy, passing through the mail, which, if it reached its destination, would expose his country to invasion and her armies to destruction, ought he not to arrest it? Yet where is his legal power to do so?

Mr. Kendall's three letters were doubtless intended to prepare the public mind for the demands of the slave States and of President Jackson for a law of Congress excluding anti-slavery papers and documents from the mails, and for a law in each free State making the publication of any anti-slavery article a misdemeanor, and providing for the delivery of any person in a free State indicted in a slave State for circulating there an anti-slavery paper, to the agent of such slave State for trial in its courts. A few of these demands by Southern Legislatures may be given as specimens of all. They were passed early in the winter of 1835–'36, most of them in December:

Resolved, That the Legislature of South Carolina, having every confidence in the justice and friendship of the non-slave-holding States, announces her confident expectation, and she earnestly requests that the governments of these States will promptly and effectually suppress all those associations within their respective limits purporting to be abolition societies. (South Carolina).

The General Assembly of North Carolina:

Resolved, That our sister States are respectively requested to enact penal laws prohibiting the printing within their respective limits all such publications as may have a tendency to make our slaves discontented.

The Alabama Legislature resolved:

That we call upon our sister States and respectfully request them to enact such penal laws as will finally put an end to the malignant deeds of the abolitionists.

The Virginia Legislature:

Resolved, That the non-slave-holding States of the Union are respectfully requested promptly to enact penal enactments or take such other measures as will effectually suppress all associations within their respective limits, purporting to be or having the character of abolition societies.

The Georgia Legislature:

Resolved, That it is deeply incumbent on the people of the North to crush the traitorous designs of the abolitionists.

The resolutions of the legislative bodies of the slave States were officially communicated to the governors of the Northern States, and by them laid before their respective Legislatures.

President Jackson, in his annual message to Congress, in December, 1835, covered so precisely the two grounds taken by the slave-State Legislatures as to demonstrate concerted action. He said:

> I must also invite your attention to the painful excitement produced in the South by attempts to circulate through the mails inflammatory appeals addressed to the passions of the slaves in prints and in various sorts of publications calculated to stimulate them to insurrection and to produce all the horrors of a servile war.

If "the misguided persons who had engaged in these unconstitutional and wicked attempts" should persist, he did—

> not doubt that the non-slave-holding States would exercise their authority in suppressing this interference with the Constitutional rights of the South.

He recommended to Congress the passage of a law that would

> prohibit under severe penalties the circulation in the Southern States, through the mail, of incendiary publications intended to instigate the slaves to insurrection.

This part of the message, on motion of Mr. Calhoun, was referred to a select committee of five, of whom four were from the slave States. The bill reported was as follows:

> Be it enacted, etc., that it shall not be lawful for any deputy postmaster in any State, Territory, or district of the United States knowingly to deliver to any person whatsoever any pamphlet, newspaper, handbill, or other paper, or pictorial representation touching the subject of slavery, where, by the laws of said State, Territory, or district, their circulation is prohibited; and any deputy postmaster who shall be guilty thereof shall be forthwith removed from office.

This bill was ordered to a third reading in the Senate by a tie vote of Senators and Vice-President Van Buren's casting vote in the affirmative.

In his report on the Senate bill, Mr. Calhoun spoke of the obligation of the States within which—

the danger [from abolitionism] originates, to arrest its further progress, a duty they owe not only to the States whose institutions are assailed, but to the Union and Constitution . . . and, it may be added, to themselves.

Early in the winter of 1835–'36 an effort was made in every free-State Legislature then in session to pass bills against the freedom of the press. These bills were substantially the same, and were so nearly alike in form as to indicate that they were drawn by the same hand. As a specimen of them I give in the note* the text of the one urged in New York. I copy it from the "Philanthropist" of June 17, 1836, which copied it from the "New York Evening Star," then one of the organs of the Administration and edited by a Federal office-holder.

---

* An act to secure to the several States a more effectual control over their slaves.

Whereas, the Government of the United States was formed in the spirit of harmony and good will, for mutual protection and benefit, and by the sacrifice of various sectional interests; and *whereas* the relation of master and slave exists in many of the States, the regulation of which constitutes an important part of their domestic policy, and that relation is liable to be disturbed, and the peace and security of their citizens to be put in jeopardy by the agency of individuals beyond their respective jurisdictions;

Now, therefore, be it enacted by the people of the State of New York, represented in the Senate and Assembly, and they do enact as follows:

SECTION 1. All writings or pictures, made, printed, or published within this State, with a design or intent, or the manifest tendency whereof shall be, to excite to, or cause insurrection, rebellion, riot, civil commotion, or breach of the peace among the slaves in any part of the United States of America, or with the design or intent, or the manifest tendency whereof shall be, to create on the part of the slaves an abandonment of

In his message of January, 1836, W. L. Marcy, Governor of New York, wrote on this subject:

Without the power to pass such laws, the States would not possess all the necessary means for preserving their external relations of peace among themselves.

The New York Legislature responded to the sentiments of the Governor by adopting a report which pledged the faith of the State to enact such laws whenever they shall be requisite. February 2, 1836, a similar bill was reported to the Legislature of Rhode Island.

---

the service, or a violation of the duty which the master has a legal right to claim, shall be deemed a *misdemeanor;* all persons who shall make, print, publish, or circulate, or shall subscribe or contribute money or other means to enable any other person to make, print, publish, or circulate any such writing or picture, shall be deemed guilty of the offense, and shall be punished by fine or imprisonment, or both, in the discretion of the court.

SEC. 2. It shall be the duty of the Executive of this State, whenever a communication shall be made to him by the Executive of any other of the United States setting forth that a citizen of this State has been engaged in publishing or circulating in any such State any writing or picture, the manifest tendency whereof shall be to cause or excite to insurrection, rebellion, riot, or civil commotion among the slaves of such State, to transmit such communication, with all proofs accompanying the same, to the district attorney of the county where such citizen shall reside; and it shall be the duty of said district attorney to lay such communication before the grand jury, which shall next be summoned in said county, and it shall be the duty of said grand jury to examine such communication and proofs, and if they shall find thereupon, or upon additional evidence, that such citizen has been engaged since the passing of this act in publishing or circulating, either personally or by an agent, within such other State, any such writing or picture, they shall so return to the court before which such grand jury was summoned, and thereupon such court shall take order for the arrest, safe custody, or forthcoming of said citizen; and the Executive of this State is authorized, upon the demand of the Executive making such communication, to cause such citizen to be surrendered and delivered up, in like manner as is provided in case of fugitives from justice, from any other State."

Edward Everett, the Whig Governor of Massachusetts, recommended the passage of a bill. He said:

> Whatever by direct and necessary operation is calculated to excite an insurrection among the States has been held by highly respectable and legal authority an offense against the peace of the Commonwealth, which may be presented as a misdemeanor at common law.

About the same time, the Hon. William Sullivan of Boston, an eminent lawyer and orator and a leading Whig, issued a pamphlet on the subject. In this he wrote:

> It is to be hoped and expected that Massachusetts will enact laws declaring the printing, publishing, and circulating papers and pamphlets on slavery, and also the holding of meetings to discuss slavery and abolition, to be public indictable offenses.

Before and during the efforts in the free States by politicians to effect the passage of laws against freedom of speech and of the press, fraternal appeals and threats of disunion came in rapid alternation from public meetings in slave States. The Southern newspapers clamored incessantly for action by the free-State Legislatures. "Up to the mark the North must come if it would restore tranquillity and preserve the Union," said the "Richmond Whig." The Governor of Alabama made a requisition in September, 1835, on Governor Marcy, of New York, for the delivery of R. G. Williams, publisher of the "New York Emancipator," to be tried under the laws of Alabama.

On the 7th of January, 1836, in the United States Senate, Mr. Calhoun made another demand on behalf of the slave power. This was the suppression of the right of petition in any matter touching slavery. He said of the petitions: "Nothing will stop them but a stern refusal, by closing the doors to them and refusing to receive them."

In the House, Mr. Pinkney, of South Carolina, obtained February 8, 1836, the appointment of a select committee on anti-slavery petitions, and, at a later date, the passage of a resolution that all such petitions should be laid on the table without being either printed or referred, and that no further action shall be had thereon.

In the summer of 1835, President Jackson sent a military force to compel the Seminole Indians to remove beyond the Mississippi from Florida, without taking with them the colored or half-breed members of the tribe. The Seminoles refused. On the 21st of January, 1836, by order of President Jackson, the Secretary of War wrote to the general commanding in Florida:

> I have to ask your particular attention to the measures indicated to prevent the removal of those negroes, and to insure their restoration. You will allow no terms to the Indians until every living slave in their possession belonging to a white man is given up.

As the Indians were most of them of mixed blood, half and quarter breeds, descendants in part of fugitive slaves, the claims could not be accepted by the Seminoles. The result was a seven years' war, at a cost to the United States of some thirty millions of dollars, brought on by President Jackson on his own responsibility. The political object was to place slavery on the footing of a national institution, to be protected by the National Government with all its power.*

The next measure on the programme of the slave power for 1835 was an insurrection in Texas. This broke out in the summer. "Committees of safety" were formed, and the organization of rebel troops pushed with great activity. Armed bodies of adventurers assembled in dif-

* For all the facts of the Seminole War, see speeches and works of Hon. J. R. Giddings.

ferent parts of the Southwest and crossed the border into Mexico without any hindrance by the authorities of the United States. From that time hostilities continued until Texas was wrested from our sister republic. No one doubts now that the movement was fomented and organized by secret emissaries from the Administration of the United States Government, with the distinct intention on the part of the political South to annex Texas to this Union as slave territory, to be divided in time into from five to ten States.

Mob violence wherever practicable was also a part of the system of operations. The mobs of July in Philadelphia and New York city were instigated and led by slave-holders who, by arrangement, had met there in large numbers. It was a meeting of this class in New York city, on July 10th, that called by advertisement and placards a general meeting of Southerners, to be held on the 20th of the month, in Tammany Hall. A reporter who was taking notes of the proceedings was promptly ejected. July 25th, Amos Dresser, an inoffensive Bible agent from the North, was publicly whipped on the bare back by a mob of leading citizens on the public square of Nashville, Tenn. July 29th was the date of burning the Northern newspapers by the first citizens of Charleston, S. C. August 11, Dr. Crandall, a respectable physician, was thrown into jail in the District of Columbia, and detained there eight months on the charge of having an anti-slavery newspaper in his trunk. September 6th, five Northern men were hung by a mob of gentlemen at Vicksburg, and a rumor was spread of an insurrection plotted among the slaves. In the resulting panic, twenty-six men, most of them Northern, were hung or shot by mobs in different parts of Mississippi. The Vicksburg murders were apologized for on the ground that the victims were gamblers, and the others were never investigated, the Mississippi press passing them without remark. The rumor was afterward admitted to have had no foundation in fact; and it was doubtless started as a pretext for the murderous raid on Northern residents and as a means of driving the slave-holders generally into a frenzied excitement against Northern men.

September 5th, a town-meeting held at Clinton, Miss., passed a resolution which was aimed at Mr. Birney's proposed paper. It was:

> *Resolved* that we would regard the establishment of an abolition newspaper among us as a direct attempt to peril the lives and fortunes of the whole population, and that it will be the duty of every good citizen to break up, by any means that may be necessary, any such nefarious design. ("Philanthropist," June 10, 1836).

September 17th, the grand jury of Oneida County, N. Y., under the promptings of a law officer of the United States, presented abolition publications as nuisances. October 15th, the Committee of Vigilance of Feliciana Parish, La., offered a reward of fifty thousand dollars for the delivery to it of Arthur Tappan. October 21st, the New York Anti-Slavery Convention at Utica was broken up by a body of men headed by Samuel Beardsly, a Democratic member of Congress, and two Federal office-holders. On the invitation of Gerrit Smith, of Peterboro, the delegates adjourned to that village, and organized there the New York State Anti-Slavery Society, with a membership of nearly a thousand persons. The object of the Utica rioters was to prevent the sitting of the convention in that city; and not to maltreat any of its members. On the same day, at Boston, a mob of "gentlemen of property and standing" assembled for the purpose of tarring and feathering George Thompson, of England, the eloquent lecturer on abolition. This gentleman had come to New England in

September, 1834, on the invitation of Mr. Garrison, and had been extremely active as a speaker on slavery as it existed in the Southern States. This intervention of a foreigner in what was regarded by most Americans as a purely domestic question excited a strong prejudice against Mr. Thompson. He was followed with persistent misrepresentation in the newspapers; and an unguarded hypothetical argument of his, making logical deductions from the Declaration of Independence, exposed him to the plausible charge of advising slaves to cut their master's throats. The excitement caused by this imprudent speech offered the pro-slavery managers a good occasion to foment a mob in Boston—a thing up to that time deemed to be an impossibility in that city of law and order, free speech, and anti-slavery sentiment. The announcement that Mr. Thompson would address a meeting of Boston ladies in the afternoon of the 21st of October caused a hue and cry to be raised by the city newspapers against "the foreign incendiary," the "English cut-throat, etc. Placards were posted over the city naming the time and place, and stirring up the mob to "snake him out," and "tar and feather" him. Mr. Thompson abandoned his intention to speak, and in the forenoon the mayor was notified of the fact. Under the supposition that Mr. Thompson's absence would be generally known, and would prevent the assemblage of the mob, the ladies met in a room adjoining the anti-slavery rooms. The doings of this mob have been celebrated in anniversary meetings of abolitionists and have been the subject of more controversy than those of any other of that period. No lives were lost, however, and very little property. It is memorable as being the only mob in Boston in the decennium ending with 1840; and as being the only one of any note in the Northern States during that period that was not caused mainly by the intrigues of politicians. An incidental good result of it was to open the eyes of thoughtful anti-slavery men to the unwisdom of inviting public speakers from England to take an active part in the agitations of our domestic politics. Mr. Thompson went back to England immediately; but, good and eloquent though he was, his visit exposed the American abolitionists for many years to the damaging charge of receiving English gold for promoting English policy. The charge appealed strongly to what was in that day a powerful popular prejudice.

The foregoing part of this chapter is a rapid and necessarily imperfect sketch of the programme devised by the slave power for its operations beginning in the early summer of 1835. Every measure was aggressive. The crusade against free mails, freedom of speech and of the press, the right of petition and trial by jury; the costly war to enslave the majority of the Seminoles, undertaken without authority of Congress; the connivance of the Administration with the organization within the United States of armed parties which avowed the purpose to conquer a province from a republic with which we were at peace and add it as slave States to the Union; the attempted ostracism, social and political, of every American citizen who would not bow the knee at the new altar erected to the dark spirit of slavery; the reign of terror at the South, with its inquisition into opinion, lynchings, expulsions, and murders of men from the free States; the mobs excited at the North by the inflammatory appeals of the political press and the active exertions of party wire-workers—these were war measures in a time of peace precipitated upon the country by an oligarchy led by able and brave men determined to rule or ruin, wielding all the powers and patronage of the Administration with the influence of the Federal judiciary, and apparently controlling the majority of each House in the Congress of the United States. They were re-enforced by pathetic appeals addressed to the humanity, fraternal affection, and generosity of Northern men and women to save Southern wives, mothers, and children from the bloody horrors of servile insurrection; by arguments to prove slavery a patriarchal and biblical institution, the beneficent result of which would be to elevate the barbarians of Africa to the high plane of Christian civilization; by new theories of the national Constitution which interpolated in that instrument guarantees for the existence and protection of slavery and stamped as misprision of treason any opposition to that institution. Quiet submission to the demands of the slave power was represented as the only means of averting the dissolution of the Union!

At the time the first of the above great measures—the destruction of the freedom of the mails—was announced, there was no organization which represented the national sentiment. The leaders of the two political parties were either involved in the great conspiracy or were "dumb dogs that did not bark." Aspirants for presidential honors dared not risk the loss of the Southern vote. The national conventions of the Democratic and Whig parties in 1836 passed in silence the pending assaults by the Executive on the liberties of the people; the party press uttered no warning; and the leading churches deprecated agitation as the forerunner of schism, and cried "Peace! Peace!"

The outlook was gloomy. Until the spring of 1836 there was hardly a rift in the dark clouds that overhung the future of this republic.

Fortunately for the progress of civilization, the sober second thought of the people is stronger under democratic institutions than any other force. Before the end of the winter the reaction had become strong enough to satisfy members of Congress of the imprudence of establishing a despotism over the mails, and to satisfy members of the

Legislatures of the free States that popular opinion would not sustain any law to muzzle the press or to make extradition of citizens for trial in slave States on charges of circulating anti-slavery documents. Mr. Calhoun's bill in relation to the United States mails was defeated on its final passage, though the Senate had voted its third reading. Not a single free State enacted the law against the press as demanded. The slave power had underestimated the strength of the attachment of the people to its liberties, and its first combined assault upon them, intended and expected to be overwhelming, had failed at the most important point.

The tidal wave of the slave power had broken into foam on the solid rock of public opinion, and receded never again to rise so high until the rebellion.

In this reaction of 1835–'36 lay the germ of the National Republican party. It was of slow but of sure growth, extending unseen its fibrous roots to all parts of the North. It first showed itself in politics with the motto, "Vote for no man who votes against freedom," and in asserting the right of petition and of trial by jury, and of freedom of the press and of speech; next in balance-of-power combinations to carry nominations in the conventions of the dominant parties, State and national; then in independent nominations for Congress and State offices; afterward in the nomination of candidates for President and Vice-President and the formation of a national party independent of any other which acted in 1840 without official name, but under the popular designations of "Free Democratic," "Abolition," "National Republican," and "Freedom" party; in 1844 giving itself the name of "Liberty party"; in 1848 and 1852 of the Free-Soil party; and in 1856, after the beginning of the Kansas-Nebraska struggle for freedom, of the "National Republican" party—maintaining under all changes of name the same principles and substantially the same platform.

The gradual growth of such a party was a necessary result of the formation in 1820 of the "Solid South," of the determined effort of the slave power in 1835–'36 to overthrow the strongest bulwarks of individual liberty, of its subsequent persistent and arrogant encroachments on the Constitution, and of its repeated attempts to extend slavery to the Territories, to establish the right of slaveholders to hold their alleged property in free States in defiance of the local law, and to make the protection, preservation, and extension of slavery the chief object of what they were pleased to call the *confederacy* of States. John C. Calhoun foresaw and predicted the formation of such a party. In his report to the Senate accompanying the bill to destroy the freedom of the mails, he predicts that, if the abolitionists should be allowed to persist, "the artful and profligate" would in time "unite with the fanatics and make their movements the basis of a *powerful political party* that will seek advancement by diffusing as widely as possible hatred against the slave-holding States."

One of the clearest teachings of the history of the United States is that the formation of a "powerful political party" to extend and perpetuate slavery and make cotton the absolute king, preceded the formation of the party of resistance. The moral reprobation of slavery by the North and the Christian world generally had never abolished that curse or seemed to affect it. Milton, Cowper, Clarkson, Jonathan Edwards, Wesley, Lundy, Bourne, Kenrick, Torrey, Rankin, Duncan, Doak, Crowe, and thousands of faithful ministers of the Gospel, had for centuries hurled against it the thunders of Divine truth and the human sense of wrong, but no man stirred to organize a national political party against it.

If the slave power had been content to maintain slavery without extending it, had treated it as local and not national, and had kept hands off the liberties of individual citizens and of the free States, no political party would have been formed against it. In its inception and growth the Republican party was one for *defense* only.

CHAPTER XXI.

THE CINCINNATI MOB OF JANUARY, 1836.

THE removal of Mr. Birney from Kentucky to the leading commercial city of Ohio was generally understood to have been made for the purpose of publishing there a weekly anti-slavery paper. He had hardly established himself in his new domicile before the leading political Southern dailies opened fire on him and his project. The most moderate article was the following by Mr. Prentice, of the Louisville "Journal":

> We have little doubt that his office will be torn down, but we trust that Mr. Birney will receive no personal harm. Notwithstanding his mad notions, we consider him an honest and benevolent man. He is resolute, too. Not having been permitted to open his battery in this State, he is determined to cannonade us from across the river. Isn't it rather too long a shot for execution, Mr. Birney?

On the 18th of October the slave-holders of Limestone County, Alabama, at a public meeting denounced him by name, printing it in capital letters, as one of the heads "of an organized band of abolition fanatics of the Northern States," and appointed a vigilance committee of twenty persons, among whose duties was that of detecting any person that may attempt to circulate among the community "any seditious publications of any kind whatever," and "upon proof of such fact to inflict upon such person or persons *death*," etc.

His visit to Cincinnati in August, 1835, for the purpose of conferring with friends there, was an occasion for the publication of unfriendly paragraphs in three of the four city dailies—the "Post," the "Whig," and the "Republican." In these the abolitionists were termed "fanatical," "miserable," and "misguided," and their papers "vile incendiary publications." "What ought to be done with them?" asked the "Post." "We would say: Send them back to the place from whence they came, and if any of their authors, or the agents of them, should be found here, *lynch* them."

The "Whig" was the recognized organ of the party whose name it bore, and the two other dailies named sustained the same relation to the Democratic party. Mr. Birney's arrival in Cincinnati in October was the signal for broadsides of malignant abuse in these political sheets, whose common object seemed to be to mark Mr. Birney as an outlaw and proper object of violence at the hands of the rabble.

It is not improbable that the united efforts of the three papers and of the politicians who supported them would have resulted in a mob in October if it had not been for the powerful intervention of Charles Hammond, the veteran editor of the "Gazette," which was the leading commercial daily in the city. Hammond was an able lawyer, a forcible writer, an old citizen, and a man of influence. He was noted for his personal independence, which exhibited itself in his refusal to wear a party yoke without trimming it to fit his neck, in wearing a long queue, and in contempt for many social usages. In the presidential campaign of 1824 he had denounced Jackson as a slaveholder and the Southern politicians as aiming at the monopoly of political power. He approved the Ohio laws that oppressed the blacks, believed in giving up fugitive slaves, and thought abolitionists mistaken and fanatical.

Per contra, he was a decided advocate of free speech, a free press, the right of petition, and resistance to the encroachments of the slave power on the rights of the free States. In many points of character and doctrine he resembled John Quincy Adams. Unfortunately for his permanent fame, he had not taken the temperance pledge. In 1835 he rose to the highest point of his career. He rebuked with dignity and force his fellow-editors for their course, censured the attempt to excite mob violence, and vindicated the rights of freedom of speech and of the press. He denounced the lynching at Nashville as a crime, published Dresser's narrative, and notified the South not to ask its Northern friends to justify or even palliate such an outrage. As to Mr. Birney, who was a gentleman of character, intelligence, and property, if he should choose to publish a paper at Cincinnati and discuss slavery, that was his right; to deny it to him, or to molest him for its exercise, would be the act of men recreant to the foundation principle of American institutions. This vigorous attack from an expected ally caused a temporary halt of the mobocratic forces.

For some weeks after reaching Cincinnati Mr. Birney was busy in furnishing his house and calling on his acquaintances. He presented his letters of membership to the Sixth Street Presbyterian Church, then under the pastoral charge of the Rev. Heman Norton. His affability and pleasing address extended rapidly his circle of acquaintances and friends, and his intelligence and social tact commended him to the best citizens. Before the end of the year he numbered among his visitors Salmon P. Chase, Samuel Eells, William D. Gallagher, the poet, Charles Hammond, Henry Starr, United States Senator Thomas Morris, Alexander Kinmont, the teacher, Dr. Drake, Dr. Nash McDowell, and other men of distinction. In October he wrote an "Address to the Women of Ohio," a pamphlet of sixteen pages, asking their participation in the anti-slavery work. This was in development of a resolution he had offered at the April meeting of the State society. On the 9th of December he published a pamphlet of forty pages, ostensibly as an answer to the denunciatory resolutions of the slave-holders of Limestone County, Alabama. This is known as his "Vindication of Abolitionists," and was generally regarded as an answer to the abusive epithets in the message of President Jackson. It went through several editions, and was republished in Boston in 1836 in a collection called "Valuable Documents." Meanwhile the political leaders were restless with anxiety to find some cause of complaint against him. Several of them made pretexts to call on him and talk of abolition, hoping to entrap him into some unguarded expression; but his habitual reticence about himself and his plans baffled while his courtesy disarmed them. On the 1st of November the city mayor, the city marshal, and the county sheriff, called on him as guardians of the peace, to complain of the publication of "a very exciting handbill" alleged to have been issued by the City Anti-Slavery Society. They assured him that it had caused great popular excitement, and that on that very night his house and the office, where the handbill had been printed, would probably be destroyed.

He answered good-naturedly, thanking them for the personal interest they had expressed for him. He took pleasure, he said, in assuring them that no handbill had been published, but that the city society had, in accordance with usage, printed its constitution. He thought that a contradiction by them of the rumor would allay any excitement, and their power was quite sufficient to suppress any mob. Then, passing to another subject, he detained them in friendly conversation, giving them no opportunity to utter the menace they had evidently come with the purpose of giving. They retired foiled and disconcerted. There was no mob that night; and Mr. Birney had expected none, but he was not surprised when, a few days later, he was notified by the mayor, that, in the event of his persisting in his design to publish an anti-slavery paper in the city, the authorities would not be able to protect either his property or his person from the fury of the mob.

This pretense of fright did not impose upon Mr. Birney. During his month's residence in the city, he had come into contact with many people of all classes; he had visited the shops and manufacturing districts, had traversed the streets in every direction, his person was well known to thousands, and he had been always treated with respectful politeness. His inference from the mayor's notification was, not that there was a strong popular feeling against him, but that the mayor would connive at violence and withhold from him and his property the protection of the police force. In this event, he would be helpless.

He began to think, therefore, that it might be expedient for him to begin the publication of the "Philanthropist" at some point outside of the jurisdiction of Mayor Davies. He was confirmed in this view by his recognition of the fact that public opinion had been affected by the constantly repeated newspaper charges against him of disloyalty to the Constitution of the United States and intention to excite the slaves to insurrection. He believed that a few numbers of the paper would vindicate him in both these respects.

On the 25th of November Mr. Birney wrote to Gerrit Smith:

The solicitations from various quarters that my paper should be published have become so importunate that I have determined to go on with such resources as I myself can command. . . . I shall commence the paper in a small village (New Richmond) about twenty miles up the river from this place; or, if not there, at one (Ripley) about fifty miles above, where I can print without being mobbed, but with the expectation of making way for the introduction of the press in a few months into this city. . . . All I expect is to keep from losing anything by the paper; but a paper out here we must have.

Having selected New Richmond as the place of publication, he issued his prospectus early in December, and spent the rest of the month in equipping a printing-office, engaging printers, writing editorials, and making a flying visit to the capital of the State. There he addressed a committee of the Legislature in opposition to the Jackson bill against the freedom of the press.

Meanwhile his enemies kept all his movements under the closest espionage. A running fire of newspaper paragraphs was kept up against him in Cincinnati during December. The following is a specimen:

Abolition Paper.—We perceive by a notice in the "Christian Journal" that James G. Birney is about to commence his abolition paper at New Richmond, Clermont County. Finding that his fanatical project would not be tolerated at Danville, Ky., nor in this city, he has at length settled himself on the border of Kentucky, and so near Cincinnati as to make the pestiferous breath of his paper spread contagion among our citizens. We deem this new effort an *insult to our slave-holding neighbors* and an attempt to *browbeat public opinion* in this quarter. We do, therefore, hope, notwithstanding the alleged respectability of the editor, that he will find the public so inexorably averse to his mad scheme that he will *deem it his interest to abandon it.* ("Cincinnati Whig," December 21.)

On the 31st December he wrote to Gerrit Smith:

The proceedings in Congress show to my judgment that the cause of freedom to the slave, as *well as to the white,* is working well. When your Northern folks have their ears pulled a little longer by the Southern aristocrats their pluck will doubtless begin to rise. I am glad the subject of abolition has been introduced in Congress *in any way*. It can not lose, no matter how it comes into debate. . . . My paper will probably be issued to-morrow. It will be received here the next day after publication. I know not how our friends in the West will support it—not well enough, I fear, to keep me from losing . . . about $1,000 or $1,200 (to which I have made up my mind) for one year's experiment.

The publication of this first number was eagerly awaited by his enemies, who hoped to find in it some passage that might be quoted to inflame the passions of the populace.

No such passage could be found. In his leading article, the editor maintained that "such publications as the 'Philanthropist' purposes to be, have become absolutely necessary for the preservation of liberty in what are called the free States. . . . The truth is, liberty and slavery can not both live in juxtaposition."

That the first number of the "Philanthropist" was unexceptionable did not prevent the renewal of the attempts to excite a mob against the editor. The Cincinnati dailies, except the "Gazette," quoted paragraphs from the Kentucky, Mississippi, and Louisiana papers, calling upon the merchants and manufacturers of Cincinnati to prevent the publication of the "incendiary" sheet. The proofs that the plot against him was confined to a few party wire-workers and their tools were so abundant that, in the second number of his paper (issued Jan. 8, 1836) he said:

It is remarkable that no mob has ever attacked the abolitionists except after special training by politicians who had something to hope from the favor of the South. The people of whom mobs are composed . . . care not a rush for the abolition of slavery, and, if left to themselves, would as soon think of attacking the phrenologists as the abolitionists. It is to the editors of a venal press, to the expectants of office, in the shape of Congressmen, judges, postmasters, etc., that we are to look for the cause of these frequent and shameful outrages.

This article will be found by the student of history to be the key to the motives of the instigators of mobs in the free States during the Jackson and Van Buren Administrations, except a few caused directly by slave-holders.

In the warfare on Mr. Birney, the Democratic and Whig newspaper organs worked in concert to inflame the populace.

January 16th, the "Cincinnati Republican," the Democratic organ, devoted an article a column long to Mr. Birney. The following is a specimen of its style:

> This new laborer in the unholy and unpatriotic cause of abolition goes even beyond Garrison or Thompson in his uncompromising hostility to slavery, and in his zeal for unqualified and immediate emancipation, and, we doubt not, the editor, *if encouraged to promulgate his abolition firebrands* among our citizens in the spirit in which he has commenced, will win for himself as notorious and infamous a character as that which now distinguishes the two individuals above mentioned. . . . But the editor of the "Philanthropist" has not the plea of ignorance; he is a man of education and talents. . . . The editor rings the changes upon "incendiary missiles" and "the dissolution of the Union."

This false and inflammatory article was republished next day in the "Whig," and the suggestion made "that a meeting of our citizens be called to take this matter into consideration." On the 22d the "Republican" appealed to the capitalists, merchants, and tradesmen to suppress the City Abolition Society; the street corners were posted with a placard, and each daily newspaper advertised a call for a public meeting, to be held that evening at the court-house, of citizens opposed "to the course now pursuing by those individuals composing abolition and anti-slavery societies." The most prominent signatures to the call were James F. Conover, editor of the "Whig"; Charles R. Ramsey, editor of the "Republican"; and W. R.

Thomas, editor of the "Post," a Democratic organ; William Burke, city postmaster; Robert T. Lytle, ex-member of Congress and Surveyor of the Land Office; John C. Wright, ex-member of Congress; Richard Fosdick, candidate for sheriff; Elam P. Langdon, Whig expectant of the post-office; Morgan Neville, Receiver of the Land Office; E. Hulse, candidate for sheriff; J. S. Benham, standing candidate for Congress—all office-holders or candidates for office, and a few merchants and property owners. The men who did not sign, but who were busy in making arrangements for the mob were N. C. Read, prosecuting attorney and Democratic aspirant to judicial office, and Timothy Walker, Whig aspirant to judicial or congressional honors.

During the day runners were sent through the foundries, machine-shops, and manufactories to secure the attendance of working men at the meeting. The towns of Newport and Covington, on the Kentucky side of the river, were beaten up for recruits. The principal managers met at the office of an ex-Representative in Congress and prepared resolutions to be passed by the assembly at the court-house. One of them was as follows: "That this meeting will exert every lawful effort to suppress the publication of any abolition paper in this city *or neighborhood.*" It was given out that the meeting would be addressed by a Whig and two Democrats—John C. Wright, N. G. Pendleton, and that fiery declaimer Gen. Robert T. Lytle; and understood that, after its adjournment, the mob should visit the anti-slavery printing-office, the book store where anti-slavery pamphlets were sold, and the house of Mr. Birney. The colored people feared that an attack would be made upon their dwellings; some of them left the city with their wives and children, others concealed themselves, and a few barricaded the doors and windows of their houses. One or two of the abolitionists, more obnoxious than the rest because of their English birth, betook themselves to the country; many of the others circulated among the leaders and runners of the mob and learned their programme for the violence of the evening. The mayor, city marshal, and sheriff, being fully informed as to the facts, refused to take any precautions whatever. A night of horrors was anticipated.

In the afternoon Mr. Birney wrote to the corresponding secretary of the Rhode Island Anti-Slavery Society:

> . . . An anti-abolition meeting is to be held this evening, called by "gentlemen of property and standing." The hand of the South has almost benumbed the spirit of freedom. . . . I can not print my paper *here*. I lectured here one evening (January 5th) to a small audience in a private manner, no notice having been given of it in the papers. This is the exciting cause of the meeting this evening. It was but yesterday that a wealthy slaveholder of Kentucky called to let me know that my press in Ohio would be destroyed by a band of his fellow-citizens, who had determined upon it, that almost the whole county would be summoned to the service, and that my life was in continual danger. A few days before a citizen of Cincinnati, a high commissioned officer of the militia, called to inform me that I would be disgracefully punished and abused and my property destroyed if I persisted in my anti-slavery movements. . . . I pray you press on. It is not a time to be indolent. If we are our children may wear the livery of the slave. If I fall in this cause I trust it will bring hundreds to supply my place. (See appendix to "Proceedings of Rhode Island Convention.")

About 6 o'clock P. M., a meeting of the men employed to do the active work of the mob was held in a store in Front Street. It was a rough crowd, composed of wharf laborers, workers in the Fulton foundries and machine-shops, and men from the towns on the Kentucky side of the river. They were divided into squads, each under a leader, whose orders were to be obeyed. The proceedings of this meeting were promptly reported to my father by a friend who came with a carriage to take him to a house in the country. His offer was gratefully declined. Other friends called to offer the shelter of their houses to him and his family. He thanked them cordially, but would not detain them. He took tea as usual, talking pleasantly with me and my mother, but making no allusion to the probable events of the evening. I knew the danger, and was suffering under painful apprehensions. After tea I followed him to his study, intending to beg him to go into the country. He anticipated me by saying, "My son, I am going to the meeting." His tone forbade me to utter my request. Waiting for him at the front door while he bade my mother good-evening, I passed out with him and walked by his side to the court-house. An immense crowd of people was already there. The approaches were thronged; men stood on the window-sills and looked through and talked in groups in the yard. Inside every place was filled, from the judge's bench to the gallery. We made our way with difficulty to the foot of the steps leading to the bench. The recreant Mayor Davies was in the chair; four politicians, two Whigs and two Democrats, including Postmaster Burke, were acting as vice-presidents, and, as we were getting through the crowd, a committee of fifteen, Surveyor-General Lytle, chairman, was appointed to report resolutions. During its supposed absence the floor was given, evidently by prearrangement, to Colonel Hale of the militia, a livery stable-keeper and ward politician. This man was an illiterate but fluent and passionate declaimer, full of bitter prejudices and proud of his selection as the orator who was to stir the people to acts of violence. He made a most inflammatory harangue against Mr. Birney, charging him with amalgamation, incendiarism, and treason to the Constitution of his country. To prove the last charge, he flourished before his audience what he called a copy of the Boston

"Liberator," and read, or pretended to read, from it one or two passages denouncing the national Constitution and advocating disunion.* In the name of all that is sacred in love of country, he called upon his hearers to prevent the "miscreant Birney" from making Cincinnati the place of his intrigues to overthrow the Constitution and plunge the South into the blood-reeking massacres of a servile insurrection. The roughs cheered him wildly, and, at the close of his peroration, were ready to rush to the work of destruction.

As the vociferous applause subsided, my father spoke in a distinct and clear voice: "Mr. President, my name is Birney. May I be heard?" The crowd was silent as he added, "My personal character and my cause have been unjustly attacked. May I defend them?" The president's answer was lost in the wild clamor and tumult that followed. Cries of "Kill him," "Down with him," "Drag him out," "Tar and feather him," drowned those of "Hear him." A few, among them the zealous livery stableman, tried to force their way toward him; but those near him resisted them, calling out "Fair play." In the height of this tumult, Surveyor-General Lytle, a man of generous and chivalrous temperament, sprang to the judge's bench and by gesture demanded silence. As he was the recognized chief of the anti-abolition movement, quiet was restored. "My friends," said he, "hear before

* For many years I thought the colonel must have read passages that were spurious, but on pages 307 and 309 of Garrison's "Life," by his sons, I find extracts from the "Liberator" of 1832 which sound like those read by the fiery speaker to goad the mob to take vengeance on Mr. Birney. In these Mr. Garrison concedes the unfounded claim of the slave-holders that there is a "compact" in the Constitution to continue and protect slavery, and calls it "a most bloody and heaven-daring arrangement, . . . a high-handed villainy," etc. He says, too, "So long as we continue one body, a *union*, a *nation*, the compact involves us in the guilt and danger of slavery."

you strike. Don't disgrace our city and our cause before the nation. I oppose abolitionism, but I honor a brave man, and Mr. Birney has to-night shown himself the bravest man I have ever seen." Then, addressing my father politely, he asked him to defer his remarks until the resolutions should be read, and pledged the audience to hear him. After the report of the committee was read and Judge Wright had spoken a few minutes, General Lytle moved that Mr. Birney be invited to defend abolition. The motion was carried by a large majority.

For three quarters of an hour Mr. Birney held the attention of the audience. The turbulent interruptions of a few were hushed. Point after point was made with telling effect. Pathos, wit, argument, and eloquent appeals followed each other in rapid succession. To the charge of amalgamation brought against him by Colonel Hale, he answered by giving a statement of the fact on which it was based. He had found, he said, Colonel Hale, a venerable person with flowing white hair, at the door of his house with a colored man. Both were strangers to him, and, supposing they came together, he had invited them to enter. The man applied for employment and was dismissed. He left it to the gallant colonel to explain why he came with such a companion. The tables were turned on the colonel, and the crowd laughed at his discomfiture and would not hear his explanation. To the charge of hostility to the national Constitution, he answered by a noble vindication of that instrument. He denied that it contained any compact with slavery or any guarantee or even any mention of it; claimed that the nearest approach to a recognition of it was the stigma placed upon it in the denial of congressional representation to two fifths of a certain class of population, and that the South would gain and not lose in the number of its members of Congress by emancipation; and in a magnificent appeal he developed the grand object of the Constitution to "secure the blessings of liberty to ourselves and our posterity." He was proceeding to arraign General Jackson, Amos Kendall, Van Buren, and Calhoun for their attempts upon the liberties of citizens, when the mayor interrupted him to say that the invitation given him extended to a personal explanation only. Mr. Birney appealed to the audience, and on vote was sustained; but the presiding officer's example was followed by the unruly, and the uproar made by the minority was so great that the speaker expressed his thanks for having been permitted to address the meeting and stepped from the stand.

His triumph, however, was complete. The subsequent efforts of orators to excite the crowd were fruitless. The meeting passed the resolutions and adjourned *sine die.* As my father left the court-room, which he did a few minutes before the adjournment, the crowd made way respectfully for him, and he was neither followed nor molested on his way home. After locking the front door behind us, we inspected each one of about forty muskets and double-barreled shot-guns that were kept on the front staircase landing and in other parts of the house, getting them ready for use, for, said he, "Though nearly all of that crowd will go home quietly, the little band led by Hale means mischief and may be down on us to-night." Then, leaving me at a front window up-stairs on the lookout, he went into my mother's room and sat chatting with and reassuring her. He was not a non-resistant. There was never a time when he would have refused or neglected to defend his wife and children.

The night passed quietly. The city papers of next morning had lost somewhat of their truculent tone. The "Whig" said:

The incidents of the meeting were exceedingly interesting and somewhat peculiar. The celebrated and fanatical abolitionist

James G. Birney had the boldness and fatuity to attend. Some observations were made by Colonel Hale of a severe character touching Mr. Birney's abolition proceedings and which were calculated to produce a very unfavorable impression toward him and to render him and his course still more odious. Mr. Birney rose to reply. Inflammable symptoms of hostility toward him were instantly manifest, and a good deal of confusion ensued. Some were for turning him out, some for compelling his silence, and others for hearing what he had to say. A vote was then taken whether he should be permitted to speak, and was decided in the affirmative by a large majority.

The "Gazette" gave a short report as follows:

A good-looking man, past the meridian of life, with hair somewhat gray, here rose and said: "My name is Birney; May I be heard?" The audience appeared confounded by such a request coming from such a source. Recovering from their surprise at the calm fearlessness of the man who dared stand unarmed in the midst of his enemies, one cried out "Down with him!" others cried, "Kill him!" others cried, "Tar and feather him," For a time there was confusion worse confounded. Mr. Birney, with entire self-possession, remarked that he would not proceed if he could not have the ear of the assembly. To go on under such circumstances would justify the charge of obstinacy that had been laid at the door of abolitionists.

At this stage, Gen. Lytle, who had great influence with the mob, rose and, at the top of his voice, cried:

"Hear before you strike." The meeting then resolved to hear.

Mr. Birney, thanking them for the unexpected favor, said that his sentiments had been misunderstood. It was no part of the design of the abolitionists to interfere with the Constitution of the country. . . . Emancipation was a work that could be carried on and consummated without touching the Constitution. . . .

He was not indifferent to the safety of his fellow-citizens of the South. He was from the South. He was born in the South. He had spent his life there. He had numerous beloved kindred who held slaves. To their safety he was not indifferent, and he certainly should pursue no course which he thought likely to put them in peril. He considered that the ultimate safety of the South was more in danger from perpetual slavery than from its abolition. See how the blacks increase upon the whites! This disproportionate increase of blacks will finally bring the very catastrophe which is now dreaded. It may be slow, but it will come if slavery is perpetuated. He desired to save his fellow-citizens of the South and his country from the horrors of that day. He had reason to believe that such appeals to his fellow-citizens on this subject would not be in vain.

When Mr. Birney concluded, he mingled among the crowd, and retired upon adjournment without further molestation. His conduct had disarmed the madness of the multitude.

For several months following the "Great Mob Meeting" held at the court-house, January 22, 1836, all was quiet at Cincinnati.

None of the dailies suggested again a resort to violence. It was quite evident that the threatened storm had blown over for a time. After this date anti-slavery publications were openly sold in Cincinnati; the City Anti-Slavery Society held frequent meetings; Mr. Birney lectured in the city and its suburbs; his well-known figure still attracted attention in his daily walks in the streets, but respect and curiosity were more marked than ill-will. To outward seeming, the enslavement of the press in the Queen City of the West had been defeated. But the snake was only scotched, not killed; it was to regain its venom and vigor in the heats of the following July. Then the excitement of the presidential campaign would be at its height and the city hotels and boarding houses would be full of sojourning slave-holders.

CHAPTER XXII.

THE EDITOR.

THE "Philanthropist" was named after an anti-slavery religious paper which had been published in 1817–'18 at Mount Pleasant, Ohio, by Charles Osborn, a preaching member of the Society of Friends. It was a folio weekly, and was well printed on good paper. At the date of its first issue, the whole number in the United States of periodical publications of all kinds, from dailies to quarterlies, was in round numbers twelve hundred, and of these about one hundred and twenty, most of them local county papers, were published in the States formed out of the Northwestern Territory. Cincinnati was the newspaper center for the West, issuing three dailies and about twelve weeklies, several of which were of a religious character. The era of steam-power printing had not then begun; all press-work was done by striking off one impression at a time on a press worked by hand. Subscription-lists were necessarily small. The average circulation of the eleven six-cent dailies then published in New York city was seventeen hundred each, their profits coming from advertising patronage. Telegraphic news was not known.

The standing of the press was not high. De Tocqueville, writing in 1835, says:

> The journalists of the United States are usually placed in a very humble position with a scanty education and a vulgar turn of mind. . . . The characteristics of the American journalist

consist in an open and coarse appeal to the passions of the populace, and he habitually abandons the principles of political science to assail the characters of individuals, to track them into private life and disclose all their weaknesses and errors. . . . The personal opinions of the editors have no kind of weight in the eyes of the public.

To this there were numerous exceptions, not numerous enough, however, to diminish the public expectation that the new paper would take high rank. Admiration of James G. Birney was not confined to the friends of his cause. The incidents at the mob meeting in January had brought into general notice his personal courage and his qualities as a leader. People began to believe that he would continue to publish his paper notwithstanding the opposition. The friends of a free press regarded him as their representative, and so did the anti-slavery men. The subscription-list, small in January, grew rapidly in February, and in three months numbered more than seventeen hundred. There were a few from the South; the rest were from all the free States, but chiefly from Ohio. Many distinguished men were on it. Among them were William Ellery Channing and Charles Sumner, Thaddeus Stevens and Governor Ritner, Joshua Giddings and Salmon P. Chase. A few wealthy men of public spirit made up a fund to pay the cost of sending three hundred copies of each number to as many influential men in State and Church for their information. Some of these were sent regularly to the same persons, but the greater number were sent to different addresses from week to week. High officials of the National Government, congressmen, governors of States, prominent members of legislatures, bishops, and eminent divines, were recipients of papers paid for out of this fund. The intention was to reach all the men who shaped public opinion and awaken them to the imminent danger of the subjugation of the National Government by the slave power. To this work Mr. Birney devoted himself with characteristic energy.

As neither the limits of this biography nor the interest of the narrative permit a detailed account of his editorial labors, their nature will be best suggested by a statement of the political situation in regard to slavery at the opening of the year 1836.

The unfavorable features of it were as follows:

1. The slave power was in possession of the patronage and power of the National Government.

On his accession in 1829, President Jackson had promptly removed from office every official known to hold anti-slavery views, and he had appointed none whose fealty to slavery was questionable. If a Northern politician was known to have become unpopular because he had voted to increase slave territory he was rewarded. Baldwin, of Pennsylvania, had voted to admit Missouri. His constituents burned him in effigy and sent him into private life. Jackson placed him in the United States Supreme Court. In 1819 Roger B. Taney, in a speech in Gruber's case, had said of slavery, "While it continues it is a blot on our national character." In 1824 he turned a somersault into the Democratic party and became the zealous advocate of the political schemes of the slave power. In 1831 Jackson made him Attorney-General of the United States, and in December, 1835, nominated him as Chief Justice. That nomination was pending until the following March. Its confirmation gave to the slave power the majority in the highest tribunal of the nation. A not unimportant part of the policy of the Jackson Administration was the corruption of the press by appointments of editors to office. More than sixty of this class were thus favored. The selections were made among those who had been most active in propagating the pro-slavery dogmas that the Constitution guaranteed the existence of slavery and authorized all legal measures necessary to its perpetuation. It was well understood that any editor or publisher who favored free discussion would not be favored by the Administration.

Means were found to give preference to friends of the South in awarding Government contracts for labor or supplies, and, as the Seminole War was being actively pushed, opportunities to do this were not wanting. This substitution of sectional politics for business principles had its natural result in the numerous defalcations under Van Buren's administration.

The military and naval academies were placed under pro-slavery administrators, and with such effect that an anti-slavery officer in either army or navy was unknown. The constitutional doctrines taught in them were pro-slavery and loyalty to State Governments.

Many of the most active and enterprising young men in the Northern States were led by money and promises to engage in forming bands of recruits for the insurgent forces in Texas.

In short, the whole influence of the National Administration was thrown aggressively on the side of the extension and nationalization of slavery.

2. The two political parties were bound hand and foot to the slave power.

In profession the Democratic party was the friend of the laboring classes, the advocate of the equality of rights of all men before the law, and the opponent of sectionalism and centralization in politics. In practice it held that two millions and a half of the laboring classes had no right to wages, or any rights whatever, sustained the only purely sectional party ever known in the United States, and was always eager to overthrow the rights of the States and vest the National Government with the power to legislate on the personal relations of inhabitants of States to each other and to authorize the seizure and transportation for trial to a distant State of a man charged with owing service to another. The Democratic party was thus a complex solecism of national extent. Its leaders were Jackson, Calhoun, Taney, and Van Buren; and it relied for success upon the slave power at the South and the Irish Catholics, free traders, and rabble at the North.

The Whig party represented the banking, manufacturing, and moneyed interests of the country. It was the political expression of the era of business enterprise and material prosperity which opened soon after the close of the War of 1812–'15. Unacceptable, because of its protective tariff views, to the cotton planters, it sought to conciliate them through its leaders. Henry Clay had been in 1819 a zealous advocate of Texas annexation, had, by his casting vote as Speaker, fastened slavery on the Territory of Arkansas, and, by his zeal and tact, effected the admission of Missouri into the Union as a slave State against the public sentiment of the North. Gen. Harrison, the candidate of the party for the presidency, was a native Virginian, and had distinguished himself as Governor in the Northwestern Territory by favoring efforts to legalize slavery in Indiana. The choice of the Whig party fell on him because of his pro-slavery record, no less than because of the simplicity and integrity of his private life and popularity as a military hero.

The common desire of both parties not to antagonize the slave power caused them to vie with each other in eager and unlimited indorsement of its most indefensible views of the national Constitution.

These views, though unsupported by history or the text of the Constitution, had spread from the politicians to the lawyers, and, in a few instances, had extended their poison to the courts. The American people are essentially law-abiding, and the corrupting influence of the false constitutional doctrines constantly inculcated upon them by men high in power, by political speakers, and a partisan press can hardly be estimated at this day. In 1836 it was no uncommon belief, even among the intelligent, that resistance to the demands of the slave power was unlawful and akin to treason.

3. Many church organizations embraced both free and slave territory and most of the good men in their membership honestly believed it of vast importance to preserve them unbroken. All the conservative influences in the national religious bodies were arrayed against a discussion which was likely to result in schism. This was true also of the large secret orders.

4. The commercial and manufacturing classes were generally hostile to agitation. The enormous development within the ten preceding years of steamboat and railroad transportation had greatly extended internal commerce; and the control of this was rapidly falling into the hands of the merchants in a few cities. With peace and quiet, large fortunes were in their grasp. They wished to be let alone.

5. The prejudice among the Northern people against negroes indisposed them to resist the slave power. It was partly racial and partly due to the ignorance and utter destitution of fugitives from slavery. They were black, fugitive, and beggared. To betray them was dishonorable; to feed, shelter for a night, and speed them on their way to Canada was a Christian duty; but to give them employment and homes was regarded as the act of a bad citizen. In all, or nearly all the free States there were laws intended to prevent the settlement of blacks within their boundaries.

These laws were disgraceful in their inhumanity. The pro-slavery advocates maintained that if emancipation should take place at the South the negroes would migrate *en masse* to the North; and this absurdity obtained general credence among the unthinking and prejudiced them against the abolitionists.

6. The prevalent aversion among moral and religious people to take part in political action greatly increased the difficulty of organizing resistance to the slave power. This was the natural result of the almost purely material character of public questions after the war, the general absence of ethical elements in them, the coarseness and scurrility of the partisan press, the widely known personal vices of men prominent in public affairs, the trickiness in the presentation of party issues, and the shameless incongruity between party professions and practice. A conscientious man was out of place in a caucus or primary meeting. The number of good men who would not go to the polls was increasing. Several small religious sects forbade their members to vote. Politics, in the language of the non-voting class, was "a dirty mire"; and, by a perverse logic, the country was to be saved by permitting all its political machinery to be controlled by bad men. The non-voters in politics were generally "Come-outers" in religion, and for all purposes of progress, were useless both in State and Church. Most of them were anti-slavery in profession, because of their habit of unstinted censure of things existing; they attended abolition meetings, but were chiefly earnest in trying to prevent anti-slavery men from voting. They were as noted for the violence of their tirades against slavery as for their stubborn refusal to go to the polls. This class, imprudent of speech and useless in action, was a hindrance to the abolition cause. They pretended to be soldiers, but refused to bear arms.

7. The incongruous and widely divergent opinions among anti-slavery men were an element of weakness in their cause. They had no coherent body of doctrine; no accepted plan of action. In regard to the national Con-

stitution, opinions ranged from conservative to revolutionary; and discussion had not yet been general enough to separate anti-slavery men into the distinct classes which were evolved at a later period. In 1836, constitutionalists, consolidationists, and disunionists, met on the same platform. Those who believed that freedom was national but that the rights of States to self-government was guaranteed; those who believed that Congress could and should, without delay, abolish slavery in the States; and those who accepted the creed of the slave power that the Constitution guaranteed the perpetuity of slavery had not yet crystallized into antagonistic groups. The sensational declamations of zealots of the two classes last named were of a nature to array patriotic feeling against abolitionists generally and were freely used for this purpose by pro-slavery speakers and editors.

8. In July, 1836, there were twenty-four States, and the only ones in which slavery did not exist *practically* were Maine, Massachusetts, Michigan, and Vermont. The census of 1840 reports slaves in all the rest, not excepting the States formed out of the Northwestern Territory. This practical survival reminded the people of the free States that they had abolished the institution without interference and gave point to the argument that the people of the slave States would soon follow their example, if not exasperated by intermeddlers. This had weight with the timid, the easy-going, and those uninformed of the political encroachments of the slave power.

Against the formidable influences tending to promote the designs of the slave power to gain permanent ascendency in the Union there were working powerful ones making for freedom. The tendency of all modern civilization to the recognition of human rights and the emancipation of the individual in both Church and state had been marked in the decay of serfdom and feudalism; in the outburst and growth of Protestantism; the decadence of absolute monarchies; the French revolution; the legislation against the African slave trade; the abolition of slavery in the French West Indies, the Cape Colony, Mexico, and all large civilized countries except Brazil and the Southern States of the Union. Equality of civil rights and the blessings of liberty had been recognized in the Declaration of Independence, the national Constitution, and the Constitution of each State. Every legal tribunal administered the law on the basis of the equal rights of individuals. Every church preached justice and human brotherhood. Every orator lauded the United States as the home of the free and refuge of the oppressed of all nations. Twelve States had broken the shackles of slavery by law. The institutions, traditions, and instincts of the people of this country were inconsistent with anything that antagonized freedom of speech, of the press, of organization, of locomotion, and of industry. Even in the far South, slavery had not been formally established by statute in any State. It was a tolerated anomaly, an incongruity, which had grown up, since 1793, under the invention of the cotton-gin and the vast development of cotton culture, into a gigantic moneyed interest, and then been transformed into a political power. The united political South did not exist before the Missouri controversy of 1820, after which its existence as a factor in national politics was masked until 1835, when it appeared openly as the slave power, aiming at the complete subjugation of the republic. It was sectional and aristocratic; consequently hostile to the genius of American institutions and repugnant to Americans generally.

Although merchants and manufacturers, intent on present gain, deprecated agitation, the influences of internal commerce worked quietly but surely for freedom. Planters neither farmed nor spun; they were not mechanics; they imported horses, mules, provisions, cloth, whips, shackles, and furniture from the North. Northern railroads traversed the South, and the steam whistles of Northern steamboats were heard on every Southern stream. Car-hands, boatmen, contractors, free laborers, merchants, drummers, and peddlers from the North were seen in every Southern village. Yankees set up shops in the Southern towns. Instead of the isolation of plantation life necessary to the slave system, there were frequent visitors canvassing for business; and these visitors were men accustomed to the wages system.

Travel of Southern men to the North had decupled within ten years. Merchants went North to buy goods; planters, to buy provisions, to take their families to watering places, and leave their sons at college and their daughters at boarding-schools; preachers to attend anniversaries, synods, and conferences; and educators to engage teachers. Interstate marriages were numerous. Commercial and social intercourse with communities enjoying the advantages of varied industries and the wealth gained in them tended to break up the provincialism of Southern life.

The marked revival of religious feeling beginning with 1815 was national. This had given a strong impulse to the formation of philanthropic societies. Among these, were the Colonization, Tract, Bible, Foreign Mission, Home Mission, Sailors' Friends, and Peace Societies. To the same cause may be attributed the foundation of numerous asylums, hospitals, libraries, and the large extension of the public-school system. All these organizations and methods for the good of mankind were the expressions of a widely prevailing quickened conscience to which the friends of freedom might appeal with hope. Probably nine tenths of the abolitionists were church-members.

Thus the battle was set. On the one side, a compact

phalanx, disciplined to obedience, trained in all the arts of political warfare, all-powerful in half the States, and wielding all the power and influence of the National Administration and tribunals. On the other, a people without recognized leaders, without unity of belief or plan, taken by surprise and sudden onslaught, wielding no weapon but the ballot, strong only in the national instincts and traditions of freedom; in the letter of national and State Constitutions; in the Declaration of Independence; in bills of rights; in the cosmopolitan influences of travel and commerce; in the industrial superiority of the wages to the slave-labor system; in the moral sense of the civilized world and the teachings of Christianity; and, more than all, in the complex and slow-moving machinery of our political institutions. The advantages of the slave power, in January, 1836, were so preponderating, that if government had been centralized at Washington, the liberties of the people would have been trampled down and the republic transformed into a slave-holding oligarchy. It was the great crisis of American freedom.

Mr. Birney placed his paper at once in the forefront of the conflict. The "Philanthropist" was a special journal; it had no room for literary or miscellaneous articles. Every line in it was devoted to the vital questions before the people and was alive with earnestness. Vituperation and declamation were excluded. His methods were fair. In exposing the designs of the slave power he made no loose charges. He allowed its representatives to speak for it. He published the text of the messages of the Governors of Georgia, South Carolina, and other Southern States; of the speeches of Calhoun, Pickens, Bellinger, and other pro-slavery congressmen; of the editorials of leading papers in the slave States; and of the laws passed in slave-State Legislatures against freedom of speech and of the press. He obtained, principally through

Hammond, editor of the Cincinnati "Gazette," a large supply of Southern newspapers, and copied from them accounts of the brandings, whippings, and hangings of Northern men at the South. He published the text of the demands made by Southern governors and Legislatures upon the free States and of the bill to muzzle the Northern press and deliver to Southern governors for trial before Southern juries every abolition editor and publisher. He printed Jackson's message on the United States mails, with Kendall's letters and Calhoun's report and speech on the same subject. Having laid the original documents before his readers he analyzed them, exposing the designs of the slave power.

He showed the spirit of slavery to be essentially and of necessity aggressive, "pushing its victories and extending its conquests." In his first number he declared, "Liberty and slavery can not both live long in juxtaposition," and he constantly insisted that the designs of the slave power were such as not to admit the existence of liberty in any part of the Union, and that the real question of the times was not the abolition of negro slavery, but the "preservation of liberty in what were called the free States."

He exposed the narrowness and inadequacy of the two great political parties, their avoidance of the real and vital questions in politics, their subserviency to the slave power, and their drifting with a current that led to rocks and whirlpools. His criticisms of leading party men were as severe as truth. Of Henry Clay, the great compromiser, he said, "He has done more for slavery and said more against it than any man in public life"; and in an article of January 8, 1836, commenting on Clay's argument that the Northern people had no right to *discuss* slavery because they had no right to *decide* upon it, he wrote: "Mr. Clay has deliberately enrolled himself among the opponents of free discussion, and consequently of the liberty of the press and of speech." He examined the records of Van Buren, White, and Harrison. Mr. Van Buren had voted in 1820 for freedom in Missouri, in 1821 for giving the suffrage to colored citizens in New York, and in 1822 to prohibit the slave trade with Florida; but he had become a parasite of the political South. Neither of the other candidates had done anything to commend him to any opponent of the slave power. One department of the paper was headed "Political," and was opened "that our anti-slavery friends may have such information on this subject as they ought to have to enable them to vote understandingly. . . . Abolitionists ought to desire to see in office men who go for right first, for expediency next, no matter in what party they may be found." (June 10.) He could not understand a man's not voting or believing one way and voting another. "Virtuous principle can not exist without correspondent action. The sun can not be separated from its light and warmth." Sept. 23, 1836, he wrote: "Neither of the candidates (for the presidency) will turn to the cause of freedom until the people turn, and either of them will when they do. . . . If abolitionists unite themselves to either of the existing parties they will weaken their influence in the great revolution that has begun. . . . In all the elections the safest rule would be to vote for those who are honest and capable and who show the most independent and unwavering regard for our laws and common liberties."

October 28th he writes: "We can not forbear making a remark as to the inconsistency of many of our abolition friends when, in the late congressional elections, they voted for Mr. Storer. How can they one day sign petitions to Congress to abolish slavery in the District of Columbia and on the next vote for one who had declared Congress ought to have nothing to do in the matter?" He warns them that such inconsistency will retard their success and possibly prevent it. Owing to the active efforts of Mr. Birney and the trifling difference in the numerical strength of parties Mr. Storer was defeated.

In Appleton's "Cyclopædia of American Biography" Mr. Storer is said to have declined a renomination. He ran and was beaten.

December 30th he tells abolitionists that under certain circumstances "it became their religious duty to resort to political action." At this period of his career there is nothing tending to prove that he contemplated the formation of an independent party. Public opinion, even among professed anti-slavery men, was not yet ripe for such a movement. Nor was it yet a necessity. It seemed practicable at that time to influence the action of existing parties by using the abolition vote as a balance of power. Taking as texts the series of resolutions passed by the Cincinnati mob meeting of January, he published a series of articles in defense of the liberty of the press. They were in the form of letters addressed to Judge John C. Wright, the author of the resolutions. The judge read them and never attended a mob meeting afterward. The articles were widely copied by the press, and their arguments contributed largely to open the eyes of publishers and editors to their own danger and to bring a sound public opinion to bear on Congress.

His most powerful editorials were given to the demonstration of the harmony of abolition measures with interstate law and the national Constitution, a demonstration never before attempted. They ran through a series of numbers, were carefully prepared, and, after revision, were reprinted in pamphlet form and distributed among anti-slavery lecturers and speakers. Partly historical and partly legal, they vindicated the founders of the Constitution from the charge of having entered into a compact to perpetuate slavery, proving by their membership of abolition societies and the early abolition laws in several of the States and by other facts that the general understanding or implied compact among the framers of the Constitution was that slavery should be abolished in all the States before or soon after 1808. Then, in an analysis of the instrument itself, he vindicated it from the charge of guaranteeing slavery. The argument in these articles was, in its main lines, identical with that so ably elaborated and published in 1845 in book-form by Lysander Spooner, of Boston. It was generally adopted by anti-slavery lecturers and writers, and it contributed greatly to keep the current of anti-slavery effort within constitutional channels. The rejection of it by a few professional reformers of the Boston school led them by easy gradations into the heresy of "the Constitution a covenant with hell" and its corollary, disunionism.

The power of Congress to abolish slavery in the District of Columbia, the freedom of a slave brought, and not escaping, into a free State, the necessity of enacting personal-liberty laws in the free States, the necessity of precautions against the annexation of Texas, and all the means of resisting the encroachments of the slave power were vigorously and frequently discussed.

The proceedings in Congress were closely watched and reported, and praise bestowed upon the members of Congress who were defending the right of petition and the freedom of the mails; among whom were Senator Thomas Morris, and Representatives Adams, Evans, and Slade. Every member of a State Legislature who stood for the right was honorably mentioned; Leicester King's speech against the "Black Laws" of Ohio was published and specially commended. The action of each church on slavery was duly noticed. The Michigan Synod, in 1836, declared itself for "immediate abolition," as also the Reformed Presbyterian Church which had admitted no slaveholder to membership since the year 1800. It was noted that the majority of preachers belonging to the New England and New Hampshire Conferences of the Methodist Church were abolitionists. The discussion of slavery in the Methodist General Conference at Cincinnati in May was reported with hearty appreciation of the noble efforts of Rev. Orange Scott and Rev. George Storrs in behalf of the right. All anti-slavery movements were chronicled. In short, the "Philanthropist," within its scope, was a well-edited paper; and, in all that related to the Constitution and laws it was the leader and representative of the conservative anti-slavery sentiment of the country. In the Northwestern States its influence was without a rival in the anti-slavery press. There were numerous laudatory notices, both in prose and verse, of the editor in the newspapers of the day, but these were never copied into the "Philanthropist" while he had charge of it. He had not the infirmity of vanity.

The judgment of intelligent contemporaries on the paper and its editor may be inferred from the following extracts taken from a pamplet letter of twenty-three pages dated November 1, 1836, written to Mr. Birney by Dr. William Ellery Channing, the celebrated Boston theologian.

My Dear Sir: I have not the pleasure of knowing you personally, but your history and writings have given me an interest in you which induces and encourages me to address you with something of the freedom of acquaintance. I feel myself attracted to the friends of humanity and freedom, however distant; and when such are exposed by their principles to peril and loss, and stand firm in the evil day, I take pleasure in expressing to them my sympathy and admiration. . . . Liberty suffers from nothing more than from licentiousness, and I fear that abolitionists are not to be absolved from the abuse of it. It seems to me that they are particularly open to one reproach—their writings have been blemished by a spirit of intolerance, sweeping censure, and rash, injurious judgment. I do not mean to bring this charge against all their publications. Yours, as far as I have seen them, are honorable exceptions; and others, I know, deserve the same praise. But abolitionism, in the main, has spoken in an intolerant tone, and in this way has repelled many good minds, given advantage to its opponents, and diminished the energy and effect of its appeals. I should rejoice to see it purified from this stain* (p. 8).

The above letter appeared in the second volume of Channing's complete works. The preface, dated December 20, 1836, begins:

The following letter was prepared for the "Philanthropist," an anti-slavery paper, published at Cincinnati, and edited by James G. Birney, a gentleman highly respected for his intellectual and moral endowments.

The first campaign of the slave-power against the liberties of the country began with the opening of Congress in December, 1835, and ended with the presidential election in November, 1836. The results may be summed up as follows:

Victories—The adoption by the House of Representatives of the rule known as the gag-law and the admission of Arkansas as a slave State.

Defeats—Failure to pass any law prohibiting anti-slavery publications or their transmission through the mails or investing the States (Calhoun's plan) with the legal right to prescribe what publications might be delivered from the post-offices within their respective limits; failure to induce any free State to pass laws for the sup-

---

* Dr. Channing's criticism was intended, no doubt, to apply to the "Liberator," published in Boston. It does not apply to the writings of Judge William Jay, or to those of Joshua Leavitt, or of Theodore D. Weld, or of William Goodell. The publications issued at New York by the American Anti-Slavery Society were marked by candor and freedom from the exaggeration of fanaticism.

pression of anti-slavery papers or for the delivery of abolitionists to slave-State governors on demand; failure to suppress any anti-slavery paper by mob violence; and failure to get Congress to vote that it had no power to abolish slavery in the District of Columbia.

The reaction at the North against the demands of the slave power indicated a state of public sentiment which made politicians afraid to vote for them; it was a very uncertain factor in the pending political elections.

The Legislature of Vermont voted that "neither Congress nor the State governments have any Constitutional right to abridge the free expression of opinions or the transmission of them through the public mails," and that Congress do possess the power to abolish slavery in the District of Columbia.

The Legislature of Massachusetts sustained by strong resolutions the right to petition, and the right of Congress to abolish slavery in the District, and declared slavery "a great social, moral, and political evil." These were voted in the House by a majority of 378 to 16.

The Judiciary Committee of the lower branch of the Pennsylvania Legislature reported (Thaddeus Stevens, chairman) the following resolution: "That Congress does possess the constitutional power, and it is expedient to abolish slavery and the slave trade within the District of Columbia."

Governor Ritner, of that State, in his annual message, reprimanded "the base bowing of the knee to the dark spirit of slavery."

There were numerous other indications of a rising spirit of resistance at the North, and the leaders of the slave power thought it wiser to postpone effort until after the presidential election. Their storming party had failed, and they proposed to proceed more cautiously.

Mr. Birney was greatly encouraged by the result. "The

people," he wrote, "are sound at heart. They love liberty at home more than slavery in the South." In a letter, published October 28th, "To the Slave-holders of the South," he says:

> If it [slavery] must be relinquished, as I now believe it will be in a very few years, I pray you that you so act in the South and so control the zeal of your friends in the North that it may be relinquished bloodlessly, peaceably, happily.

In his public speeches about that date, he expressed his conviction that slavery would not endure more than about twenty-five years; that the encroachments of the slave power would be resisted step by step by a constantly increasing force; that it would gain no more clean victories, and would finally be overwhelmed; that the struggle would be prolonged if Florida and Texas should be admitted as slave States; and that it might end in war unless public opinion in the free States should speedily be reformed so as to exclude "dough faces" from Congress and place the National Government firmly on the side of freedom. To restrict slavery to its existing limits, add free States as the growth of population might require, and enforce the law of freedom in the Territories and District of Columbia, was sufficient in his view to lead to the abolition of slavery by the voluntary action of the slave States themselves.

For the first ten months of 1836 Mr. Birney's labors were chiefly editorial. His duties, however, in connection with the executive committees of the State and national anti-slavery societies and as a public speaker became so imperative that, in the summer, the minor duties of the editorial department were devolved upon Dr. Gamaliel Bailey. In October, Dr. Bailey was announced as assistant editor; and although Mr. Birney retained the control of the course of the paper until he removed to New York in the last week of September, 1837, his contributions gradually became limited to the leaders only. On his removal Dr. Bailey * succeeded to the editorship.

---

* The doctor had been reared by pious parents. They were members of the Methodist Protestant Church, which had never admitted slave-holders to membership or the communion. From boyhood he had been an immediate abolitionist. In 1834 he had fraternized with the Lane Seminary students. In 1847 he transferred his paper to Washington city, changed its name to the "National Era," and managed it with great ability as the organ of the political abolitionists. "Uncle Tom's Cabin" was first published in his paper in chapters.

CHAPTER XXIII.

THE MOB AT CINCINNATI, JULY, 1836—PRO-SLAVERY MOBS.

SOON after the mob meeting at the court-house in January, the editor of the "Philanthropist" announced in its columns that after the month of March the paper would be printed and published at Cincinnati. It had been found impracticable to rent a building in the city at an earlier date. At the appointed time the office was opened in the upper stories of the building on the north-east corner of Main and Seventh Streets. The situation was central and on the chief business street. The removal of the press and types was effected by daylight and without concealment. It excited little interest. A policeman looked on from the opposite side of the street. Passers-by asked a few questions, but there was no interference.

From that time until the 12th of July following the paper was published without molestation. A sign about eighteen feet long and bearing the words "Anti-Slavery Office" was conspicuous on the Main Street front of the building. Abolition pamphlets and books were kept for sale, and buyers and subscribers were constantly passing in and out. Mr. Birney was there almost daily. His figure was a familiar one on Main Street and in the central part of the city. He resided on the west side of Race Street, the second door above Eighth. He lectured in the city and the suburbs, attended the Sixth Street Presbyterian Church regularly, and was known by sight to thousands of the inhabitants. He was uniformly treated with respect, though he could not but be aware that he was often pointed out to strangers as a person to be looked at. For two months and twelve days not a single paragraph appeared against him in any city newspaper and no movement was made against his press. July 12th (we quote from the "Narrative of Riotous Proceedings"):

> At midnight a band of thirty or forty men, including those who stood as sentries at different points on the street, made an assault on the premises of Mr. Pugh, the printer, scaled a high wall by which the lot was inclosed, and with the aid of a ladder and plank mounted the roof of the press-office. They then made their way through a window on the roof into the room below, intimidated into silence by threats of bodily violence a boy who was asleep there, covered his head with the bed-clothes to prevent him from seeing who were the perpetrators, tore up the paper that was prepared for that week's number of the "Philanthropist," as well as a large part of the impression of a number that had not been mailed, destroyed the ink, dismantled the press, and carried away many of its principal parts.

Although about two hours were occupied in this violence and the premises were on one of the principal streets of the city and the noise made was great, no policeman made his appearance. Three of the operatives in this raid on property came from Covington, Ky., and a large number of the band was made up of slave-holders who were temporarily stopping at the city hotels. Joseph Graham, a city salesman in the Southern trade and member of the Texas Aid Committee, was an active participator.

On the morning of the 14th, a handbill headed "Abolitionists beware!" and menacing the abolitionists if they should "re-establish their press," was placarded on the street corners. It transpired afterward that this was written by Joseph Graham and printed in Covington. In the afternoon the "Evening Post," edited by South Carolinians, published an inflammatory article repeating the threats of the handbill. On the 15th the "Philanthropist" appeared at its usual hour. In the afternoon Mr. Birney and two friends called on Mayor Davies, and, on his promise to issue a suitable proclamation, deposited one hundred dollars with him as a reward for the detection of the rioters. The proclamation appeared next day and contained the following paragraph:

> And I do earnestly entreat those persons whose proceedings, it is alleged, have prompted to the commission of the riot complained of, as they value the quiet of the city, to abstain from the further prosecution of such measures as may have a tendency to inflame the public mind and lead to acts of violence and disorder, in contempt of the laws and disgraceful to the city.

This manifesto, so well calculated to assure the rioters of his sympathy, reminded abolitionists that Mayor Davies had presided at the mob meeting in January and had done his best at that time to excite to violence. It appeared also that in private conversations he had frequently declared his hopes that Mr. Birney would be mobbed, and that on the night of the 12th instant the policeman on the beat including the Anti-Slavery Office had been sent, by the mayor's orders, to another part of the city. An interview with Mayor Davies to protest against his proclamation left the conviction on Mr. Birney's mind that no interference with the mob could be expected from that official. On the 17th a handbill signed "Old Kentucky" was posted up in the streets, offering a reward for the delivery of "one James G. Birney." That, too, was afterward shown to have been the literary work of young Graham. On the 18th the executive committee published a vigorous address to the people of Cincinnati. Its closing words were:

> We have now in some degree, from the force of circumstances, committed to our custody the rights of every freeman in Ohio, of their offspring, of our own. Shall we as cravens voluntarily offer them up, sacrifices to the spirit of misrule and oppression, or as American citizens contend for them till a force which we can not withstand shall wrest them from our hands? The latter part of the alternative we have embraced with a full determination by the help of God to maintain unimpaired the freedom of speech and the liberty of the press, *the palladium of our rights.*

The interpretation put upon this address was that it meant resistance by force. The little band of mobocrats halted and called for recruits. The politicians came to their aid. The "Whig," the "Republican" and the "Post" published inflammatory articles daily. The "Gazette," Charles Hammond, editor, said nothing editorially, but published anonymous cards as advertisements. One of the articles in the "Whig" suggested "dangling from a bough" and a "dress of tar and feathers." An anonymous advertisement appeared in the papers calling a meeting of citizens at six o'clock, Saturday evening, the 23d, at the Lower Market, "to decide whether they will permit the publication or distribution of abolition papers in this city," and naming forty-two * respectable citizens to prepare resolutions to be voted on. The place and time indicated an intention to get together a crowd of workingmen and Kentuckians and have the mob after the adjournment. No public meeting had ever been held at the Lower Market. The meeting was not more than one third part as large as was expected by its projectors—not more than

* Of those named, twenty-nine took no part in preparing the resolutions or in the meeting or in the mob proceedings.

one thousand persons were present, including boys, market-dealers, passers-by, drawn by the music of a band, the idly curious and a goodly number of abolitionists; the mob party, including Kentuckians, numbered between two and three hundred. The respectable merchants who had been expected to act as officers were not present. A change of programme was, therefore, made; William Burke, the Democratic city postmaster, Morgan Neville, the Democratic receiver, and Timothy Walker, a prominent Whig and expectant office-holder, were elected president, vice-president, and secretary.

After passing resolutions prepared, it was said, by Mr. Neville, including one pledging the persons present to "use all lawful means to discountenance and suppress every publication in this city which advocates the modern doctrines of abolitionism," it was thought best to postpone the suppression. An impromptu resolution was accordingly passed, authorizing the chair to appoint a committee of twelve, which, with the officers of the meeting, should "wait upon James G. Birney and his associates . . . to remonstrate with him," etc.

This unexpected move was designed, no doubt, by Burke, Neville, and Walker, to force prominent Whigs to come to the front and take their part of the responsibility. The chair appointed twelve citizens, nine of them Whigs. Two of the twelve did not act. The other ten were Jacob Burnet, Josiah Lawrence, Robert Buchanan, Nicholas Longworth, O. M. Spencer, David Loring, David T. Disney, Thomas W. Bakewell, John P. Foote, and William Greene. Most of these were wealthy men, identified with politics and contributors to the funds of their respective parties. Having been forced by Burke's adroitness into a false position, the Whigs had not the manhood to refuse to stand in it. David T. Disney was a Democratic politician, and both he and William Greene, with

Joseph Graham, were then actively engaged in forwarding arms and men to aid the Texans. The committee began its remonstrances, every member of it knowing that Mr. Birney would not lay down his rights at their bidding. A week followed of correspondence and interviews, with a running accompaniment of daily incendiary articles in the "Whig," "Republican," and "Post," ending in a peremptory demand by the committee of discontinuance, and a firm negative answer by the executive committee of the Anti-Slavery Society. A part only of this answer was published by the Market House Committee. The following is one of the omitted paragraphs:

> We believe that a large portion of the people of Cincinnati are utterly opposed to the prostration of the liberty of the press, and that there is among us, whatever may be said to the contrary, enough of correct and sober feeling to uphold the laws, *if our public officers faithfully discharge their duty.*

On the morning of July 30th, it being Saturday, and the night the best of the week to get up a mob, the Market-House Committee published in every city daily (except the "Gazette," which refused to publish it before Monday) the failure of its "remonstrances." With the conventional hypocrisy of the mobocrats of the period, they closed their announcement in the following words:

> They owe it to themselves and those whom they represent to express the utmost abhorrence of everything like violence; and earnestly to implore their fellow-citizens to abstain therefrom.

How slyly these Tartuffes must have smiled together when they signed that passage!

After tendering to the mayor, on Friday, the services of themselves and friends for the preservation of order as special policemen, and being unable to obtain from him any assurance that he would take any steps whatever against the mob party, the majority of the executive committee decided to leave to him the entire responsibility. Mr. Pugh, the owner of the printing-press and type, was a Quaker, and he absolutely refused to have any armed resistance made to the expected mob.

At six o'clock P. M., a preparatory meeting of the mob operators was held, Joseph Graham presiding. It was resolved: 1, that the press should be destroyed and types thrown in the street; and, 2, that Mr. Birney should be notified to leave the city in twenty-four hours. About fifty persons were present, mostly clerks and Kentuckians. Of these, ten or twelve were stout workmen, who took no part in the proceedings, and had the air of men receiving orders to do work for which they were paid. The following account of the mob was given in the "Gazette" of the following Monday:

Destruction of Property.

On Saturday night, July 30th, very soon after dark, a concourse of citizens assembled at the corner of Main and Seventh Streets in this city, and, upon a short consultation, broke open the printing-office of the "Philanthropist," the abolition paper, scattered the type into the streets, tore down the presses, and completely dismantled the office. It was owned by A. Pugh, a peaceable and orderly printer, who published the "Philanthropist" for the Anti-Slavery Society of Ohio. From the printing-office, the crowd went to the house of A. Pugh, where they supposed there were other printing materials, but found none nor offered any violence. Then to the Messrs Donaldson's, where ladies only were at home. The residence of Mr. Birney, the editor, was then visited. No person was at home but a youth,*

* I was the youth and seventeen years of age at that time. I was alone, my mother with the younger children being then on a two months' visit to relatives in Kentucky, and my father having gone to Lebanon, Ohio, to deliver the third of a series of Saturday evening anti-slavery lectures. On seeing the crowd approaching, which it did without outcry, and quietly as if under control of leaders, I stepped out of the front door, closing it behind me and remaining on the door-sill. Joseph Gra-

upon whose explanations the house was left undisturbed. A shout was raised for Dr. Colby's, and the concourse returned to Main Street, proposing to pile up the contents of the office in the street and make a bonfire of them. Joseph Graham mounted the pile and advised against burning it, lest the houses near might take fire. A portion of the press was then dragged down the Main Street, broken up, and thrown into the river. The Exchange was then visited and refreshments taken. . . . An attack was then made upon the residence of some blacks in Church Alley; two guns were fired upon the assailants and they recoiled. . . . It was some time before a rally could be again made, several voices declaring that they did not wish to endanger themselves. A second attack was made, the houses were found empty and their interior contents destroyed. It was now about midnight, when the party parading down Main Street was addressed by the mayor, *who had been a silent spectator of the destruction of the printing-office.* He told them they might as well now disperse. A dispersion to a considerable extent followed.

The mayor's speech was reported in full. It was short. The most striking passage was:

We have done enough for one night. . . . The abolitionists themselves must be convinced by this time what public sentiment is, and that it will not do any longer to disregard or set it at naught. . . . As you can not punish the guilty without endangering the innocent, I advise you all to go home.

Sunday evening, a small crowd of persons collected on Main Street, opposite the Franklin boarding-house. It was rumored that Mr. Birney was there. The "Gazette"

---

ham, who appeared to be in command, asked me: "Who are you?" I gave him my name. "Where is your father?" "In Warren County." "Is anybody else in the house?" "No." He turned to consult with his friends, and I stepped quickly inside, turned the key in the door-lock, and took my stand on the first stair platform, to give a due reception to the expected intruders. I had within reach about forty rounds. After consulting several minutes, the crowd moved away quietly. From beginning to end, there was in its manner no indication of popular excitement.

of August 4 reported the following most extraordinary act on the part of Mayor Davies: The mayor, with one or two citizens, "officiated as a domiciliary committee to examine the house, and reported that the object of search was not there." Mr. Birney returned to the city on Monday, and remained there without molestation.

The extraordinary conduct of the mayor illustrates the folly of placing in command of a city police force a person of neither social standing nor pecuniary responsibility nor regard for law. Davies was a servile parasite of the politicians who had placed him in office. On Monday, however, public opinion declared itself strongly against his course. Several volunteer companies organized to preserve order, and the mayor reluctantly swore them in as special policemen. Disorder ceased at once. Forty leading citizens, including Charles Hammond, Salmon P. Chase, William D. Gallagher, Thomas H. Shreve, E. Hulse, M. Lyon, E. W. Chester, James Calhoun, and J. M. McCullough, and not including a single political wire-worker, signed the following call:

PUBLIC MEETING.

The friends of order, of law and the Constitution, having no connection with the Anti-Slavery Society, and who are opposed to the action of a mob under any possible circumstances, are requested to meet this afternoon (Tuesday) at three o'clock at the court-house.

It is useless for our purpose to enter into further details relating to this mob. A "Narrative of the late Riotous Proceedings," etc. (forty-six octavo pages) was written and published soon after by Mr. Birney, and was widely circulated throughout the country.

Several facts must be evident to every careful reader of the foregoing statements: 1, that the movement was begun by Southern visitors and a few irresponsible and obscure persons in trade and would have failed if it had not been countenanced by three political daily newspapers and by persons prominent both in trade and politics; 2, that the operatives were men hired to do the work and not men who volunteered for the purpose under a strong popular excitement; and, 3, that the success of the mob was assured in advance by the countenance and co-operation of the mayor.

In the leading editorial of the first number of the "Philanthropist" issued after the mob, it is stated:

> A good-looking young man, while the mob were in the office, proclaimed from a conspicuous place if six others would join him, he would put a stop to the violence. But it was known the mayor was there, that he was a quiet spectator of what was doing. This discouraged all. Had he summoned aid he would have been instantly joined by hundreds.

In the same article Mr. Birney stated that no Irish Catholic,* or Englishman, or German was concerned in the mob. At that time about half the population of Cincinnati were foreigners. The Germans alone numbered about ten thousand. He estimated the adult American male population of the city at five thousand, and of this number that not more than two hundred and fifty could be found willing to join in destroying an anti-slavery printing press. This was a dispassionate view of the facts. And yet Cincinnati, by its proximity to Kentucky and its large Southern trade and great number of Southern visitors, especially in the summer, was more liable to mob violence than any other city in the free States. That city and Alton, Ill., were the only two Northern cities in which a prominent abolitionist could reasonably

* Bishop Purcell, afterward archbishop, was an Irish Catholic and favored anti-slavery opinions. His younger brother, a priest and an able man, was an abolitionist of the O'Connell type.

entertain apprehensions of any attempt upon his life or person.

And here, in the interest of historical truth, I wish to enter a protest against the customary conventional exaggerations of the Northern mobs in "abolition times." Having lived in Cincinnati eleven of the years between 1835 and 1848, and having seen every mob in that city and a good many in the other parts of Ohio, and heard the facts touching those in other States during that period, I must say they were, as a general thing, not dangerous either to life or limb, or beyond the power of the police to suppress. Meetings were assailed by missiles thrown by thoughtless boys, prompted secretly by their elders. The smashing a few panes of glass in a church or town-hall was not uncommon. It was a good practical joke to throw eggs into a congregation and run away to escape punishment. Speakers were rudely interrupted. But these minor forms of mobocratic annoyance were in a ratio probably of less than one to a hundred anti-slavery meetings. More serious ones, though much talked of, were very rare. "Tar and feathers" figured largely in newspaper articles and pro-slavery speeches; but of the thousands of anti-slavery lecturers one only was subjected to that indignity, and that was as early as 1834. Not a man was hurt seriously in New England. The profuse rhetoric of certain Massachusetts writers about "abolition martyrs" might lead a careless reader to imagine that hecatombs of men were slaughtered on the altar of slavery; but I remember no abolitionist but Lovejoy who lost his life. The mobs were misdemeanors at law and political crimes, being aimed at the freedom of the press and of speech, but very few persons were hurt. The famous Utica mob of 1835 did no physical damage to anybody. Pennsylvania Hall was burned in 1838, and the houses of the Tappans were sacked in 1834; but these mobs were especially dangerous because they consisted chiefly of slave-holders and their hirelings, aided by the idle rabble always ready for any excitement which is without danger.

Though homicidal in intent, they in fact made no martyrs. In the dangerous class of mobs must be placed those excited against Englishmen where traditional patriotic hatred whetted to keenness pro-slavery zeal. If the Boston mob of October, 1835, had seized George Thompson, he would probably not have escaped alive; but no Boston pro-slavery mob from 1830 to 1850 ever harmed any one personally. The most dangerous mob at Cincinnati was the one in 1841, against the English confectioner, Burnett. He was a zealous abolitionist, bold as a lion, and had a sharp tongue which he used freely against slave-holders and their abettors. He was generous and genial, and had warm friends. Having rescued a slave girl and sent her safely to Canada, he jeered at the masters and some constables who were seeking for the fugitive. The anti-English mania was aroused. A mob collected on three successive evenings to take Burnett from his house and hang him. He disdained to run; besides, his person was so generally known that he could hardly have escaped. Twelve friends helped him and his two sons to defend his house. The numerous assaults were repulsed by throwing lumps of stove coal from the upper windows. A large quantity was daily transferred from the cellar to the upper floors. Firearms were reserved for the last resort. Donn Piatt, late editor of "Belford's Magazine," was one of the garrison, and the writer personally knows he did his duty. Many of the assailants were severely injured; but the assailed, owing to the adjustment of slanting barricades in front of the windows and the great strength of the lower door and window blinds, escaped with a few bruises. On the third night, at a very late hour, the mayor interfered; but not until the garrison had threatened to use its firearms. Such a conflict never took place, it is believed, in any other city. Mayor Spencer was a brother of O. M. Spencer. He was a bitter anti-abolitionist, and probably thought it desirable that Burnett and his friends should be worsted. At any rate, he let the mob run for three nights, and the "anti-Burnett mob" took rank with the "anti-bank mob" of a previous date.*

In several accepted accounts of the early struggle against the slave power, James G. Birney is represented as having often suffered from mob-violence; this is not true. No man ever laid an unfriendly hand upon him during his public career. A few of his meetings were interrupted or disturbed; and, on one occasion some missiles were thrown at him from a distance as he rode out of a town, but he was untouched. He used to say that, notwithstanding statements of the great number of anti-abolition mobs, not a single abolitionist had been mobbed half as often as John Wesley, the preacher of Methodism—a comparison which he thought was honorable to the American people. He published a list of more than thirty mobs against Wesley. If he had survived until the present time, he might have proved that the saloon interest has quadrupled the mobs excited in the North by the slave power and its parasites; and that the prohibitionists number three martyrs among their prominent men to one on the roll of abolitionists. While he exposed the persecutions directed against himself and other abolitionists, he did not exaggerate them or celebrate them in anniversary meetings; and he checked a certain tendency among his friends to place him on the pedestal of a martyr. He refused to pose in that way. The numerous rewards offered in the South for the abduction of leading abolitionists caused

* In the mobs against negroes in Northern cities many lives were sacrificed. The remarks in the text are not intended to apply to them or to the fighting in Kansas.

him no apprehension. He regarded them as attempts at intimidation made by weak men. An abduction, he argued, would be a serious blunder on the part of the slave power, and the leaders would not permit it; nothing would have been easier than to seize him by night and take him into Kentucky, but such an act would rouse the whole North as one man. All he could possibly apprehend was assassination, perpetrated by some slave-holding zealot, crazed by drink or under cover of some mob disturbance—an act that would be promptly disclaimed by the pro-slavery leaders with suitable expressions of abhorrence.

For a short time after the re-establishment of his paper in September, 1836, he exercised some caution in exposing himself at night; but this soon ceased. His temperament did not make him susceptible to panic terrors.

After the destruction of his paper in July, the notices of the leading papers of the country were generally kindly. We have room for two only. The New York "Evening Post" said:

> He is a man of great ardor and resolution of character, and is not likely to give up his design but with his life. . . . His enemies will probably find that nothing short of murder will effect their object.

The New York "Journal of Commerce" said:

> Judge Birney's paper was ably conducted, and, although an advocate of abolition, was managed with far greater moderation than several papers at the East we could mention engaged in the same cause. Judge Birney himself is a man of very estimable character and possesses talents of a high order.

Webb, of the "Courier and Enquirer," was characteristically truculent and coarse:

> They are a poor miserable set of driveling dastards who are as bold as so many Parolles at a distance from danger, but who

always *run into the shavings** like William Lloyd Garrison when their own poor pates are in danger.

The popular reaction against the mob was general through the North. Mr. Birney wrote in November, "The great majority of the people are sound on free discussion and a free press."

After the October elections, the Dayton "Republican," a Whig paper, rejoiced that "the Whig mobocrats" of Cincinnati had been rebuked "at the polls. Not a mother's son of the whole batch of Whig candidates in Hamilton County is elected." It expressed the hope that "leading and influential Whigs" would not again act as "mobbers."

The estimate of Mr. Birney in 1836 by his anti-slavery contemporaries may be inferred from the following extracts from important documents. In the next annual report of the American Anti-Slavery Society six pages were given to the mobbing of the "Philanthropist." Of that paper it was said:

> Though fully and unflinchingly advocating the doctrines of this society, it could never be reproached for want of forbearance or courtesy in its language. Even its enemies were obliged to concede that its *mode* of conducting the discussion was unexceptionable.

The New England Anti-Slavery Convention of that year, in a formal resolution, mentioned Mr. Birney as one

---

* This allusion to Mr. Garrison's concealment of himself in a carpenter's shop from the Boston mob in 1835 is inaccurate. Mr. Garrison, in his account of the mob, says: "We then went up-stairs, and, finding a vacancy in one corner of the room, I got into it and he and a young lad piled up some boards in front of me to shield me from observation." (See his "Life," ii, 20.) In 1833 Mr. Garrison had written an article beginning: "To the charge made against me by the cowardly ruffian who conducts the 'Courier and Enquirer,' and by the miserable liar and murderous hypocrite of the New York 'Commercial Advertiser,'" etc. (Garrison's "Life," ii, 387.)

"who so nobly volunteers to jeopard his life in the midst of dangers and persecutions," and declared "That the convention give their unqualified approbation to that distinguished friend of the slave, James G. Birney," etc.

The New York Anti-Slavery Society, through its executive committee, published an address of sympathy with its Ohio coadjutors. In this it said:

> The well-known character of the press and editor, . . . the universal meed of approbation for candor, courtesy, and kindness that have been awarded them from all parties—from opponents as well as friends—enhances in no small degree the moral force and virtue of the demonstration that has been made. . . . You are in the forefront of the battle. . . . Your brethren are looking anxiously toward you.

CHAPTER XXIV.

LIFE IN CINCINNATI.

1836–1837.

SOON after Mr. Birney's removal to Cincinnati he had been made a member of the executive committee of the State Anti-Slavery Society. As he possessed the entire confidence of his associates and was the only member who gave his time and attention to the common cause, the management of the business naturally fell into his hands. It is no easy matter at this day to appreciate the delicacy of his varied duties. One of them was to select lecturers and give them the stamp of official approval, thus indirectly discrediting numerous volunteer speakers who were working without good results or who did not properly represent the anti-slavery cause. In the preceding ten years certain zealous anti-slavery clergymen had wasted much precious time in expounding the true meaning of *doulos* in the Bible, and expended much learning on slavery among the Jews in the time of Moses and much energy in arguing against race prejudice as a sin, as if such a prejudice had ever yielded to argument. A few of the speakers were eccentrics. In that era of religious and reformatory excitement and new ideas of progress, material and moral, the natural drift of highly emotional persons of ascetic temperament and defective logical power was into abolitionism, and beyond it into fads and whimseys without end.

When fluency of declamation and the vanity of notoriety were added to their other qualities it was very difficult to keep them from the abolition platform. Lacking knowledge of history, politics, law, and the Constitution, they resorted to personalities, abusive epithets against slave-holders, the Church, and the national Constitution, and to logical inferences from the Declaration of Independence and the Revolution of 1776 of the right of slaves to rise and cut their masters' throats, thus exasperating public sentiment against the abolition cause by giving prominence to false or collateral and unimportant issues which were offensive to good taste, humanity, and patriotism. These men did great harm to the abolition cause. Some of them were eccentric in their personal appearance. One believed he resembled Christ, and wore long hair parted in the middle and flowing in curls over his shoulders; another sported a sombrero hat and a long beard like a Mexican bandit; and a third wore no hat at all. Some had adopted Dr. Sylvester Graham's recently advanced theories of living. They ate coarse bread and fruits but no meat, drank no stimulants, not even tea and coffee, and, even if delicate, took cold shower-baths every morning, winter and summer. Some abjured marriage; others thought it wrong to punish or even restrain children. One anticipated the Christian Scientists of the present day. He was becoming perfect like Christ, and expected to be able in time to cure disease and work miracles. He was as abstemious as an Oriental hermit. All these well-meaning persons, who were bringing abolition into discredit with people of common sense, were quietly and tactfully laid aside by Mr. Birney. They were not invited to meetings or conventions, and if they appeared at them were ignored. He believed the staff of accomplishment was in other hands. The men he selected to represent the cause to the public were men esteemed for practical ability, integrity, and knowledge of public affairs. They were Messrs. Thome, Streeter, William T. Allen, of Alabama, Lyman, Weed, Barber, Timothy Hudson, and Rev. John Rankin. These were the paid lecturers. All of them were able speakers and did much to lay deep and broad foundations for future anti-slavery action. He adopted a system of appointing as local lecturers without pay good men in the different counties of the State. On this list were such men as Hon. Thomas Morris, Rev. Henry Cowles, Albert A. Guthrie, Rev. James H. Dickey, Rev. Dyer Burgess, and Dr. W. W. Bancroft. These names are given from memory. There were many others.

As a result of this systematic effort in Ohio, eighty anti-slavery societies were formed in that State in the twelve months beginning with May, 1836. In Indiana, where no such effort was made, one society only was formed in the same period.

One of the most active lecturers in Ohio was Mr. Birney himself.

The "Philanthropist" contains almost weekly announcements of his engagements. He lectured in almost every town of southwestern Ohio without giving occasion for any hostile demonstrations worthy of special notice. At Cummingsville and Fulton, suburbs of Cincinnati, he had good audiences. At Fulton he delivered a series of lectures in the Presbyterian church of which the Rev. John Dudley, father of Colonel W. W. Dudley, of Indiana, was pastor. No other church in Cincinnati opened its doors to him.

Mr. Birney made it a point to form the acquaintance of editors in Ohio whenever occasion served. He had personal friends among them in all parts of the State, and was sure of a kind reception in their respective localities if they could secure it for him. His social relations embraced a great variety of persons. Among the guests who enjoyed his hospitality at Cincinnati were Benjamin Lundy, Elijah P. Lovejoy, and Rev. Alexander Campbell, an extremely able controversialist and the founder of the "Church of the Disciples." Mr. Campbell had a public debate with Bishop Purcell on the interpretation of the prophecies, in which he attempted to prove that the Roman Catholic Church was the "scarlet woman," and also, as well as I recollect, the little horn of the beast in Daniel. I had the honor of accompanying Mr. Campbell and my father to the debate on one of the evenings. Mr. Campbell and Bishop Purcell were very learned theologians, but my father was much amused with the debate, and expressed to me his wonder that such men should spend time on such trivialities. He did his best to interest Mr. Campbell in the anti-slavery cause, but with little success. He accomplished more with Bishop Purcell, whom he visited repeatedly.

About this time a learned Jewish rabbi sought to interest Mr. Birney in the "testimony of the targums" in relation to slavery, but failed to impress him with the practical importance of that branch of curious learning. To young men of good morals, ability, and promise, Mr. Birney made himself agreeable, seeking to win them to his cause. Among these were the lawyers Samuel Eells, John Jolliffe, and Salmon P. Chase. Mr. Eells died in early manhood; Mr. Jolliffe became and remained through a long life a thorough political-action abolitionist; Mr. Chase, afterward Chief Justice of the United States Supreme Court, did not connect himself publicly and formally with the anti-slavery movement until he joined the Liberty party in 1841, but he adopted Mr. Birney's legal and constitutional opinions on slavery in 1836. His conversion was not rapid. The acquaintance growing out of the ordinary relation of lawyer and client became one of personal friendship and intimacy in the autumn of 1835, and continued on that footing. Mr. Chase spent many of his evenings in my father's library, and I was present on most of these occasions. As I remember the conversations, they turned chiefly on the legal aspects of slavery. Mr. Chase was my father's junior by sixteen years, and, although a good practitioner, had made no special study of slavery. He was a most attentive listener. I have a vivid remembrance of my father's vindication of a decision by Justice Hornblower, of New Jersey, that a person claimed in one State as a fugitive slave from another had a right to a trial by jury; and of one by Justice Shaw, of Massachusetts, that a slave taken into a free State by the master becomes free. His arguments were as elaborate as if made to a court, and were illustrated by cases read from books taken from the library shelves.* They were impressed upon my memory by the reproduction of them by Mr. Chase in his argument, in March, 1837, in what is known as the case of the girl Matilda Lawrence, claimed as a slave, and the elaboration of them in my father's subsequent defense of himself when indicted under the "Ohio black laws" for harboring her. It was my good fortune to hear both of these arguments, so noted in their day; and it derogates nothing from the future Chief Justice that James G. Birney was his first and only instructor in anti-slavery law. Mr. Chase did not abandon the Whig party until 1841, but from that time cordially

---

* In his eloquent funeral oration on Chief-Justice Chase, Judge Hoadley dates the beginning of Mr. Chase's anti-slavery action in 1829–'30, while he was teaching school in Washington city. This is a mistake. I knew Mr. Chase intimately from 1841 to 1848, and he never alluded to such early action. I have also inquired closely into his life in Washington in 1829–'30, and find no evidence tending to sustain Judge Hoadley. The facts that he spent a vacation in Virginia as a guest of slave-holders, and that his pupils were nearly all sons of slave-holders, are inconsistent with the assertion that at that time he was an active abolitionist.

supported Mr. Birney as a candidate for the presidency, taking a very active part in the campaign of 1844.

The case of Matilda Lawrence illustrates the extent to which the great property interest of slavery, though alien to the spirit of republican institutions was able to overbear the common sentiments of humanity and chivalry, the principles of law, and the Constitutions of Ohio and of the United States. Her father, a resident of southern Missouri, was a rich planter. He was an elderly man, unmarried, and a testy invalid. His daughter, an octoroon, had been brought up in his house as his servant and dependent. At sixteen she lost her mother and succeeded her as housekeeper. At twenty she was a beautiful brunette. There was nothing in her personal appearance to excite suspicion of the fatal taint in her blood, but her origin was known in the county of her residence, and she was not admitted to the society of the white people in the neighborhood. Her father forbade her to associate with the blacks. She belonged to neither race. For four years she lived in isolation. She had learned to read, and her chief solace was in poring over the few books in her father's library. In the winter of 1836 he decided to spend a year in New York for the purpose of consulting eminent physicians. Being unwilling to lose her services as his nurse and attendant, or to meet the many inconveniences inseparable from her going with him as his servant, he determined to take her with him and represent her as his daughter. He was rich enough to disregard the additional expense, and cynical enough to enjoy the mystification. Her neat apparel, quiet manners, and apparent intelligence caused his representations to pass without question; she was received at hotels with the respect due to the daughter of a wealthy Southern gentleman. Her remarkable beauty attracted admirers, her pensiveness and modesty being additional charms. In these unusual circumstances her intelligence developed rapidly. She availed herself of opportunities to learn what she might about the rights of individuals at the North. She was a woman, and no doubt conscious of the newly discovered power of her beauty. She began to chafe at her servile condition and false position, and to importune her father to set her free. She begged not to be taken back to Missouri and the isolation of plantation life, with the dreary prospect of the auction block at her father's death. Mr. Lawrence, alarmed at this unexpected result of his freak, and unwilling to grant her request, lost no time in starting for Missouri. Arriving in Cincinnati, he stopped at a hotel near the wharf, intending to take passage on the first steamboat bound for St. Louis. After a vain effort to persuade him to give her "free papers," in which case she promised to go with him and serve him faithfully, she left the hotel and found a refuge in the house of a colored barber who was well known as a friend of the unfortunate of his race. This was in May, 1836. A few days later Mr. Lawrence left for St. Louis. It is quite doubtful whether he authorized the proceedings for seizure taken in the following March in his name by one John W. Riley, a notorious negro hunter and kidnapper, no proof of authority having been submitted, except the affidavit of Riley himself.

After remaining a few days in concealment, Matilda Lawrence obtained employment as a servant in a white family and, in the following October, was engaged by my mother as chambermaid and nurse. She was a modest, industrious girl, of respectful manners and affectionate disposition, and in a short time became a favorite with my mother and the children. We thought her white. She was reticent in regard to her past life. She told us that she was born in Missouri, that her family and relatives lived there but were too poor to help her, that her mother was dead, and she did not wish to live with her father and would rather not say why, and was happy to be able to gain her own living. During the five months of her stay with us she gained the esteem of all the members of the family.

Early in March, having gone into the street on some errand, she came rushing back, pale and trembling with fright, and begged my mother to save her from being seized as a slave. A man she had never seen had spoken to her roughly, charging her with being a runaway negro slave. Then came the pitiful story in all its details, the story of a friendless woman hunted to her hiding place. My father was absent from home at the time of the above occurrence, but was told all the facts on his return next day. They gave him great concern. While he knew she was free, having been taken by her master into a free State, he had little faith in the even poise of the scales of justice when they were held by appointees of the slave power.* He therefore advised that Matilda Lawrence should secrete herself from pursuit for the present and until she could reach the home of one of his friends in western New York. The house was watched constantly, however, by Riley and his men. Matilda was seized, March 10th, on a warrant issued by one Doty, a justice, acting under color of the law of 1793, since pronounced unconstitutional by the Supreme Court of the United States. Mr. Chase, who had been retained by Mr. Birney for the purpose, applied to Judge D. K. Este for a writ of habeas corpus. The writ was issued by William Henry Harrison, then clerk of the Common Pleas Court. Judge Este was a silver-gray Whig, whose strongest sentiments were consciousness of his own supreme respectability and veneration for the

* That slavery can have no legal existence outside of the territory of the State that sanctions it or in the territory of the State that interdicts it had been decided in England (Somerset's case), in Massachusetts, in Louisiana (Lunsford's case, 14 Martin), and in Kentucky (Rankin's case, 3 Marshall).

claims of slave-holders. The attorneys for Riley were three leading Democrats—M. N. McLean, Gen. Lytle, and N. C. Read. The learned and able argument of Mr. Chase was heard by Este with the ostentatious courtesy of a judge who had already made up his mind. The refusal to discharge was from the first a foregone conclusion. As soon as it was pronounced by the judge, the young girl, sobbing in her terror, was seized by three stout hired ruffians, hurried through the crowd, placed in a carriage in waiting, driven rapidly to the wharf, and taken by ferry-boat to Covington, where she was put in jail for safe keeping. The same night she was transferred to a steamboat bound to New Orleans. There she was sold at public auction to the highest bidder. What became of her afterward was never known. The price she brought was large, and, rumor said, was divided equally between the kidnapper and his three attorneys. None of the blood money was offered to Judge Este, who performed his part of this crime against humanity and law without fee or reward and with perfect decorum; and, probably, none of it went into the hands of the father. In sending this hapless girl to a fate worse than death, the judge disregarded all laws human and divine. He presumed that she was a colored person when the law of Ohio declared white all persons of more white blood than a mulatto; that she was a slave, though the Ohio Constitution and the Ordinance of 1787 prohibited the existence of slavery within the State limits; that she was a slave who had escaped from Missouri into Ohio, though the evidence proved the contrary; and that Riley represented her former owner, though there was no proof of this except Riley's own oath.* But in that era

* Judge Caldwell, the Democratic successor of Judge Este, administered the law as it was. In several cases, brought before him between 1842 and 1848, he did not hesitate to issue certificates of freedom to slaves brought into Ohio by their masters.

of political subserviency to the slave power it was not uncommon that a judge should facilitate the operations of professional kidnappers.

Matilda Lawrence having been judicially declared a slave, the next step of Mr. Birney's political enemies, headed by Lytle and Read, was to procure an indictment against him for harboring her. This was tried before Judge Este. The writer was subpœnaed and examined as a witness against his father, proving the facts substantially as above narrated. The court-house was crowded. The accused spoke about three hours in his own defense, admitting the facts, and maintaining that Matilda Lawrence was in law a free woman. His argument made many converts, especially among the younger members of the bar. Judge Este attempted to answer it in his charge, and came as nearly as possible to directing the verdict of guilty. On appeal, the Supreme Court of Ohio quashed the indictment as defective. The majority of the judges would have decided the case for the defendant, on his exceptions, if that course had been necessary. Chief-Justice Hitchcock was well known to indorse cordially the propositions of law made by Mr. Birney in the case. He was an old-time abolitionist and a good lawyer, and possessed uncommon independence of character.

Thus failed the last great effort of the politicians to crush Mr. Birney at Cincinnati. It was noticeable that the political dailies of the city, except the "Gazette," set on and incited the persecution against him, but not one of them was shameless enough to approve the seizure of the unfortunate woman. The sympathy excited by this case throughout the North was one of the potent causes of the passage by free-State legislatures of "personal-liberty laws," designed to secure the right of trial by jury to every person claimed as a slave, and to punish as kidnappers all persons aiding or abetting in delivering as a slave any person not proved to have escaped from a slave into a free State. To aid in procuring such laws, Mr. Birney printed a large edition of a pamphlet containing Mr. Chase's argument, and distributed it among lawyers and members of legislatures.

About the 1st of May, 1837, he went to New York to attend the fourth anniversary of the American Anti-Slavery Society, and to seek to harmonize leading anti-slavery men on important doctrines and methods of work. From the outset of his public career, he had been in favor of using "all lawful means" to accomplish the restriction and final extinction of slavery. In the first number of his paper he had spoken slightingly of those non-voting abolitionists "who think to accomplish the end without using the means." He had steadily maintained the duty of political action. December 30, 1836, he wrote as editor:

> Slavery in the District and Territories and the domestic slave trade are under the control of political action; by political action alone can they be terminated. . . . non-interference would be criminal.

His patience was severely tried by men who professed to be abolitionists but continued to vote for their old parties, or who refused to vote at all, preferring to "entreat" Whigs and Democrats for abolition measures, or to petition Congress for them, or to indulge in wordy denunciations of men and things. Such abolitionists, he thought, were brambles without fruit; a million of them would effect nothing. They fought like a Chinese army, rattling tin pans to frighten the enemy. He regarded diffusion of information, promotion of discussion, and formation of public opinion against slavery as the proper functions of voluntary anti-slavery societies; while, from their very nature, they were not adapted to organize practical political movements. It was wrong in such societies to throw their influence against any lawful means of resisting the slave power. To obtain for some of his views on kindred subjects the indorsement of the executive committee, he wrote for the "Annual Report of 1837" the first paragraph of the part of that report headed "Political Action" (see page 113). The following sentences condense his views:

> Our immediatism has led us to appeal to that religion which will go immediately to work *by all lawful and right means*, trusting that it will *enlarge and deepen itself* by its own action. . . . The opinions and feelings of the people will not be felt in their legislatures till some effort is made to carry them them there. . . . That sympathy for the oppressed which does not, from the instant of its birth, operate to reform and purify the abused and perverted law *is thrown away*, etc. . . . Political action there must be. . . . That religion which makes a man shrink from his political responsibilities when the foundation principles of justice are to be brought to their position in the structure of human society—when the liberties of millions are at stake—will not, we are constrained to believe, prove a support to the soul when God shall ask, Where is thy brother?

This was too strong a stroke at the non-voting abolitionists. The executive committee dulled its edge by inserting after the above passage the advice to abolitionists: "While they firmly refuse to vote for a man who will not support abolition measures to avoid setting up candidates of their own." This solecism in the reports reveals the want of harmony then existing among anti-slavery leaders.

The weak advice of the committee implied that no abolitionist was fit to hold office, and was based upon an opinion widely prevalent among religious men of that day of the inherent depravity of all attempts by citizens to elect to office men who agreed with them in politics.

Administration of government was to be abandoned to

political enemies in the hope that they would not act and legislate on their own views!

Mr. Birney was treated with great respect by his fellow-members. He presided at three of the seven business meetings, Gerrit Smith presiding at two others, and made the leading speech at the public anniversary meeting. He availed himself of the occasion to place himself publicly on record as in favor of "all lawful means." He said:

> There is now a large and rapidly increasing number of the most estimable, patriotic, and intelligent of our countrymen who, agreeing on the evils of slavery, on . . . the danger with which they threaten all that is valuable and worthy to be cherished among us—freedom of speech and of the press, the right to investigate truth, to publish its results, and to act consistently with them—aye, the Government, liberty, and religion itself—who, thus agreeing, are resolved, before it be too late, to act *by all lawful means*, for the removal of these evils.

In this speech he declared that the Colonization Society, though wrong in principle, had been a step in the necessary evolution of anti-slavery opinion. He demonstrated also the impolicy of gradual emancipation of slaves in the Gulf States by showing that freedmen in large numbers could not be employed as laborers by the side of slaves.

He was elected the Ohio vice-president of the society. After a short lecturing tour in New York and the New England States he returned home.

CHAPTER XXV.

THE NO-GOVERNMENT VAGARY.

IN his visit to New York and New England, in May and June, 1837, Mr. Birney's chief object had been to restore harmony among anti-slavery leaders on doctrines and measures and especially to check a tendency, already marked in Massachusetts, to burden the cause with irrelevant reforms, real or supposed. With this view he had attended the New England Anti-Slavery Convention held at Boston, May 30 to June 2, inclusive, accepted the position of one of its vice-presidents and acted as a member of its committee on business. Rev. Henry C. Wright, the leader of the No Human Government, Woman's Rights, and Moral Reform factions, was a member of the convention, but received no appointment on any committee. Mr. Garrison, who had adopted the new theories of Mr. Wright, was a member of the committee on business.* But neither of these gentlemen brought their peculiar views before the convention in any offensive manner. Mr. Garrison, to whom the duty had been assigned by the business committee, advocated resolutions calling upon statesmen, political parties, and legislatures to oppose the admission of Texas to the Union, and recommending measures to secure the votes of Congressmen against such admission. In his speech he advised the people of the non-slave-hold-

---

* This was the first and only time Mr. Birney was ever brought into any personal intimacy with Mr. Garrison.

ing States to "unite their entire political strength" in opposition to Texas annexation. This language was inconsistent with the "no human government" notions then held by Mr. Garrison, and created the belief on the part of Mr. Birney that Mr. Garrison would not use his newly adopted vagaries to the injury of the abolition cause. He returned to Cincinnati confident that harmony in New England would be maintained. His confidence was, however, of brief duration.

Exciting events occurred in New England in rapid succession. June 23, the "Liberator" denounced human governments. July 4, Mr. Garrison, in a speech at Providence, spoke, as if approvingly, of the overthrow of the nation, the dismemberment of the Union, and the dashing in pieces of the Church. July 15, an association of Congregational ministers issued a "pastoral letter" against the new doctrines. August 2, five clergymen, claiming to represent nine tenths of the abolitionists of Massachusetts, published an "appeal" which was directed more especially against the course of the "Liberator." August 3, the abolitionists of the Andover Theological Seminary issued a similar appeal. Among the complaints were some against "speculations which lead inevitably to disorganization, anarchy, unsettling the domestic economy, removing the landmarks of society, and unhinging the machinery of Government." About the same time a new anti-slavery society at Bangor passed the following:

Resolved, That while we admit and maintain the right of free and full discussion of all subjects, yet, in our judgment, individuals rejecting the authority of civil and parental governments ought not to be employed as agents and lecturers in promoting the cause of emancipation.

August 17th, the Rev. J. T. Woodbury, of Acton, published a letter in which he said:

I am an abolitionist and I am so in the strictest sense of the term, but I never swallowed William Lloyd Garrison and I never tried to swallow him. . . . I have seen, as I think, in Mr. Garrison a decided wish, nay, a firm resolve, in laboring to overthrow slavery to overthrow the Christian Sabbath and the Christian ministry. His doctrine is that every day is a Sabbath and every man his own minister. There are no Christian ordinances, there is no visible Church. Here I would add also the notion of his that the people have no right under God to frame a government of laws to protect themselves against those who would injure them, and that man can apply physical force to man rightfully under no circumstances, and not even the parent can apply the rod to the child and not be in the sight of God a trespasser and a tyrant. . . . Good men say we are abolitionists and would go with you most heartily if your lecturers and writers did not attack the Sabbath and the Christian ministry and the churches and all civil and family government. . . . We are not willing, for the sake of killing the rats, to burn down the house with all it contains.

August 14th, the Quaker poet Whittier wrote to the sisters Grimké:

I am anxious, too, to hold a long conversation with you on the subject of war, human government, and church and family government. The more I reflect upon the subject the more difficulty I find and the more decidedly am I of opinion that we ought to hold all these matters aloof from the cause of abolition. Our good friend H. C. Wright, with the best intentions in the world, is doing great injury by a different course. He is making the anti-slavery party responsible in a great degree for his, to say the least, startling opinions. . . . But let him keep them distinct from the cause of emancipation. This is his duty. . . . To employ an agent who devotes half his time and talents to the propagation of "no human or no family government" doctrines in connection—*intimate connection*—with the doctrines of abolition is a fraud upon the patrons of the cause. Brother Garrison errs, I think, in this respect. He takes the "no church and no human government" ground, as, for instance, in his Providence speech. Now in his prospectus he engaged to give his subscribers an anti-slavery paper, and his subscribers made their contract with him on that ground. If he fills his paper with Grahamism and no governmentism he defrauds his subscribers.*

To the vigorous protests against the course of the "Liberator," Oliver Johnson, the temporary editor, made a caustic answer, and Mr. Garrison treated them as "sedition," and "rebuked" and "chastised" the authors. In his efforts to suppress the "sedition," Mr. Garrison wrote to New York, demanding the aid of the executive committee of the American Anti-Slavery Society. He wanted a manifesto from that body crushing the dissenters, thought it could not fairly stand aloof, and that silence on its part was not magnanimous. His devoted follower, Maria W. Chapman, was aggressive and menacing. She wrote to a friend in New York in the peculiar style affected by her:

> If the executive of the National should yield! I pray God that I may not be unduly suspicious; but, I beseech you, call it a virtuous sin if I do say that I suspect them. . . . Why will they think they can cut away from Garrison without becoming an abomination? . . . I pray they may not fall to confessing Garrison's sins. . . . If this defection should drink the cup and end all, we of Massachusetts will turn and abolish them as readily as we would the Colonization Society.

The National Committee refused to take part in the Massachusetts quarrel. Its reasons for this course are given in a letter from Lewis Tappan, published in full in Garrison's "Life" by his sons. (See Garrison, i, 163.) In the kindest language, Mr. Tappan expressed his disapprobation of the "appeal" and of the spirit in which it had been met by Oliver Johnson and Mr. Garrison, and the opinion that "principles and feelings are at work in Massachusetts in the abolition ranks that are unknown elsewhere," that the discussion of the Sabbath question was

---

* See "Grimké Sisters," p. 203.

injudicious, and the doctrines on national and family government wrong.

Other members of the National Committee expressed themselves with equal frankness. Elizur Wright wrote to Garrison:

I could have wished, yes, I have wished from the bottom of my soul, that you could conduct that dear paper, the "Liberator," in the singleness of purpose of its first years. . . . without broaching sentiments which are novel and shocking to the community. . . . I can not but regard the taking hold of one great moral enterprise while another is in hand and but half achieved as an outrage upon common sense, somewhat like that of the dog crossing the river with his meat. . . . To tell the plain truth, I look upon your notions of government and religious perfection as downright fanaticism, as harmless as they are absurd. . . . My heart sickens over your letter to Woodbury. . . . You meet him in a way which my whole soul tells me is *sinful.* You exalt yourself too much. . . . I am as confident as of my existence that a few more such letters would open a bottomless gulf of distrust between you and the abolitionists. . . . Let the Sabbath and the theoretic theology of the priesthood alone for the present. . . . Let the Government alone till, such as it is, all are equally protected by it. . . . But, if all this can not be done, why come out plainly and say you have left the old track and are started on a new one, or rather two or three new ones at once.

At a later date Elizur Wright wrote to Mr. Phelps:

I have just received a letter from Garrison which confirms my fears that he has finished his course *for the slave.* At any rate, his plan of rescuing the slave by the destruction of human laws is fatally conflictive with ours. (Garrison, ii, 169.)

Theodore D. Weld uttered his protest against the new doctrines:

If you adopt the views of H. C. Wright . . . why, then, we are in one point of doctrine just as wide asunder as extremes can be. . . . When the devil is hard pushed and likely to be run down in the chase, it is an old trick of his to start some smaller game, and thus cause his pursuers to strike off from his own track on to that of one of his imps.

And again:

Every reform that ever foundered in mid-sea was capsized by one of these gusty side winds. (Grimké Sisters, p. 209–212.)

August 24, Gerrit Smith wrote to William Goodell:

I am glad to see, by the "Friend of Man," that you have laid your hand on one of H. C. Wright's extravagances. . . . I see no way for quitting the old team.

September 1, H. B. Stanton wrote to the same editor:

I am glad to see that you have criticised Brother H. C. Wright. I have just returned from a month's tour in eastern Massachusetts, and he has done *immense hurt there.* Plain, yet kind reproofs from your pen will do great good. . . . And such remarks and disclaimers are much needed now, and we owe them to the community and the cause. You see that everybody—Tray, Sweetheart, etc.—is seizing hold of H. C. Wright's notions to injure our precious cause. . . . No harm, I think, will come out of the Eastern schism, though the defection is widespread.

The apprehensions felt by A. A. Phelps, the able general agent of the Massachusetts A. S. Society, were expressed in several letters written in August and September, and also in one from Boston, dated October 20. I quote from the last:

I write you this in great grief and yet I feel constrained to do it. The cause of abolition here was never in so dangerous and critical a position before. Mutual jealousies on the part of the laity and clergy are rampant; indeed, so much so on the part of some of our lay brethren that, let a clerical brother do what he will, it is resolved as a matter of course into some sinister motive. If he goes with us it is because it is popular, or something of the kind; if he opposes us, his salary or something of the kind is the reason;

and if he opposes any practical measure, it is clerical jealousy or sectarianism. Such a thing as a good motive does not seem, in the judgment of some of our friends, to be capable of dwelling beneath a black coat.

Of this stamp, more than ever before, is friend Garrison. And Mrs. Chapman remarked to me the other day that she sometimes doubted which needed abolition most—slavery or the black-hearted ministry.

For this cause alone we are on the brink of a general split in our ranks. . . . And as if to make a bad matter worse, Garrison insists, notwithstanding repeated remonstrances, on yoking perfectionism, no governmentism, and woman preaching with abolition, as part and parcel of the same lump. See the last two "Liberators." Now, for one, I can not stand this. I can not merge everything in my abolition; and if he insists on thrusting his peculiar views across mine, mine will and must stand on the defensive. . . . The whole question is fast becoming a question of persons; and that, not whether we will sustain W. L. Garrison, the abolitionist, but whether we will sustain him in the other things named. . . . The danger is, and it is by no means small, that the quarrel will go through the whole country. Garrison threatened some time since to come out upon the American Society for their silence. . . . I should not be surprised if the matter comes up at the annual meeting in New York in the spring. We have not seen the end of it yet. (MS.)

At the outbreak, in July, of the storm in Massachusetts, the executive committee of the American Anti-Slavery Committee consisted of fiye clergymen, four merchants, a college professor, an editor, and Elizur Wright, Jr., an ex-professor of mathematics, a writer of keen wit, and, in after days, a famous insurance actuary. John G. Whittier was the secretary. Judge William Jay, the corresponding secretary of the society, was the only statesman and lawyer connected with the New York management; and his judicial duties and out-of-town residence prevented him from devoting his time to the business of the society. In the new turn of affairs Judge Jay wrote to Mr. Birney, urging him to come to New York and take the helm, and offering to resign in his favor the office of corresponding secretary. This letter was followed by others of similar tenor from members of the executive committee. Mr. Birney was loath to assume the responsibilities of the position offered him; his relations with Western abolitionists were exceedingly pleasant, and he was established in a comfortable home of his own at Cincinnati. After several weeks of consideration, the Eastern troubles growing meanwhile, he finally decided to go. Under his advice the National Committee cautioned the public "not to confound their doctrines with such as individual members may occasionally advance," and acknowledged their "obligation not to permit the funds of the society to be used for the promotion of any principles or objects whatever, except those specified in the constitution," and declared their determination to avoid any just censure "in regard to the agents they employ and the publications they issue." It is probable that this important paper was drawn up by Mr. Birney. It was a notice to Mr. H. C. Wright that he could no longer act as agent and a disclaimer of the novel doctrines "sifted into" the "Liberator." In the "Philanthropist" of September 15, Mr. Birney published an editorial on "The Boston Controversy." In this he pointed out indiscretions on both sides. The article was just and conciliatory; the language of Messrs. Fitch and Towne, though unjustly inculpatory of Oliver Johnson, did not justify the language and style of Mr. Johnson's retort. An editor should rule his spirit and be a peace-maker. "With the spirit that breathes through Mr. Garrison's reply we have no sympathy." Neither Mr. Garrison nor any other abolitionist is authorized to judge and rebuke as Christ did.

We are much disappointed in the course Mr. Garrison has pursued on the present occasion—and we are grieved because we are disappointed. . . . At New York, in 1835, when Charles Stuart introduced the subject of abstaining from the products of slave labor, and in Boston, last spring, when the Peace Question was brought up before the convention, we had evidence of Mr. Garrison's considerateness and self-control that inspired us with high confidence in the course he would pursue should he ever be placed in circumstances where much was placed at hazard. By his reply to Messrs Fitch and others, we have been much disappointed and our confidence in his prudence much weakened.*

September 22, Dr. Bailey announced at the head of his editorial columns, that Mr. Birney with his family was on his way to New York. "A conviction that his efforts will be more influential there than here in behalf of abolition reconciles us in a degree to the loss of his society, counsel, and aid."

It is not probable that at that time Mr. Birney comprehended the nature of the difficulties which were to be thorns in his path. His social environment in Kentucky, New Jersey, Pennsylvania, Alabama, and Ohio, differed widely from that existing in Boston, and his acquaintance with professional reformers of all mundane evils had not been intimate. His visits to New England had been hurried and his mind had been fully occupied with the great end he had in view—the abolition of slavery—with very little regard, it must be admitted, to the metaphysics of reform movements generally. He was eminently of a practical turn of mind. For the next few years he was to be brought into close contact with the New England reformers, a class exceedingly numerous between 1815 and

* The two instances in which Mr. Garrison, in Mr. Birney's presence, had refrained from disturbing conventions with irrelevant subjects, are here specified as the reasons for confidence that he would be equally considerate in the future. The passage does not justify the inuendo that Mr. Birney had former confidence in his judgment and prudence (Garrison, ii, 166).

1840 and noticed by Emerson, in his Amory Hall lecture, as follows:

The Church or religious party, is falling from the Church nominal, and is appearing in temperance and non-resistant societies, in movements of abolitionists and of socialists, and in very significant assemblies called Sabbath and Bible conventions, composed of ultraists, of seekers, of all the soul of the soldiery of dissent, and meeting to call in question the authority of the Sabbath, of the priesthood, and of the Church. In these movements, nothing was more remarkable than the discontent they begot in the movers. The spirit of protest and of detachment drove the members of these conventions to bear testimony against the Church, and, immediately afterward, to declare their discontent with these conventions, their independence of their colleagues, and their impatience of the methods whereby they were working. They defied each other, like a congress of kings, each of whom had a realm to rule, and way of his own that made concert unprofitable. What a fertility of projects for the salvation of the world! One apostle thought all men should go to farming; and another, that no man should buy or sell; that the use of money was the cardinal evil; another, that the mischief was in our diet, that we eat and drink damnation. These made unleavened bread and were foes to the death to fermentation. It was in vain urged by the housewife that God made yeast as well as dough, and loves fermentation just as dearly as he loves vegetation; that fermentation develops the saccharine element in the grain and makes it more palatable and more digestible. No; they wish the pure wheat and will die, but it shall not ferment. . . . Others attacked the system of agriculture, the use of animal manures in farming, and the tyranny of man over brute nature; these abuses polluted his food. The ox must be taken from the plow, and the horse from the cart, the hundred acres of the farm must be spaded and the man must walk wherever boats and locomotives will not carry him. Even the insect world was to be defended; that had been too long neglected, and a society for the protection of ground worms, slugs, and mosquitoes, was to be incorporated without delay. With these appeared the adepts of homœopathy, of hydropathy, of mesmerism, of phrenology, and their wonderful theories of the Christian miracles! Others assailed particular vocations, as that of the lawyer, that of the merchant, of the manufacturer, of the clergyman, of the scholar. Others attacked the institution of marriage as the fountain of social evils. Others devoted themselves to the worrying of churches and meetings for public worship.

Mr. Emerson notes in the movement a tendency to—

an assertion of the sufficiency of the private man. Thus it was directly in the spirit and genius of the age, what happened in one instance, when a church censured and threatened to excommunicate one of its members on account of the somewhat hostile part to the Church which his conscience led him to take in the anti-slavery business; the threatened individual immediately excommunicated the church in a published and formal process. . . . Many a reformer perishes in his removal of rubbish—and that makes the offensiveness of the class. They are partial; they are not equal to the work they pretend. They lose their way; in the assault on the kingdom of darkness, they expend all their energy on some accidental evil, and lose their sanity and power of benefit. It is of little moment that one or two or twenty errors of our social system be corrected, but of much that the man be in his senses. The criticism and attack on institutions which we have witnessed has made one thing plain, that society gains nothing while a man, not himself renovated, attempts to renovate things around him; he has become tediously good in some particular, but negligent or narrow in the rest; and hypocrisy and vanity are often the disgusting result. . . . The reason why any one refuses his assent to your opinion, or his aid to your benevolent design, is in you; he refuses to accept you as a bringer of truth, because, though you think you have it, he feels that you have it not.

Another writer, adopting the style of a medical formula, describes the character of the representative reformer of the period under treatment:

Add to his blood a drop of malignity, to his disposition a tinge of melancholy, to his self-worship vanity, to his love of reform a prominent desire for notoriety, and you have an irrepressible "crank," the curse to any reform he may select for his sphere of action, a stumbling block to the timid and conservative.

When the seed was sown for the crop of New England reformers, and how it grew and yielded a plentiful harvest, will be the subject of the next chapter.

CHAPTER XXVI.

THE PHILOSOPHY OF BOSTON VAGARIES.

During the eighteenth century the psychological philosophy commonly known as Locke's governed the thought of the English-speaking world. Its accepted doctrines were that the world external to man has a substantive existence; that knowledge is derived from the senses; that true ideas originate in experience and are not innate; and that the best traditions of the human race are more trustworthy for guidance than the intuitions, imaginary and illusory for the most part, of individual minds. Its abuses were to honor inductive reasoning overmuch and restrain progress by its slow processes; to exaggerate the value, in social and political life, of expediency, conventionalism, and conservatism; and to elevate dogmas, rites, and church organizations above the spiritual part of religion.

About the close of the last century a reaction against this sensual system began in New England under the influences of the new doctrines taught by Kant and other German philosophers, and it gradually extended until in the next forty years it embraced the leading thinkers of Boston and affected every form of social life in New England.

The new school reversed the doctrines of its predecessors. It held that the only reality is subjective, or, in plain words, that objects commonly thought to be external to man exist only in his consciousness; that all ideas are intuitions, that the soul is the only creator, being divine, receiving inspiration immediately from God and accepting truth from the moral necessity of its own nature; that the true man should look to intuitive and inspired principles without the aid of facts, and, if necessary, in disregard of them; that he should be a law unto himself and obedient to his own heart, mind, and conscience without regard to the intuitions or desires of other men; that his primary duty is self-culture, by means of which he could "unfold" himself to perfection according to his inward nature; that the human soul, being divine in its essence, is allied to omnipotence, and "the simplest person who in his integrity worships God becomes God."

This philosophy asserting so strongly the dignity of human nature, the inherent worth of the individual man, his supremacy over his surroundings, and his natural right to think and act independently of all other men, appealed with power to the leading minds of a country fresh from the formation of State and National Governments and the creation of the only great republic. In 1800 an American was conscious of his immense superiority, in achieved privileges and possibilities of eminence, to the inhabitant of any other country, and an educated citizen of Massachusetts was conscious of his advantages over all other Americans. Hence the rapid spread in that State of the new ideas.

Their workings were soon visible in the increase of dissent. The belief that religion is the "soul's own sense of things divine" discredited the orthodox Church and the received dogmas of Bible interpretation. Some of the churches discontinued the worship of Christ. Afterward, in 1805, the Divinity chair in Harvard University passed into the hands of a Unitarian professor, and in 1815 the Congregationalist Church was split in twain by the secession of the Unitarian congregations.

Other churches lost members by the growth of antinomianism, resulting in schisms more or less important. The most striking illustration of the effect upon churches of the new sentiment of the supreme dignity of the individual man and his right to express without restraint his aspirations, no matter how changeable, is found in the men who separated themselves from the Church and were known as "Come-outers." They "had no distinguishing tenets, but held opinions of every radical type, taking their name from the mere circumstances of their having 'come out' from the regular churches." Frothingham, in the seventh chapter of his life of Theodore Parker, describes some of them. "Brother Jones was to hold forth . . . on the second coming of Christ in 1843." "There was Joseph Palmer, a man with a meek face and a fine gray beard six or eight inches long, clad in fustian trousers and a clean white jacket. He had been a butcher, but had renounced that calling, partly from the convictions of the wrongfulness of eating flesh. Alcott found him full of 'divine thoughts.' He wore his beard because God gave it to him, doubtless for some good end." He thought a man got into the Church by giving to the poor, and no man but himself could put him out. "Nickerson and Davis were two preachers among the Come-outers, two as rough-looking men as you would like to meet on a summer's day; but their countenances were full of the divine. Their hands, their dress, their general air, showed that they belonged to the humblest class in society." "Mr. Bearse was a plain Cape Cod fisherman, a skipper probably, of bright, ruddy, cheerful countenance." He was opposed to all sects and to the Church universal, calling them "little Babels" and it "one great Babel."

These men thought little of rites. Said Mr. Bearse: "Sometimes a brother wishes to be baptized, and, if the spirit moves me, I baptize him, . . . any one into whom

God puts the desire may do it." The Lord's Supper they held in light estimation. "All our meals are the Lord's Supper if we eat with a right heart. . . . Whoever wished to join their company did so without ceremony. No questions were asked about his creed. He subscribed to no confession, set his name to no paper, was free to come and go." Should an unbeliever offer to speak in meeting, they heard what he had to say, and if he could convince them they were ready to be convinced. They had no rules for worship; each spoke as moved. They had no church edifices and their ministers received no salary. They did not consider the Bible inspired, but used it as a help. "Men worshiped the Bible just as the old pagans worshiped their idols. . . . The Bible is a scripture of the Word, not the Word itself. . . . They held that men were inspired in proportion as they had received the truth, and they received the truth through obedience." In all this the new philosophy appears in a religious garb put upon it by uncultured men.

But the most intellectual men were not free from the spirit of "comeouterism." Emerson would not vail his bonnet to circumstance or violate his own moral intuitions; and he resigned his pastorate and abandoned the pulpit rather than administer the communion to members of the church. Rev. George Ripley, after preaching for fifteen years, threw off his clerical frock in order that his soul might not be hampered by possible misunderstandings on the part of his parishioners. Nothing would content him but freedom to embrace the absolute right as he should see it. Both these gentlemen believed that the inviolate soul is in perpetual communication with the source of events. Rev. W. H. Furness is said to have believed that the man perfected by obedience is capable of working miracles.

After the close of the war in 1815, the new philosophy

was taught in Harvard, with limitations, of course, as to its logical results. But the generation growing up at that time showed many converts in after days. Among them was A. Bronson Alcott, who was the first to apply the spiritual views to the practical work of education. His first school was established in 1825. Having faith in the soul and believing that the soul of a child antedates its body, and that its ideas are inspired by God, his object as a teacher was to entice the indwelling deity in the child forth by sympathy. Instead of being taught, the pupils were to evolve all knowledge out of their own consciousness. All, even the youngest, were required to keep diaries. To maintain the free development of the individual soul, no punishment was inflicted; but, if absolutely necessary, Mr. Alcott suffered it vicariously—a method that proved satisfactory to the pupils. Becoming convinced that eating beef encourages bovine qualities in man, he renounced flesh diet, and thereafter confined himself to a food composed of fruits, vegetables, and bran bread. His strong anti-slavery sentiments led him to study the condition of laboring men, including slaves, and having arrived at the conclusion that the wages system is but a modification of chattel slavery, and that the root of the evil in servitude is the divorce of labor and culture, he determined to unite these in his own person and preach abolition by his personal example. Thenceforth he supported himself by manual labor, chopping wood in winter and working in the fields and gardens in summer. In his view the allegiance of the free soul was due to God alone; he was unwilling that any human government should intervene between him and God; he asked nothing from the State and thought the State had no right to ask anything from him; he therefore refused to pay his taxes and went to jail in the serenity of spirit worthy of a philosopher. To make actual his ideal of a perfect social life he established a community. This lasted during one summer and autumn.

He was one of the best talkers ever produced in Massachusetts; could hold forth for hours after the style of Coleridge; was the soul of several Boston and Concord clubs, formal and informal, for two generations, and a brilliant and plausible lecturer. His mystic sayings were puzzles in his own age and are hardly yet understood. "The poles of things are not integrated," and "Love globes, wisdom orbs all things," are examples. He had many admiring friends and hearers, among whom were Samuel J. May, Edmund Quincy, and Willliam L. Garrison.

A very able man of the same class, but not so well known as Alcott, was Rev. Samuel Johnson. Among his sayings was the following, "Man is divinely prescient of his infinity of mind as soon as he begins to meditate and respire."

Between 1832 and 1844 Orestes A. Brownson ran at Boston the brilliant part of his career. He had been a Presbyterian, a Universalist, and a labor reformer. He was then a Unitarian, and passed from that through infidelity, and finally, in 1844, into the bosom of the Roman Catholic Church. He was editor of the Boston "Quarterly," and for several years an apostle of the intuitive school. He gained great notoriety by his extravagant phrases and incisive style, which he studied to make startling and paradoxical; but he had generally the good taste to shun personalities. His manner of writing was imitated by many feebler men who were anxious to attract public notice to themselves. As intuitions may change with lightning-like rapidity, Brownson never took the trouble to apologize for inconsistencies. One of his admirers says of him: "That others thought as he did was enough to make him think otherwise; that he thought as he had six months before was a signal that it was time for him to strike his tent and move on."

Brownson was a forcible speaker. It was said, in the height of his celebrity, that if one wished to become a perfect orator, he should unite Brownson's strength with Edward Everett's diction and delivery. He was an iconoclast, and sympathized with the most advanced advocates of destructive reforms.

While all who had drunk the new wine were filled with a supreme disgust of the actual, the action of each was modified by his personal qualities. The sensitive, fastidious, and dreamy Thoreau, averse to contact with abuses, cultivated the divine in himself; he built a hut in a wood on the edge of a lake, and communed with Nature and his own soul at an annual outlay of some fifteen dollars. George Ripley and his associates, benevolent, abhorring oppression, desirous of superseding the actual and establishing an ideal society in which there should be no slaves, no menials, and no drudges, dazzled by the day-dreams of St. Simon and Fourier, and having boundless confidence in their own intuitions of the practical and a corresponding contempt for the teachings of human experience, established the famous community of "Brook Farm." This attempt to reconstruct the social order, with a view to the symmetrical development of men as rational beings, exhibited so much self-denial, perseverance, and hopefulness on the part of the men who made it that it holds the first place in the long list of American Utopias.

It was preceded by the more distinctly anti-slavery community of Hopedale, Mass. This was formed by abolitionists who were also Universalists. In an account of it, written by Adin Ballou, its principal founder and republished in the "History of American Socialisms," by J. H. Noyes, himself a Communistic Socialist, we find the following: "No precise theological dogmas, ordinances, or ceremonies are prescribed. . . . It enjoins total abstinence from . . . all intoxicating beverages; . . . all slave-holding and proslavery compromises; all war and preparations for war; all capital and other vindictive punishments; . . . all voluntary participations in any anti-Christian government, . . . whether by doing military service, commencing actions at law, holding office, voting, petitioning for penal laws, aiding a legal posse by force, or asking for public interference for protection which can be given only by such force. . . . It is a moral suasion temperance society on a teetotal basis. It is a moral-power anti-slavery society, radical and without compromise. It is a peace society on the only impregnable foundation of Christian non-resistance. It is a sound theoretical and practical woman's rights association."

A similar community, omitting Universalism, was formed about the same time at Northampton, Mass.

These organizations were outgrowths of the all-pervading anti-slavery sentiment in Massachusetts, ripened into rankness by the warmth of the new philosophy. For proof read the following passage from a speech by Charles A. Dana:

> We have an association at Brook Farm, of which I now speak from my own experience. We have there abolished domestic servitude. This institution of domestic servitude was one of the first considerations; it gave one of the first impulses to the movement at Brook Farm. . . . It was a deadly sin—a thing to be escaped from. (Noyes, p. 222.)

The communities were not organized until after 1840, but they were crystallizations of opinions and aspirations which had been growing into definite form since 1830. One path to them began in anti-slavery Unitarianism and passed through Fourierism; the other began in anti-slavery orthodoxy and passed through perfectionism. This was the one followed by Mr. Garrison. At the beginning of his career he was a Calvinistic Baptist in theory, though not a church-member or professor of personal religion. Having become hostile to the Sabbath and other Christian ordinances and to all church organizations, he became an easy convert to perfectionism. J. H. Noyes, afterward the founder of the Oneida Community, but in 1837 the editor of the "Perfectionist" (New Haven, Conn.), called on Mr. Garrison on March 20th of that year. Of this interview Mr. Noyes (see G. ii, 145) writes:

> He spoke with interest of the perfectionist, said his mind was heaving on the subject of holiness and the kingdom of heaven, and he would devote himself to them as soon as he could get anti-slavery off his hands. I spoke to him especially on the subject of government, and found him, as I expected, ripe for the loyalty of heaven.*

This last was the cant phrase of the period for disavowing all allegiance to human governments and declaring one's allegiance to God alone. Human laws and institutions had no binding force on a man in whom "the God-life was infolded." March 22d, Mr. Noyes developed his views in a letter to Mr. Garrison abounding in delicate strokes of flattery and betraying a reasoned hostility to the Government of the United States. Among other things he said: "My hope of the millennium begins where Dr. Beecher's expires, viz., at the overthrow of this nation." He claimed authority "to stand in readiness actively to assist in the execution of God's purposes." (G. ii, 147.)

April 16th, Mr. Garrison, in a letter to H. C. Wright, then in New York, avows his no-human government prin-

* That Mr. Garrison wished to abandon the anti-slavery cause about this time, and to devote himself to his new hobby of no-human government, is proved by the concurrent testimony of Mr. Noyes, Angelina Grimké, Lewis Tappan, H. B. Stanton, and others. It is probable that nothing was lacking except money. Capital is shy of anarchical doctrines.

ciples and ultra-pacific views, and says of his "religious views": "My own are very simple, but they make havoc of all sects and rites and ordinances of the priesthood of every name and order." (G. ii, 149.)

August 26th, Mr. Garrison wrote to his brother-in-law: "I feel somewhat at a loss to know what to do, whether to go into all the principles of holy reform and make the abolition cause subordinate or whether still to persevere in the one beaten track as hitherto." (G. ii, 160.) The next day Angelina Grimké, having just received a visit from Mr. Garrison, in which she had gained his adhesion to woman's rights, wrote to Mr. Weld: "What wouldst thou think of the 'Liberator' abandoning abolitionism as a *primary* object and becoming the vehicle of all these grand principles?" (G. ii, 161.)

Mr. Weld would doubtless have been much gratified to have the abolition cause disburdened of the "Liberator," but the plan was impracticable, probably for want of pecuniary means, the friends of the "grand principles" of Nihilism having no money to support another newspaper organ.

It is a noteworthy fact in the evolution of ideas that the men who favored sweeping away all human governments and institutions generally ended by organizing on a small scale governments and institutions of their own. Mr. Noyes, it has been already said, became the founder of the Oneida Community, but he was preceded several years in this kind of work by a bosom friend of Mr. Garrison's. The Skaneateles Community had its tap-root in the very office of the "Liberator." We quote from Noyes's "History of Socialisms" the following:

It was time for anti-slavery, the last and most vigorous of Massachusetts nurslings, to enter the socialistic field. . . . John A. Collins, the founder of the Skaneateles Community, was a Boston man, and had been a working abolitionist up to the summer of 1843. He was, in fact, the general agent of the Massachusetts Anti-Slavery Society, and in that capacity had superintended the one hundred national conventions ordered by the society for that year. During the latter part of this service he had turned his own attention and that of the conventions he managed so much toward his private schemes of association that he had not the face to claim his salary as anti-slavery agent. His way was to get up a rousing anti-slavery convention and conclude it by calling a socialistic convention to be held on the spot immediately after it. At the close of the campaign he resigned, and the Anti-Slavery Board gave him the following certificate of character :

"*Voted*, That the board, in accepting the resignation of John A. Collins, tender him their sincercest thanks and take this occasion to bear the most cordial testimony to the zeal and disinterestedness with which at a great crisis he threw himself a willing offering on the altar of the anti-slavery cause as well as to the energy and rare ability with which for four years he has discharged the duties of their general agent, and in parting offer him their best wishes for his future happiness and success." (P. 163.)

As Mr. Collins was leaving Mr. Garrison's board for the purpose of establishing his community, and Mr. Garrison himself had attended the series of conventions, this certificate must be regarded as an indorsement both of Mr. Collins's proposed enterprise and of the bold fraud upon the anti-slavery public by which he had sought to identify abolitionism and communism. What the creed of the new society was may be inferred from the following passages copied from it as published in Noyes's "History of Socialisms" (p. 163). After styling it a "community of property and interest by which we may be brought into love relations," the "fundamental principles" are stated:

1. *Religion.*—A disbelief in any special revelation of God to man touching his will and thereby binding upon man as authority in any arbitrary sense ; that all forms of worship should cease ; that all religions of every age and nation have their origin in the

same great falsehood, viz., God's special providence. . . . We regard the Sabbath as other days, the organized Church as adapted to produce strife and contention rather than love and peace, the clergy as an imposition, the Bible as no authority, miracles as unphilosophical, and salvation from sin . . . through a sacrificed God as a remnant of heathenism.

2. *Governments.*—A disbelief in the rightful existence of all governments based upon physical force, that they are organized bands of banditti whose authority is to be disregarded. Therefore we will not vote under such governments or petition to them, but demand them to disband; do no military duty, pay no personal or property taxes, sit upon no juries, refuse to testify in courts of so-called justice, and never appeal to the laws for a redress of grievances, but use all peaceful and moral means to secure their complete destruction.

3. That there is to be no individual property, but all goods shall be held in common.

The Chicago Anarchists of our day have never put these doctrines in a clearer light. That Mr. Collins learned them in the four years of his service in the Anti-Slavery Office at Boston is certain. Before he became agent there his friend Mr. Garrison had declared himself as follows:

We can not acknowledge allegiance to any human government, neither can we oppose any such government by a resort to physical force. . . . Our country is the world, our countrymen are all mankind. We love the land of our nativity only as we love all other lands. . . . We can allow no appeal to patriotism to revenge any national insult or injury. . . . If a nation has no right to defend itself against foreign enemies, no individual possesses that right in his own case. . . . We register our testimony not only against all wars, whether offensive or defensive, but all preparations for war, . . . we deem it unlawful to bear arms or to hold a military office. . . . As every human government is upheld by physical strength, and its laws are enforced at the point of the bayonet, we can not hold any office. . . . We therefore voluntarily exclude ourselves from every legislative and judicial body and repudiate all human politics, worldly honors, and stations of authority. If we can not occupy a seat in the legislature or on the bench, neither can we elect *others* to act as our substitutes in any such capacity.

It follows that we can not sue any man at law to compel him by force to restore anything which he may have wrongfully taken from us or others. . . . The triumphant progress of the cause of temperance and of abolition in our land . . . encourages us to combine our own means and efforts for the promotion of a *still greater cause.* (See "Declaration of Sentiments of the Peace Convention," September, 1838, Writings of Garrison, p. 72.)

Mr. Garrison had entered his "solemn protest against every enactment" forbidding labor on Sunday (see "Writings," p. 99), and declared against the clergy and the Church.

The views of H. C. Wright, expressed in and after 1837, are summed up in his book, entitled "Ballot-box and Battle-field." A few extracts will show their character:

Suppose the abolition of slavery throughout the world depended on a presidential election, and that my vote would throw the scale for abolition. Shall I vote? . . . I may not vote for the war system that is founded in guilt and blood and utterly wrong in its origin, its principles and means, even to abolish slavery.

The ranks of impracticables in Massachusetts were swelled by Second Adventists, Mesmerists, Grahamites, Fourierites, Spiritualists, and advocates of free love, and of the substitution of barter for the use of money. All of them were few in number compared with the whole population, and their extreme notions, tolerated at first, soon grew offensive or ridiculous in the eyes of nine tenths of the people of New England. Emerson shot at them a few of his bolts of satire:

They withdraw themselves from the common labors and competitions of the market and the caucus. . . . They are striking work and calling out for something worthy to do. . . . They are not good citizens, not good members of society; unwillingly they bear their part of the private and public burdens. They do not even like to vote. . . . They filled the world with long words and long beards. . . . They began in words and ended in words.

Frothingham says of their self-culture that they carried it "to the point of selfishness, sacrificing in its behalf sympathy, brotherly love, patriotism, friendship, honor, producing a 'mountainous me,' fed at the expense of life's sweetest humanities."

Their strongest aspiration was to express in stinging epithets and vituperative language their infinite devotion to the cause of the slave; but they were serenely indifferent to its success or failure. They would not cast a ballot if the act would free three million slaves!

CHAPTER XXVII.

THE SCHISM OF THE GARRISONIANS.

1837–1840.

AFTER his arrival in New York Mr. Birney devoted his attention partly to checking the no-government defection at Boston. The evil proved, however, to be much more deeply seated than he had thought. Its progress must be indicated here in a very cursory manner

November 16, 1837, A. A. Phelps wrote from Boston:

If I can get on without a public censure upon friend Garrison I will do so ; if not, I shall give full and free expression to my dissent. . . . I had not noticed Garrison's omission of the paragraph you mentioned. I think he has omitted other things—not many—of the same character. If I mistake not, Judge Jay sent him a letter about his Providence speech, which has never yet appeared.

About this time Lewis Tappan went to Boston on a peace mission, to confer with the authors of the "Clerical Appeal" and restore harmony. November 17th he wrote:

We kept the appeal out of the discussion until the last day. Mr. Garrison and Mr. Oliver Johnson were violent against Fitch, Towne & Co., calling them "hypocrites," "traitors," etc. . . . At the last moment Mr. Garrison, at the instigation, it is said, of his brother-in-law Benson, introduced a resolution condemning the appeal. It was thought best not to oppose it. Think of his introducing it ! a party concerned and not a member of the society ! Every one I heard speak of the matter, even O. Johnson, regretted its introduction.

In Mr. Garrison's remarks he was full of perfectionism doctrines. It is evident that *that* is the absorbing thing with him at present. In Boston Mr. Knapp told me that Garrison would, after January, relinquish the "Liberator" or change its character, unless the controversy should be continued, and then he would think it his duty to continue the "Liberator" as now on that account. . . . Messrs. Towne and Fitch, so far as I could learn, have no intention of lowering the abolition standard ; but they say that Garrison is so much disliked by the orthodox in Massachusetts on account of his views on the Sabbath, on government, etc., that none of them will join the Anti-Slavery Society while he holds the reins here. . . .

I endeavored to show Towne, etc., that if Mr. Garrison is hauling off to engage in other hobbies—*as he will if they let him alone*—a glorious opportunity presented itself of taking hold of the old society with new vigor. . . . I believe they (the appellants) simply intended to show that the views and spirit of the "Liberator" were such that they could go no further with its editor as the leader of the society in Massachusetts. . . . W. L. Garrison attacks the clergy as such, when the fact is they have come into the anti-slavery ranks ten to one compared with any other class of men, A. A. Phelps says. . . . W. L. Garrison told me a year since, that as soon as he saw the anti-slavery cause going on without the need of his labors, he should attend to *some other objects he deemed paramount.* He then opposed family prayer, a regular clergy, etc. ; of late his views have been more developed. As an abolitionist, therefore, his zeal is on the wane. . . . Oliver Johnson, agent of the Rhode Island Society, will do well "if he does not sympathize too much with the new *isms* of W. L. Garrison."

February 8, 1838, Judge William Jay writes from Bedford :

Having sworn to support the Constitution of the United States, I could not hold communion with any society that was seeking to violate it.

What Mr. Garrison was doing about the same time is pictured in a letter written nearly two years later by John

E. Fuller, of Boston. Mr. Fuller was one of the original members of the New England Anti-Slavery Society (1832), had been counselor and treasurer of the Massachusetts Anti-Slavery Society, one of the supporters of the "Liberator," and a friend of Mr. Garrison in time of need. (G. ii, 12, 47, 69.) The accuracy of the statements in the letter was never questioned by Mr. Garrison or his biographers. November 25, 1839, Mr. Fuller writes to the editor of the "Massachusetts Abolitionist":

Satisfied that the present state of the anti-slavery cause demands a publication of the facts in the case, I do not feel at liberty to shrink from the responsibility of giving them to the public in answer to your inquiries. They are briefly these:

Some two years since Mr. Garrison received a letter from Mr. James Boyle of Ohio,* which was subsequently published in the "Liberator" (March 23, 1838), under the caption of "A Letter to William Lloyd Garrison touching the Clerical Appeal, Sectarianism, and True Holiness."

The character of the letter may be judged from the following extracts: "For your independent expression of your sentiments respecting human governments—a pagan-originated Sabbath (Sun's day)—your wise refusal to receive the mark of the beast either in your forehead or in your right hand, by practically sanctioning the irreligious sects which corrupt and curse the world, your merited denunciation of these sects, of the sordid, dough-faced popish leaders; but, above all, for your Christ-exalting poetry, 'Christian Rest,' you are in my heart.

"It would seem from the sympathy manifested by clerical men in this country toward the religion and priesthood that were abolished in France that they would rather have a priesthood from hell than none at all.

---

* Mr. Boyle was from New England. He was an ex-clergyman and perfectionist. He afterward became a quack doctor in New York city, and advertised himself by wearing on the streets a cocked hat, long black frock coat, colored silk knee-breeches, large gold buckles on his shoes, and gold-rimmed spectacles. A very long and large gold-headed cane completed his equipment.

"I have observed of late that you have become satisfied that *moral influence will never abolish slavery in this country.* [In a note Mr. Fuller says : "This was Mr. Garrison's opinion at that time."] Of this I have long been certain. The signs of the times indicate clearly to my mind that God has given up the sects and parties, political and religious, of this nation into the hands of a perverse and lying spirit, and left them to fill up the measure of their sins."

In publishing this letter Mr. Garrison said (editorially): "It is one of the most powerful epistles ever written by man. We alone are responsible for its publication. It utters *momentous truths* in solemn and thrilling language, and is a testimony for God and his righteousness which can not be overthrown."

Mr. Garrison had the letter on hand some time previous to its publication, and read it repeatedly to individual and particular friends. On one occasion, before its appearance in the "Liberator," myself and several others were invited to meet at a room in the Marlborough Hotel to hear it read. Mr. Garrison, having read it, spoke of it in terms of the highest commendation, saying in substance that, however unpopular its doctrines, they were true and would yet be received by the people. That they were not now prepared for them—that if a new publication were started for the purpose of promulgating them (a measure which he had had under consideration some months before, and in respect to which he consulted some of his most confidential friends), it would not get sufficient circulation to sustain it ; that the abolitionists, indeed, were the only class of the community that had been so trained to free discussion as to bear their discussion, and, therefore, said he, "as our enemies say," referring to the charge of Mr. Woodbury some time previous, "we must *sift it into the* 'Liberator.'" This is the substance of what he said.

The impression I received from it at the time was that it was then his deliberate design to take advantage of the abolition character of his paper to "sift" his peculiar opinions on other subjects into public favor . As I had never before believed that Mr. Garrison had any such design, and had repelled the charge as a slander upon him, I was of course surprised at this avowal of it by himself. That he made what amounted to such an avowal I am sure from three facts :

1. I mentioned it to Mrs. Fuller the same evening.

2. My confidence up to that time in Mr. Garrison's integrity was entire and implicit, and from that time it began to be shaken. And

3. The columns of the "Liberator" have since been in exact keeping with such a design. . . . I make these statements in no ill-will to Mr. Garrison, but solely because I believe that the cause of truth and freedom demand it.

Yours for the bondman, JOHN E. FULLER.

Mr. Fuller promptly refused to march under false colors with Mr. Garrison. Many other abolitionists followed his example; the people of Massachusetts held aloof from the cause, and before the anniversary of the American Anti-Slavery Society, held at New York, May 2–8 inclusive, it had become plain that the no-government faction, though in possession of the "Liberator" and the machinery of the State society, would not be able to control the majority of the abolitionists of the State. Under Mr. Birney's counsel the national society, after refusing to renew H. C. Wright's commission as agent, forbore to take part in what was still a purely local affair. The cause was progressing so well in the other Northern States that it was highly desirable to avoid dissension at the anniversary meeting. The no-government leaders attended in force—Henry C. Wright, Oliver Johnson, Edmund Quincy, Samuel J. May, Orson S. Murray, W. L. Garrison, George W. Benson, and A. Dresser, were all present. Their only demonstrations were to offer a resolution expressing a desire that agents and members should not defend themselves by physical strength against violence, which was defeated, receiving only nineteen votes; and another to appoint a committee which should "announce the judgment of the American Anti-Slavery Society concerning the *common error* that our enterprise is of a political and not religious character." The explosion of this bomb-shell was prevented by an adjournment. Oliver Johnson offered another deprecating the imposition by any anti-slavery society of "a religious or political test for the purpose of rendering the anti-slavery cause subservient to the interests of a sect or party, or of opposing existing organizations." What this meant was not understood then and can not be understood now; it was ambiguous enough to satisfy everybody, and was not voted against by anybody. Mr. Garrison tendered the olive branch by moving the acceptance and publication of the annual report, saying it ought to be circulated through the length and breadth of the land. Most of the report had been written by Mr. Birney. It gave many facts to show that abolitionism was "rapidly becoming a part of the religion of our country," quoting the abolition resolutions of Methodist and Free-Will Baptist conferences, of two Presbyterian synods, and of five Congregational associations. The Connecticut clergy were complimented. "The Methodist Episcopal Church in the Northern States is rapidly coming upon abolition ground. In six out of sixteen conferences there is already a majority of abolitionists, and in four a very large majority." Thirty-five pages were devoted to the political aspects of the situation. The supremacy of the laws and Constitution was implied in every page. On "the right use of suffrage" the report said:

> As honest and determined men abolitionists will not fail seasonably to exercise this right, and he is not worthy the name of an abolitionist who does not put the anti-slavery qualification above any and all others in selecting the candidate to receive his vote. The principle of *using our suffrage* in favor of emancipation while we neither organize a distinct party nor attach ourselves to any already existing is vital to our cause. . . . Every party predilection must be merged or the cause is lost.

That Mr. Garrison, with his declared views of the clergy, the Church, the laws, the Constitution, and voting, should indorse the report without reservation, or indorse it at all, was an inconsistency startling to persons of common sense, but quite to be expected from a philosopher of the intuitive school. Such a one acts from supposed divine inspiration at the moment; but whether Mr. Garrison did so or not, in this instance he did right. He relapsed after his return to Boston.

The "no-government" men made up in activity what they lacked in numbers. While refusing for themselves to vote at the ballot-box, they voted in conventions and formed coalitions with women who wished to vote at the ballot-box. January 25, 1839, H. B. Stanton wrote from Boston:

> An effort was made at the annual meeting of the Massachusetts society, which adjourned to-day, to make its annual report and its action subservient to the non-resistant movement, and, through the votes of the women and of Lynn and Boston it succeeded.

February 18th, Mr. Stanton wrote to William Goodell from Haverhill, Mass.:

> I have taken the liberty to show your letter to brothers Phelps, George Allen, George Russell, O. Scott, N. Colver, and a large number of others, and they highly approve its sentiments. They, with you, are fully of the opinion that it is high time to take a firm stand against the non-government doctrine. They are far from regarding it merely as a humbug.
>
> No! coming out, as it does, attached to our glorious cause and ushered into being under the sanction of Brother Garrison, it will be subscribed to from that simply by hundreds without examination. But though great evil will result from it, yet, thank Heaven, the practice of these men will be much better than their theory.
>
> The non-government doctrine, stripped of its disguises, is worse than Fanny Wrightism, and, under a Gospel garb, it is Fanny Wrightism with a white frock on. It goes to the utter overthrow of all order, yea, and of all purity.

When carried out it goes not only for a community of goods but a community of wives.

Strange that such an infidel theory should find votaries in New England! . . . And then the name and influence of the "Liberator" and its editor have greatly forwarded its destructive ends.

I fully concur with your remarks as to the influence of praise upon the mind of Brother Garrison. It has, indeed, bewildered him. Had it not been for the self-confidence with which this has inspired him he might have been held back from his wild notions of government. . . . Brother Garrison is now using weapons we have thoughtlessly placed in his hands, and the cause we love is feeling the wounds. . . . How humiliating to his admiring friends that we are compelled to say he has departed from the standards!

Same to same:

BOSTON, *April 8, 1839.*

. . . You will see by the last "Liberator," containing the letters of O. Scott, Birney, and myself, the state of things here. We were compelled to say thus much in self-defense. Brother Garrison seems sometimes almost reckless of the truth of his statements if so be he can excite prejudice against such as take ground against him on his no-government doctrine. Our cause in this region is in a sad plight. . . . Garrison told Whittier two or three days since that, at the annual meeting of the American Society, he should move to amend the Constitution by striking out all which relates to the power of Congress, . . . in a word, all that relates to political and governmental action, etc. . . . After this alteration who would remain in the society? Birney [Jay], Phelps, Scott, Colver, Allen, the Tappans, Leavitt, Whittier, Weld, E. Wright, *et id genus omne*, would quit it instantly. Not a member of the executive committee at New York would remain, I presume. . . . I beg you to notice the last clause in Birney's letter in the "Liberator," . . . where he speaks of the anti-slavery cause in New England being greatly embarrassed by attaching to it other and irrelevant matters. He speaks what I know to be true; and as to separating our cause from these wild ultraisms — non-government, perfectionism, anti-clergy, anti-church, anti-marriage, anti-money, etc.—I agree with him fully.

And I wish I were not compelled to utter what I religiously believe, viz., that W. L. Garrison, H. C. Wright, and others are determined to rule or ruin, to make the anti-slavery cause, and especially the associations, subservient to their ends or destroy the latter. Of this I have not a shadow of doubt. . . . Some men are fond of new theories simply because they are new. Some have taken hold of abolitionism merely because it ministered to their appetite for intense excitement. Mobs, etc., having passed away, the present excitement on that subject is not strong enough for them, and so they must get up something else.

In Massachusetts the breach between the no-government faction and the mass of the abolitionists was rapidly widening. In December, 1838, Henry C. Wright published a characteristic document, intended no doubt as an assault upon voting. In a letter of December 23d (G. ii, 253) Garrison wrote of him:

He has prepared a tract on human governments which when published will doubtless *stir up the feelings of community*. It shows in a simple and lucid manner that national organizations as now constructed are essentially anti-Christian.

Edmund Quincy wrote to H. C. Wright, December 31st:

I received your missive, full of combustible matter enough to set the whole United States mail on fire, in due course. I was well content with the doctrine therein laid down.

The voting abolitionists were not idle. Some anti-slavery conventions held in January resolved in favor of going to the polls and voting, and recommended to the State Anti-Slavery Society to establish a weekly paper to sustain this policy. Garrison responded with his customary arrogance and insinuations against persons. Charles T. Torrey replied with anger, speaking of Garrison's "brassy brow." Alanson St. Clair pronounced Garrison's references to himself "an unprovoked and vile attack on one you professed to regard as a friend," and said: "I shall take the liberty to appeal from your imperial decision."

Amos A. Phelps replied, claiming a right to work for the cause "without doing it through your paper and without coming and kneeling devoutly to ask your holiness* whether I may do so or not." He said that Mr. Garrison's charges were natural to "one whose overgrown self-conceit had brought him into the belief that his mighty self was abolition incarnate."

In another letter to Mr. Garrison Mr. Phelps said: "You seem still to be possessed with the old idea that you and your paper are abolition incarnate, so that no man can dislike or reject either without disliking and rejecting abolition." (See G. ii, 270.)

John Le Bosquet thought Mr. Garrison might be "so elated with his elevation as to think that he was monarch of all he surveyed." Daniel Wise reported Mr. Garrison to have spoken "as if he were whip-master-general and supreme judge of all abolitionists, as though he wore the triple crown and wielded an irresponsible scepter over all the embattled hosts of anti-slavery troops." George Allen declared Mr. Garrison resolved "to cripple the influence of all who will not come under the yoke which he has bent for their necks." Benjamin Lundy, who had for several years lost his confidence in Mr. Garrison, wrote in his paper of the course of the "Liberator" as "erratic and dogmatical," "whimsical and unreflecting," and of its editor as arrogant. Mr. Garrison answered by charging Lundy with being "jealous and envious."

February 7, 1839, the first number of the "Massachusetts Abolitionist," a paper "devoted exclusively to the discussion of slavery," appeared. In the first three months

---

* This was an allusion to the nickname of *Pope*, commonly applied to Mr. Garrison in derision of his egoism.

the subscribers to it outnumbered those to the "Liberator." March 26th, the Massachusetts Society met in Boston. Messrs. Birney and Lewis Tappan were present from the National Committee. Mr. Tappan advised a division of the society into two parts. Mr. Birney approved the establishment of the newspaper, and declared that under the constitution of the national society every member who was a legal voter was morally bound to go to the polls, and if he had conscientious scruples against so doing ought to leave the society. He said also that the cause ought to be relieved of all the extraneous questions which had been connected with it during the past year or two. The meeting settled no differences.

After his return to New York in April, Mr. Birney prepared "A Letter on the Political Obligations of Abolitionists." It appeared May 2d in the "Emancipator" over his signature and afterward in a pamphlet of twelve pages. This was generally regarded as an unofficial declaration by the National Committee, and excited the most lively interest in the abolition world. Its sub-title was "View of the Constitution of the American Anti-Slavery Society as connected with the 'No-Government' Question." It was an expansion of his views expressed at the recent Boston meeting and which had been misrepresented in the "Liberator." A very brief statement of points made, with a few extracts, must suffice for our notice of this closely reasoned and powerful tract of the times. "The *object* of the American Society was the entire abolition of slavery in the United States. The *means* for effecting it were:"

1. The admission that each slave State has the exclusive right to *legislate* on its abolition.

2. Arguments against slavery.

3. "In a constitutional way to influence Congress to put an end to the domestic slave trade; and

4. To abolish slavery in the Territories and in the District of Columbia; and

5. To prevent the extension of slavery to new States.

Under the terms of the constitution of the society no person can be a member of it who does not consent to the above principles.

Influencing the action of Congress "in a constitutional way" implies of necessity the use of the elective franchise.

The declaration of sentiments, signed by the makers of the constitution of the society, contains the following passage:

> We also maintain that there are at the present time the highest obligations resting upon the *people* of the free States to remove slavery by moral and *political action* as prescribed in the Constitution of the United States.

The constitution of the Massachusetts Society binds the members "to endeavor by *all means* sanctioned by *law*, humanity, and religion," etc.

In 1834 the editor of the "Liberator" voted in person and strenuously upheld in his columns the propriety of abolitionists carrying out their principles at the ballot-box. The constitutions of none of the State societies are inconsistent with political action. No opposition worthy of mention was made to this means of furthering abolition until recently. He says:

> Within the last twelve or eighteen months, it is believed after efforts, some successful some not, had been begun to affect the elections, and while the most indefatigable exertions were being made by many of our influential, intelligent, and liberal friends to convince the great body of the abolitionists of the necessity—the indispensable necessity—of breaking away from their old "*parties*" and uniting in the use of the elective franchise for the advancement of the cause of human freedom, . . . at this very time, and mainly, too, *in that part of the country* where *political action* had been most successful, and whence from *its promise of*

soon being wholly triumphant * great encouragement was derived by abolitionists everywhere, a sect has arisen in our midst where members regard it as of religious obligation in *no case to exercise the elective franchise.*

This persuasion is part and parcel of the tenet which it is believed they have embraced, that as Christians have the precepts of the Gospel to direct, and the spirit of God to guide them, all *human governments*, as necessarily including the idea of *force* to secure obedience, are not only superfluous, but unlawful encroachments on the Divine government as ascertained from the sources above mentioned.

Therefore they refuse to do anything voluntarily by which they would be considered as acknowledging the lawful existence of human governments. Denying to civil governments the right to use force, they easily deduce that family governments have no such right. Thus they would withhold from parents any power of personal chastisement or restraint for the correction of their children. They carry out to the full extent the "non-resistance" theory. To the first ruffian who would demand our purse or oust us from our houses they are to be unconditionally surrendered unless *moral suasion* be found sufficient to induce him to decline from his purpose. Our wives, our daughters, our sisters, our mothers, we are to see set upon by the most brutal without any effort on our part except argument to defend them! And even they themselves are forbidden to use in defense of their purity such powers as God has endowed them with for its protection if resistance should be attended with injury or destruction to the assailant!

In short, the "no-government" doctrines, as they are believed now to be embraced, seem to strike at the root of the social structure, and tend, so far as I am able to judge of their tendency, to throw society into entire confusion and to renew, under the sanction of religion, scenes of anarchy and license that have generally heretofore been the offspring of the rankest infidelity and irreligion!

---

* John Quincy Adams and several other members of Congress owed their election to abolition voters, who held the balance of power in their respective districts.

To the supposed objection that non-voting persons had joined the society and were still members of it, Mr. Birney answered that, under the constitution, anybody who chose might join and no method of expulsion had been provided. In this state of things the honorable course for no-government men was either to move to amend the constitution or withdraw from membership. To the claim that voters and no-government men could get along together quietly he answered:

> But is this really so? Is the difference between those who seek to abolish any and every government of human institution and those who prefer *any* government to a state of things in which every one may do what seemeth good in his own eyes . . . so small that they can act harmoniously under the same organization? When, in obedience to the principles of the society, I go to the polls and there call on my neighbors to unite with me in electing to Congress men who are in favor of human rights I am met by a no-government abolitionist inculcating on them the doctrine that Congress has *no rightful authority* at all to act in the premises, how can we proceed together? When I am animating my fellow-citizens to aid me in infusing into the Government salutary influences which shall put an end to all oppression my no-government brother calls out at the top of his lungs "All governments are of the devil," where is our harmony?

He denied that no-government men could consistently petition Congress or advise people, who believed in voting how to vote, comparing this last to angels advising devils how to sin for the glory of God. He concluded:

> But it is high time that something was done to bring this subject directly before the great body of the abolitionists, in order that they may relieve their cause from an incubus that has so mightily oppressed it in some parts of the country during the last year. It is in vain to think of succeeding in emancipation without the co-operation of the great mass of the intelligent mind of the nation. This can be attracted only by the reasonableness, the *religion*, of our enterprise. To *multiply causes of*

repulsion is but to drive it from us and insure our own defeat—to consign the slave to perdurable chains, our country to imperishable disgrace.

JAMES G. BIRNEY.

Of this essay, the tone was judicial and dispassionate. Mr. Garrison was not mentioned by name. The only allusion to him was as "editor of the 'Liberator.'" But he answered in a pamphlet twice as long as Mr. Birney's. The allusion to him was noticed as follows:

I am quoted by Mr. Birney as "having set the example of voting for a professed abolitionist and encouraging others to do the same." As to this citation, *cui bono?* I humbly conceive that it concerns no man, or body of men, to know how many or how few times I have voted since the adoption of the anti-slavery constitution; or whether I have, or have not, changed my views of politics within a few years.*

Mr. Birney had carefully and fairly stated the tenets of the new sect as to human and divine governments, but in his sub-title had used the phrase "no-government question," and had applied the same hyphened adjective to the words "scheme," "enterprise," and once only to the word "party." Mr. Garrison answers in the following strain:

He calls us a "no-government" party. He might as honestly style us a banditti. . . . We deny the accusation. We religiously hold to government—a strong, a righteous, a perfect government, a government which is indestructible, which is of Heaven, not of men. . . . How monstrous, then, the representation, that we are "for destroying *all* government?

In such verbal cavils and simulated rage, Mr. Garrison took pleasure. His want of logical power struck Von Holst, the German historian of this country, as "wonder-

* Up to 1835, Mr. Garrison had not only voted, but advocated the formation of an anti-slavery political party. (See testimony of Whittier and other proofs given in the "Second Annual Report of the Massachusetts Abolition Society.")

ful," nor did he let slip the opportunity for writing about himself. His answer bristles with capital *I's* and *my* and *me.* In the last four sentences of one paragraph there are nine of these croppings-out of egotism. The last sentence is: "But how coldly, how invidiously, how like an abhorred Samaritan, have I been treated by many in the anti-slavery ranks, on account of my religious opinions!"

The feelings of the New York leaders toward Mr. Garrison were the natural result of his waywardness, unreliableness, splenetic temper, jealousy of others, scheming disposition, and arrogant vanity, and not at all of his "religious opinions." Such misrepresentation must have sorely tried the Christian patience of the orthodox Lewis Tappan, who had done all in his power to get the much younger Garrison to work kindly in abolition traces! Again he writes:

> It is quite remarkable that some of those who have been foremost in protesting against being reckoned my followers, . . . who have been unwilling that I should be regarded as the mouthpiece of the Anti-Slavery Society in any sense, who have repelled the slightest intimation from the enemies of abolition, that the society is responsible for the sayings and doings of the "Liberator"—I say, it is quite remarkable that all at once, in the eyes of those persons, I have become an official organ, an unerring oracle, the *magnus* Apollo of the whole land.

To impute to Mr. Birney such an estimate of Mr. Garrison was an inference much too wide for the premises. The same may be said of Mr. Garrison's argument for "non-resistance," drawn from the advice given to slaves by the national society, not to vindicate their rights by physical force, meaning insurrection. If every man who shudders at the massacres of a servile war, thinking peaceful abolition attainable, or advises unarmed Ireland not to declare war against the British Empire, may be held to be a non-resistant in any and all circumstances, it is only in that "wonderful" Garrisonian logic.

There are passages of plausible reasoning in the answer, and Mr. Birney might have replied to them, but they were seasoned with so many epithets, such as "unfair," "improper," "libelous," "absurd," "folly closely allied to cool effrontery, "ridiculous," " a disorganizing spirit," "untrue," that a reply was out of the question. Mr. Birney never bandied epithets. Besides, Mr. Garrison's admissions made a reply unnecessary for intelligent readers. He said:

> As men, as citizens, as Christians, we confess that we have advocated the heaven-originated cause of non-resistance, . . . *but not as abolitionists.** . . . Non-resistance is destined to pour new life blood into the veins of abolition . . . though not necessarily connected with it.

An example of the peculiar boldness of Mr. Garrison in controversy is his assertion (see page 35 of pamphlet) that, at its annual meeting in 1838, the national society had adopted a resolution appointing a committee of nine to prepare a declaration of the judgment of the society "concerning the common error that our enterprise is of a *political* and not *religious* character." Mr. Garrison's very positive assertion is not sustained by the published minutes of the meeting (page 16). The resolution was offered, but does not appear to have been adopted. No such committee ever met; and no such declaration was ever prepared or presented. Mr. Garrison was one of the nine members named to constitute the committee, and should have known these facts.

---

* This subtle distinction between what Mr. Garrison did as an abolitionist and what as a private gentleman, reminds one of the distinction made in the "Mikado" between Poohbah's action in the different capacities of Lord High Treasurer and Lord Chief Justice.

The chasm between the no-government faction and the leaders of the constitutional movement was too broad and deep to be bridged. Separation was inevitable. When and how it should be effected were the only questions. Instead of quietly withdrawing, the no-government men decided to seize upon the organization of the national society. This was made easy by the provision of its constitution, which in effect enabled any one to vote as a member who would sign that instrument and contribute any sum, however small, to the funds of the society. All that was necessary was to get voters enough. The no-government men decided to do this at the anniversary meeting in May, 1840. The practical work of this movement was placed in the hands of that active no-government man and Communist John A. Collins, with Oliver Johnson as his assistant. Mr. Collins raised a fund and chartered a steamboat for the cheap or gratuitous transportation of their voters from Boston to New York. In regard to the number, the "Liberator" afterward said: "On making an enumeration, it appeared there were about four hundred and fifty anti-slavery men and women in our company, of whom about four hundred were from Massachusetts. Probably one hundred went by other routes."

Goodell, in his history "Slavery and Anti-Slavery," says of this:

> This would make 550 in all. The proceedings afterward showed only 1,008 recorded votes from all in attendance from all the States. Of these, Mr. Garrison's rally of 550 would, if unanimous, secure a majority of 92, without any votes from any of the other States. Yet the business to be transacted was that of a society scattered in all the free States, and numbering, perhaps, one or two hundred thousand, the majority of whom antici pated nothing of what was going forward; and if they had known, could have had no opportunity of attending.

The character of the Garrison raid in 1840 can be inferred from the number of Massachusetts members of the national society in the seven years of its existence. In the respective years between 1834 and 1840 inclusive, the delegations from that State numbered as follows: 6, 22, 26, 18, 22, 118, and 550.

It goes without saying that the no-government men captured the machinery * of the national society. They captured nothing else. The pro-government men retired quietly. Some of them formed a new national society; but the abolition cause had already outgrown the crude methods of its earlier days and was becoming a part of the political life of the nation. Outside of Massachusetts and in New York and the great West, among men who knew little and cared less about the dissensions in and around Boston, who had never seen the "Liberator" or its editor, there was rapidly extending a sentiment that the existing political parties could not defend the republic against the slave power and that a necessity existed for laying the foundations of a party broad as the Constitution itself and enduring as the republic. Before describing the growth of this new party we will devote a chapter to the non-government sect and its leader.

---

* This they accomplished by a coalition with women suffragists. The real issue of Nihilism *versus* Government and Law was adroitly kept in the background.

CHAPTER XXVIII.

"*THE SMALL EXTREME WING.*"

In his remarkable work on the "Constitutional History of the United States," Prof. Von Holst, the German historian, says: "The abolitionists generally were held responsible for every word uttered by Garrison, who, after all, was only the leader of *the small extreme wing.*"

In its annual report (page 14) for 1851, the Glasgow (Scotland) Female New Anti-Slavery Association, speaking of the relative number of the Garrisonians to the whole number of American abolitionists, says: "Mr. Garnet [Henry Highland Garnet, the eloquent colored preacher] unhesitatingly declared that they do not amount to one in one hundred and fifty."

The Rev. John Guthrie, of Scotland, in a pamphlet (1851) on the subject, said: "We stated last week, in order to keep thoroughly within bounds, that the Garrisonians, as compared with the evangelical abolitionists in America, are not *one* in *ten.*"

In a letter of July, 1839, Lewis Tappan speaks of "W. L. Garrison and his *clique*," and in August of the same year Amos A. Phelps wrote from Boston: "Mrs. Chapman's influence in this city is dead. At the last meeting of the Boston Female Society, on a test vote, she could muster but eighteen colored people in all, and six of the eighteen were members of her own family. The same is true to a considerable extent in regard to Garrison. The sober, serious, prayerful, and religious abolitionists are mostly with us in the city. The weight of character is with us in the country." (MSS.)

In 1839 the Massachusetts Anti-Slavery Society (old organization) declared in a manifesto the doubt of its managers "whether the one hundredth part of its members held the peculiar views of Mr. Garrison." (Goodell, page 462.)

The son of Samuel Lewis, the eloquent Ohio abolitionist, in his biography of his father (1857) speaks of "that largest portion of the abolitionists who acted with the Liberty party." He says also: "The fact was that the Garrison party formed the smallest segment of the abolitionists; but the opponents of the abolitionists, either from ignorance or convenience, found it the easiest method to confound the two and lay the opprobrious character of disunionists upon all," etc. (page 339).

In a pamphlet entitled "Truth vindicated" (1883), A. T. Rankin, of Ohio, an old abolitionist and brother of John Rankin, says: "Mr. Garrison did some good in the cause of anti-slavery, but it is a question whether he did not do it more damage than good. . . . On page 119 of his book of selections are recorded ten curses he hurled at the Government of the United States. For bitterness of hate they are rarely equaled. Any lover of his country who reads them will not wonder that good men fled from him. . . . When the Anti-Slavery party divided, *only a fragment adhered to him.*"

If Mr. Garrison had not possessed a peculiar faculty for gaining the personal friendship of the few whom he wished to conciliate, he would have had no following whatever. Miss Martineau says of his conversation: "It has none of the severity, the harshness, the bad taste of his writing." Throughout his career a few persons of wealth adhered to him, furnished him with money when necessary, and the poet Whittier, though often obliged to dissent from and rebuke him, always continued to him his friendship. The same may be said of the gentle Quaker Lucretia Mott. To his friends he knew not how to stint his praise. He wrote verses in their honor and commended them in his speeches. Some of them reciprocated, especially Quincy and Wendell Phillips, and the *clique* became known as "the mutual admiration society."

But Mr. Garrison had never been able to gain the confidence of the public or of abolitionists generally. His first newspaper, the one at Newburyport, had failed partly because of his reckless personal attacks on eminent men in the State. He had been rebuked in the newspapers of Boston in 1827, because, although he had resided there but six months and was an unknown and very young man, he had had "the impudence" to appear in a Federal party congressional caucus, composed of prominent citizens and party leaders, and nominate before nominations were called for a successor to Daniel Webster. At Bennington the "Gazette" nicknamed him "Lloyd Garrulous" and said of him: "He is withal a great egotist, and when talking of himself displays the pert loquacity of a blue jay."

In 1829 he made a speech at Boston, and the "Traveler" of that city described him as "of quite a youthful appearance and habited in a suit of black, with his neck bare and a broad linen collar spread over that of his coat."

When in Baltimore he wrote the libel on his townsman and former acquaintance Francis Todd, for which he was indicted and sentenced to pay fifty dollars and costs, he incurred the blame of all judicious persons who knew the facts. Mr. Allen, of Newburyport, under whom he had served his apprenticeship and who knew Mr. Todd, "thought that in assailing Todd he had stepped aside to wound those who were not and never would be guilty of joining in the traffic, and that his charge had been based on vague rumor, hasty conversation, and scattered facts." (G. i, 185.)

Moses Sheppard, an anti-slavery Quaker, resident in Baltimore, was still more severe. He said that Garrison "had promulgated statements utterly destitute of the slightest foundation in truth in relation to a transaction of which, as it took place at his very door, the most careless inquiry would have supplied him with the correct details." (See his pamphlet, 1834.)

That the anti-slavery Quakers of Baltimore agreed with Mr. Sheppard is proved by the fact that not one of them came forward to relieve Mr. Garrison from imprisonment, though he lay in jail forty-nine days and until Arthur Tappan paid the small fine.

In the "Genius" for May, 1832, Benjamin Lundy, in answering an attack made on him in the "Liberator," gave his opinion of Garrison in the following language: "His course is sometimes rather headlong and reckless. When mounted on his favorite hobby, scorning to touch the reins and leaning forward with his cap extended in one hand and a barbed goad in the other (to say nothing of the rowels at his heels), he thinks of neither rocks nor quagmires, but rides as though he would distance the winds. It is true he may be safe in pursuing the path that *others have beaten*."

The pressing need of another anti-slavery newspaper in 1831 would have made the "Liberator" a success from the first if its editor had abstained from sensational personalities and indiscriminate vituperation. Remonstrances were unavailing, and the paper was obliged to depend for its small circulation nearly altogether upon the colored people. In 1842, eleven years after its first number, Mr. Garrison, writing of the "Liberator" and its want of success, said that it had "sunk one or two thousand dollars per annum over and above its receipts." (G. ii, 332.)

In its whole course the "Liberator," it is said, never paid expenses. As early as 1832 Arthur Tappan wanted Garrison to employ himself in promoting the education of colored youth. (G. i, 313.)

In 1833 a proposition had been made to merge the "Liberator" in the "Philadelphia World," and later the national executive committee had suggested merging it in the "Emancipator." In 1832, when Garrison was about to sail for England, he made himself a laughing-stock by having himself locked up for three days at New Haven and as long at New York to prevent the colonizationists from *abducting* and *destroying* him! The *rôle* he played in England was that of a reformer who had narrowly escaped becoming the victim of a murderous plot. A pretty full account of this pretended panic is given in the biography of him by his sons. Before December, 1833, between twenty-five and thirty abolition newspapers had been started in the Northern States, and none of them, it is believed, imitated the style peculiar to the "Liberator." That paper was regarded by abolitionists generally as a fire-ship in the abolition fleet, unmanageable, and dangerous to its friends rather than to the enemy, and its editor had the reputation of being erratic and without judgment. This state of opinion is clearly indicated in Lewis Tappan's speech before the convention that organized the American Anti-Slavery Society in December, 1833. In it he said: "There is good evidence to believe that many professed friends of abolition would have been here had they not been afraid that the name of William Lloyd Garrison would be inserted prominently in our proceedings." (G. i, 402.) (See also G. i, 457, for Lewis Tappan's letter of January 2, 1835.)

The formation of a national society had been called for

since 1830 by the abolition sentiment of the country, and Mr. Garrison had sought to take the initiative by making a motion, at the meeting of the New England Anti-Slavery Society in January, 1833, to authorize the managers to call a convention for the purpose; but no call was issued, the managers becoming aware, probably, that it would not be responded to. The call was issued in October by the officers of the New York City Anti-Slavery Society. It had not been shown to Mr. Garrison nor had he been asked to sign it. Both Lewis Tappan, in his life of his brother Arthur, and William Goodell in his history, narrated the facts relating to the call for the convention, and neither of them mentions or alludes to any connection of Mr. Garrison therewith. Every precaution was taken by the men who called the convention to prevent Mr. Garrison from obtaining undue prominence in its proceedings. He was not made one of the officers nor placed on the committee on credentials nor made chairman of any committee. His friend, R. B. Hall, was indignant when he found that Garrison was not to be one of the permanent officers of the society, and demanded that if there was no office for Garrison to fill, "one ought to be *and must be made.*" (G. i, 415.)

Under this pressure the office of secretary of foreign correspondence was created and Garrison elected to it; but he was soon informed that his official "letters must first be submitted to the executive committee." The project, too, of discontinuing the "Liberator" was again suggested. (G. i, 415.)

Mr. Garrison's feelings were deeply wounded, and he promptly resigned the office. No one conversant with anti-slavery history and familiar with the proceedings of conventions can look over the minutes of the convention of 1833 without rejecting the thesis so stoutly maintained by the Garrisonian writers that Mr. Garrison was the founder of the American Anti-Slavery Society. A single fact condemns it. *The constitution formed was in direct contradiction to Mr. Garrison's declared opinions* on the Federal Constitution. Our view is confirmed by the fact that from 1833 to its disruption in 1840, the American Anti-Slavery Society never elected Mr. Garrison either president or one of the many vice-presidents or secretary or member of the executive committee. He rose no higher than to be one of the managers for Massachusetts. At the seven public anniversaries of the society held during the same period, he appeared but twice on the platform, once to make a speech of twelve lines, and once to make a motion and a speech which is reported in four lines. (1st Rep., 16; 5th Rep., 18.) In the hundreds of pamphlets, newspapers, magazines, almanacs, records, and reports of the society, it is barely possible to find Mr. Garrison's name. In the annual report of 1836 it appears in necessary connection with the Boston mob of 1835, but without commendation either of the "Liberator" or the methods of its editor. In those days it was an open secret that the leaders of the national society were averse from giving to Mr. Garrison the prominence he sought while they recognized him as a factor in the local movements in Massachusetts. They were unwilling to be responsible for his words or acts. As a boy writer he had taken Junius for his exemplar and libeled like his English prototype. His earliest ambition was to be the American Junius without being anonymous. His vanity displayed his name at its full length on all occasions. The same sentiment caused him to multiply drawings, paintings, photographs, sketches, and busts of himself. While he was a printer's apprentice he spent part of his earnings in having his portrait painted, representing him in fashionable garb and ruffled shirt. During his flight and concealment in 1833 from the imaginary abductors and assassins hired by the Colonizationists, he sat twice for his portrait, once in Philadelphia and once in New Haven. He was then twenty-seven years of age. It goes without saying that he was a subject for English artists. He had his portrait engraved and put on the market. Copies were placed in every anti-slavery book-store for sale on commission. He practiced all the arts of personal notoriety. To be talked of, no matter how, seemed to be his aim in life. A dramatic situation was his delight; he posed at the grave of Calhoun and in the gallery of the World's Convention. At twenty-one he had published in a Boston paper, "If my life be spared my name shall be known to the world," and a year later he had repeated this gasconade. It seemed to matter little to him whether his professions and practice were in accord. In early manhood he quoted Scripture and talked religion like a clergyman, but he was not then and never became a communicant in any church. (G. i, 56.) He advocated immersion, but was never immersed. Claiming to be a Christian, he denied the inspiration of the Bible and the divinity of Christ, and said at the second decade anti-slavery meeting in 1853: "We are infidels, are we? Well, who would be recognized otherwise in a land like this? Who that is honest, manly, humane, who that loves God and loves his race, would desire for one moment to pass current in this blood-stained nation as a religious man? He who is willing to be popularly recognized as such ought to hang his head for shame and hide himself until he is willing to come out and be branded as an 'infidel.'" ("Proceedings," page 90.)

His professions at one time were in conflict with those at another. He called the Sabbath "our moral sun," and apostrophized it as follows: "If thou wert blotted out . . . earth would resemble hell." Afterward he did his best to blot it out, denouncing it as fervently as he had praised it.

In a printed address in 1831 (page 15) he bursts into

ejaculations of enthusiasm for the Federal Constitution: "Thanks be to God that we have such a Constitution!" He called it a "high refuge from oppression." In 1832 he called it "the most bloody and heaven-daring arrangement ever made by man" (G. i, 308); and later in his career he flaunted at the head of his newspaper the gibe that it was a "covenant with death and agreement with hell." His inconsistencies in action and frequent changes of doctrine gave an air of unreality and insincerity to his professions as a reformer. This was added to by his numberless whims and the facility of his adoption of novelties in belief.

His sons speak of the "faith in advertised remedies which was ever characteristic of him" (G. i, 37). Many amusing stories were told of his use of quack medicines. He was an easy convert to all the crotchets of his day, among which were Grahamism and Spiritualism. It is said, he was a firm believer in photo-spiritism and the materialization of spirits, following in this the example of H. C. Wright. We learn from Oliver Johnson's biography of him that he was "thoroughly satisfied that he had received many communications from friends in the spirit world" (page 376).

Von Holst, in his "Constitutional History" (vol. i, page 225), gives a carefully studied appreciation of Mr. Garrison:

> With a mind capable of logical thinking neither by natural endowment nor from education, his judgment, in the hand of his unbridled feeling, was lost in a labyrinth of senseless abstractions. . . . Clambering upon the ladder of his wonderful logic toward pure principles, without looking to the right or the left, he soon completely lost the ground of the real world under his feet.

After the separation of the Garrisonians from the main body of the abolition army, the tendency of their doctrines became more marked. Senseless abstractions led to extravagances in language and conduct. The fine-spun casuistries of "no-human government" unsettled some of the finest intellects in New England. N. P. Rogers, the poet-editor of New Hampshire, and who for years had been an efficient worker in the anti-slavery cause, fell a victim to the cloudy metaphysics of religious nihilism. He would have no president, no secretary, no business committee, no resolutions, at his meetings; each man was to act as he might think best, without being influenced by others. Among the converts to the same doctrine was the logical Palmer, who refused to touch coin or note or bond, or to pay taxes or recognize human government in any manner. Trade was to be conducted by barter. There were enough like him to start a small paper as their organ, but its existence was brief, there being trouble in paying and collecting subscriptions. Some, of whom Abby Folsom was the type, became crazed on free speech. A meeting for humanity was everybody's meeting and, of course, everybody had a right to speak. As Abby wanted to speak all the time and others wanted a part of the time, there was conflict. Meetings were broken up. This becoming unbearable, the principle was suspended, and Abby was lifted up gently and carried out of doors. On one occasion, when she was being carried out by Oliver Johnson, W. A. White, and Wendell Phillips, she cried out: "I am more blessed than my lord; he had but one ass to carry him and I have three."

A favorite speaker of the sect was flattered into a conceit that his profile resembled Christ's. He parted his hair in the middle, let it grow until it covered his shoulders, cultivated a rather scanty beard, and with liberal use of crimping-irons, curling-tongs, and "thy incomparable oil, Macassar!" effected a transformation of himself which would have been creditable to a theatrical costumer. His audiences had the pleasure of frequent profile views of the orator. At a later period, a blonde rival, equal to him in every point except the curled and tufted beard, divided with him the admiration of æsthetic souls.

"Father Lamson," who, in his better days, was noticed by Theodore Parker as a "beautiful soul," went clean daft under the pressure of the new ideas. He had long white locks which he wore uncovered, and being deeply impressed with the necessity of mowing down this wicked world and its ways, procured a large scythe with a long handle to perfect his resemblance to Time. He was a frequent attendant at the Garrisonian meetings, where, if permitted, he stood upon the platform, leaning on his weapon and looking sadly at the audience.

If it had not been a principle of this sect of professional reformers to say and do shocking things for the purpose of attracting attention, the sanity of several of their leaders might well be doubted. The language of H. C. Wright increased in violence as he grew older. In the "Liberator" for October and November, 1849, were published letters from him which savor of a disordered intellect. Of the Christian's God, he says: "Such a being is to me a devil," etc. . . . What they call 'God' is but an almighty convenience to slave-holders and warriors and their allies." There is other language too indecently blasphemous for reproduction here. At what was called a "Peace Meeting," he offered the following: "Resolved that fidelity . . . demands that we should deny the existence and scorn the worship of any being as God, who ever did, or ever can, sanction war or authorize the destruction of human life at the hand of man for any cause."

That was the kind of resolution passed by non-resistants at their meetings, in order, as they said, to create "moral power" in behalf of their cause! It was, however, the expression of a sympathetic nervous excitement caused by an intense and narrow fanaticism of the same generic class as the "jerks" prevalent in Kentucky, in a single sect, in the early part of the century. Parker Pillsbury was worse, if possible, than Wright; he compared churches to gambling houses and brothels ("Liberator," November 2, 1848). Pillsbury's book, "Acts of the Anti-Slavery Apostles" (1884, 503 pages), gives a very frank and interesting, though confused, account of the doings of himself and five or six other Garrisonian lecturers in New England, beginning about 1839. They hit upon a new plan of "creating moral power"; it was to go into churches at the time of regular services and lecture the congregations without leave and until put out by force! On this plan, they acted systematically, regardless of the indignation excited among the persons whose rights they so recklessly invaded. Indeed, they do not appear to have imagined that other persons had any rights to be respected. They were ejected, of course; sometimes gently, sometimes roughly. Fines were inflicted upon them by magistrates, and imprisonment on non-payment. This they called persecution for righteousness' sake. These cranks must have been intolerable nuisances to the people; and it is wonderful that they escaped with little bodily injury. One of these very aggressive non-resistants was S. S. Foster, the author of a vigorous assault on the Church and clergy entitled "The Brotherhood of Thieves." If there had not been a strong anti-slavery sentiment among the people, and a certain tenderness toward the trespassers as persons supposed to be crazed by the abolition agitation, Messrs. Pillsbury, Foster, and their colleagues would have fared badly.

Before the end of 1843, the Garrisonians found they were flailing thrice-thrashed straw. Perfectionism, non-resistance, and no-human government theories had been condemned by the common sense of the public. Americans rejected doctrines that left wives and daughters without protection from ruffians and prevented the weak from associating themselves to restrain the strong. That shallow fallacy, "the world is my country" the motto of the "Liberator," did not rouse the heart like the lines:

> Breathes there a man with soul so dead
> Who never to himself hath said
> *This* is my own, my native land!

"In 1841 or 1842 it was alleged that there were not, probably, more than one or two hundred non-resistants in all New England." (Goodell's "History," page 462.)

The distinctive doctrines of the Garrisonian faction would have caused its early extinction. It was kept in existence by its continued professions of desire to abolish slavery. As, however, every convert refused to vote, it was plain that if two thirds of the people of Massachusetts became Garrisonians the political power of the State would be wielded by the pro-slavery minority and the Legislature and members of Congress would be chosen from among the most pliant tools of the slave power. Discussion had laid bare the absurdity of denouncing the national evil and refusing to take the only practical action to get rid of it, and in 1843 it had become evident that a change of programme was indispensable to the further vitality of the faction. Internal divisions also threatened disaster. Wendell Phillips and his friends, possessing the best ability and constituting the large majority of the faction, had never accepted Mr. Garrison's peculiar notions about government, and they reprobated the disorderly assaults of Pillsbury, Foster, and others upon the churches. A compromise between these conflicting elements was effected. *Secessionism* was adopted as the future platform. This lay half-way between the contracting parties. Phillips, it is evident from the result, waived his liberty of resorting to constitutional methods to gain abolition, and Garrison waived his no-government and non-voting theories and consented to advocate a political movement that involved State action and much voting. This compromise was a last and desperate struggle of a moribund faction for life. Oliver Johnson, in "Garrison and his Times" (page 337), describes what Garrison did in this matter :

> He began with the Massachusetts society in January, 1844, but even that society was not then quite ready to follow his lead. He brought the subject before the American Society in May, and, after a long and very exciting discussion, that society, by a vote of 59 to 21,* put itself *squarely on the ground of disunion.* The New England Convention followed two weeks later, voting the same way, 250 to 24. Then the whole Garrisonian phalanx swung solidly round to the same position, and the movement thenceforth carried aloft the banner No Union with Slave-holders.

This was in May, 1844, and the campaign for the presidency was in progress. The Whig newspapers, from one end of the North to the other, immediately charged secessionism and disunionism upon the Liberty party as its logical result if not its avowed doctrine, and the charge was reiterated by the numerous speakers of that party. The members of the Liberty party defended by denial and by the countercharge that the passage of the secession resolution in the American Anti-Slavery Society was an electioneering trick concocted between Garrison, a former Whig and ardent friend of Henry Clay, and Horace Greeley, the Whig manager, to whom had been assigned the task of defeating the Liberty party and winning the anti-slavery vote for Clay. They pointed also to the fact that David Lee Child, an intimate friend of Garrison and editor of his anti-slavery organ at New York, had aban-

* This falling off in the numbers reveals the decadence of the American Anti-Slavery Society under Garrison's rule. It had lost its hold on the country at large.

doned his post in order to devote his whole time to promote the success of Henry Clay and to the further fact that the negroes of Boston and the non-resistants generally were ranging themselves in the Whig phalanx. In after years they regarded Mr. Greeley's frequent praise of Garrison and the appointments on the "Tribune" staff of several sub-editors of the "Liberator" as so many recognitions by Mr. Greeley of his secret political obligations to Mr. Garrison. Von Holst intimates obscurely his belief in such a bargain when he says of Mr. Garrison's heresies: "These differences and heresies were, so to speak, *traded in open market* from the very beginning" (page 225).

If traded at any time it was in 1844. The result of the move, however, was that the Liberty party was generally held responsible for the treasonable declarations of its bitterest enemy and was greatly damaged in public estimation.

From this time to the breaking out of the rebellion the true leader of the Boston secessionists was Wendell Phillips. The humble *rôle* of his companion on lecturing tours was filled by Garrison.

Nature had endowed him with wonderful gifts as an orator, and his youthful aspiration was to excel Edward Everett and win the fame of being the most eloquent American. He found the needed theme in slavery and identified himself with abolitionists before their separation. Hereditary wealth gave him leisure, which he used in the preparation of his speeches. He sharpened and polished his phrases until they were keen as razors and bright as diamonds. He would not speak before he was quite ready, and his speech was an event. Though lacking the pathetic element he attracted as large crowds as Ingersoll. He spoke seldom and generally in the large cities. He had no talent or taste for organization. He was *vox et preterea nihil.* There was no disunionist party at the North except, perhaps, Vallandigham and the Knights of the Golden Circle, and Wendell Phillips advocated secession from a standpoint which was not theirs. He was the only prominent advocate of a withdrawal of the Northern States from the Union, Garrison in this matter being merely a foil to his brilliant companion. To the people generally the proposition appeared unpatriotic and treasonable, and the moral power of the North was arrayed against the phrase-maker whose sole object in life seemed to be to burn down the temple of liberty by shooting blazing arrows upon its roof. When the agitations of the incipient rebellion began to shake the country, the Northern people ceased to tolerate Phillips's set speeches as innocuous oratorical displays. For the first time in Boston he was in danger of mob violence. When he announced his great disunion speech for Sunday, January 20, 1861, in the Boston Music Hall, a popular outbreak became imminent. The authorities took every precaution to maintain the public peace and order. Police officers were scattered through the crowded hall, and a large reserve force was secretly held ready a few rods distant. The Governor, the adjutant-general, the county sheriff, and the mayor of the city, were stationed close by. Mr. Phillips was well protected from the fury of the populace. He advocated letting "the erring sisters go in peace." He exclaimed:

> Sacrifice anything to keep the slave-holding States in the Union! God forbid! We will rather build a bridge of gold and pay their toll over it, accompany them out with glad noise of trumpets and "speed the parting guests." Let them not stand on the order of their going, but go at once! Take the forts, empty our arsenals and sub-treasuries, and we will lend them besides jewels of gold and jewels of silver, and Egypt be glad when they are departed.

The Union was termed a "monstrous nightmare."

For the first three years of the war Wendell Phillips and his corporal's squad of secessionists gave "aid and comfort" to the rebels by persistent efforts to undermine the influence of Abraham Lincoln. Their choicest sneers and epithets* of ridicule were reserved for him. At the last hour, when the doom of slavery had been sealed and the triumph of the Government assured, they somersaulted awkwardly into the Union camp, joined in the national huzzas for Lincoln, stripped themselves of their tattered non-resistant and secession garments, donned hastily the Union uniform, and have ever since boldly claimed that all their professions of disunion sentiments for twenty years before the war were false, and they were at heart loyal citizens, and ready to take arms for their country!

Not a single distinctive doctrine of the Garrisonian "extreme wing" was ever accepted by the American people or Government. It was the most utter abortion known in the history of this country. It advocated the abolition of the clergy, the overthrow of the Church, of the Union, of the Government; but the clergy are still numerous, the Church stands firm, the Union is preserved, and the pillars of the Government are as solid as those of the earth. It besought men not to take up arms, but to abjure their manhood and yield their rights to the violent. Free Americans responded by defending with Sharp's rifles the free soil of Kansas and stretching their line of battle against rebellion from ocean to ocean. It opposed slavery as it opposed imprisonment for crime or parental coercion of children because it was one form of *force* which they held to be sinful *per se.* The Government abolished it because it was a political monster dangerons to the safety of the republic. The

---

* One of these was "bloodhound of slavery."

only use Garrison found for the national Constitution was to burn it at Framingham on a Fourth of July; but Abraham Lincoln found in it the war powers under which he put an end to slavery by military order. Garrison spent the best years of his life in trying to transform American citizens into political eunuchs, urging them not to vote or organize a political party against slavery. The people have answered by building up a political party based upon the Constitution he burned.

Historians will follow the lead of Von Holst in his estimate of "the small extreme wing." They will assign to it the same relation to the anti-slavery movement which is borne by the dynamite faction of O'Donovan Rossa to the legitimate movement for Irish home rule. They will declare it to have been from its inception, about 1836, to its final recantation and disappearance in the civil war an unmitigated curse to the abolition cause, acting in its name, but discrediting it by noisy crotchets and blatant treason. They will adopt as true the saying of Charles Sumner: "An omnibus load of Boston abolitionists has done more harm to the anti-slavery cause than all its enemies."

CHAPTER XXIX.

THE LIBERTY—FREE SOIL—REPUBLICAN PARTY.

A PERMANENT national party in a republic governed by suffrage must be in harmony with the genius of the institutions and laws of the country. In this essential element the slave power was wanting. Unceasing struggle was the condition of its existence, and from its birth, in 1820, it was doomed to perish soon or late—peaceably or in the struggles of civil war.

That its antagonist, the Constitutional Anti-Slavery party, embodied all the elements of final success, is evident from its record. It was a powerful national sentiment which in the winter of 1835–'36 forced a reluctant Congress to defeat the attempt of President Jackson and Senators Calhoun and Preston on the freedom of the mails, and to enact a law punishing with fine and imprisonment any postmaster guilty of tampering with them; which brought an average of sixty-six representatives to vote against each of the four "gag" rules passed by the House in 1836, 1837, and 1838; which brought Vermont and Massachusetts boldly to the front in 1836 and 1837, as favoring abolition in the District of Columbia, the vote in the Legislative Assembly of the latter standing 378 to 16. Beginning in 1836 with efforts in some localities to affect the choice of members of State Legislatures and to punish pro-slavery candidates for re-election to Congress, it grew stronger from year to year, acting first as a "balance-of-power" party, and voting for the best Whig or Democratic candidate until the sycophancy of the two great parties to the slave power compelled it to place its own candidates in the field. From that time it gained steadily in influence, compelling the passage of personal-liberty laws in all the Northern States, electing Governors, United States Senators and Representatives, and casting an increasing vote for its candidate at each presidential election, until its success in 1860.

In round numbers, its presidential vote was as follows, subject to allowance for votes not counted in the first four elections:

1840	Birney......................	7,100
1844	Birney......................	62,300
1848	Van Buren / Gerrit Smith	300,000
1852	John P. Hale	155,900
1856	Fremont....................	1,341,000
1860	Lincoln.....................	1,900,000

A party of such steady growth had its roots deep down in national soil; and it rapidly grew strong under the fierce heat of Southern aggression. James G. Birney did not plant it. Nor was he the first who unfurled the banner of "political action." Rufus King, Talmadge, and others, had unfurled it in 1820; Governor Coles, in Illinois, in 1824; Lundy and Raymond, in Maryland, in 1826, 1827, 1828, and 1229; and William Jay, Joshua Leavitt, and their coadjutors, in the constitution of the American Anti-Slavery Society, in 1833. But when historians shall have cleared away the rubbish heaped by vanity, ignorance, and family pride upon the facts of the early opposition to the slave power, they will award this honor to James G. Birney; that he saw more clearly than any other one man of his times the true path, followed it more closely, kept the end more steadily in view, and by common recognition of friends and enemies, became, and remained until the sudden close of his public career, the trusted and honored leader of the party of constitutional resistance.

Some marked changes in the practical operations of the national executive committee followed immediately upon the removal of Mr. Birney to New York, in September, 1837. The organization of auxiliary local societies by means of agents was discontinued, the cause being sufficiently advanced to leave this to the spontaneous action of the people. The result was the voluntary formation of 644 auxiliaries in less than two years, in addition to the 1,006 already existing, and of many other societies, not auxiliary. All of these, without distinction, were encouraged to be active in independent propagandism, by means of the circulation of documents, placing the best anti-slavery books in town and school libraries, and causing their best talkers to take part in debates and public discussions on topics relating to slavery. As a part of the same policy, the committee resorted to the employment of a large number of local agents (Annual Report, 1838, page 47). These were most of them professional men who lectured in their respective neighborhoods. Encouragement was given in the summer of 1837 and the ensuing winter to petitioning Congress, with a result of 414,571 signatures to petitions presented in the House in the six months following the 1st of December. After that session, it was regarded as safe to leave this means also of influencing public opinion to the spontaneous action of the people.

Increased care was given to the character of the publications of the society. The year 1838 was remarkable for the value and timeliness of the anti-slavery books. Among them were the admirable argument of T. D. Weld, on the power of Congress to abolish slavery in the District of Columbia, and his famous book " Slavery as it is," a collection of facts from Southern newspapers; Thome and Kimball's report of the results of emancipation in the West Indies; and Judge Jay's view of the "Action of the Federal Government in behalf of Slavery." Each of these ran through several editions. The number of issues in the twelve months ending with April, 1838, was 646,-502; and in the following year, 724,862. By unceasing effort, these were distributed, through agents, friends, and societies, into every nook and corner of the Northern States.

One of the greatest dangers to the anti-slavery cause was warded off by Mr. Birney at the May anniversary of the national society, in 1838. Alvan Stewart, Esq., of Utica, N. Y., a devoted abolitionist and eloquent speaker, had written him that he would offer a resolution to amend the society constitution, by striking out the cause asserting that, by the Constitution of the United States, each slave State had the exclusive right to legislate in regard to the abolition of slavery in its own limits. He asserted the right of Congress to abolish slavery in the South. Mr. Birney, on the other hand, believed, with the consensus of nearly all jurists, that Congress had no such power in time of peace. For four years he had maintained, in speech and in the press, that the Constitution had been formed by States independent of one another, no one of them having any right to legislate on slavery in any other, and that such a right could be acquired only by express grant; that while by the Constitution freedom was stamped as law upon all territory under national jurisdiction, the States, all * of them being slave-holding in practice, had entered in that instrument into no compact, in

* This has been denied in regard to Massachusetts; but see "Notes on the History of Slavery in Massachusetts," by George H. Moore, published by D. Appleton & Co.; also authorities cited by Mr. Moore in an article in the "Historical Magazine," December, 1866.

regard to slavery in the States, except to grant the power to Congress to prohibit the importation of slaves and suspend its exercise until 1808; and that though what may be done by a nation for self-preservation is practically unlimited, war powers are not to be regarded as ordinary constitutional ones. He thought it revolutionary to hold that Congress could establish or abolish slavery in a State, and that the passage of Mr. Stewart's resolution would be such a radical change in the anti-slavery constitution as to amount to a breach of faith with members and would greatly damage the cause; and entreated him not to present it. Mr. Stewart persisted. An arrangement was made by Mr. Birney with Judge Jay, under which both of them made careful preparation to meet Mr. Stewart's arguments. The question was debated for two days and was finally decided affirmatively.* The vote stood 46 yeas to 38 nays. It fell short of the two-thirds vote required by the constitution. This unexpected defeat greatly shook the confidence of Mr. Birney in the good judgment of many of the men who habitually attended the annual meetings, not as delegates selected for their sound sense, but as volunteers abounding in zeal. From that date he redoubled his exertions to popularize the movement and make it independent of the influences of a central society whose membership and policy were alike unstable.

The famous "Elmore Letter," though written by Mr. Birney in March, 1838, was not published until nearly the last of the following May. The correspondence is of historical value. Mr. Elmore was a member of the House from South Carolina, and an intimate friend of John C. Calhoun. In January Mr. Birney had sent an anti-slavery

---

* The writer had the good fortune to hear all this debate. It was extremely able on both sides. Mr. Garrison was present but said nothing.

publication to Mr. Calhoun with a note, stating that it was sent because Mr. Calhoun had appeared more solicitous than most other Southern politicians to get accurate information about anti-slavery movements, and adding: "We have nothing to conceal, and should you desire any information as to our procedure, it will be cheerfully communicated on my being apprised of your wishes."

This note was handed to Mr. Elmore. Thereupon the slave-power Representatives in Congress, after conferring together, appointed a committee to obtain authentic information touching anti-slavery associations, and Mr. Elmore was selected as the South Carolina member of the committee. February 16th Mr. Elmore addressed Mr. Birney a courteous letter, quoting from his note to Mr. Calhoun and asking full information "as to the nature of yours and similar associations." May 5th, in a letter closing the correspondence, Mr. Elmore refers as follows to his reasons for soliciting the correspondence:

> I heard of you as a man of intelligence, sincerity, and truth—who, although laboring in a bad cause, did it with ability and from a mistaken conviction of its justice. . . . I was induced to enter into a correspondence with you, who, by your official station and intelligence, were known to be well informed on these points, and from your well-established character for candor and fairness would make no statements of facts which were not known or believed by you to be true.

This tribute of respect paid by a South Carolina Congressman to the leading abolitionist of the country, tends to exonerate the public men of the South from the common imputation of underestimating their opponents. There is no doubt that Mr. Elmore expressed the sentiment of Mr. Calhoun and the other slave-holding representatives.

In his first letter Mr. Elmore propounded fourteen questions, searching and exhaustive in regard to the nature, object, numbers, methods of propagandism, printing-presses, funds, and hopes of the anti-slavery associations. They were answered fully and in their order by Mr. Birney. The lucid statements made by him have passed into every history of the times; they need not be repeated here. We make an exception, however, of one or two expressions in regard to the national Constitution:

> The abolitionists regard the Constitution with unabated affection. They hold in no common veneration the memory of those who made it. They would be the last to brand Franklin * and King and Morris and Wilson and Sherman and Hamilton with the ineffaceable infamy of intending to ingraft upon the Constitution, and therefore to *perpetuate*, a system of oppression in absolute antagonism to its high and professed objects (p. 28). . . . In the political aspect of the question they [the abolitionists] have nothing to ask except what the Constitution authorizes —no change to desire but that the Constitution may be restored to its pristine republican purity.

The distance between these sentiments and the motto of the "Liberator," "The Federal Constitution—a covenant with Death and agreement with Hell," is the measure of the chasm that already separated the abolitionists of the country from the Garrisonian *clique*.

The number of members of anti-slavery societies was estimated at one hundred and twelve thousand four hundred and eighty; but it was added, that *now* societies are "not deemed so necessary for the advancement of our cause" (page 7). . . . "Within the last ten months I have traveled extensively in both these geographical divisions

---

* In a letter to a bosom friend Franklin apologized for consenting to a Constitution which left the abolition of slavery in the control of the States. He said: "It is a little sop to Cerberus, the best thing that can be done at present. It (slavery) can not last long, there is too much virtue in the country. As fast as men become honest they will drop slavery." He was president of the Pennsylvania Abolition Society.

(the Northern and Middle free States). I have had whatever advantage this, assisted by a strong interest in the general cause and abundant conversations with the best informed abolitionists, could give for making a fair estimate of their numbers. In the Northern States, I should say, they are *one in ten;* in New York, New Jersey, and Pennsylvania, *one in twenty*, of the whole adult population."

The Elmore correspondence was published in a neat pamphlet of sixty-eight pages, in a very large edition, and a copy of it was placed in the hands of every public man, especially of every Southern member of Congress.

A large share of Mr. Birney's attention was devoted to legislative bodies. In the winter of 1837–'38 he visited every State capital, from Maine to Ohio and Michigan, in which the legislative body was in session, and he obtained a hearing everywhere. The results of his labors and of more general causes contributing to the rapid extension among politicians of sound opinions on slavery and correlated political questions may be summed up as follows: A jury trial was secured in Massachusetts and Connecticut to every person claimed as a slave; Connecticut repealed her black act; and the Legislatures of Maine, Vermont, Massachusetts, Rhode Island, New York, Ohio, and Michigan passed vigorous resolutions in favor of the right of petition and against the admission of Texas, every Democratic member except one of the Lower House in Ohio, voting with the majority. Mr. Birney was encouraged by these signs of the times. In the "Annual Report" made in May, 1838, he said: "We have never for a moment despaired of republicanism or of our country" (page 97).

With characteristic energy and tact he applied himself to political action to affect the result of the fall elections in 1838. Agents lectured in Rhode Island creating a popular sentiment that resulted in the election as Governor of William Sprague, the only candidate who had placed himself squarely on the anti-slavery platform. The earnest support given to Luther Bradish, the Whig anti-slavery candidate in New York for Lieutenant-Governor, hardly sufficed to compensate for the loss of the votes of the pro-slavery men of his party. A decided and successful effort was made to defeat the re-election of Governor Vance, of Ohio, who had hastily surrendered John B. Mahan to the Governor of Kentucky, to be tried for abducting slaves. It was considered very important to keep in the United States Senate that noble abolition Democrat Thomas Morris, of Ohio; but this was not found feasible. The election of Benjamin Tappan, brother of Arthur and Lewis Tappan, as Morris's successor, was, however, a compromise by the Democratic party with anti-slavery sentiment.

The main effort of the campaign was to accomplish the return to the House of Representatives of several anti-slavery members. Mr. Birney was wont to say:

> One good Congressman can do more for our cause than a hundred lecturers. He has almost daily occasions for agitation, and he speaks to the whole people. We can reach the South through no other means. The slave-holders gain their advantages in national politics and legislation, and should be met in every move they make.

With these views he used freely the agencies under his control to influence public opinion in the Congressional districts represented by John Quincy Adams and by William Slade, of Vermont. The election of both these was regarded as certain. It was desirable, however, to give them able coadjutors. The nomination by Massachusetts Whigs of James C. Alvord, who was distinguished as an anti-slavery writer and orator, was arranged, and he was elected by a large majority. Mr. Alvord died before taking his seat. In the Genesee district (New York) the anti-slavery voters holding the "balance of power," compelled the nomination of Seth M. Gates, and carried his election triumphantly. Mr. Gates was re-elected in 1840. During the four years of his service in Congress he was a tower of strength to the abolition cause. In the Western Reserve District, Ohio, settled chiefly by men from Connecticut and other New England States, the people were opposed to slavery by tradition and education. Abolition lecturers from Lane Seminary had visited them in 1834 and 1835 and enlightened them on the religious aspects of the subject. In 1836 and 1837 Mr. Birney, under his matured policy of gaining representatives in legislative bodies by gaining districts, had sent into the Western Reserve the best political lecturers in the employ of the Ohio Anti-Slavery Society. He had himself lectured in the principal towns. The eloquent T. D. Weld had traversed every part of the district. When Elisha Whittlesey resigned his seat in Congress, in 1838, it needed but a few letters to leading abolitionists in the district to show them their opportunity. The Whig managers felt the political necessity of nominating a candidate who would receive the anti-slavery vote. Their convention nominated and the people elected Joshua R. Giddings, one of Mr. Weld's converts. From the time Mr. Giddings took his seat in Congress he stood shoulder to shoulder with William Slade, and both of them were in advance of John Quincy Adams. In December, 1839, the accession of Seth M. Gates completed the "Big Four" of the early anti-slavery agitation in Congress. While these successes were won by the anti-slavery party by the judicious use of the "balance of power," defeats and disappointments were the general rule. The plan of questioning the candidates nominated by Whigs and Democrats was proved by the experience of three years to be a mistake. If both the opposing candidates answered fairly, abolitionists voted each for his old party ticket; if they answered defiantly, abolitionists stayed at home on election day. In either case no special anti-slavery influence was exerted in politics. In nearly every instance of the election of a State Legislator or a Congressman by an anti-slavery "balance-of-power" vote, the office-holder regarded his obligations to his party as paramount. And as the fixed policy of the Whig and Democratic parties was to conciliate the favor of the slave power and secure the vote of the South, members of those parties could not redeem pledges made by them to abolitionists. Beginning with 1836, the anti-slavery voters were known as a party in politics. For the first three years it worked on the radically vicious plan of having no candidates of its own, and voting for the least hostile candidates nominated by its enemies; and in that time it had made little progress in gaining representatives in Congress and the State Legislatures. The necessity of abandoning that plan and adopting the more effective one of nominating from its own body, was apparent to those leaders who were in earnest to accomplish the proposed end. Such a change, it was evident, would cause the falling away of talkers who would not vote, and of that large class of men who were manœuvring for position between the anti-slavery and pro-slavery parties; but a Gideon's band was likely to accomplish more than a discordant crowd.

The occasion and one of the causes of Mr. Birney's adoption of the plan of independent nominations was the announcement, January 21st, in the House by John Quincy Adams, that he was not prepared to favor the abolition of slavery in the District of Columbia! He regarded this as unfaithfulness. Mr. Adams's usefulness to the anti-slavery cause he regarded as ended forever. This opinion was justified by the subsequent course of that leading Whig in regard to slavery. This was reviewed in 1843 by Mr. Birney over his own signature, with his accustomed candor, courage, and power; and as Mr. Adams will not reappear in these pages, we copy from the article the following extracts:

His course, in my judgment, has been eccentric, whimsical, inconsistent; defended in part by weak and inconclusive, not to say frivolous, arguments; and taken as a whole thus far, is unworthy of a statesman of large views and a right temper in a great national conjuncture.

He cites facts to prove that, while Mr. Adams had professed sympathy with the abolitionists, he had opposed each of their special measures, and that they, in violation of their rule, had put confidence in his words, though flatly contradicted by his deeds.

This departure in Mr. Adams's case from the rule has been followed by the consequences that usually attend . . . departures from rules which have been deliberately adjusted for the management of large affairs. The abolitionists in electing Mr. Adams made him their *own* witness, hoping, like an eager but an inexperienced litigant, that his testimony would be favorable to them, because he was heard to speak freely of the bad character of their adversary. But the upshot of the matter is that everything *substantial* in his testimony is favorable to their adversary. To them he gives words—words—words.

Do the abolitionists assault slavery in Florida—in the District of Columbia? *There* is Mr. Adams, the main reliance of their adversary, placed in his position of power by abolitionists, playing "fast and loose" at pleasure between the contending parties —amusing the one with speeches and letters against slavery, all very interesting and eloquent to be sure, but serving the other day and night defending the citadel of their abominations.

Do the abolitionists labor so to correct public sentiment that Congress, possessing unlimited discretionary power in the premises, shall be persuaded to refuse Florida admission into the Union as a slave State? Mr. Adams is unceasingly impressing on the public mind that this would be a breach of the national faith.

Do they toil to produce the general conviction that slavery can not long withstand the influence of a fast rising public sentiment against it? Mr. Adams, in his cold response to the warm greetings of the colored population of Cincinnati, assures us that "as long as Africa encourages slavery it is impossible to put an end to it in America. . . . The abolitionists insist on *immediate* emancipation as the most practicable and safest mode for all parties." Mr. Adams dispatches it as a "moral and physical impossibility." . . .

For the logic by which Mr. Adams, after asseverating in almost every variety of form our language can supply that no law can confer or sanction *property in human beings*, has arrived at the conclusion that this barbarian, brutal usurpation ought to be endured at the heart of the Government until the wrong-doers voluntarily relinquish their hold on their victims; that Florida ought to be admitted into the Union with a slave-holding Constitution; . . . that immediate emancipation is a moral and physical impossibility; that slavery must first be abolished among the Mohammedan and pagan chiefs of Africa before it can be possible to put an end to it in Christian America; for such logic, I say, I can entertain but little respect. . . . Mr. Adams owes much of his present popularity —may I not say nearly all—to his connection with the anti-slavery agitation. Abolitionists have contributed more than any other class of persons to swell the tide of his influence. That influence is now active in fortifying against them every practicable point at which they have attacked slavery in this country, and his *quasi*-sympathy with them gives it an independent and unusual force. There is no one who is doing so much—I assume not to say it is so *intended*—to deaden the awakening sensibilities of our countrymen against the private iniquity and public disgrace of slavery, as Mr. Adams.

This arraignment of Mr. Adams was made by a man who had supported him earnestly up to his sudden change of front on the 21st of January, 1839. The surprising declaration of Mr. Adams shook the confidence of many thoughtful abolitionists in the wisdom of voting for candidates nominated by the other political parties. He had been regarded as the "faithful among the faithless." The idea of independent nominations received another strong impulse from Mr. Clay's speech on the ensuing 7th of February. He said:

> It is because these ultra-abolitionists have ceased to employ the instruments of reason and persuasion, have made their cause political, and have appealed to the ballot-box, that I am induced upon this occasion to address you. . . . That is property which the law declares *to be* property. Two hundred years of legislation have sanctioned and sanctified negro slaves as property.

He was answered by that stout old abolition Democrat, Thomas Morris, United States Senator from Ohio:

> I have noticed for some time past that many of the public prints in this city, as well as elsewhere, have been filled with essays against abolitionists for exercising the right of freemen.
>
> Both political parties, however, have courted them in private and denounced them in public, and both have equally deceived them. And who shall dare say that an abolitionist has no right to carry his principles to the ballot-box? . . . Let me then proclaim here from this high arena to the citizens not only of my own State, but to the country, to all sects and parties who are entitled to the right of suffrage: *To the ballot-box!* . . . Fear not the frowns of power. It trembles while it denounces you.

Mr. Clay's strong pro-slavery speech shocked the anti-slavery Whigs and was the chief cause of his losing the party nomination in the following December. Senator Morris's "trumpet call" found the abolition leaders ready to buckle on their armor for the battle. The system of independent party nominations had already been discussed in New York. James G. Birney, Joshua Leavitt, Elizur Wright, H. B. Stanton, and others, had declared in its favor, and an active private correspondence to promote it had already been entered upon with prominent anti-slavery men in different parts of the country. In February Alvan Stewart urged it upon the executive committee of the New York Anti-Slavery Society. About the same time, in a private letter to a prominent abolitionist, Mr. Birney wrote:

> Our political movement heretofore may be compared to the wake of a vessel at sea, never increasing in length no matter how many thousands of miles she may sail. But the present movement shows that we have discovered our mistake ; that there is enough life and spirit among us to attempt its correction ; that we are willing to act as well as to talk, to overshadow with this great question minor ones that have for a long time distracted portions of our friends and alienated them from each other ; and that, instead of resting satisfied with still longer committing our sacred cause to the hands of its enemies or of mere partisans who almost uniformly thus far have either baffled, befooled, or betrayed us, we have confidence enough in it and in ourselves to take the political as well as the other parts of it into our own keeping and under our own management. I look on the independent party movement as proof not only of the greater force and energy of the anti-slavery cause, but of its greater expansion, and I am not more surprised at it than I would be at seeing the young of a noble bird, grown too large for the nest and feeling its strength and courage equal to the attempt, committing itself to the bosom of the air and training its powers in the region of thunders and lightnings and storms.

In this letter Mr. Birney expressed the conviction which was felt by that small number of men who, regarding resistance to the slave power as the paramount political duty of the time, had been as individuals casting their votes as the "balance-of-power" party. Having no separate organization they could not act in concert, and in general anti-slavery meetings they were greatly outnumbered by men who still adhered to the old political parties or who for different reasons would not go to the polls. In every political campaign the rumor was industriously circulated that the anti-slavery men would vote every man for the candidates of his old party. The mutual distrust excited by this prevented the increase of the abolition vote. Its gains since 1836 were scarcely perceptible. The necessity began to be felt strongly of cutting loose from non-voting abolitionists and from those who voted with their former parties. The policy of independent anti-slavery nominations for State officers and congressmen was readily and generally concurred in by voting abolitionists before the month of July, 1839, the responses to a lithographed circular sent out from New York and urging it having been for the most part favorable.

To the nomination of a candidate for the presidency, the expenses incident to a national political campaign and a thorough organization presented difficulties apparently insurmountable. It was therefore not contemplated by any respectable number of persons until after Mr. Clay's pro-slavery speech in February and the resulting alienation from him of anti-slavery Whigs. This apparent defection looked like a permanent one, and occasioned one of equal or larger proportions from the ranks of the Democrats. The propriety of national nominations began to be talked of. With discussion the sectional policy of the Whig and Democratic parties, their unlimited servility to the slave power, endangering the republic by the admission of new slave States and the erection of slavery into the law of the nation, were impressed more deeply upon the minds of leading abolitionists as making imperative the organization of a separate and permanent national party upon the principle, "freedom national, slavery local."

This tendency of opinion was shown in the resolutions passed at a national anti-slavery convention of some five hundred delegates held at Albany, N. Y., July, 31, 1839, to vote for no man who would not avow his immediatism, entreating all abolitionists to vote and to adopt such a course in respect to presidential nominations as seemed best for the cause in each section. In the last proceedings of the convention a resolution was passed looking to independent nominations for President and Vice-President. On the 28th of September following the Monroe County (N. Y.) convention adopted a series of resolutions and an address in favor of nominating a national ticket for abolition suffrages. These were prepared by Myron Holley, who since the 1st of January of that year had taken an active interest in the anti-slavery movement. He was a public man who had earned the gratitude of the people of his State by his devotion to its greatest internal improvement, the Erie Canal. His public spirit, ardent temperament, and moving eloquence designated him as a proper person to advocate a movement which had already been decided upon by Alvan Stewart, Gerrit Smith, William Goodell, Joshua Leavitt, Elizur Wright, and other leading men.

October 23d, at a national anti-slavery convention of four hundred delegates held at Cleveland, Ohio, the subject was discussed on a resolution offered by Myron Holley proposing a nominating committee; but, as it had not been mentioned in the call and nearly all the delegates were from Ohio, the convention being for special objects, it was laid on the table, the friends of independent nominations voting for this disposition of it. November 13th, a State convention of about five hundred delegates met at Warsaw, N. Y., and *unanimously* nominated James G. Birney for President.

This action indicated the strength of the new movement, but it was not that of a national convention. On that ground Mr. Birney declined the nomination. There were two other grounds not mentioned—the inexpediency of nominating before the Whig party had done so and his desire that Judge William Jay should be the anti-slavery standard bearer if it should be necessary to choose one. In the event of the nomination of Henry Clay or any other slave-holder by the Whigs, he thought the Whig abolitionists might be relied on; but that if the Whig party should nominate General Scott, who was known to be opposed to the extension of slavery and admission of Texas as a slave State, and to be willing to approve a bill for the abolition of slavery in the District of Columbia, the Whig abolitionists would support the Whig candidate. This would cause a stampede of Democratic abolitionists to their old party, and the independent ticket would fall to the ground.

In view of this state of things, he would not have regarded it as expedient to nominate an independent ticket if General Scott had been the Whig candidate.

Matters remained therefore at a standstill until after the Whig convention of December 4th at Harrisburg had nominated General William Henry Harrison. It is conceded by Henry Clay's friends that he was dropped because of his unpopularity at the North, caused by his pro-slavery speech in February and his identification with the cause of the United States Bank. There was in the free States a strong repugnance among intelligent men to an alliance through Clay between the great moneyed power of the country and the slave power of the South. Abolitionists especially feared Clay because he was plausible and adroit and would be able not only to procure the admission of Texas to the Union, but the division of the territory into several slave States. General William H. Harrison was nominated without a platform; but he was a Virginian by birth, had antecedents as favoring the re-establishment of slavery in the Indiana Territory while he was Governor there, and had declared the discussion of slavery unconstitutional and that "the schemes of the abolitionists were fraught with horrors upon which an incarnate devil only could look with approbation."

Nothing could be hoped for the anti-slavery cause

from either Harrison or Van Buren, and there was imminent danger that if an independent nomination were not made the anti-slavery voters would disappear altogether. The campaign promised to be one of extraordinary virulence and vigor on both sides. The Democrats were struggling to retain power, but were weakened by the numerous defalcations of office-holders and the "hard times" caused by the bad condition of the banking system.

The Whigs were emboldened by the distress of their adversaries, and were already preparing to win by a campaign not of political principles, but of secret anti-slavery promises made to be broken and of clamor, log-cabins, hard cider, and coon-skins. To the abolitionists it had become a vital necessity to keep together. If they were swallowed up in the pro-slavery parties their cause was lost. Independent nominations were the only means to maintain the identity and perpetuation of the anti-slavery party in politics. January 28, 1840, a State convention, held at Arcade, N. Y., issued a call for a national convention to be held April 1st at Albany, N. Y., for the purpose of deciding whether nominations should be made for President and Vice-President. In spite of a very inclement season delegates from six States were present. After a full discussion the convention decided to make the nominations. In the selection of candidates no one was mentioned for the presidency except James G. Birney. He was unanimously nominated. Thomas Earle, of Philadelphia, was put on the ticket as nominee for the vice-presidency. No name was given to the new party. For several years it was known by sundry names, and in 1844 it was christened "Liberty," which was dropped in 1848 for "Free Soil." Its organization cleared the abolition cause of do nothings, trading politicians, and false friends, brought about concert of action, gave to every man something practical to do, swelled local contributions, deepened interest, put a stop to Northern mobs, and increased discussion a hundred fold. Mere talkers gave way to workers. Under the new impulse the old anti-slavery societies fell into decay and active local clubs sprang up over the country. As an independent party opening a convenient refuge for the dissatisfied it exerted a largely increased influence over the nominations by the Whigs and Democrats. The appearance in politics of such men as Charles Sumner, Henry Wilson, David Wilmot, and Thaddeus Stevens, was due to it. At one time the New York Barnburners, at another the Wilmot Proviso men came to it, and at last, when all reasons for the further existence of the Whig party had ceased, that party dissolved. Its pro-slavery members found a congenial home in the Democratic party, and its freedom-loving members went naturally into the party formed in 1840 to repel the aggressions of the slave power. For many years the bad effects of the "balance-of-power" policy in its embryonic days weakened the general confidence in the stability of the new party, and many looked to see it absorbed into one or the other of the old organizations. New converts were not steadfast; but as time wore on it became clearer that the principles of the new party were the only broadly national ones, the only ones strong enough to curb the slave power and prevent the enslavement of the laboring classes and the overthrow of the wages system and of the republic. When the slave power attempted to seize upon Kansas, the sentiment created by the Free-Soil party was strong enough to resist and conquer it. This conflict caused the reformation of political parties and the absorption of the Whig into the two others. The election of Lincoln, proving to the slave power that it could no longer dictate the national policy, led to secession. The Government took up arms to preserve the Union, and, as one of the means to that end, the abolition of slavery in the States was effected chiefly by military power. Though slavery was the cause of the war, the United States did not take up arms for the purpose of abolishing it. If the controlling power in the slave States had been willing in 1860 to accept restriction of slavery to its existing limits, freedom in the Territories, in all new States, and in the District of Columbia, it is probable that slavery would still exist in the Southern States. The final abolition of it was a political not a moral measure, adopted for national unity and peace, not as benevolence to the negroes; but it became necessary, because the slave power would not submit to the reasonable and constitutional policy declared in the constitution of the American Anti - Slavery Society in 1833, by the Anti-Slavery party in 1840, the Liberty party in 1844, the Free-Soil party in 1848 and 1852, and the Republican party in 1856 and 1860.

Many volumes have been written on the history of the anti-slavery political movement between 1840 and 1862. The plan of this sketch does not embrace that period.

A brief notice of the campaign of 1844 will close the political portion of our task.

The three candidates for the presidency were James K. Polk, Henry Clay, and for the abolitionists, James G. Birney, who had again been unanimously nominated by a national convention. Mr. Polk carried *seven* free, and *eight* slave States and a popular majority of about 39,000; Mr. Clay carried *five* free, and *six* slave States; and 62,300 votes were returned * for Mr. Birney. After the election the claim was made by Horace Greeley that the abolitionists ought all to have voted for Mr. Clay, and if they had

* A few thousand votes more were certainly given; but the election laws were weak, party spirit high, and the judges were all Whigs or Democrats. From many precincts where abolitionists had voted no votes were returned; from Rhode Island, where many abolition votes had been cast, only five were returned.

done so Mr. Clay would have been elected. Mr. Greeley had the manliness to retract this afterward and to attribute Mr. Clay's defeat to the right cause*—his pro-slavery record and his several disingenuous letters on the Texas question; but the claim is still made by some superficial politicians. It might be answered in the same spirit by saying that if all who voted for Clay had voted for Birney the latter would have been elected; and that if the 874,534 Whigs who voted for Fillmore in 1856 had voted for Fremont the latter would have been elected. Such hypotheses are puerile. A better answer is that if the abolitionists had all voted for Clay the strong probability is that, with his tact and personal and official influence, he would have probably secured the admission of Texas as five or more slave States, and thus given the political preponderancy to the slave States. This would have been the logical extension of his record in gaining the admission of Missouri as a slave State and the congressional recognition of slavery in Arkansas. The true and sufficient answer is that the abolitionists were engaged in laying the foundations of a permanent national party and ought not to have abandoned that work for any transient reason whatever. Their action has been fully justified by the subsequent triumph of the Republican party.

The contest of 1844 was one of the most closely contested in the history of presidential elections. As the campaign waxed hot and chances were seen to be about

* In 1860 Mr. Greeley in a letter to Hiram Ketchum, published in the "Tribune," referred to the Whig defeat of 1844 thus: "Unfortunate as you and I thought because Mr. Clay interposed to derange our order of battle and prevent our fighting it on the anti-slavery ground we had chosen." In the "Tribune" of January 7, 1864, Mr. Greeley wrote: "It has long been my decided conviction that but for Mr. Clay's own unfortunate and sadly perverted letters to Alabama, with regard to the annexation of Texas, his election could not have been prevented."

equal, Democrats and Whigs alike appealed to the anti-slavery men for votes. As the election drew near and Clay's chances were seen to be growing less, the appeals of the Whigs became almost frantic. Horace Greeley, then a violent Whig partisan, but who had for years, in the New York "Tribune," adopted a friendly tone toward the abolitionists, and who had thought himself able to deliver their votes to his chief, Mr. Clay, redoubled his entreaties, arguments, and appeals. David Lee Child, editor of the "Anti-Slavery Standard," the Garrisonian organ at New York, threw his influence publicly for Clay. The Whig papers abounded in false statements. Mr. Birney was abused and cajoled by turns. The last resort of the Whigs was the "Garland forgery," concocted by the Whig Central Committee of Michigan. It purported to be a letter from James G. Birney to one Garland, a resident of his legislative district in Michigan, soliciting the Democratic nomination for the Legislature, and declaring his democracy and his intention to defeat Henry Clay. It purported to be duly sworn to and to be printed on an extra of the "Oakland Gazette." This infamous document was printed at New York by the Whigs in immense quantities, and sent in packages to active Whigs in every county in the Northern States, with instructions not to circulate it until after the 1st of November. In western New York it was withheld until the 3d, on which day it was known that Mr. Birney, who had been in the State for about a month, expected to leave Buffalo in a steamboat for Detroit. Owing to the accidental detention of the boat, he did not leave on that day, and a copy of the forgery fell into his hands. As far as possible he contradicted it; but it was too late to expose the political crime fully. In those days railroads and telegraph lines were few. The "National Intelligencer," "Portland Advertiser," and "Ohio State Journal" were among the papers that published this forgery, and the Whig State Committee of Indiana issued a public address containing it; but the original contrivers of the forgery were doubtless at New York. The probable knowledge by Horace Greeley of this electioneering trick and the evasiveness of his disclaimer put an end to the friendly relations between him and Mr. Birney. Mr. Greeley gave orders that Mr. Birney's name should not be mentioned in the "Tribune" thereafter,* and carefully avoided all mention of it in his large work on the history of the anti-slavery conflict, except in the election returns. His malice ended only with Mr. Birney's death. The effect of the "Garland forgery" probably was to diminish Mr. Birney's vote at least half. In Ohio, where it was not exposed except in one or two counties of the northeastern part of the State, Mr. Birney lost several thousand votes, most of which went to Mr. Clay. The Whigs carried the State by a plurality of more than six thousand. In New York the Whigs gained largely, cutting down to 15,812 the Liberty party vote of 16,275 cast in 1843 at the State election. In spite of the forgery the Liberty party polled 62,263 votes in all the States.

This campaign was the last in Mr. Birney's public career; it left the party well organized, harmonious, hopeful, and nearly nine hundred per cent stronger than in 1840. What it might have accomplished under his wise and able leadership, if his health had been spared, how many false moves and schisms it would have avoided, can only be conjectured. In the summer of 1845 he was disabled by an accident. From that time to his death he was an invalid. He had given twelve years of his life to save the country of his love from slavery, disunion, and

* This is stated on the authority of Mr. Robert Carter, then one of the sub-editors of the "Tribune."

civil war. Becoming aware in 1833 of the dreams of political ascendency in the Union or of secession and a Southern empire cherished by the leaders of the slave-power, he had devoted himself to the task of transforming Kentucky and Virginia into free States. Finding it too late to accomplish this or to maintain a foothold in his native State, and that liberty in the Northern States was menaced, he addressed himself to the task of arousing the country to a sense of its danger. After the freedom of mails and of the press was made sure, he strove to rally the North against the extension of slavery. The weakness shown by Northern Congressmen in the admission of Arkansas, in 1836, was to him ominous of further disasters in the probable admission of Florida and Texas as slave States. With each added slave State, he knew that the aggressiveness of the slave power would be increased and the peaceable solution of the slavery question made more improbable. He did not doubt that slavery would go down, if the Union were dissolved; but he knew it would go down in blood. For his country, he feared the horrors of civil war. Hence the intensity of his reprobation of John Quincy Adams for refusing to vote against the admission of Florida as a slave State and for the abolition of slavery in the District of Columbia. Such weakness he regarded as contributing to the chances of civil war—it was unstatesmanlike and unpatriotic. Mr. Birney knew Southern men, their aspirations, plans, and power, better than any other leading abolitionist. He never depreciated them. If he had succeeded in the movement to exclude Florida and Texas as slave States, and to stamp freedom upon the national territory and national policy, the civil war, with its horrors, might have been averted. The last years of his life were saddened by the thought that slavery would not be peaceably abolished.

CHAPTER XXX.

TRAITS OF CHARACTER.

THE facts already narrated illustrate some of the qualities of James G. Birney. They do not show the whole man. From the date of his first marriage to the death of his wife in 1839, he lived with her in harmony and love. His manner to her was always expressive of respect and affection. The children were taught to honor and obey her. There was no divided authority. Her orders were never interfered with. She was his best friend, aiding him with her counsel and encouraging him with her sympathy. In his moods of depression—for he was human and subject to discouragement—she would sit by him, clasping his hands in hers, and read to him softly from the Psalms of David or the promises of Scripture. This chased away the evil spirit. How much of his strength and courage he owed to her brave heart the world can never know.

In early manhood he spent much of his time with his children. He joined them in their boyish sports, taught them many games of manly exercise, and entered heartily into their glee. His uncommon bodily activity made him enjoy running, jumping, and the games at ball then in vogue. He showed them how to ride and to row, to make bows and arrows, snares and traps, to handle the shot-gun, and to hunt game. A broad veranda in the rear of his dwelling was used for play in rainy weather, being furnished with swings and trapezes, battledores and shuttlecocks. He was fond of music and played the flute. In every innocent way, home was made attractive to the children.

After he began his career against slavery, his cheerful religious faith gradually deepened into Puritan gravity, the joyous companion gave way to the earnest man, and the children pursued their sports without his guidance. But to them he was always the object of love and veneration. His wishes were their law, the penalty of rare violation being a look varying from grave to severe. The art of command was to him a natural faculty. As he grew older and years of conflict began to tell on him, he was less demonstrative of affection, but the undercurrent ran always deep and strong. To his only surviving daughter,* he gave his whole heart. When she was ten years old, the writer, passing through Detroit, where she was at boarding-school, found her on the eve of an unexpected holiday and took her with him to Bay City. She was not expected. We reached our father's house after dark, and seeing a light in the study, tapped at the door. Florence entered first. When her father saw her, he clasped her to his breast and sobbed as if his heart would break with joy. It was the only time the writer ever saw him lose utterly his self-control. His love for the motherless little girl was one of the deep passions of his strong nature.

In the spring of 1841, he married Miss Fitzhugh, the sister of Mrs. Gerrit Smith, and reassembled his younger children under his own roof-tree. This marriage, also, was a happy one. The lady had a large property. This was secured by Mr. Birney, against her expressed wishes, to her separate use and control; and he ever after refrained from using any part of it, or doing anything in

* Now Mrs. Florence B. Jennison, of Bay City, Michigan.

regard to it, except advising as to investments and management.

His own fortune, largely increased by judicious investments after leaving Kentucky, was mostly spent in his public career. When he returned from England in November, 1840, he found his means so much reduced that it was necessary for him to replenish. He effected this by purchasing a large quantity of land on the Saginaw River, Michigan. Part of it is now within the limits of the flourishing Bay City. The rise in value of these lands placed him in comfortable circumstances and enabled him to convey, during his life, a moderate property to each of his children, reserving enough for his own ample support. He thought this much better than devising it to them by will. In his business arrangements, he was exact. His papers were drawn with legal skill, and his bargains were made so clearly that differences were avoided. So far as the writer knows, Mr. Birney was never party to a civil suit, either as plaintiff or defendant. Between 1840 and 1845 he sold in small parcels, partly for cash and partly on time, some fifteen thousand acres of land in western Ohio and eastern Indiana. Many of the purchasers defaulted on the deferred payments, and some had lost their bonds for title; but he had duplicates of the papers, and the whole business was adjusted without complaint on the part of the debtors. He was a generous creditor.

Very early in life he adopted the maxim, "Pay as you go." He had no store accounts, no small debts, except the grocer's bill, which was paid weekly or monthly. He gave no notes, except on large transactions, and these were met punctually. So were the wages of employés.

We copy from the "Life of Birney," published in 1844, the following:

In August, 1839, Mr. Birney's father closed his earthly career. A father and a son—an only son—seemed to have regarded each other with a true and tender love. The great enterprise to which the latter was devoted and which could not be endured in Kentucky had for a long time withdrawn them from each other's presence. Just before his father's death, Mr. Birney visited him and was received by him, as well as by other friends, with all cordiality. He was intent on making such arrangements as would bring his son into the bosom of his old age, where he might feel the soothing and sustaining influence of his many virtues. But all such designs, however warmly cherished, death defeated. In the division of his father's estate, his slaves—twenty-in number—were, at Mr. Birney's request, all set off to him; and set off to him that to their benefit he might apply the principles by which he was controlled. Accordingly, he at once restored to them the freedom of which they had been robbed. The deed through which their emancipation was effected—a substantial and ever enduring monument of his philanthropy, a decisive and emphatic proof of his wisdom and integrity—can not be read without the most grateful emotion and the most heathful impressions. Here it is :

KNOW ALL MEN BY THESE PRESENTS,

That, I, James G. Birney, late of Kentucky, but now having my residence in the city of New York, believing that slave-holding is inconsistent with natural justice, with the precepts and spirit of the Christian religion, and with the Declaration of American Independence, and wishing to testify in favor of them all, do hereby emancipate, and forever set free, the following named slaves which have come into my possession as one of the heirs of my father, the late James Birney, of Jefferson County, Kentucky, they being all the slaves held by said James Birney, deceased, at the time of his death.

Then follow their names and descriptions, and the deed concludes:

In testimony of the above, I have hereunto set my name and affixed my seal this third day of September, in the year of our Lord one thousand eight hundred and thirty-nine.

[SEAL.] JAMES G. BIRNEY.

The only condition on which he could effect this arrangement with his co-heir was that twenty thousand dollars should be set off against the value of the slaves. This was much in excess of their value in the market. He knew them all well and that they expected freedom for such of them as should be inherited by him, and he was unwilling to abandon any of them to the chances of slavery. He did not leave Kentucky before he had procured employment and made a moderate pecuniary provision for them all, and in after years he ever took a kindly interest in their welfare.

In manner, language, and action he was always natural. There was no approach to affectation or eccentricity. He had the refinement which comes from usage in society, extensive knowledge, absence of selfishness, regard for the rights of others, and a strong feeling of piety. He had no egotism. Without appearing to avoid it he never spoke of himself except when necessary. In all his public life he never compared himself with his fellow-workers in the anti-slavery cause. It is true that, in a report of remarks made in 1837 by Mr. Walker at an anti-slavery convention in Boston, Mr. Birney is represented as having said that his "trumpet would never have roused the country, Garrison alone could do it." Some statement of the kind may have been made by Mr. Walker or it may have been due to the zeal and imagination of the secretary, Mr. Garrison, or the person who condensed his long speech into a few lines. Mr. Walker's object was to obtain aid and relief for the "Liberator," which was then in a moribund condition, and Mr. Birney's indorsement was a valuable one. Mr. Walker must have spoken from hearsay among the friends of Mr. Garrison, with whom *trumpet* and *trumpet call* were pet phrases. He gave neither time nor place nor occasion of the imputed remark, and Mr. Birney was in the West when Mr. Walker made his speech.

No one who knew Mr. Birney would believe that he ever spoke of his "trumpet" or compared himself with any other worker in the abolition cause. His modesty and dignity both forbade it.

That he ever approved the peculiar methods of Mr. Garrison is untrue. In 1833, in a published essay, he had applied the term "rhapsodies" to Mr. Garrison's "Thoughts" (see page 126). In 1835, in a speech at Boston, he had deprecated the use of personalities by anti-slavery writers, and the implied estimate of Mr. Garrison was never modified in any of his letters, reports, speeches, or pamphlets. If he had changed his opinion he was magnanimous enough to say so, and there were numerous occasions when he might have done so publicly; but his kindness of heart never led him to say or write what he did not believe.

He took pleasure in speaking well of prominent anti-slavery men and of their writings and labors. There was no trace of jealousy in his nature. He was appreciative of the talents of Bailey, Chase, Sumner, the Tappans, Weld, Stanton, Phelps, Alvan Stewart, Samuel Lewis, Goodell, and others. The fiery poetry of Whittier awakened all his enthusiasm, and the pathetic tenderness of Mrs. Stowe touched his sensibilities. In regard to Mr. Garrison, however, he was silent. The only departure from this course remembered by the writer was in his answer to an urgent demand by a friend for his opinion. It was, in effect, that Mr. Garrison was sincere in his convictions.

He cultivated social relations with anti-slavery leaders. For them he kept open house after the fashion of old Kentucky hospitality. Nearly all of them were his guests during his residence in New York. Among the few exceptions Mr. Garrison must be numbered.

A remarkable peculiarity in Mr. Birney's character

was his freedom from censoriousness. On religious principle he judged not. In his family he discountenanced disparaging remarks about acquaintances. Gossip was offensive to him. Thinking evil, he was wont to say, grows on us by speaking of it. Avoid both.*

Mr. Birney had no quarrels with his coadjutors. He had no slights to resent, no controversies to fight out, no personal grievances to avenge. He was true to his friends and they were true to him. To the enemies of his cause he was urbane and just. In all his relations with his fellow-men he well sustained "the grand old name of gentleman."

He had no personal vanity. Though he kept himself in vigorous physical condition and was always faultless in his dress, he was shy of daguerreotypers, photographers, portrait painters, and sculptors. The only two engravings of him were both made without his knowledge or consent —the first from a replica surreptitiously made by the artist of a portrait,† for which he sat at the request of a very dear friend, a wealthy merchant of Cincinnati, who wanted it for his parlor, and the second from a daguerreotype taken for a friend in New York. While he esteemed highly the appreciation of good men he was not accessible to flattery, and his look of amused surprise was enough to arrest at once the gushing language of a sycophant. In the days of his celebrity he received many poems of praise, printed and written, from enthusiastic admirers; but he

* Garrison's sons (1 G., page 431) charge Mr. Birney with having been active in "poisoning the English mind against Mr. Garrison" in 1840. No proof is given, and the charge is absurd. Garrison had discredited himself in England by refusing to sit in the World's Convention because it declined to admit women as members and by taking at its daily meetings a conspicuous position in the gallery with the rejected women around him. This attitudinizing for notoriety was not pleasing to the English.

† See frontispiece.

published none of them and preserved none except Whittier's. He used to say that a reformer was like an orator, unable to do his best work unless he was wholly unconscious of the "little me." He assumed no honors not his due and did not permit them to be thrust upon him. On one occasion he entered the World's Convention while O'Connell was speaking. The Irish orator, who had conceived a high regard for him, welcomed him with, "I see my friend Judge Birney coming in." The answer came promptly, "I am not a judge." "You well deserve to be one," replied O'Connell amid the cheers of the audience.

Mr. Birney was one of the vice-presidents of the World's Convention of 1840, having been unanimously designated for that honor by the American delegates. His reputation as an honorable presiding officer had been already established. He had in rare degree that combination of dignity, firmness, courtesy, promptitude of decision, tact, and knowledge of parliamentary rules which enables a man to guide the proceedings of large deliberative bodies, a combination which few speakers of the American House of Representatives, except Henry Clay and James Gillespie Blaine, have possessed. The last act of his public life was to preside over the Southern and Western Liberty Convention, held at Cincinnati, June 11th and 12th, 1845. Two thousand delegates were present and as many more spectators. A stormy discussion was anticipated over the proposed "Address to the People of the United States." This important paper had been prepared mainly by the Hon. S. P. Chase, and had been submitted by him to the executive committee of the Ohio Liberty party. Several members of that committee, the writer included, had strongly disapproved certain passages which they thought would be interpreted as overtures to the Democratic party for coalition. Mr. Chase was well known to favor such a movement. Under the counsel of

Mr. Birney, who had read Mr. Chase's paper, a motion was passed to appoint a committee to prepare an address to the people. That body promptly expurgated Mr. Chase's production and reported it without mention of the omitted passages. It was adopted by acclamation. As published it is one of the best political essays of the period.*

The convention, under the wise guidance of Mr. Birney, was a gigantic and harmonious popular demonstration. Arthur Tappan was accustomed to say of Mr. Birney that he was the best presiding officer in the country for large conventions.

An amusing account, somewhat colored by prejudices contracted by the author in her after life, is given of him by Mrs. Elizabeth Cady Stanton, the leader of the woman's suffrage movement, in her recently published "Reminiscences." The reader should bear in mind that Henry B. Stanton was one of Mr. Birney's most intimate friends, that the two were on their way to a convention composed chiefly of grave Englishmen, and that the young wife was a spirited American girl, whose gay and frolicsome humor was not restrained by conventionalities. She has forgotten to put into her "Reminiscences" the fact that on a public occasion she had pinned papers to her husband's coat and joined in the laugh at his expense. Imagine her doing such a thing at the World's Convention! She certainly "needed considerable toning down before reaching England." Mr. Birney enjoyed her playful badinage very much, and ever after spoke of her with high appreciation of her intellect and kind regard for her personally. He gave her credit, too, for being the pink of propriety while in England. Here is what Mrs. Stanton says:

---

* See edition of 1867, published by Bancroft & Co., Philadelphia.

James G. Birney, the anti-slavery nominee for the presidency, joined us in New York, and was a fellow-passenger on the Montreal for England. He and my husband were alike delegates to the World Anti-Slavery Convention, and alike interested themselves in my anti-slavery education. They gave me books to read, and as we paced the deck day by day it was the chief theme of our conversation.

Mr. Birney was a polished gentleman of the old school, and excessively proper and punctilious in manner and conversation. I soon perceived that he thought I needed considerable toning down before reaching England. I was quick to see and understand that his criticisms of others in a general way, and the drift of his discourses on manners and conversation had a nearer application than he intended I should discover, though he hoped I would profit by them. I was always grateful to any one who took an interest in my improvement, so I laughingly told him one day that he need not make his criticisms any longer in that roundabout way, but take me squarely in hand and polish me up as speedily as possible before the end of the voyage. Sitting in the saloon at night, after a game of chess, in which perchance I had been the victor, I felt complacent, and would sometimes say :

"Well, what have I done or said to-day open to criticism?"

So, in the most gracious manner, he replied, on one occasion :

"You went to mast-head in a chair, which I think very unladylike ; still worse, you rolled up a bread-ball at dinner and hit Captain Montgomery square on the nose. I heard you call your husband 'Henry' in the presence of strangers, which is not permissible in polite society. You should always say 'Mr. Stanton.' You have taken three moves back in this game."

"Bless me," I replied, "what a catalogue in one day! I fear my mentor will despair of my ultimate perfection."

"I should have more hope," he replied, "if you seemed to feel my rebukes more deeply, but you evidently think them of too little consequence to be much disturbed over them." . . .

As the voyage lasted eighteen days—for we were in an old-fashioned sailing-vessel—we had time to make some improvement, or at least to consider all friendly suggestions. However, as we traveled with Mr. Birney for nine months in England,

Scotland, and France, and had the advantage of his strict ideas of etiquette at every turn, we really were improved in many minor points of manner we had considered unimportant. Mr. Birney often quoted Chesterfield's remarks. Being asked the secret of success in life, he replied : "It depends, more than any one thing, on manner, manner, manner." Hence I conjure all my young readers to cultivate polite affable manners. . . .

When within sight of the distant shore a pilot-boat came along and offered to take any one ashore in six hours. I was so delighted at the thought of seeing land that after much persuasion Mr. Stanton and Mr. Birney consented to go. Accordingly we were lowered into a boat in an arm-chair, with a luncheon consisting of cold chicken, a bottle of wine, and a few pickles. Thus provisioned, we started with just wind enough for that light craft in the direction we were going ; but instead of six hours we were all day, and as the twilight deepened and the last breeze died away the pilot said : "We are now only two miles from shore, but the only way you can reach there to-night is by a row-boat."

As we had no provisions left and nowhere to sleep, we were glad to avail ourselves of the row-boat. It was a bright moonlight night, the air balmy, the waters smooth, and with two good, stout oarsmen we glided swiftly along. As Mr. Birney made the last descent and seated himself, doubtful as to our ever reaching the shore, turning to me, he said, "The woman tempted me and I did leave the good ship." However, we did reach the shore at midnight and landed at Torquay, one of the loveliest spots in that country, and our journey to Exeter the next day lay through the most beautiful scenery in England.

While in England Mr. Birney visited different parts of the kingdom and addressed audiences under the auspices of the British and Foreign Anti-Slavery Society. In answer to a claim made in behalf of the American churches that their influence was thrown against slavery, he published in a London daily paper authentic evidence of pro-slavery acts of some of the leading churches. It is believed that no error of diminution, exaggeration, or misstatement was ever attributed to this document. He was careful to give due credit to several sects for their anti-slavery action. In conclusion he asked the reader to—

bear in mind that the foregoing presents but one side of the anti-slavery cause in the several churches whose proceedings have been considered, and that in them all there are abolitionists earnestly laboring to purify them from the defilements of slavery and that they have strong encouragement to proceed. . . . Lastly, we take pleasure in assuring him that there are *considerable portions of the Methodist, Baptist, and Presbyterian Churches*, as well as the entire membership of some of the smaller religious bodies in America, that maintain a commendable testimony against slavery and its abominations.

This is the language of a friend of the Church, anxious for purity first, then peace. The article made a sensation. It was published in pamphlet-form in London, and was subsequently republished in several editions in this country.

When Parker Pillsbury, Garrison, S. S. Foster, and others, made their onslaught on the Church itself, they sought to cover themselves under the authority of Mr. Birney and identify him with their cause. They made some impression on the public mind by quoting the title which had been given to the pamphlet, "The American Churches the Bulwarks of American Slavery." This quotation was misleading. Mr. Birney had no sympathy with Mr. Pillsbury and his associates. Up to 1840 it was probably true that ninety-nine abolitionists out of a hundred were church-members and that the clergy as a body contained more abolitionists than any other class in proportion to their number. This was recognized fully by Mr. Birney.

After he left England, the executive committee of the British and Foreign Anti-Slavery Society passed the following resolution:

That this committee are deeply sensible of the services rendered to the anti-slavery cause by their esteemed friend and coadjutor James Gillespie Birney, Esq., while in this country, in a course of laborious efforts, in which his accurate and extensive information, his wise and judicious counsels, and his power of calm and convincing statement, have become eminently conspicuous.

He shared the hospitalities of many of the eminent men of England and became widely known. Two years afterward President Kellogg, of Illinois, traveled through England. On his return he described as follows the impression left there by Mr. Birney:

It was truly refreshing to me while I was in Great Britain, amid the many complaints against my countrymen to which I was obliged to listen, to hear our excellent friend James G. Birney so frequently spoken of and always in terms of unqualified approbation and respect. The mention of his name in those circles in which he was known, and they were both numerous and extensive, invariably imparted pleasure, and many were the inquiries which were made in respect to his welfare. I could not but observe that intelligent men both in England and Scotland very highly appreciated him for that trait in his character which I have always from my first acquaintance with Mr. Birney regarded as exhibited by him in a remarkable degree. You will doubtless understand me as referring to his candor. He never deals in exaggeration or sophistry. In his public addresses and discussions, which were numerous in that country as well as in his private conversations, by the sobriety of his own views, by the fairness and fullness with which he stated the positions and arguments of his opponents, and by the manliness with which he met and refuted them, he ever impressed his auditors with a conviction of the soundness of his sentiments and of the perfect reliance which might be placed upon his statements. The visits of such men to foreign lands are an honor to our country, and leave behind them a savor which is grateful to an American citizen.

The quality of character which made such a lasting impression on the English was recognized by his own countrymen. The Rev. Beriah Green, D. D., writing of him in 1844, testified as follows:

> He had access to great numbers of his fellow-citizens, upon whom he was enabled to urge the claims of the enslaved. The influence he exerted was as benign as it was powerful. His intelligence, truthfulness, and candor, his magnanimity and fidelity, all who had the privilege of an acquaintance with him were not a little struck with. They were admitted to be noteworthy traits of his character. He was generally listened to with respectful attention. If his doctrines were not subscribed to his character was admired. We well remember that an old lawyer from New England, after a discussion with him on points on which they were at variance, exclaimed, "He is the most candid man I ever saw!" On those who were often in his presence and enjoyed his confidence his words and deeds made the impression of great wisdom. They looked up to him for counsel. Wherever he applied his hand they expected well-advised plans and valuable results.

In familiar conversation he was a sympathetic listener and good talker. A delicate humor, inherited it may be from his Irish ancestors, a gentle irony pointing a repartee or suggesting an argument, a human interest in all subjects, and entire freedom from biting sarcasm, scandal, and censoriousness made him a delightful companion. He was not a man of one idea. Intelligent women liked to talk with him. Sometimes he was epigrammatic, condensing much wisdom in a few words. To one of his sons he said:

> When you are conscious that it will gratify you to say something to the discredit of another don't say it.

To a man who asked him why he did not go South to fight slavery, he answered:

> If a man were hired to kill a den of venomous snakes it would show that he was insane if he jumped into the den.

His opinion of good story-tellers was thus expressed:

One who can keep the whole company in a roar while the muscles of his own face are entirely under his control ought not to be sought as a friend. He will be found wanting in heart.

His views on the civil service were in advance of his times:

Rotation in office is radically unsound as a dogma. Offices are created for the public good, not for the incumbents.

He admired Daniel O'Connell as a man, but thought he failed because he had made the mistake of relying on the Roman Catholic Church as his main auxiliary. Said he:

O'Connell has had his heels tripped up by the politicians, Peel, and the Pope, and he must submit to it.

He criticised Daniel Webster for eulogizing the deceased General Jackson, and thought it inconsistent with Webster's declaration in 1830 that "Jackson always looked as if he were anxious to escape from the society of gentlemen," and also with Webster's published opinions respecting Jackson's Administration.

The following illustrates his shrewdness of observation:

An eccentric man, one affectedly so, is pleased with your notice of his peculiarities. One who is really so laments them and is mortified when they are pointed out to him, looking on them, as they truly are, as evidences of a want of good sense.

One or two other sayings of his must close our selection:

Working for the benefit of the human race is a surer path to true fame than high office is. Jesus Christ is better known than Pontius Pilate. . . . *Moral suasion*, as it is called, is about as ineffectual and ridiculous as any plan can be for putting down slavery. It makes its advocates appear as if they were very ignorant of men, of large affairs, or of the just powers of government. It is only fit for visionaries. . . . The Whig party in Congress gives what men and money Mr. Polk calls for to carry on with Mexico a war which they say is unconstitutional. This is a mistake. Mr. Polk will be as sure to conquer Mexico and compel her to give a large portion of her territory to us as a remuneration for our expenses as might prevails over right; and in final success the nation will condone his faults.

In endeavoring to present the leading traits of one so dear we have deferred to the prejudices of general readers against biographies written under the bias of filial affection and relied upon facts and the representations of friends who knew him. We close this part of our subject with an extract from page 116 of the "Life of Birney," written by Beriah Green, President of Oneida Institute, New York:

> An affectionate regard for the Divine authority cherished in a manly soul is the root of every human virtue. It is the secret of sound character. Wisdom, strength, and beauty—these are the natural fruits. Where this is, there you may find veracity, simplicity, modesty, candor, united with courage, decision, fidelity; there you may find disinterestedness, generosity, and magnanimity. And we demand of those who are best acquainted with him, for which of these qualities is not James G. Birney remarkable?

CHAPTER XXXI.

TWELVE YEARS AN INVALID—CONCLUSION.

In August, 1845, on the invitation of my father, I spent a few weeks with him at his home on the Saginaw River, Michigan. He was in fine health and spirits, and joined me in the sports of hunting and fishing. The rice grass on the farther side of the river was a favorite feeding-ground for ducks. Through this we worked our way in a light canoe, getting shots as the birds rose into the air. He was generally successful in dropping them just as they turned to a horizontal flight from an upward movement to clear the tall grass. When we had bagged game enough for next day's dinner he would take the paddle and speed the frail vessel homeward. At other times he would troll for large fish. In this sport a line from fifty to a hundred feet long, with a strong triple hook covered with bits of red and white flannel, is trailed behind the canoe. To this the simple muskallonge rises, seizing the deceptive bait and rushing away with it. A pull upon the line, strong enough if it were made at right angles to upset the unstable bark, shows the game is hooked. Then the battle begins. Skill and judgment are on one side, desperation and strength on the other. The man "plays" out his line and avoids all direct contests; the great fish dashes to the bottom of the river and exhausts its strength in vain efforts to free itself by flight from the barbed torment in its mouth. Then it is brought to the surface by a steady pull on the line. As it nears the canoe, its glaring eyes and great wide open red mouth garnished with double rows of sharp teeth seen amid the foam made by the flurries of its tail give it the aspect of a monster. A scoop net passed adroitly under it aids in getting it into the canoe, where it is quickly dispatched with a hatchet. Into this sport my father entered with great zest. He generally took the line while I kept the canoe in proper position, no easy task. The capture of one or two fish ended the excursion for the day. He took no more than enough for the supply of his own family. If there was a surplus it was sent to some neighbor.

Part of each day was devoted to the cultivation of the garden and the labor of burning the brush and logs from a lot near the house. His tastes, expertness, and strength made these employments pleasant to him. His evenings were generally spent in his library, and were given to correspondence, study, and conversation.

A favorite amusement of his was riding on horseback. He owned a pair of jet-black Canadian ponies. They were swift and moved well under the saddle. Mounted on these we galloped over the prairies, enjoying the bracing air of early morning or the breezes of the evening. On our last ride we were moving rapidly, side by side. My father, with extended hand, was pointing out to me a vessel in the distant horizon making her way under full sail when a prairie chicken rose with a whirr from under the feet of his pony. The animal shied, springing to one side, and my father was thrown heavily to the ground. I dismounted and ran to him. He was already on his feet. To my inquiries he answered, "It was a bad jolt, my son, but no bones are broken." He held my bridle while I caught his pony. Declining my assistance he remounted. The place of the accident was about two miles from home. We rode back at an easy gallop, my father making no complaint.

Two hours later he had a stroke of nervous paralysis. This was the beginning of the end. For the rest of his life, twelve years and three months, he was an invalid. Partial recoveries alternated with relapses. All that medical science could do for him was done. The best specialists in nervous diseases were consulted but were unable to effect more than partial and intermittent relief. While for several years his general health was apparently unimpaired and his physical strength little diminished, he was subject at long and irregular intervals to recurrences of paralysis or to sudden and painful affections of the digestive organs. These were so violent that for years before his death he predicted one of them would prove fatal, and his prediction proved true. Another effect of the disease was to deprive him of the power of articulate speech. His tongue refused its office. The man whose enunciation had been so distinct that his every word could be heard by thousands was unable in the more severe states of his complaint to make himself intelligible to his wife and children, or in his best condition to any except to them and very intimate friends. His only medium, except gesture, of communication with others was in writing. Even this was impracticable much of the time owing to the tremulousness of his hand, which he was unable to hold steady except by grasping the wrist with his left hand. This physical difficulty was greater or less according to the state of his nerves. In their best condition writing was for him a slow and laborious process, and his penmanship lacked the firm lines of former days; in their worst he could scarcely write his name legibly.

The news of his disability brought several of his old personal friends and some of his political supporters to his bedside. The mingled pleasure and pain to him of these visits may be imagined by the reader. He grasped each one by the hand and looked his grateful appreciation, but his answers to their kind speeches were conveyed by a deprecatory wave of the hand or a look toward one of the family which was a request to speak for him. Gerrit Smith, who was a beloved friend, had not until his visit comprehended the extent of the calamity and gave way to his feelings. My father was much moved, but by a simple gesture expressed his resignation to the Divine will.

Before the winter of 1845 he had visited the Eastern cities for medical advice, and became convinced that he would never be able to speak again in public and probably never to articulate well enough for the purposes of conversation. From that time by all practicable means he made known to the members of the Anti-Slavery political party that he had absolutely and permanently withdrawn from public life, and of his friends he made the special request to prevent the offering or passage by anti-slavery conventions of resolutions of sympathy with him. He gave this matter in charge to me for Ohio, and it was not without difficulty that Salmon P. Chase, Samuel Lewis, and other leaders, were persuaded to comply with his request. From the time of his paralysis to his decease he never made or attempted to make a speech in public or attended or wrote a letter to any anti-slavery meeting or convention or signed his name to any publication of a nature to influence political action. Though often urgently requested to be present or to give his counsel in writing, he thought it best not to interferfere with the men who were actively engaged in the cause.* The clear-

---

* In the index to Garrison's "Life" by his sons, under the name of James G. Birney, there are the following entries: "Secedes from Liberty party." The passage referred to (vol. iii, p. 211) reads thus:

"In the second week in June [1847] a fourth party had gone out from it [the Liberty party], forming a Liberty League at Macedon Lock, N. Y., under the auspices of James G. Birney."

The next index entry is "neglected as nomince," with reference to a passage on page 215 of the same volume:

ness and vigor of his mind did not perceptibly diminish. In his writing intervals he jotted down his thoughts in a

---

"Birney's claims, too, whether for perpetual nomination or for incense or (now that he was physically disabled) for sympathy, were wholly ignored by the convention (at Buffalo, January, 1847). All this furnished food for conversation between Wright and Garrison as they journeyed eastward."

The next index entry is "favors colonization," vol. iii, p. 362, where it is charged that Mr. Birney in 1852 "scandalized his old associates by counseling expatriation. . . . Mr. Garrison felt it incumbent on him to make a set speech against colonization."

The charges made and insinuated in the above extracts are that James G. Birney made claims upon the Buffalo Convention for nomination, incense, or sympathy; that, not getting what he wanted, he seceded from the Liberty party and aided in the establishment of another party; and that he recanted his opposition to the Colonization Society as a proposed remedy for slavery. It is hardly necessary to state that the above scandals, published twenty-two years after the death of James G. Birney, have no foundation in fact. There were in the Buffalo Convention at least a hundred of his warm friends, every one of whom knew that he had permanently withdrawn from public life and desired that his name should not be mentioned in that or any other convention. That he was at Macedon Lock or took any part in the formation of a fourth party or seceded from the Liberty party is untrue. With the exception of Martin Van Buren, in whose sincerity he lacked confidence, he voted the Free Soil and Republican tickets, State and national, as long as he lived. The charge touching colonization is a violent misrepresentation of a letter written by him in answer to some colored men who wrote to ask his advice as to their emigration to some other country. He thought that, in view of the bitter prejudice in the United States against the blacks, each one of them should act in that matter as he might think best for the interest of his family. Not one word was said in favor of the Colonization Society or of colonization as a remedy for slavery. (See *ante*, p. 268.)

If it were not plain from the context that these scandals emanated from William Lloyd Garrison, their insidious malice and blundering inaccuracy would indicate him as the author. Much of his life was spent in misrepresenting the acts and blackening the character of his coadjutors. He wronged Benjamin Lundy so deeply that an eager offer to write his biography was indignantly rejected by Lundy's relatives. His partner in the "Liberator" for eight or nine years was Isaac Knapp;

blank-book or wrote short articles, always anonymous, for leading newspapers. In 1850 he managed to write, a few

---

but in a private letter in 1842 to a lady in London he brands Knapp as a gambler and drunkard. (G., iii, p. 41.) Knapp had charged him with "selfish and deceptive conduct." (G., iii, p. 38.) He professed warm friendship for N. P. Rogers, but aided in depriving him of his newspaper and broke his heart. (G., iii, p. 127.) He professed friendship for Frederick Douglass, but abused him without stint when Douglass refused to follow him in his secession movement in 1844. He spoke harshly of the sisters Grimké and provoked Sarah's retort:

"His spirit of intolerance toward those who did not draw in his traces and his adulation of those who surrendered themselves to his guidance have always been exceedingly repulsive to me." ("The Sisters Grimké," p. 220.)

Among those whom he libeled in the "Liberator" were Dr. William E. Channing, Henry B. Stanton, Elizur Wright, Amos A. Phelps, Henry Ward Beecher, Lewis Tappan, and Arthur Tappan. These were but a few of the whole number. The jealousy with which he looked upon the unprecedented success and influence of "Uncle Tom's Cabin" is reflected in his biography. (G., iii, p. 364.) Of such a man the poet Churchill drew the picture when he wrote:

"With that malignant envy which turns pale
And sickens even if a friend prevail,
Which merit and success pursues with hate,
And damns the worth it can not imitate."

Mr. Garrison had a peculiarity which his sons pass over with the following euphemism:

"As he had a very poor memory for past events even in his own experience, he seldom indulged in reminiscence." (G., iv, p. 334.)

Other writers have not been so lenient. Rev. Leonard G. Bacon, in a review of his "Thoughts," charged him with garbling and false statements; Rev. R. R. Gurley with being indebted "to his imagination for his fact" (*ante*, p. 126); and between him and Frederick Douglass there was an issue of veracity (G., iii, p. 211). It would have been much better for Mr. Garrison's reputation if he had never "indulged in reminiscence," for he was one of those unfortunate individuals in whose memory facts have no fixity of outline; especially should he have avoided indulging in it in relation to James G. Birney, toward whom he bore a deadly hatred which grew stronger with years, and which he appears to have transmitted in all its venom to his descendants.

sentences at a time, his "Examination of the Decision of the United States Supreme Court in the Case of Strader et al. *vs.* Graham." This was legibly copied and published in pamphlet-form with his name on the title-page. It is the argument of an able lawyer. The labor of its preparation aggravated his malady, and he finally abandoned a long cherished scheme of writing a historical work on slavery in the United States.

His interest in the anti-slavery struggle was not abated. He followed the proceedings in Congress and the course of public men on the subject. His fears that civil war would result were ripened into certainty by the outbreak of the troubles in Kansas. Deploring this as a national calamity which might have been averted by wisdom and manly courage on the part of statesmen, he thought it should be used for the suppression of the slave power and the immediate abolition of slavery; and he wrote his hope that his descendants would all do their duty when the conflict should come.*

The monotony of his isolated life at Bay City was varied by frequent visits to his married sons, to Gerrit Smith, and Theodore D. Weld. About 1853, he broke up

---

* When the rebellion broke out there were six of James G. Birney's descendants who were of age to bear arms. *James*, the eldest son was acting Governor of Michigan and was afterward actively employed in sending regiments to the field. His son, *James Gillespie*, a youth of twenty, went as cavalry lieutenant, became captain, and served as staff officer for both Custer and Sheridan. *William* enlisted, was elected captain and rose to be brevet major-general, serving in all the intermediate grades. *David Bell* entered as lieutenant-colonel, and rose by regular promotion to be major-general (see his biography by O. M. Davis). *Dion*, a physician, was lieutenant and captain. *Fitzhugh* left Harvard University to join the army. He served on McClellan's staff and rose from lieutenant to colonel (see his biography by Prof. Cutler). All these, except the writer, died, in or soon after the war, of wounds received or diseases contracted in the service. Without exception, they were deeply imbued with the principles and patriotic spirit of James G. Birney.

housekeeping and removed to Eagleswood, near Perth Amboy, N. J. At this place Mr. Weld had established his celebrated school, or academy, occupying for that purpose one end of an immense building. The other end and the very long central part was built in "flats." These were occupied by the families of patrons of the school. Mr. Birney leased and furnished one of the best suites of apartments in the building and occupied it during the rest of his life. His youngest son was a pupil in the school. His surroundings in this place freshened up his life. The daily visits of his friend Weld cheered him. He attended the debates and literary exercises of the students, the Saturday evening lectures delivered by distinguished strangers, and the eloquent Sunday morning religious addresses by Mr. Weld. Occasionally he went to the opera or visited other places of public amusement or listened to some celebrated preacher at New York. In this mode of living he was comparatively free from the curiosity of the vulgar who wished to know to what degree his organs of speech were affected, a curiosity which he was not disposed to gratify. His attempts to articulate were reserved for his family and very intimate friends, and with them were generally for the purpose of discovering whether he was improving or not.

Under his affliction his temper became more genial. The sternness which had been contracted in the latter part of his active career disappeared altogether. He took pleasure in listening to the conversation of the intelligent, the lively talk of young ladies, and the prattle of children. With these last, he was a great favorite. My children liked nothing better than to have a romp with their grandfather. He understood perfectly the rare art of making himself an agreeable visitor for a long time, being considerate of the feelings and circumstances of others and with sure intuitions of the right thing to do. His daughters-in-law loved him as dearly as his sons did. He was never morose or impatient or low spirited; nor did he complain of his affliction. He controlled himself so as not to distress those who loved him. The only expression during his long malady of his desire to die was made to me as I sat by his bedside, holding his hand after one of his excruciatingly painful attacks, "I had hoped this would be the last."

His resignation was due to his piety. The Bible was his constant companion and a part of each day was spent by him in silent prayer. But God heard him. After more than twelve years of bodily and mental suffering and anguish, in which he showed how a sincere Christian should bear affliction, his spirit was released from its earthly prison. On the 25th of November, 1857, he died at Eagleswood, New Jersey, surrounded by his wife, children, and friends.

APPENDIX A.

As an answer to the claim that Mr. Garrison was the first to reveal to Americans the nature of slavery, and that the reader may have something like an adequate idea of the quantity and comprehensiveness in 1830 of the American literature relating to slavery, I subjoin an incomplete list of publications then extant on the subject. A perfect list would probably comprise from ten to twenty times as many. The rapidity with which pamphlets and even books disappear is well known to every man who has attempted to make a collection on any special subject; they perish like autumn leaves. Important American works on slavery published before 1830, such as those of George Bourne, John Kenrick, Jesse Torrey, James Duncan, John Rankin, and George M. Stroud, which expressed the best anti-slavery convictions of the day and contributed greatly to purify public opinion and sentiment, have become exceedingly rare. Many of the works published in England circulated freely in this country. The most important ones were republished here—some in Philadelphia, others in Kentucky, and Elizabeth Heyrick's in Baltimore and Philadelphia. The following list, incomplete as it is, may aid some bibliographer to make a perfect one. The one given in the appendix to the "Proceedings of the Third American Anti-Slavery Society Decade Meeting" contains twenty-three items only; it was published under the auspices of Mr. Garrison.

Books and pamphlets on slavery, published or republished before the year 1831 in the United States. No English works are included unless they were republished or had large circulation in this country. French ones are omitted.

Godwyn, Rev. Morgan. "The Negoes' and Indians' Advocate," treatise, 1650.

Baxter, Richard. "Friendly Advice to Planters," "Negroes' Complaint," etc., about 1651.

Southern. "Oronooko," a tragedy, 1696.

Sir Richard Steele's story of "Inkle and Yarico" was published about 1715.

Sandiford, Ralph, Philadelphia. "The Mystery of Iniquity," 1729.

Atkins, Surgeon. "Voyage to Guinea and the West Indies," 1735.

Whitefield, George. "Address to the Inhabitants of Maryland and Virginia," 1739.

Hughes, Rev. Griffith. "Natural History of Barbadoes," 1750.

Benezet. "Tracts on Slavery," 1750 to 1774.

Woolman, John. "Considerations on the keeping of Negroes," 1754 to 1762.

Jeffery, Thomas. "Account of a Part of North America," 1761.

Sharp, Granville. "Memoirs and Representation of the Injustice of Slavery," 1769.

Anthony Benezet's writings on slavery, with extracts from the writings of several noted authors on the subject of slavery, viz., George Wallace, Francis Hutcheson, James Foster, and Granville Sharp, and from an address to the Assembly of Virginia, Philadelphia, 1771.

Lay, Benjamin. "Treatise on Slave-keeping," 1773.

Rush, Benjamin. "Address to the Inhabitants of the British Settlements on the Slavery of the Negroes," 1773.

Wesley, John. "Thoughts on Slavery," 1774.

Pennsylvania Abolition Society. Act of incorporation. Instituted in 1775; incorporated in 1789; 1775 and 1789.

Day, Thomas. "Slavery of the Negroes," 1776.

Miller, Prof. "Origin of Ranks," 1777.

"A Serious Address to the Rulers of America on the Inconsistency of their Conduct respecting Slavery," etc., by a farmer, London, 1783.

Woods, Joseph. "Thoughts on the Slavery of the Negroes," 1784.

Gregory, Dr. "Essays, Historical and Moral," 1784.

Ramsay, James. "Essay on the Treatment and Conversion of the African Slaves in the British Sugar Colonies," 1784.

Clarkson, Thomas. "Essay on the Slavery and Commerce of the Human Species," 1786.

Jefferson, Thomas. "Notes on Virginia," 1787.

Cowper, poet.

Sharp, Granville. "Law of Retribution," 1778.

Newton. "On the Slave Trade," 1788.

"Constitution of a Society for abolishing the Slave Trade," Providence, 1789.

"Oration upon the Necessity of establishing at Paris a Society for the Promotion of the Abolition of the Trade and Slavery of the Negroes." By J. P. Brissot de Warville, 1789. Republished in Philadelphia in 1791 (translation).

"Memorial Presented to Congress by the Different Societies instituted for the Promotion of the Abolition of Slavery, etc., in the States of Rhode Island, Connecticut, Pennsylvania, New York, Maryland, and Virginia," 1790 to 1791.

"Debates on the Slave Trade," 1791, 1792.

Buchanan, George. "Oration on Slavery," 1791, Baltimore, Md.

Edwards, Jonathan, Jr. "Injustice and Impolicy of the Slave Trade," 1791.

Rice, David, Rev. "A Kentucky Protest against Slavery," 1792. (Immediate abolition.)

"Proceedings of Conventions of Delegates from the Abolition Societies of the United States," 1794 to 1828.

"Memoirs of Waimbamma, an African Priest," 1799.

Collins. "Professional Planter," 1804.

"Congressional Debates on the Slave Trade," 1806 and 1807.

Rev. Archibald Cameron's "Slavery justified by Scripture" ("Monitor"), Lexington, Ky., 1806.

Branagan, Thomas. "The Penitential Tyrant, or Slave-Trader Reformed." A pathetic poem in four cantos. 290 pp. New York, 1807. (Immediate abolition.)

"Select Speeches" (including some of Wilberforce, Fox, North, and Pitt, on slavery), published by N. Chapman, M. D., Philadelphia, 1807.

Clarkson's "History of the Abolition of the Slave Trade," republished, 2 vols., octavo, pp. 455, 468, Philadelphia, 1808.

Dickson's "Mitigation of Slavery," 1814.

Rev. David Barrow's pamphlet against slavery (out of print), Paris, Ky., 1815. (Immediate abolition.)

Pinckard's "Notes on the West Indies," 1815.

Rev. George Bourne (Va). "The Book and Slavery Irreconcilable," Philadelphia, 1816. (Immediate abolition.) Also author of "Picture of Slavery in America."

Watson. "Defense of Methodist Missions in West Indies," 1816.

Coster "On the Amelioration of Slavery," 1816.

Kenrick, John. "Horrors of Slavery," Boston, 1816.

Thomas Clarkson's "Essay on the Slavery and Commerce of the Human Species, particularly the African." Republished, Georgetown, Ky., by J. N. Lyle, 1816.

Torrey, Jesse, physician. "A Portraiture of Domestic Slavery in the United States, etc., including Memoirs of Facts on the Interior Traffic in Slaves and on Kidnapping," Philadelphia, 1817.

Thorpe, Robert, LL.D. "Present Increase of the Slave Trade," 1818.

"The Exclusion of Slavery from the Territories and new States," 1819.

"Memorial to Congress on Restraining the Increase of Slavery," 1819.

"The Bible justifies Slavery." By Duff Green, St. Louis, 1819.

Robert Walsh's "Appeal from the Judgments of Great Britain respecting the United States," etc. 512 pp. Philadelphia (pro-slavery), 1819.

"Dialogue on Slavery." By the Rev. James Gilliland, Ripley, Ohio, 1820. (Immediate abolition.)

Congressional speeches of Rufus King, J. Tallmadge, Jr., and others on the admission of Missouri, with numerous pamphlets on the subject (most of these have perished), 1818, 1819, and 1820.

Sharp, Granville. "Memoirs," etc., reprint from 1769, 1820.

Raymond, Daniel. "Political Economy," 2 vols., octavo, Baltimore, 1820 and 1823.

Learned, Joseph D. "View of the Policy of permitting Slaves in the States West of the Mississippi," 1820.

Plumer, M. C. "Speech on the Missouri Question," 1820.

"Achates," Charleston, S. C. "Reflections concerning Late Disturbances in Charleston," 1822.

Cropper's "Letters to Wilberforce," 1822.

Singleton's "Report of the State of Sierre Leone," 1822.

Rev. John Rankin's "Letters on Slavery in America." (Immediate abolition.) 118 pp., 1823–'24.

Hodgson. "Letter to Say on the Comparative Expense of Free and Slave Labor," 1823.

"Declaration of the Objects of the Liverpool Society for abolishing Slavery," 1823.

Wilberforce. "Appeal to the Religion, Justice, and Humanity of the Inhabitants of the British Empire in behalf of the Negro Slaves in the West Indies," 1823.

Clarkson, Thomas. "Thoughts on the Necessity of improving the Condition of Slaves in the British Colonies," etc., 1823.

Cooper. "Letter to R. Hibbert, Jr., Exposure of Falsehood," etc., 1823.

Cooper. "Facts Illustrative of the Condition of the Negroes in Jamaica," 1823.

Cropper, James. "Support of Slavery investigated," 1823.

"Impolicy of Slavery," illustrated; 1823.

"Pictures of Slavery in the West Indies, United States, and especially in Jamaica." Published by the Anti-Slavery Society, 1823.

Gloucester, Jeremiah. "Oration on the Abolition of the Slave Trade," 1823.

Birkbeck, Morris. "An Appeal to the People of Illinois on the Question of a Convention," 1823.

"Brief View of the Nature and Effects of Negro Slavery as it exists in the Colonies of Great Britain." Committee of the Methodist Wesleyan Conference.

"First Report of the Committee of the Society for the Mitigation and Gradual Abolition of Slavery," June 25, 1824 and 1825.

Stephen, James. "The Slavery of the British West India Colonies delineated," 1824.

"East India Free Labor Sugar," 1824.

"Information concerning the Present Condition of Slave Trade," 1824.

"Treatise on Slavery." By Rev. James Duncan, of Kentucky, Vevay, Ind., 1824. (Immediate abolition.)

Remarks to Citizens of Illinois on the Proposed Introduction of Slavery," 1824.

"An Impartial Appeal to the People of Illinois on the Injurious Effects of Slave Labor," 1824.

"Hayti, Rural Code of," 1826.

Heyrick, Elizabeth. "Immediate not Gradual Emancipation," London, 1824. Republished December 3 and 10, 1825, in Lundy's "Genius"; first edition in Philadelphia in 1824, second in 1836. (See preface to latter.) "Thoughts on the Extinction of Colonial Slavery." By Miss Heyrick.

Quoted from by Miss Chandler and indorsed in "Genius" of January 1, 1830.

Clarkson, Thomas. The argument "That the Colonial Slaves are better off than the British Peasantry," 1825.

"Brief View of the Nature and Effects of Slavery," 1825.

"Impolicy of Slavery illustrated," 1825.

"Negroes' Memorial or Abolitionist's Catechism," London, 1825.

Lundy, Benjamin. "Life of Elisha Tyson," a Maryland abolitionist, 1825.

"Picture of Slavery, drawn by the Colonists themselves," 1825.

Stroud, George M., Philadelphia. "Sketch of the Laws relating to Slavery in the Several States of the United States of America," 1827.

"Minutes of the Twentieth Session of the American Convention for promoting the Abolition of Slavery," held in Philadelphia, October 2, 1827.

"Remarks on Slavery in the United States," 1827.

Dyer Burgess's "Pamphlet against Slavery," Ripley, Ohio, 1827. (Immediate abolition.)

Wilson's "Thoughts on Slavery," 1827.

Wilberforce's "Appeal."

Winn on "Emancipation," 1827.

"Sketches and Anecdotes of Persons of Color." By A. Mott, York, England, 1828.

"Scripture Evidence of the Sinfulness of Injustice and Oppression," London, 1828.

"Anti-Slavery Petitions," 1828.

"Anti-Slavery Monthly Reporter" from 1825 to 1827 and 1829.

"Investigator," Providence, October 11, 1827.

"Philanthropist and Investigator," Boston, January 16 to August 26, 1829.

"Investigator and Genius of Temperance," October 28, December 30, 1829.

"Treatise on the Patriarchal System of Slavery," 1829.

Walker. "Appeal," Boston, 1829.

Walsh, Rev. Dr. "Notes on the Brazils," 1830.

Godwin. "Lectures on Slavery," 1830.

Hicks, Elias. "Remarks on Character of," 1830.

Hodgson on "Free and Slave Labor," 1830.

New York. "Selections from the Revised Statutes of Laws relative to Slaves and Kidnapping," 1830.

"Negro Slavery Tracts," Nos. 1 to 17, 1830.

"Address to the Churches," by the Chillicothe (Ohio) Presbytery, excluding slaveholders from the communion, 1830.

APPENDIX B.

BENJAMIN LUNDY.

BENJAMIN LUNDY (1789–1839), editor and publisher of the "Genius of Universal Emancipation," was the most conspicuous abolitionist in Maryland during the six years beginning with October, 1824. His anti-slavery work began in 1815 in Ohio, and ended in 1839 in Illinois, having been prosecuted in the mean time in Tennessee, Maryland, and Pennsylvania. His prominent anti-slavery contemporaries prior to 1830 were Dr. Doak, Charles Osborn, John Rankin, and Jesse Lockhart, of Tennessee; the Kentucky Presbyterians David Rice, James Duncan, and John Finley Crowe; the Kentucky Baptists, "Friends of Humanity," David Barrow, Carter Torrant, John Sutton, Donald Holmes, Jacob Gregg, and George Smith; William Swaim and R. Mendenhall, of North Carolina; James Gilliland, of South Carolina; Edward Coles and George Bourne, of Virginia; Elisha Tyson, Daniel Raymond, John Needles, and Edward Needles, of Baltimore; the ministers of the seventeen "emancipating Baptist churches" of Illinois and of the Methodist Reformed Church; with Rufus King, J. Tallmadge, Jr., and the other opponents of the admission of Missouri as a slave State. Lundy's place in abolition history is unlike that of any other man. To understand it his career must be studied.

He was born and reared a Quaker in New Jersey. His education was of the narrowest—a little reading and ciphering and a great deal of hard work. Having injured his health and permanently impaired his hearing by trying to do as much work as any man on his father's farm, he left home in 1808. At Wheeling, Va., he remained four years, working at the saddler's trade and reading diligently. Owing to the suppression of the African slave trade the Southern demand for Virginia slaves was becoming active, and Lundy while apprentice and journeyman saw many chained coffles of slaves on their way to the Southern market. His pity for them made him an abolitionist. This was about 1810. Having married and established himself in his trade at St. Clairsville, Ohio, he called a few friends together at his house, in 1815, and organized for anti-slavery purposes "The Union Humane Society." It is significant of the liberal public opinion of that day that in a few months the number of members had increased to "nearly five hundred," among whom were "most of the influential preachers and lawyers." * Under date of January 4, 1816, he published an address to the philanthropists of the United States, recommending the general formation of anti-slavery societies under a common title and constitution, with co-operation and, for important business, a general convention. At the close he stated that he "had had the subject long in contemplation, and that he had now taken it up fully determined never to lay it down while he breathed or until the end should be obtained." †

In 1817 he began his work as editor. On the 12th of September in that year, Charles Osborn, the Quaker preacher from Tennessee, issued at Mount Pleasant, Ohio, the first number of the "Philanthropist," a weekly paper of a religious tone and intended to aid in the warfare then waged by reformers generally against the three great national evils—war, slavery, and intemperance. Two years before that date, Charles Osborn, John Underhill, Jesse Willis, John Canaday, John Swain, Elihu Swain, David Maulsby, and Thomas Morgan had formed the Tennessee Manumission Society. Either because of a difference of opinion on the question between immediatism and gradualism or to leave all members at liberty as to the manner of emancipation, the constitution was silent on the subject. The three first named, however, were in favor of immediate, uncompensated emancipation on the soil. Osborn removed to Ohio in 1816, and Underhill and Willis to Indiana at a later day. Osborn was a preacher, his editing taking a minor place in his life. In his first number he hopefully declares in regard to slavery that the time "is fast ap-

---

* Earle's "Life of Lundy," p. 16. † Ibid., p. 17.

proaching when the United States shall no longer be stained with this foul pollution." In his sixth he thus speaks of the Colonization Society:

"The editor has great doubts of the justice of the plan proposed. It appears to him calculated to rivet closer the chains that already gall the sons of Africa and to insure to the miserable objects of American cruelty a perpetuity of bondage."

Osborn found in Lundy a kindred spirit and trustworthy man, and encouraged him to send to the paper selected and original articles on slavery. In 1818 he proposed a partnership in the printing business. Lundy accepted, asking time to get rid of his stock in trade. To effect this he made two trips to St. Louis, reaching that city on the second trip late in the fall of 1819, when the Missouri controversy was at its height. He engaged in it with all his energy, writing numerous articles on the evils of slavery for the newspapers of Missouri and Illinois. He remained at St. Louis until about the 1st of December, 1820, at which time, having lost nearly all his property and exhausted the patience of Charles Osborn, who sold his paper before Lundy's return, he set out on foot to return home. On the road he heard of the death (December 4, 1820) of Elihu Embree, the editor of the "Emancipator," of Jonesborough, East Tennessee. Osborn's successor did not come up to Lundy's standard of anti-slavery doctrine, and he decided to establish a monthly periodical at Mount Pleasant, Ohio, under the title of "The Genius of Universal Emancipation," a sounding name suggested by a passage in one of Curran's speeches. The first number was issued in January, 1821. "In four months," he says, "my subscription list had become quite large." At that time he was well aware that the best vantage ground for attacking slavery was the State of Maryland. In his "proposals," published in the number for July 29, 1824, of "The American Economist and East Tennessee Statesman," he says:

"I had fully determined on removing to Baltimore as soon as necessary arrangements could be made. . . . But finding that the Manumission Society of Tennessee had procured a press for the purpose of exposing the pernicious effects of slavery and disseminating the principles of universal emancipation, and that they were likely to fail in the attainment of their object for the want of assistance in conducting their printing establishment, I concluded that, perhaps, it was a duty incumbent on me to render them my feeble aid in so laudable an undertaking, especially as I had received an invitation from them to that purport."

Lundy could not do as he would. He had no money and owned neither press nor types ; his monthly edition was printed ten miles off and he lugged it home on his back. He went, September, 1821, to the press and types in East Tennessee, and there he learned the practical part of a printer's business and established at Greenville a weekly local and a monthly agricultural paper besides the "Genius." In the winter of 1823–'24 he attended the biennial convention of the American Abolition Society at Philadelphia, and became acquainted with some of the Eastern abolitionists. Encouraged by the increasing circulation of his paper and disgusted with the irregularities of mail transportation* in the South, he resolved to carry out his original design of publishing in Baltimore. Having issued at Greenville his number for August, 1824, he started eastward on foot. *En route* he delivered numerous anti-slavery lectures in North Carolina and Virginia, forming several abolition societies. One of the places in which he spoke was Raleigh. He says :

"Before I left the State (North Carolina) there were some twelve or fourteen anti-slavery societies organized."

Several others were formed in the middle section of Virginia. The public impression that, prior to Jackson's first term, there was in the South no freedom of speech on slavery is contradicted by Lundy in these words :

"I afterward, during that visit to North Carolina, held some fifteen or twenty anti-slavery meetings at different places. My discourses were similar to all that I have since delivered in other parts of the United States, and as ultra-orthodox in anti-slavery sentiment as any of modern times." †

The establishment of the "Genius" caused no excitement in Baltimore. The abolitionists received Lundy "civilly enough." ‡ His personal presence was not imposing. He was of medium height, plain in dress, hard of hearing, and not fluent in speech.

* See the "proposals" for publishing the "Genius" in Baltimore.

† "Life," p. 22. ‡ Ibid., p. 23.

It took time for the public to appreciate the scrupulous truthfulness, good judgment, firmness, industry, and sledge-hammer style of the unpretending Quaker. His initial article painted in lively colors the impending dangers from the "grievous curse" of slavery, adding :

"Yea, all Nature cries aloud that *something must be done* to appease the kindling wrath of outraged humanity and violated justice ere the fate of ancient Egypt or of modern St. Domingo shall be ours."

He pledged himself to expose the vile management of those who endeavor "to uphold and perpetuate the horrors of the system" that men might see "what manner of *Christians or republicans* are those who cherish the infamous practice of enslaving their fellow-mortals." He declared that nothing less was contemplated than the "complete and final extinguishment" of slavery.

The first number was an excellent paper. It contained the editor's address, an article on Hayti, "Backing out," triumph of principle in Illinois, accounts of the formation of six new emancipation societies, notices of General Lafayette, slavery in Brazil, Rev. James Duncan's new work on slavery, Manumission Society of North Carolina, letter from Illinois, revivals in North Carolina, the constitutions of six abolition societies, "Mr. Adams and Slave-holding," the black list, on kidnapping, etc., Hayti circular, British anti-slavery meeting in London, poetry on Hayti and Africa, and notices to patrons and correspondents.

To get out this number required all Lundy's pluck and spirit of self-sacrifice. He had neither money nor type nor press. He worked as journeyman for the printer in whose office the "Genius" was set up and struck off ; lived cheaply, paid as he went, and kept out of debt—a rule which he always conscientiously observed. The paper made a good impression ; subscriptions came in rapidly; the editor was a good canvasser; the funds for the publication of the following six numbers were easily obtained. Prospects were so bright that in the March number proposals were published for a weekly edition of the paper. The monthly was a sixteen page octavo, of which the printed matter on each page was about 4½ by 7½ inches. The weekly was to be a sixteen page quarto, the size of the printed page to be 6¾ by 9½ inches. The first and specimen number of the weekly was issued July 4, 1825, and its regular publication began September 5, 1825, and was continued until January 3, 1829, having been enlarged July 4, 1827, to 8½ by 11 inches printed page. The monthly paper was not again published after September, 1825, until April, 1830. The pecuniary success of the paper was large enough in the first three years to encourage Lundy greatly. He brought his family from Tennessee and went to housekeeping, rented a good printing-office, furnished it with cases, type, and press. He employed several journeymen printers, did a fair job business, and published a book (the "Life of Tyson") and sundry pamphlets. His income was from subscriptions and job-work. There is no trace of his having received donations or pecuniary aid of any kind. His prosperity was solid, being based upon a public sentiment represented in 1826 by 974 abolition votes at the Baltimore polls. It appears to have steadily increased in 1825, 1826, and in 1827, until the October election, which defeated the Adams candidates and placed Jackson Democrats in the Legislature.

From that time the "Genius" was doomed. The signs of the times indicated the overthrow of Adams, a non-slave-holder, under whom free discussion had been the rule, and the incoming of Jackson, the slave-holder, with the ascendency of the slave power. Time-servers and trucklers were preparing to change parties. Fence men descended on the Southern side. Timid men did not like to have it known that they took Lundy's paper, and business men who were abolitionists thought it prudent to be so secretly. The subscription list fell off and old subscribers did not pay up.

In March, 1828, Southern patronage had fallen off to such an extent that it was necessary to do what Lundy had never before done—appeal to the North. In March, 1828, he visited Philadelphia, New York, Providence, and Boston, seeing Arthur Tappan, William Goodell, and other well-known friends of the slave. March 17th he explained his views to eight Boston clergymen. They "cordially approved," and Mr. Garrison, "who sat in the room, also expressed his approbation of my doctrines." ("Life," page 25, and "Life of William Lloyd Garrison," page 93.) Having been successful in getting subscriptions he returned home.

In a few weeks he made a second * and last visit to the North. His journal, the substance of which is published in his "Life" by Earle (pages 26, 27, and 28) shows that he started May 1st and returned to Baltimore October 25th, having held forty-three public meetings, going as far as "New Hampshire, Maine, and New York," and having "considerably increased his subscription list."

The relief from Northern subscriptions was but temporary. The heavy ground swell of the slave-power democracy in 1827 had become a tidal wave in 1828, and the little bark, the "Genius," already loosed from its moorings, was driven high and dry on shore, a hopeless wreck. The election of Jackson, a slave-holder and cotton-planter, over Adams by a vote of 178 to 83 struck the chill of the grave into Maryland abolitionism. Lundy found himself on the road to bankruptcy and suspension. He was obliged to mortgage his press and type and to let the press and part of the type go to his creditors.

---

* It was on this "second" visit that Mr. Lundy says he invited Mr. Garrison to be his assistant editor, which invitation was declined. (See Earle, p. 28.) Writing from memory, he errs in fixing the date of the visit in "November" and saying that Mr. Garrison was then "conducting a paper in Vermont from which he could not then disengage himself." The second visit is shown by his published diary (Earle, p. 26) to have continued until the 25th of October. As Lundy's public meetings in Boston were held on the 7th and 11th of August and were attended by Mr. Garrison, the two meeting doubtless every day, and as Mr. Lundy needed an assistant at that time, an offer was quite in the natural order of things, as was also the refusal by Mr. Garrison because of his engagement to go to Bennington. (Compare Earle and Garrison's "Life" for the dates.)

The story so often repeated by Mr. Garrison and his friends of Lundy's traveling afoot, staff in hand and knapsack on back, to Bennington, Vt., to invite Mr. Garrison to join him, is romantic and sensational, but it has no foundation in fact. It was not told during his life and his relatives reject it. He was never in Bennington. That city was six hundred miles from Baltimore by the nearest roads, and forty days of foot travel would not have been undertaken by Lundy to accomplish what he could have done as well by letter. The foot-trip was never mentioned in either of the papers edited by the parties or by Mr. Garrison until after Lundy's death.

The last number of the "Genius," before its suspension, was issued January 3, 1829. In it he shows his indomitable pluck by declaring his intention to resume its publication at a future day, and that "it shall never be abandoned while the labor of his own hands will support life and produce a revenue *sufficient to print and publish one sheet per annum.*"

Such a cry of desperate failure was not of a nature to bring in subscriptions. The next eight months were spent in preparations to resume, with the exception of the time taken for a trip to Hayti. He renewed, doubtless by letter, his invitation to Mr. Garrison to join him, and gained his promise to do so. By diligent canvassing he managed to get a few new subscribers and collect some arrears of old subscriptions, so that he was ready to begin again on the 5th of September. It was, however, on a reduced scale. Having no printing-office, he had the printing done by contract in the office of Lucas & Deaver, who were abolitionists. By the use of larger type he cut down the cost of composition. By adding the space of fourteen lines to the length of the column he gave the paper a better form, though it did not contain as much printed matter as before the suspension. The old subscription price was retained.

The Baltimore public did not respond to Lundy's appeal. The wind was raw and chilly. The shadow of the incoming slave-holding President darkened the sky. Money was scarce, and in order to live Lundy was forced to sell the remains of his former office. In the number of January 22d the assistant editor wrote :

"The voluntary remittances of our subscribers for more than four months do not exceed the sum of fifty dollars."

As the terms were "three dollars per annum, payable in advance," the attempt to resuscitate the weekly* "Genius" was

* In a speech at the third decade meeting of the American Anti-Slavery Society, Mr. Garrison, speaking of editing the "National Philanthropist" at Boston, in 1827, says:

"Among my exchange papers I received a *little, dingy monthly periodical* called the 'Genius of Universal Emancipation,'" etc.

And again, speaking of Lundy's invitation to join him in editing "the little, dingy monthly," he says :

"The proposition upon his part was that we should convert the *little* evidently a disastrous failure from the very first. It was abandoned after a trial of six months. The octavo monthly was resumed by Lundy alone in April, 1830.

It was published in Baltimore until the end of that year, then nominally for a few months and really after that time at Washington city until October, 1833, when its further publication there was to be effected only at the daily risk of life, and it was removed to Philadelphia.

The historical value of Lundy's paper for the period beginning with 1821 and ending with 1830 can hardly be overestimated. It is the repository of all plans for the abolition of slavery, of all laws, opinions, arguments, essays, speeches, and views, statistics, constitutions of societies, etc., manumissions, congressional proceedings, notices of books and pamphlets, colonization efforts, political movements, in short, of everything relating to slavery. To such a writer as Von Holst it would be a rich mine of suggestive information.

As a newspaper it is better than any reform journal of the same period. The "Harbinger of Peace" compared with it is a rush-light to the sun. It is interesting. The style of the editor improves from year to year. So does his taste in making selections. The reader becomes insensibly absorbed in gazing upon the life-like panorama presented to him of the doings of a former

---

monthly into a large and handsome weekly paper. (See "Third Decade Proceedings," p. 120.)

This authority is followed by Oliver Johnson and the sons of Mr. Garrison ("Life" of W. L. G., p. 120). It is incorrect in every particular. At the time spoken of (1827 and 1828) there was no monthly in existence, and had not been since September, 1825, and the weekly, though the columns were a little longer, contained no more matter and was not "handsome." *I write with the files of the "Genius" on the table before me.*

In the same speech Mr. Garrison claims that he ruined Lundy's paper by advocating immediate emancipation. As Miss Heyrick's pamphlet had been published in the "Genius" in December, 1825, and the doctrine constantly presented in the paper from about that time, and as Miss Chandler had devoted more space to it than Mr. Garrison, his conscience might well have been easy on that score. Mr. Lundy never attributed his failure to Mr. Garrison.

generation, and when he at last lays aside the paper it is with genuine respect for the noble sincerity, unselfishness, and sure judgment of Benjamin Lundy. His paper bears no trace of personal quarrels, of envy or jealousy of co-workers.

"He did not find his sleep less sweet
For music in some neighboring street,
Nor rustling hear in every breeze
The laurels of Miltiades."

This was one of the causes of his success. His single purpose made him see clearly. In Osborn's "Philanthropist" (1817) he took ground against colonization. December 20, 1825, he says of the Colonization Society:

"Its direct effect, even to remove the nominally free blacks, is next to nothing; . . . as a means to do away the system of slavery, . . . it furnishes not the least hope."

The same year (vol. v, No. 5) he denounces it as aiming at the "expatriation of the free people of color" and as "*inadequate* to the object I have ever kept in view and the attainment of which is the end and aim of all my exertions, viz., the total abolition of slavery in the United States."

In this opinion he never wavered. His soundness on the doctrine of immediate emancipation has been slurred by Mr. Garrison and questioned on the same authority since his death; but a few remarks on this subject may aid to a more just conclusion.

The doctrine was not new to him. Milton had asserted it:

"But man over man
He made not lord; such title to himself reserving,
Human left from human free."

That "slavery is a sin," imposed, in theology, the duty of immediate abandonment. Wesley had said, "*Instantly*, at any price, were it the half of your goods, deliver thyself from blood guiltiness."

In 1789 Bishop Burgess had advocated immediate abolition and denounced those who wished to "modify" and "ameliorate" slavery. (See "Anti-Slavery Monthly Reporter," 1829.)

In 1792 David Rice had delivered an address to the Kentucky Convention, urging it "to resolve *unconditionally* to put an end to slavery in this State."

To his anti-slavery poem, "The Penitential Tyrant," published in New York in 1807, Branagan had added a note (page 280):

"I deny that, in the sight of God, any human being can be the property of another."

In 1816, Rev. George Bourne (Virginia), in "The Book and Slavery Irreconcilable," had said :

"The system is so entirely corrupt that it admits of no cure but by a total and *immediate abolition.*"

From about 1824 immediatism was accepted by the majority of English abolitionists. In 1824, Rev. James Duncan (Kentucky), in his "Treatise on Slavery," showed the fallacy of gradualism and advocated immediate abolition on the soil without compensation to the master. (See G., i, p. 144.)

In the same year, Rev. John Rankin (Tennessee, Kentucky, and Ohio), in his "Letters on Slavery," had argued that "less inconvenience and danger would attend their liberation at the present than at any future time" (page 25).

The same doctrine had been preached in Ohio many years by the Revs. James Gilliland, Jesse Lockhart, J. Dunlavy, John Rankin, the two Dickeys, and by Charles Osborn. It was, therefore, a familiar one to Lundy ; but his intention was to effect practical abolition through manumission by masters and through legislation by slave-holding States, compelling masters to emancipate, and he went into those States to accomplish his object. His appeal to masters was always, Manumit at once, for slave-holding is a sin. His appeal for compulsory statutes was, Fix a time now. He recognized the fact that the States already free had adopted the gradual plan, and that it would be impracticable to obtain from any State unconditional and instantaneous emancipation on the soil. He expressed this well in his "proposals" for issuing his paper at Baltimore. These appeared in his Greenville weekly local paper of July 29, 1824. In them he declares himself in favor of means whereby slavery, "may be completely annihilated," and adds, "The editor is well aware that this must be effected *gradually.*"

In this he refers rather to what *will* be than to what *ought* to be ; to what *can* be done rather than to what is *best* to be done. In all his writings, it is believed, he never pointed out any bad results likely to flow from unconditional emancipation by law, but thought such a proposition to the Southern people was chimerical. As time wore on, however, he modified his views on this point. In the "Genius" for December 3 and 10, 1825, he republished the whole of Elizabeth Heyrick's pamphlet, "Immediate, not Gradual Emancipation," and about the same time he republished Rev. James Duncan's book and aided actively in circulating it. In 1827 he proposed to issue in book-form a reprint of Miss Heyrick's second book, "The Prompt Extinction," etc. (See "Genius" of September 11, 1827.) In the later prospectuses of his paper (see those of September 2, 1826, and June 16, 1827) he omits all mention of gradualism. In the number of August 5, 1826, he publishes an article from a Presbyterian preacher advocating immediate abolition. The following lines show its tenor:

"What has God told you about crime or sin? To desist from it or to persevere? To desist, when? Now! now! . . . We are required to do it immediately."

In August and September, 1826, he copies six radical articles from the (New York) "Recorder and Telegraph." They contain such passages as these: "The point to be aimed at is the entire, speedy abolition of slavery, for whether we choose it or not the thing will be done. . . . Emancipation must take place on the spot where slavery exists. . . . The slave has a right to immediate liberty paramount to every claim of his master."

November 11, 1826, a North Carolina correspondent urges as "the next step" to call on the legislatures "to make an immediate, unconditional, and indiscriminate destruction of the slave market."

Miss Elizabeth M. Chandler, who in 1825 had written "The Slave Ship," a prize poem, and, after writing literary pieces for the "Genius" in 1826, had become, early in 1827, a frequent contributor to it of articles on slavery, showing the tender heart of woman and rare poetical genius, had never penned a line in favor of gradualism. She was always in favor of immediate abolition. In her second letter "to the ladies of Baltimore" she says: "What is wanted, therefore, is not so much an acknowledgement of its wickedness as a general desire for its *immediate extinction*," etc. ("Memoir," page 45.)

In his memoir of her, written in 1836, Lundy says: "She was the first American female author that ever made this subject the principal theme of her active exertions. . . . She ranked as second to none among the female philanthropists of modern times who have devoted their attention to it, if we except the justly celebrated Elizabeth Heyrick, of England."

During the six months' effort in 1829–'30 to re-establish the "Genius," she freely advocated in her department of the paper the doctrine of immediate abolition, devoting at least twice as much space to it as Mr. Garrison did, and quoting freely from the last and most able work of Miss Heyrick * on the subject.

Mr. Garrison announced the doctrine in his salutatory and approved it in some half-dozen other articles, none of which were elaborate. He qualified it, however, as follows: "Let me here remark that I do not advocate total and instantaneous abolition without at the same time urging the duty of the States to make liberal provisions and suitable regulations *by law* for the maintenance and government of the emancipated blacks. For every imaginary or real evil I propose a safe antidote."

That Mr. Lundy not only acquiesced in but cordially approved the doctrine is proved by his republication, in the "Genius" of December, 1825, of Miss Heyrick's pamphlet, by his indorsement (September 11, 1827) of that lady's second work on the same subject, and of Rev. James Duncan's book, by his continued publication of Miss Chandler's articles, by numerous "enunciations" of it by other writers, and by his special indorsement of Garrison's articles in the last number (March 5, 1830) of the "Genius," which was edited by them jointly. In reference to these articles he says: "I fully acquit him [Garrison] of intentionally inserting anything *knowing that it would be thus disapproved.*"

---

* In his speech at the "Third Decade Meeting" (p. 121) Mr. Garrison says: "From the moment that the doctrine of immediate emancipation was enunciated in the columns of the 'Genius,' as it *had not been up to that hour*, it was like a bombshell," etc. In comparison with the columns themselves, with which Garrison was familiar, this statement is seen to be without foundation in fact. These bombshells had been exploding during the five years preceding Mr. Garrison's arrival in Baltimore. Had Mr. Garrison never seen the files of the "Genius"?

As the doctrine had been fully discussed between them and was of the first importance, as the "Genius" had advocated it for four years and Lundy had acquiesced for six months in its editorial advocacy by both Mr. Garrison and Miss Chandler and continued for the rest of his life to advocate it himself, and as he made an arrangement soon after with Garrison to join him in editing the "Genius" at Washington, the above indorsement fully covers Garrison's articles on immediate abolition. He knew that Benjamin Lundy would approve them,* and that in all matters regarding slavery they were united. In his parting editorial notice Garrison says: "Although our partnership is at an end, I trust we shall ever *remain one in spirit and purpose* and that the cause of emancipation will suffer no detriment."

---

* The articles inserted in Mr. Lundy's absence and of which he disapproved were on sundry political subjects, especially those favoring Henry Clay for the presidency. He had no faith in Mr. Clay as a statesman, and had so stated in the "Genius." Mr. Garrison's faith in Clay was ardent. In his prospectus of August, 1830, for a paper at Washington, Mr. Garrison says: "I shall give a dignified support to Henry Clay and the American system." (See vol. i of "Life," p. 201.)

Mr. Lundy, on the contrary, regarded Mr. Clay as chiefly responsible for the admission of Missouri as a slave State, the greatest error in American statesmanship up to that time, and he treated him as an enemy of the cause of the slave.

In his "Third Decade Speech" (1863) Mr. Garrison attributes his signing his editorials in the "Genius" with his initials to the common desire of himself and Mr. Lundy that the latter should be relieved from responsibility for the doctrine of immediatism. At the time that speech was delivered Mr. Lundy had been in his grave twenty-four years and could file no caveat against Mr. Garrison's attempt at pre-emption. If Mr. Garrison had signed his initials to no other editorials than the very few on immediatism, his statement might be accepted; but the fact that he signed them to his numerous notices of books, magazines, newspapers, and sermons, and to articles long or short on embezzlers, Indians, swift steamboats, Mr. Clay, intemperance, popular bombast, his own birthday, etc., indicates vanity of authorship and not a desire to assume exclusive responsibility for unpopular views. The fact that in the same numbers of the "Genius" immediatism was advocated in the ladies' department without initials, proves that Benjamin Lundy was not shirking responsibility for that doctrine.

This contemporaneous, mutual recognition of their unity refutes the insinuations made by Garrison against Lundy in his life which have grown into definite charges since his death.

In 1831 he copied in full Garrison's explanation of the doctrine and indorsed it as plainly as he could. To an imputation made in 1832 by Garrison against his soundness of doctrine he answered:

"My sentiments have ever been adverse to the principle that tolerates the monstrous anomaly in our free institutions that man can be viewed as the property of man. I deny its correctness *in toto.* I have asserted, and the assertion has been recorded a hundred times, that no man can in justice *hold another as a slave a single moment.*" ("Genius" for 1832, page 208.)

In Earle's "Life of Lundy" (page 308) his half-sister writes:

"He was much grieved that the advocates of the cause of emancipation seemed not to enter into the view of Elizabeth Heyrick respecting immediate emancipation as he did. He talked much to me about it and lamented it, for, said he, the view was a sound one. . . . He has sometimes been represented as opposed to the measure of immediate emancipation. This, I believe, *was not true.*"

That Lundy was sound to the core on all questions affecting human liberty will not be doubted by any unbiased, intelligent reader of the "Genius." In the matter of political action against slavery he was in advance of most of his contemporaries. From a very early date, even during his residence in Tennessee, he advocated a resort to the ballot-box, and in Maryland he aided in the most effective movement of the kind made before 1830 except the exclusion of slavery from Illinois by popular vote in 1824. He was one of the first in 1828 and 1829 to expose the designs of the Jackson party managers to acquire Texas and to answer the articles in which Thomas H. Benton, Duff Green, and the "Richmond Inquirer" advocated the creation of six to nine new slave States and the ascendency of the slave power. After his return from Mexico his pamphlet against the annexation of Texas and the abundant information on that subject given by him to John Quincy Adams were among the strongest causes (after Guerrero's abolition of slavery in Texas and his refusal in 1829 to sell that Territory to the United States) of the temporary defeat of that measure of the slave power.

In the prosecution of his reform he steadily invoked the active aid of the women of the country. He established free labor produce stores in several cities and accomplished a great deal, particularly among the Friends, in the matter of abstention from the products of slave labor. Though he was not an eloquent public speaker, he lectured on slavery to more than two hundred assemblies of people, moving them to action by his thorough knowledge of his subject, his earnestness, and his array of facts; but his permanent reputation must rest on his journal, which is the most valuable record of anti-slavery opinions and movements in the times of which it treats.

Between the close of the war in 1815 and the year 1830 there were published the following journals which avowed the extinction of slavery as one, if not the chief one, of their objects:

1. The Philanthropist (Ohio), 1817.
2. The Emancipator (Tennessee), 1819.
3. The Abolition Intelligencer (Kentucky), 1822.
4. The Genius of Universal Emancipation (Ohio, Tennessee, and Maryland), 1821.
5. Edwardsville Spectator (Illinois),* 1822.
6. Illinois Intelligencer,* 1823.
7. The African Observer (Philadelphia), 1826.
8. Freedom's Journal (New York city), 1827.
9. The Investigator (Goodell's), 1827.
10. The National Philanthropist (Boston),† 1827.
11. The Journal of the Times (Vermont), 1828.
12. The Liberalist (New Orleans), 1828.

This list does not include the "African Repository" (1826) and other distinctively colonization papers. Of the twelve, "The Genius of Universal Emancipation" must be assigned to the head of the column for substantial merit.

The only way to form an adequate idea of the extent and

---

* See Washburne's "Sketch of Edward Coles," p. 167.

† In "The Genius of Universal Emancipation" of March 3, 1827, is the following extract from an editorial in the "National Philanthropist":

"We had in view when we adopted it (our title) the three great evils with which the world is cursed—*war*, *slavery*, and *intemperance*, especially the latter."

depth of anti-slavery sentiment in the United States in the period under consideration is to glean from these papers the articles expressing it which are copied from other newspapers. Charles Osborn republished in the "Philanthropist" anti-slavery articles from the following papers: Chester and Delaware Federalist, Federal Republican and Baltimore Telegraph, Alexandria (Va.) Gazette, Providence Gazette, Westchester Record, and Freeman's Journal.

Lundy copies similar articles from the following: Richmond Whig, Alexandria Gazette, Winchester (Va.) Republican, Village Record (Pennsylvania), Baltimore American, The Berean, United States Gazette, Abolition Intelligencer, New York Recorder, Christian Observer, Saturday Evening Post, New York Observer, American Economist, Western Luminary (Kentucky), Richmond Family Visitor, Freedom's Journal, American Farmer, Ohio Repository, Saturday Evening Chronicle, Maryland Republican, Zion's Herald, Greensborough (N. C.) Patriot, New Lisbon Patriot, Frederick (Md.) Political Examiner, Washington (Pa.) Examiner, National Advocate, Russellville (Ky.) Messenger, New York Daily Advertiser, Pennsylvania Gazette, Baltimore Gazette, Visitor and Telegraph, Genius of Temperance, Baltimore Patriot, African Repository, American, National Philanthropist, Lebanon Gazette, Democratic Press, Cincinnati Gazette (Hammond's), Journal of the Times (Vermont), Vertical Press, and the New England Enquirer. (43.) (For books, etc., during and before this period on slavery, see Appendix A.) Considering that the American press was then in its infancy, the era of the "Herald" and the "Tribune" and other modern journals not having then begun, that Lundy had few exchanges and probably did not copy for want of space in his paper more than one tenth of the anti-slavery articles published, it is clear that the sentiment of the American press, except in the extreme South, was against slavery between 1817 and 1830. This harmonizes with the fact that within that period the legislatures of three States (Ohio, Pennsylvania, and New Jersey) passed joint resolutions recommending the abolition of slavery by national compensation to the masters and professing willingness to bear their proportion of the expense.

It would be a departure from the plan of this book to enter

into any biographical details in regard to Mr. Lundy except such as illustrate the public opinion of his day. He richly merits a revised and improved edition of the hastily written sketch by Thomas Earle. We must part here with the heroic Quaker.*

---

* The confidence inspired by the personal character of Lundy was so great that a large number of slaves, in one case eighty-eight, were manumitted and sent to suitable refuges under his advice. In that day nearly all, if not all, the free States had what were called "Black laws," prohibiting under heavy penalties the bringing of negroes within their limits, while of the slave States that permitted manumission at all some required heavy bonds, with sureties for their good behavior and support, and others, for instance North Carolina, required them to leave the State within ninety days under penalty of being sold again into slavery. The freed negroes were left without a safe refuge from persecution except in Canada. Lundy's heart was deeply touched by their wretched condition. He went twice to Hayti in their behalf and made arrangements for their reception. By his means, direct and indirect, about two thousand slaves were manumitted and placed in security. These acts of noble devotion to the oppressed have been tortured by jealousy into a foundation for the charge against him of being a colonizationist, a charge refuted by the "Genius," but necessary to Mr. Garrison's claim to pre-empt the doctrine of anti-colonizationism. Let Lundy have his laurels! Is there not glory enough for all abolitionists? It is noteworthy that the three individuals who in the history of the struggle for abolition effected freedom for the largest number of slaves were Elisha Tyson, Benjamin Lundy, and Levi Coffin, the president of the Cincinnati Underground Railroad Company. Each wrought by his own methods, and not one of them probably ever saw either of the two others.

APPENDIX C.

ASSOCIATIONS OF A NATIONAL CHARACTER TO PROMOTE THE ABOLITION OF SLAVERY.

In the first forty years after the formation of the national Constitution abolition societies were active in nine of the original thirteen States. There were none in Massachusetts and New Hampshire because there was no need of them, or in Georgia and South Carolina because those States were completely under the control of the slave-holding interest. Either they or the influences that created them abolished slavery in the five States of Rhode Island, Connecticut, Pennsylvania, New Jersey, and New York, ending with the last named on the 4th of July, 1827. They failed in the four States of Maryland, Delaware, Virginia, and North Carolina.

Originally each of these organizations acted in the State in which it existed. Practically it did not need the co-operation of the others for its special purposes. There was, therefore, no affiliation between them until the common sentiment in favor of putting an end to the African slave trade made them feel the absolute necessity of a closer union. In December, 1791, the abolition societies of Rhode Island, Connecticut, New York, Pennsylvania, Maryland, and Virginia, sent separate memorials to Congress praying for action against the slave trade. In the House these papers were referred to a special committee. No further action was had, a neglect which excited the indignation of the memorialists. A correspondence between them ensued which resulted in an agreement of the societies to send delegates to meet in convention at Philadelphia on the first day of January, 1794. The societies represented on this occasion were the six above named and those of New Jersey, Delaware, Wilmington (Del.), and Chestertown (Md.). With the exception of 1799, 1802, 1805, and 1807, similar conventions of delegates were held every year until 1808, after which, owing partly to the abolition of the African slave trade in that year, but chiefly to the troubled condition of the country—the embargo and the war with Great Britain—they were not resumed until 1814. Beginning with that year they were regularly held biennially until 1824. Though the system of stated conferences of delegates of local societies, without organization during the long intervals of adjournment, without funds, newspaper presses, or lecturers, was the natural one so long as the object of each society was to abolish slavery in the State within which such society existed, that system was altogether inadequate to meet the necessities of the situation after the great upheaval of the North in the Missouri controversy. William Goodell, the historian of "Slavery and Anti-Slavery," says: *

"If Henry Clay could but have known how many were made uncompromising abolitionists by their disgust with that unholy compromise he would have found less occasion to congratulate himself with the results. The present (1852) anti-slavery excitement may be distinctly traced in part to the earnest debates among the people elicited by that same Missouri Compromise. The 'settlement' of the question by Congress was only the signal for its agitation among their constituents."

Of Rhode Island, the State of his residence at that time, Mr. Goodell says:

"Party lines for the time being were well nigh erased and the terms 'anti-slavery' and 'pro-slavery' took the place of Federalist and Republican. The files of newspapers, particularly the Providence 'Gazette,' bear testimony that the discussion became as 'radical' then *as it is now*, and that nearly the same arguments *pro* and *con* were then in use. Some who commenced writing against slavery and compromise *then* † have not ceased

---

* Page 384.

† William Goodell, Joshua Leavitt, Rev. James Duncan, and John Rankin, began to publish articles against slavery about that time. Benjamin Lundy issued his "Genius" in 1821, and John Finley Crowe "The Abolition Intelligencer" (Kentucky) in 1822.

writing against them still. The author may be permitted to record himself among these." (Page 384.)

The year 1824 was marked by the removal of Lundy's press to Baltimore, the anti-slavery victory at the polls in Illinois, the declaration of the Ohio and New Jersey Legislatures in favor of abolition by national legislation, and the election of John Quincy Adams to the presidency. Under the magnetic influence of these favorable events the anti-slavery societies wakened into vigorous activity. The annual conventions of delegates were resumed and were held in each year of the Adams Administration. The tendency in them to the assumption of the relation of parent society to auxiliaries became more and more marked ; but they could not rid themselves of the original feature of the delegate principle. Their operations were not openly indorsed by the Administration nor were they discountenanced. To be an abolitionist was no disqualification for office under the National Government under Adams. Among the agents for Lundy's paper there were nine postmasters, most of them in the South, and their names were published in its columns. Among the officers and delegates of the abolition conventions there were several men of national reputation who were noted friends of the national Administration. William Rawle (president), Horace Binney, and John Sergeant, of Philadelphia ; William L. Stone, Hiram Ketchum, and Cadwallader D. Colden, of New York, were of this number, and they attended or were officers of the conventions in 1824, 1825, 1826, and 1827. When the political skies began to darken over Adams in the disastrous presidential campaign of 1828, and it became manifest that Clay with his slaveholding policy would succeed to the Whig leadership, the above-named gentlemen with one accord abandoned the abolition movement. Not one of them appeared at Baltimore in the delegate convention of 1828, and not one of their names is mentioned in the proceedings of that body. The convention itself was a failure. Both the president and vice-president were absent, and of the thirteen delegates present six were residents of the city of Baltimore. Evan Lewis was there from New York. Thomas Shipley was elected president *pro tem.*, and Edwin P. Atlee secretary. Both of these were from Philadelphia. This sudden and unexpected defection of the Whig politicians must have been extremely discouraging to the societies. Its full meaning, that Herod and Pilate were about to combine against Christ, they may not have comprehended and measured in its probable results. The hundred and six Southern auxiliaries still remained. These could not be deserted.*

Another convention (the twenty-first) was called to meet at Washington city, December 3, 1829. This was the expiring effort of the delegate system. Not only were the Whig politicians absent, but there was not a single delegate present from any of the societies formerly existing in the slave States south of the District of Columbia. In 1827 there had been more than a hundred of these. Lundy was there. He was ashamed to own the dismal failure of the convention. In the "Genius" of December 25, 1829, he says the number present was "smaller than had been anticipated." It must have been very small. The general defection of the Southern societies, following upon that of the Whig politicians, should have opened the eyes of the few who remained faithful. Left without leaders or constituency, having achieved the abolition of slavery in the Northern States, but having no strength to lift the gage of battle for national supremacy through Texas annexation which had been thrown down by the slave power in the election of Jackson, they should have abdicated the leadership, terminated the delegate system, and joined in an effort to unite all the abolitionists of the country in an army strong enough to fight the national battle then imminent.

But they did not see. Men cling long to outworn forms. The old abolition societies which had supported the delegate system for forty years could not give it up at once. They could not believe that the prospects of emancipation in Maryland, Virginia, and North Carolina which had been so bright in 1827

* These were distributed in 1827 as follows: Delaware, 2; District of Columbia, 2; Kentucky, 8; Virginia, 8; Maryland, 11; Tennessee, 25; and North Carolina, 50. The membership comprised 6,625 persons. There were 12 auxiliaries in Illinois, and 12 more in Pennsylvania, New York, and Ohio. All these were reported to the American Abolitionist Convention in 1827. (See "Proceedings.") Of unreported anti-slavery societies there were probably between 50 and 70. Consult Poole's pamphlet, p. 72.

were utterly overclouded in 1828. Nor could they comprehend that in electing General Jackson without previous discussion of slavery extension and Texas annexation the country had practically changed its policy, and the nation had without shout of command or blare of trumpet executed a left wheel upon its center, marched into the camp of the slave power, and surrendered at discretion ; and so, being blind, they issued a call for another convention. But this never convened. The delegate system had had its day ; *it was dead.*

From the time of the Missouri controversy, which had revealed the inherent weakness of the delegate system, the abolition sentiment of the North was growing away from it. In the exciting battle of 1822–'24 for the rescue of Illinois, the convention was not known in the leadership of the anti-slavery forces ; nor was its primacy acknowledged by the greater number of the societies which were organized between 1820 and 1830 under the names of Abolition, Aiding Abolition, Manumission, Emancipation, Gradual Emancipation, Anti-Slavery, Constitution, Free Labor, Free Produce, Union Humane, Benevolent, African Protection, Friends of Humanity, Moral and Religious, and others more or less expressive of their anti-slavery character. The assumption that the few societies which sent delegates to the convention were almost the only ones of the kind in existence before 1830 is an error into which many worthy writers have fallen. In truth, from the time of the revival of anti-slavery action in 1814, the discussion of slavery increased from year to year in geometrical progression, and until 1830 the formation of societies kept pace with the discussion ; nor did the convention contribute in any perceptible manner to the triumphs of anti-slavery sentiment in the legislatures of the Northern States. Between 1824 and 1827 the General Assemblies of Ohio, Pennsylvania, and New Jersey, had each passed resolutions in favor of the abolition of slavery by national legislation, and professed willingness that those States should bear their respective proportions of the necessary expenditure. In 1828 the Pennsylvania Legislature, by an almost unanimous vote, "*Resolved*, That the Senators of this State, in the Senate of the United States, are hereby requested to procure, if practicable, the passage of a law to abolish slavery in the District of Columbia in such a manner as they may consider consistent with the rights of individuals and the Constitution of the United States." *

On the 28th of January, 1829, the New York Assembly "*Resolved*, If the Senate concur herein, that the Senators of this State in the Congress of the United States be and are hereby instructed, and the representatives of this State are requested to *make every possible exertion* to effect the passage of a law for the abolition of slavery in the District of Columbia." †

On the 9th of January, 1829, the House of Representatives, United States, "*Resolved*, That the Committee of the District of Columbia be instructed to inquire into the *expediency* (not the *right*) of providing by law for the gradual abolition of slavery in the District in such manner that no individual shall be injured thereby." ‡

The statement that "after the Missouri Compromise of 1820 a paralysis fell on the anti-slavery sentiment of the country" (G., i, 90) is not justified by the facts. The truth is that for substantial anti-slavery victories no subsequent decade up to 1850 can compare with the one ending in 1830. The final exclusion of slavery from Illinois in 1824, its total abolition in New York in 1827, the formation of more than a hundred abolition societies in slave States, and the anti-slavery action of three Northern legislatures in and before 1829, are facts which alone should vindicate the healthy state of anti-slavery opinion in the North during that decade. The old convention system did not expire because anti-slavery sentiment was suffering "paralysis," but because it was inadequate to meet the demands of the vigorous sentiment which dated from 1820. The old shell was sloughed off that the new life might have free play. The sickle gave place to the mowing-machine; the stage coach to the railroad train.

The quotation in Appendix B from the "Genius" of July, 1831, proves that "men of wealth and influence are [were] about to engage in forming an American Anti-Slavery Society." The project was delayed in its execution by the Nat Turner insurrection of August 21st, the expectation of a successful emancipation movement in Virginia during the winter of 1831-'32, the intense

* Jay's Inquiry, p. 161. † Ibid., p. 161. ‡ Ibid., p. 161.

activity infused into anti-slavery movements by the attempt of President Jackson in March, 1829, to purchase Texas, the reluctance of the convention men to assume a leadership not recognized by the recently formed societies, and the necessity of correspondence and interviews between the many persons interested. Meanwhile, between 1829 and November, 1833, many new anti-slavery societies* had been formed; about thirty newspapers † were actively advocating the abolition cause; in 1829 Mexico had foiled President Jackson by abolishing slavery; on the 1st of August, 1833, the Parliament of Great Britain had passed the act for emancipation the following year in the British West Indies; and the whole North was stirred to its depths on the slavery question. To bring all the societies and presses into effective

---

* The lists of auxiliaries published with the annual reports of the American Anti-Slavery Society for 1836, 1837, and 1838, show *by dates* that 36 had been organized before the national society, and enumerate more than twice as many without date of organization. Of this last class at least 50 were in existence before December, 1833. Not reckoning the 130 auxiliaries of the Abolition Convention, there were nearly if not quite 100 anti-slavery societies whose organization antedates that of the American Anti-Slavery Society.

† In the annual report of the managers of the New England Anti-Slavery Society, read January 15, 1834, and probably written at an earlier date, there is the following note:

"The following is an imperfect list of the newspapers and periodicals in the United States which advocate the cause of abolition: 'Philanthropist,' Brownsville, Pa.; 'Observer,' Lowell, Mass.; 'State Journal,' Montpelier, Vt.; 'Anti-Masonic Enquirer,' Rochester, N. Y.; 'Workingman's Press,' New Bedford, Mass.; 'Rights of Man,' Rochester, N. Y.; 'Free Press,' Hallowell, Me.; 'Gazette,' Haverhill, Mass.; 'Friend,' Philadelphia, Pa.; 'Emancipator,' New York city; 'Massachusetts Spy,' Worcester, Mass.; 'Unionist,' Brooklyn, Conn.; 'Record,' Lynn, Mass.; 'Evangelist,' New York city; 'Canonsburg Luminary,' Pennsylvania; 'New England Telegraph,' North Wrentham, Mass.; 'Genius of Universal Emancipation,' Washington, D. C.; 'Christian Watchman,' Boston, Mass.; 'Messenger,' Indiana; 'Liberator,' Boston; 'Palladium,' Bethania, Pa.; 'Freeman,' Greenfield, Mass.; 'Reporter,' Watertown, N. Y.; 'Philanthropist,' Providence, R. I.; 'Christian Secretary,' Hartford, Conn.; 'We, the People,' Plymouth, Mass."

unity was the need of the hour. It is believed that every anti-slavery society and press then in existence favored the formation of a national society. Several resolutions to that effect had been passed. On the 21st of January, 1833, about eighteen months after the notice quoted in our thirteenth chapter from the "Genius," the New England Anti-Slavery Society had authorized its managers "to call a national meeting of the friends of abolition for the purpose of organizing such a society [national] at such time and place as they shall deem expedient." (Report of 1833, page 8.) But as the managers, in their report for 1834 (page 12), mention the formation of the American society without reporting any action of their own contributing to it, the inference is unavoidable that they took none.

During the summer of 1833, the general demand for a new national organization suited to the wants of the times and controlling funds and presses became so urgent that meetings were held among the abolitionists in Philadelphia to consider the subject. Those of them who had figured prominently in the old convention were Thomas Shipley, Dr. Edwin P. Atlee, James Mott, David Paul Brown, Isaac Barton, Peter Wright, Thomas Earle, Thomas Parker, Jr., Abram L. Pennock, Dr. Joseph Parrish, Isaac Parrish, Dilwyn Parrish, William S. Hallowell, Evan Lewis, Enoch Lewis, and Charles S. Cope.* It was agreed in their conferences that Evan Lewis, who had formerly resided in New York city, should go to that city and urge the Tappans to take the lead in the formation of a national society. He went upon this mission in the summer of 1833, saw the Tappans, and prevailed upon them to take the matter into consideration.

For many years Arthur Tappan had been known throughout

---

* All these favored immediate abolition and were identified with the cause both before and after the formation of the new society. It is believed, indeed, that, with the exception of the Southern delegates and the six Whig politicians named in the text, all the able and energetic men who had acted as delegates to the old conventions continued their anti-slavery efforts in the new organization. Evan Lewis, Edwin P. Atlee, Edwin A. Atlee, Thomas Shipley, Peter Wright, John Sharp, Jr., and Isaac Barton, were among the men who formed it, and Edwin A. Atlee and Evan Lewis were among its vice-presidents.

the country as a wealthy merchant, fervent Christian, and liberal contributor to the Church and to the Bible, Tract, Missionary, Education, and other religious and benevolent associations. He was an officer in several of them. He was widely known, too, as opposed to slavery. In the twenties he aided the Colonization Society. He subscribed to Lundy's paper, and in 1828 he made a small donation of money to help it out of its embarrassments. In 1830 he was elected a vice-president of the African Education Society and paid Garrison's fine at Baltimore to release him from prison, and in 1831 he endeavored to establish an African high school at New Haven. In March, 1833, he and his brother Lewis established the "Emancipator" (Goodell's "Slavery and Anti-Slavery," p. 392), which soon gained an extensive circulation. He aided the "New York Evangelist," which was both Presbyterian and anti-slavery. About the same time he printed and circulated at his own expense five thousand copies of Whittier's excellent pamphlet against slavery. Goodell (page 392) says : "By co-operation between the Messrs. Tappan and a few others, very large issues of anti-slavery tracts were circulated monthly during the greater part of this year and sent by mail," etc. Lewis Tappan adopts this statement in his brother's "Life" (page 168). It was chiefly through the munificence, discretion, and activity of the Tappans, aided by the counsel of William Jay and the editorial ability of William Goodell, Joshua Leavitt, and Elizur Wright, that before General Jackson's first presidential term had expired New York had become the head center of abolition influence. By general recognition of the public Arthur Tappan was the leader, and his brother Lewis ranked next. Arthur's strength lay in his wisdom, firmness, discretion, and liberality ; Lewis's in his ready tact, will-power, strong convictions, and indefatigable activity. Arthur was not a public speaker ; Lewis was fluent, clear, and forcible. Arthur had no taste for public business ; Lewis, if he had been elected representative in Congress, would have led the house. There was no jealousy between the brothers, and the two were strong enough to lead the strong men who composed the abolition army between 1829 and 1834.

The visit of Evan Lewis to New York was the abdication of the Philadelphia abolitionists who had led to the Tappans who were to lead. The former capital ceded precedence to the new metropolis. The project was discussed in August and September, but no definite action was taken before the *New York city Anti-Slavery Society* was formed. How, when, and why this occurred we will let Lewis Tappan tell. He says:

"The abolitionists of the city had made such progress in the diffusion of their sentiments that they were encouraged in the belief that the time had come to form a society and thus combine and extend their influence. Accordingly a call was made for a meeting of the friends of immediate emancipation, to be held at Clinton Hall on the second day of October, 1833. The notice was published in the papers of the day and by show-bills put up in the streets and on public buildings." *

He then gives an account of the mob, the manner in which it was foiled in its purposes, the formation of the society at Chatham Street Chapel, and the names of its officers. These were Arthur Tappan, W. Green, John Rankin, Elizur Wright, Charles W. Denison, Joshua Leavitt, Isaac T. Hopper, Abram L. Cox, Lewis Tappan, and William Goodell.

In the last half of September brief intimations were made through the anti-slavery papers that a convention was to be held to form a national anti-slavery society and a future official notice was promised. Referring to the formation of the New York city Anti-Slavery Society, October 2, Lewis Tappan writes:

---

* "Life of Arthur Tappan," p. 168. The honor of causing the formation of this society is claimed for Mr. Garrison by his sons on the ground that, on the eve of sailing for England, May 2, he directed it. "It *must* be organized, he said, and his words gave the needed resolution." (G., i, 346.) The authority for this claim is given in a foot-note, "Related by William Green in 1880." As the supposed order lay five months without execution and forty seven years without being testified to, it can not be taken against Lewis Tappan's plain statement; nor was this claim intimated at the time by Mr. Garrison, though in October, 1833, he noticed the formation of the New York city Anti-Slavery Society several times in his paper and copied its constitution in part. The Tappans, Leavitt, Isaac T. Hopper, Wright, Goodell, and others who did form that society were men of undaunted courage, and the inuendo that in the preceding May they were hesitating to act because "of a hostile and lawless public sentiment" (G., i, 346) is unjust to them. Imagine Isaac T. Hopper, the lion-hearted, charged with timidity!

"Shortly afterward Mr. Tappan met with a few friends to consider the propriety of issuing a call for an anti-slavery convention to form a national society." ("Life of Arthur Tappan," page 175.)

An unsigned circular, nearly a newspaper column in length, written, it is said, by Joshua Leavitt and Lewis Tappan, and setting forth the reasons for such a step, was published in the first week of October. It mentioned neither time nor place, being intended to elicit expressions of opinion by societies, newspapers, and individuals. These were favorable. The time was come.

The call was issued under the auspices of the New York city Anti-Slavery Society on the 29th of October. It was signed by Arthur Tappan, President, Joshua Leavitt, one of the managers, and Elizur Wright, Jr., Secretary, and was published in the anti-slavery newspapers, while letters were addressed to friendly individuals in different parts of the country inviting their attendance.

In the first paragraph of the official report of the proceedings of the convention, made out by Lewis Tappan and John G. Whittier, secretaries, the statement is made that the delegates and other friends of emancipation had convened at Philadelphia "on the fourth day of December, Anno Domini, 1833, for the purpose of forming a national anti-slavery society *pursuant to an invitation* from the *New York city Anti-Slavery Society.*"

The official report of the "roll of the convention" shows names* as follows: From Maine, 5; New Hampshire, 1; Vermont, 1; Massachusetts, 12; Rhode Island, 3; Connecticut, 5; New York, 9; New Jersey, 3; Pennsylvania, 22; and Ohio, 3. From ten States, total, 64. Of the members, three were colored men—Purvis, Barbadoes, and McCrummell. The religious element was largely predominant, if it did not absorb all others.

---

* Sixty-two names are signed to the Declaration of Sentiments, as published in the "Proceedings of the Second Decade Meeting" (1853), p. 169. Of these, *three* (Daniel S. Southmayd, George Bourne, and James Mott) do not appear on the official roll, and six that do appear on the roll are wanting, to wit, Thomas Shipley, Peter Wright, Isaac Barton, Edwin Fussell, Sumner Stebbins, and W. H. Johnson.

There were at least twenty-one Presbyterians or Congregationalists, of whom six were preachers (not counting George Bourne, who was not present at the convention), nineteen Quakers, and one Unitarian preacher (S. J. May). It is probable that every person present was a member of some religious denomination except Mr. Garrison. He was not. (G., i, 56.) Every one of the seven preachers and a dozen or more of the others, it is believed, were platform speakers, and some of them were distinguished as such. There was not a single statesman or man of experience in public affairs. There were merchants, theological students, a college president, an ex-professor, and a poet. It was an assembly of remarkably intelligent and sensible men who were without experience in practical politics and whose bias was to give undue prominence to the religious aspect of the anti-slavery movement.

The dominating influence was that of the Tappans, John Rankin, William Goodell, Beriah Green, and Elizur Wright. Arthur Tappan had counseled great discretion, and Judge William Jay, the only statesman at that time identified with them, had written urging them to make an explicit declaration of sound political principles. (See page 134 of "Third Decade Proceedings.") The charges generally brought against the abolitionists were that they advocated—

1. Violation of the national Constitution ;
2. Dissolution of the Union ;
3. The right of Congress to abolish slavery in the States ; and
4. Insurrection of the slaves.

To meet these charges three distinct propositions were incorporated into the constitution of the American Anti-Slavery Society, viz. :

1. That each State in which slavery exists has by the United States Constitution the exclusive right to *legislate* in regard to its abolition in said State.

2. That the society would endeavor in a constitutional way to influence Congress to prohibit the interstate slave trade, to abolish slavery in the Territories and the District of Columbia, and to prevent the extension of it to any State that might be admitted to the Union.

3. That it would not countenance any insurrection of slaves.

The constitution is an instrument in ten articles, preceded by an elaborate preamble. It covers three and a quarter pages of the official pamphlet report. The fact that it was reported at the first session of the convention and promptly adopted without amendment indicates previous and careful preparation. Tradition says that it had been drafted by Judge Jay. The doctrine of immediate * emancipation is contained in the preamble.

The criticism of more than half a century has failed to detect a flaw in this admirable instrument. The doctrines of constitutional law embodied in it were reiterated by the anti-slavery men in all the stages of their grand struggle as a Liberty party in 1840 and 1844, a Free Soil party in 1848, and a Republican

---

* The expediency of taking this position is well set forth in the following letter to Dr. E. P. Atlee, written twenty days after the convention adjourned. The original lies before me:

"New York, 26 *Dec.*, 1833.

"My dear Sir: Illness has prevented an earlier reply to your esteemed favor of the 11th inst. I have read your letter once and again, and it has been read in the executive committee.

"We differ with you in opinion that it is incumbent on us to present a specific plan for the government of emancipated slaves or that it is advisable to recommend the separation of a territory exclusively for that class of our fellow-citizens. The moment we offer a *plan* objections will be made to it by those who are in favor of perpetual slavery (and they are not a few), and the minds of the community will be turned off from the great duty of emancipation to altercations about the mode in which it shall take place and the measures to be taken in consequence. By presenting any specific plan, we pledge ourselves to it when time might unfold a better plan which we could not advocate without a charge of inconsistency. If we recommend a separate territory we admit that a *removal* of the colored (people) is expedient, a doctrine we have over and again denied. Thus we aid the argument of colonization and introduce division into our own ranks.

"By advocating simply the doctrine of emancipation we move on with united hearts; but whenever we propose plans of subsequent measures we produce division. . . . These are the reasons, so far as I think of them, that seem to oppose the design you have suggested. Perhaps on further reflection they will have weight on your mind. . . .

"Very truly yours, Lewis Tappan."

party in 1856; and they were finally adopted by the nation in the election of Abraham Lincoln to the presidency on a platform containing them.

After the convention had adopted the constitution and elected its officers, and at the close of its first day's session, a motion was made to appoint a committee to draw up for the signature of members a declaration of principles of the society. This had not been in the regular programme of intended proceedings; but as it was understood that Mr. Garrison had prepared one a committee of ten, including him, was appointed. Dr. Atlee was chairman, and Elizur Wright, John G. Whittier, and William Goodell, were members. The first draft was rejected. Another was prepared during the night by Mr. Garrison. This was amended first by a sub-committee, then by the committee of ten, and finally by the convention in committee of the whole. Naturally enough it bears traces of hasty preparation, and also of its mixed authorship. In more than one instance the wrong word is used, or a passage inserted out of its proper place. The recapitulation of divers human measures to secure success is followed, oddly enough, by our "trust for victory is *solely* in *God*." The style is partly terse and partly turgid; the imitation of the literary form of the Declaration of Independence is in bad taste; and the statement of doctrines of constitutional law, though embracing those already adopted by the society, is more rhetorical than precise.* Why six members of the convention did not sign the declaration does not appear. With its obvious faults it was a noble document as finally adopted. The following sentence, though open to verbal criticism, was worthy of a place as a motto at the head of every anti-slavery paper in the country: "We also maintain that there are, at the present time, the highest obligations resting upon the people of the free States, to remove slavery by *moral* and *political action*, as prescribed in the Constitution of the United States."

Of this declaration Mr. Garrison said at the third decade meeting ("Proceedings," etc., page 22), "It is a collection of the merest truisms." Some of his friends, attributing to him

---

* The right of the National Government to suppress a slave insurrection by proclaiming freedom might have been mentioned.

the exclusive authorship, exaggerate its merits, and the truth seems to lie about half-way between the two. In the same speech he says: "The result" (of the adoption and signing of the declaration) "was the immediate formation of the American Anti-Slavery Society, which," etc.

This is a mistake; the official record shows that the society was formed and the officers elected Wednesday, and that the declaration was not reported until Thursday, the 5th. S. J. May, in his "Recollections," (page 88), says it was reported in the afternoon of Thursday and signed on Friday. The American Anti-Slavery Society had then been in existence two days.

The officers chosen were Arthur Tappan, President; twenty-six vice-presidents, representing ten States; Elizur Wright (New York), Secretary of Domestic Correspondence; W. L. Garrison,* Secretary of Foreign Correspondence; Abraham L. Cox (New York), Recording Secretary; W. Green (New York), Treasurer; and seventy-two managers, representing ten States.

---

* Mr. Garrison was at once placed by the executive committee under the "vexatious restriction" of submitting to it for approval all his official letters before sending them. He resigned the same month or early in January. His friend R. B. Hall, who was a member of the convention, wrote to him January 21, 1834, upon hearing of his resignation: "I will give you succinctly the history of that office. When the committee to form a constitution at Mr. Sharpless's were about to retire, I had reason to suppose that the form of constitution *which they had in their hands* provided but one secretary to the society. I knew, too, *what was to be the management* about that office, *that Mr. Wright was to fill it*, and thus be the mouth of all anti-slavery men in the United States. This did not exactly suit me. *I knew your claims.* I knew, too, that you would be placed on the board of managers or as vice-president—in other words, would be *second fiddle*—and this did not suit me. I laid hold on the committee, and urged and entreated them to create the office to which you were subsequently appointed." . . . (G. i, 415).

Mr. Hall's testimony shows that the men who framed the constitution and formed the society had no intention to put Mr. Garrison into any important position. They yielded to Mr. Hall's insistence, but the "vexatious restriction" immediately imposed on him as secretary shows they were determined that Mr. Garrison should not only play "second fiddle," but no tunes except of their choosing.

The convention adjourned on December 6th, and the National Society entered at once upon its wonderful career of agitation. Arthur Tappan made an annual subscription of three thousand dollars*; John Rankin, the New York merchant, one of twelve hundred ; and each paid in promptly the first installment. Other parties subscribed and paid smaller amounts. Men like William Jay were pleased with the conservative and law-abiding character of the society, and gave it earnest support. Up to the date of its disruption, in 1840, the activity of the American Anti-Slavery Society was unparalleled among the reformatory associations of the United States.

* This was increased in 1835 to five thousand dollars.

APPENDIX D.

To Colonel Stone—

Sir : A few days since I was told by a friend that he had read in the New York "Spectator," of which you are the editor, this assertion : "Mr. Birney is not the only brawler who has sold his slaves and turned abolitionist." He had not the paper with him, but he assured me that I might rely on the substantial accuracy of the words as above quoted. The accusation it involves is a serious one to myself individually, and may, if unanswered, have an injurious influence on the cause of human liberty, in which, with many others much more distinguished than myself, I am employing the humble powers with which it has pleased God to endow me. It is only in the latter view—for, as to myself, I believe I could bear patiently the wrong you have incautiously inflicted—that I have thought it proper to transmit to you for publication the following statement, which I ought not to doubt, from your Christian profession, you will take pleasure in laying before the public through the same medium you used in acquainting them with your accusation.

At the time (1818) I determined to remove from Kentucky to Alabama. I was the holder of a few slaves, principally domestics or house-servants, given to me by my grandfather, my father, and the father of Mrs. Birney. Intending to engage in planting, I sold nearly all my property in Kentucky with the view of investing the proceeds in slaves and land in the South. Including those obtained by purchase and those already mentioned, I had on my settlement in Alabama as a planter, as nearly as I can now remember, about thirty. Two or three years afterward I received from my father *five* more.

My habits at this period of my life tended more to the dissipation than to the accumulation of wealth. In a few years my circumstances became embarrassed, though not insolvent, and I found it necessary to resume the practice of the law, which from the time of my removal to Alabama I had relinquished. It became necessary, also, in order to meet my responsibilities and preserve my credit, that I should sell my land and slaves. Before making any contract for the sale of the slaves I informed them of my situation, and consulted their wishes in their selection of a purchaser. They had less aversion to being sold than they would formerly have had, because I had found it necessary to the prosecution of my professional pursuits to remove from my plantation to Huntsville, sixteen miles distant, thus leaving them for the last year entirely in the charge of an overseer. In the sale I made a short time afterward to a planter whose land adjoined mine, and whose character as a humane master was well known to my slaves, I reserved my domestic servants, five in number, a man, his wife, and their three children. This sale was made in 1824, at a time when my opinions on the subject of slave-holding did not materially differ from those which prevailed among the generality of planters. My religious profession and connection with the Church took place in the spring of 1826.

For several years I had no other slaves than the five I have mentioned as domestics. In the autumn of 1829, an elderly man and his wife, held by an innkeeper at whose house I usually boarded while attending a neighboring court, became solicitous that I should buy them. The innkeeper was addicted to fits of intemperance, and while they were on him he would compel the old negro to amuse him by exercising his skill—acquired in his younger days—in playing vulgar tunes on the fiddle. The old man being a member of the Methodist Church, and an occasional exhorter, considered his participation in such things as inconsistent with his religious station, and felt the *necessity* under which he was placed as a great grievance. This, in addition to other reasons, induced me to purchase him and his wife at the price set on them by the innkeeper. They were not very long in my possession till the husband found in Huntsville an old acquaintance in a gentleman who was about removing from Huntsville to the neighborhood of Louisville in Kentucky. They expressed a desire to remove with him, on account, as they stated, of their being thus brought into the neighborhood of some of their friends and relatives who resided near Louisville. They persuaded the gentleman to offer for them the same price I had given, though it was not all to be paid in cash, as I had paid it. A part of it was to be paid in furniture, for which I had no pressing necessity. However, this was made no impediment to the accomplishment of their wishes, though they would doubtless have brought much more had they been set up for sale to the highest bidder.

Up to 1831 my professional business had been profitable, and my pecuniary means had again begun to accumulate. I determined to expend them, together with a gift of money I had received from my father about this time, in the establishment of a *stock*-farm, because it could be conducted with comparatively few slaves. To this end I bought, partly from an individual and partly from the Government, several hundred acres of cheap land. In November of that year I bought from a Tennesseean a negro woman with her child, a little girl about four years old. Before I had made any other purchases of slaves, a lady in Huntsville, who had secured to her several slaves, proposed to me, through her husband, to pledge to me two of them for a sum of money of which he stood in need. The sum to be advanced was supposed to be their value, taking into the estimate the risk of their lives during the time the money should be retained. I acceded to the proposition, took into my use the two slaves, and kept them on this contract till within a short time of my removal to Kentucky, in the autumn of 1833. The money was then returned and the slaves redelivered to the lady. In the beginning of 1833 I hired from an administrator for that year five slaves, a man, his wife, and their three children. They remained on my farm till I was about leaving Alabama, At the proper time they were delivered up to the gentleman from whom they were hired. These circumstances in relation to the pledged and hired slaves are mentioned to correct misrepresentations that have been frequently made at the North by some of my Southern acquaintances as to the extent of my connection with slavery at the time I prepared to remove from Alabama. They have represented me as holding slaves to some considerable extent, and as selling all or nearly all of them in order to avoid loss in my conversion to abolitionism. These misstatements have doubtless been often made inconsiderately and ignorantly by those who would do more to injure the cause of emancipation than they would to injure me. Yet in a few instances, if my information be correct, they have been made by persons whose knowledge of my circumstances at that time takes away every excuse which charity can plead for them on the ground of *ignorance.*

At this time, the autumn of 1833, I held as slaves the woman and child above mentioned and five house-servants. I was then, and had been more than a year before, the agent and advocate of the American Colonization Society. I do not now remember that my views as to the *right* of the slave to his liberty and the *duty* of the master to emancipate were much in advance of those usually entertained by colonizationists. Certain it is I looked forward to no time, I anticipated no circumstances which would ever bring me to consider them as I now do. I had then no expectation that I should at any period of my life deserve the name of an abolitionist or draw on me persecutions of sufficient rigor to banish me from Kentucky, where I was born—persecutions from which the constitutional ægis of the free State of Ohio have not yet availed to defend me.

Before breaking up my establishment in Alabama, I proposed to the woman to send her and her child to Liberia, after she had, by the services she had already performed and by her future hire, returned me the price I had paid for her. She objected utterly to going to Liberia. I then proposed to bring her with me to Kentucky, where, after being remunerated by her services for the sum I had paid for her, I would manumit her and her child without any condition of removal, in the mean time giving to the child such education as I could under existing circumstances. To this, so far as she herself was concerned, to my great surprise, she objected, urging that she was an entire stranger in Kentucky, and that she did not wish to leave the acquaintances she had made since her residence in Alabama. Believing her conduct to be altogether injudicious, I said to her, that while I felt no desire to compel her to either of the courses I had proposed, I could not permit her to make for the child the election of remaining behind. So far from being displeased with this she expressed her full concurrence, saying she *knew her child would be well taken care of, and every provision made for her that could be expected.*

She preferred being *sold* to being *hired*, on account of the better treatment she would receive from a master than from a hirer. I permitted her to select her own master, and in order that she might have no difficulty in inducing such a one as she might select to purchase her, I put her price at eighty-five dollars less than I had given for her and her child. The advance on the price of negroes at this time would have enabled me to have sold her alone at public sale for from seventy-five to one hundred dollars more than the sum I asked. The gentleman whom she selected, and of whose character for humanity to his slaves I had received, on inquiry, satisfactory assurances, purchased her without hesitation. I was not informed of the reasons for her conduct—so singular, as it appeared to me—till she had rejected both my propositions leading to her ultimate manumission. I was afterward told by my overseer, who was warmly attached to my interests, and who, I believe, thought that I was already somewhat fanatical in my desire to oblige the woman who wanted me to sell her, believing if I took her to Kentucky I would finally emancipate her, that her conduct proceeded from an attachment she had formed for a negro man who, he supposed, had persuaded her to object to every proposition which contemplated her removal from that part of the country. The little girl, her child, I brought with me, together with the domestic servants already mentioned, to Kentucky in 1833.

I had already lost much of my first confidence in the efficacy of colonization principles for the extirpation of slavery among us. I assisted, in December, 1833, in the organization at Lexington of a gradual emancipation society, thinking its principles were somewhat stronger than those of colonization and would be more effectual. I entered on this scheme with ardor and became its active advocate. A short trial of it soon convinced me of its inefficacy to move the hearts of men. During this winter and the ensuing spring my mind was deeply interested in the whole subject of slavery. I read almost every work I could lay my hands on ; I talked much of it in public and in private. In the month of May, 1834, I became so fully convinced of the *right* of my slaves to their freedom and of my *duty* as a Christian to give it to them that I prepared, as well as I now remember, on the first day of June, a deed of emancipation for the six I brought with me from Alabama and had it duly entered of record in the office of the county court of the county in which I lived. They all remained with me, receiving such wages, with the exception of the little girl, as were customary in the country.

In the previous month of January or February, a young negro man held by the executors of the late Judge Boyle, of Kentucky, earnestly solicited me to buy him lest at the sale of the estate he might be sold to some person of whose character and temper he knew nothing. At first I objected on the ground that I intended never again to purchase a slave to be held in the absolute sense. He left me, but returned again, bringing as an aid to his own importunity the recommendation of the brother-in-law of Judge Boyle, who held as slaves some other members of the family. He prevailed on this second application, and I paid the price of him to the executors. Before I consented to do so we had this understanding, that, so soon as by the allowance of fair wages he should return me the money I had advanced he should go free; that in the mean time I would have taught him to read, and, if he proved apt to learn, writing and the elementary rules of arithmetic; that I would ask of him no unreasonable services, but that if he should fail to perform with fidelity what I required of him I should return him to the state of absolute slavery from which I considered I was taking him. It was but a short time before I became satisfied that his character had been grossly, though I will not suffer myself to think intentionally, misrepresented to me. He proved trifling, lazy, and troublesome among the rest of my servants. Especially provoking to me was his reiterated harsh treatment of the little girl above mentioned, for whom, as she had no relative near her, I felt almost a parental tenderness. After bearing with him for several months, and often persuading and admonishing him, I found it was out of the question to keep him about me any longer. In the month of July, I think it was, I gave him a writing authorizing him to obtain for his master any one who would give me within one hundred dollars of the price I had paid for him, although I think it probable had I offered him for the highest price without regard to the character of the purchaser I might have received for him one hundred dollars *more* than I gave. It turned out that the gentleman who had unwarily recommended him to me offered to become the purchaser if I would grant a longer credit for part of the sum than I had proposed in my written note. To this I assented. The same gentleman had a short time previous become the owner by purchase of the farm belonging to the estate of Judge Boyle, so that the young man was returned to the very place from which I had taken him. Before the last payment fell due I became convinced, notwithstanding what I had done was nothing more than a literal execution of the arrangement to which he had *assented* (if such a thing can be predicated of a *slave*), that I had done wrong in selling him. I wrote to the gentleman who had bought him that I wished to repurchase the slave that I might give him his freedom. His reply informed me that he was out of his power, as he had sent him down the Mississippi with a Southern planter. This case has given me more uneasiness of mind than any of the others. While most persons under the same pressure of influences which was then bearing on me would probably have acted as I did, yet do I not seek to justify it. The influences which warped and obscured my moral vision I ought to have resisted.

The above statement shows my connection with slavery for nearly twenty years. There has been no concealment or suppression on my part of any of the facts since I have become an abolitionist. I have often repeated them to friends who have inquired concerning them. The enemies of abolition have often perverted or misunderstood them and trumpeted them to the world in a manner not unlike that which it has pleased you to adopt. I should have published them in the journals of the country had I not thought it would be impertinent to consider such small matters as at all affecting the magnificent and awful cause which has brought in opposition the friends of liberty and the upholders of slavery. At present I think differently. An importance has been given to my conduct which renders an exposition of it necessary. While God has granted me, as I trust, repentance for its errors, he has not altogether withheld from me the humility which can bear their exposure.

Had you been as careful as it seems to me you ought to have been before venturing so deadly an assault on the reputation of a Christian brother, you would either previously have asked of me if the facts on which it was to proceed were true or you would have given the authority on which you have made your injurious accusation. Hereafter, sir, should you deem any part of my private history worthy of publication through the journals under your control, I will at your request, and on my own consent to its propriety, furnish you with statements which will stand any test your friends or mine may choose to apply to them.

With due respect, JAMES G. BIRNEY.

CINCINNATI, *May* 2, 1836.

APPENDIX E.

THE facts alluded to in the text, although well known to many of the old inhabitants of Indiana and Ohio, have been ignored by most of the writers of abolition history. They possess a value, however, that entitles them to permanent record. It is to be hoped they will all be preserved in the local annals of the counties of those States so that the future historian may trace the strong currents of anti-slavery opinion early in the century. The limits prescribed to this volume do not permit the author to group any facts except a few of those relating to immediate abolitionists in the adjoining counties of Adams, Brown, Clermont, and Highland in Ohio. These will suffice, however, to throw light on the times treated of in the text. An equally interesting statement might perhaps be made in relation to the county of Belmont, in which in 1815 Lundy organized the *Union Humane Society*, an abolition organization that soon numbered five hundred members, to Jefferson County, in which in 1817 Charles Osborn published his abolition paper the "Philanthropist," or to Warren County or Wayne County (Indiana), the homes of numerous Quakers, who in early days were stanch friends of the slave. The author's selection is determined mainly by personal knowledge gained during a long residence in Ohio of many of the facts and the facility of ascertaining the others from reliable persons and local publications.

Before 1805 the following families had migrated from slave States into Brown County: The Ellisons, the Shepards, the Campbells, the Dunlavys, and the Dunlops. All these were immediate abolitionists and Presbyterians, and with the exception of two individuals remained such. Rev. Dyer Burgess, one of the most noted abolitionists in Ohio between 1800 and 1840, married a Miss Ellison. He was for about forty years pastor of the Presbyterian church at West Union, Adams County. His sermons against slavery were uncompromising, and for years before 1817 he had refused to admit slave-holders to the communion-table.

The Shepards were numerous. The original settlers of that name had three sons—John, Abraham, and Jacob. The Rev. J. Dunlavy from Virginia preached in Brown County against slavery from 1790 to 1805. There were six Campbells who came from Virginia in 1796. The sons were Joshua W., Charles, Joseph N., and Samuel—all men of standing.

William Dunlop migrated from Fayette County, Kentucky, to Brown County in 1796, bringing a large number of slaves with him. He set them free and established them on land about three miles north of Ripley. When the Rev. John B. Mahan was kidnapped and taken to Kentucky for trial on the charge of abducting slaves, Mr. Dunlop went on his appearance bond for $1,600 and paid the money rather than have Mahan go back to sure condemnation.

Dr. Alexander Campbell (1769–1857) was a native of Virginia ; began the practice of medicine at Cynthiana, Ky. ; served as representative in the Kentucky General Assembly in 1799-1800 ; favored a free Constitution ; removed to Ripley, Ohio, in 1803, taking with him several slaves and giving them their freedom ; was a member of the Ohio Legislature in 1806, Senator of the United States from 1810 to 1813, and State Senator for the following ten years ; and was always an unwavering immediate abolitionist. In 1835 he was made the first of twenty-one vice-presidents of the Ohio Anti-Slavery Society.

Thomas Morris (1776–1844), a Virginian, removed to Ohio in 1795, resided in Clermont County from about 1800 to the time of his death, was a member of the Ohio Legislature from 1806 to 1830, chief judge of Ohio from 1830 to 1833, Senator of the United States from 1833 to 1839, and during his whole life a sturdy, uncompromising immediate abolitionist. In 1838 he refused to follow his party in its subserviency to slavery and cut loose from it, preferring to sacrifice his office to his principles. His speech in 1839 in opposition to Clay's on abolition was manly and able. In 1840 he was nominated for Vice-President by the Anti-Slavery, then called Liberty, party. Though a Virginian he never owned a slave.

Rev. James Giililand (1769–1845) was born and brought up in South Carolina. His teacher in boyhood was the Rev. William C. Davis of that State, and from him he learned to regard slave-holding as a sin. He was graduated at Dickinson College, Pennsylvania, in 1792, licensed to preach in 1794, and ordained as pastor of the Broadway church in 1796. Twelve members of the congregation presented to the presbytery a remonstrance against his ordination, charging him with preaching "against the Government." This he denied. He admitted, however, that he had preached against the sin of slavery both before and after his call to the Broadway church. The case was taken by him to the synod on appeal. A minute of that body, at its session of November, 1796, is in these words:

"A memorial was brought forward and laid before the synod by the Rev. James Gilliland, stating his conscientious difficulties in recognizing the advice of the Presbytery of South Carolina, which has enjoined upon him to be silent in the pulpit on the subject of the emancipation of the Africans, which injunction Mr. Gilliland declares to be in his apprehension contrary to the counsel of God. Whereupon synod, after deliberation upon the matter, do concur with the presbytery in advising Mr. Gilliland to content himself with using his utmost endeavors in private to open the way for emancipation so as to secure our happiness as a people, preserve the peace of the Church, and render them (the slaves) capable of enjoying the blessings of liberty. Synod is of the opinion that to preach publicly against slavery in present circumstances and to lay down as the duty of every one to liberate those who are under their care is that which would lead to disorder and open the way to great confusion." (See 4, Sprague's "Annals of the American Pulpit," page 137.)

Mr. Gilliland obeyed the mandate of his Church until 1804, not ceasing meanwhile his private teachings against slavery. Unable to endure longer the restrictions placed upon him, he resigned his pastorship, took his credentials to Washington Presbytery, and traveled West in search of a free pulpit. Hearing of the state of opinion in Brown County, Ohio, he went there in 1805, and was the pastor of Red Oak church for thirty-nine years. During all that time he preached the doctrine of immediate abolition without dilution. About 1820 he published a pamphlet, setting it forth in the form of dialogue. His church, made up in great part of ex-slave-holders and immigrants from slave States, including South Carolina, adhered to him, and the four Presbyterian churches of Ripley, Russellville, Decatur, and Georgetown, known through Ohio for their stalwart abolitionism, were offshoots from the one at Red Oak. That the Rev. Mr. Gilliland, during his whole term as the pastor of Red Oak, often preached abolition and always "immediatism" is a Brown County tradition, and the fact would be testified to by every old resident. In a letter to me of May 2, 1884, one of his sons writes that his father was preaching immediate abolition before Garrison was born. Of the thirteen children of Mr. Gilliland one is a clergyman and two are lawyers. Like most abolitionists of Southern origin Mr. Gilliland was an advocate of political action against slavery and voted the Liberty party ticket. He was an effective speaker and a good man and the membership of his church was large. From 1805 to 1822 he was the recognized abolition leader in southern Ohio. In 1835 he was placed second on a list of twenty-one vice-presidents of the Ohio Anti-Slavery Society.

In 1806 the Rev. William Williamson moved from South Carolina to Adams County, Ohio, bringing his slaves with him and emancipating them. He sent the younger ones to school; to two of them he gave a liberal education. One of these, Benjamin Templeton, studied theology and was licensed to preach by the Chilicothe Presbytery.

In the same year Colonel Thomas Means moved from South Carolina to Adams County. He was a man of wealth, had many slaves, freed them all, taught them to read and write, and was true as steel to the cause of liberty.

Thomas Kirker left Kentucky in 1806 to escape the evils of slavery. He settled in Adams County, and in time became Governor of Ohio. He and Messrs. Williamson and Means were members of Dyer Burgess's church. Colonel Means was an elder. Governor Kirker had five sons: William, John, James, Thomas, and George. All of them became respectable citizens.

Rev. Jesse Lockhart migrated from Tennessee to Brown County, and was for forty years pastor of the Presbyterian church at Russellville. He was a zealous coadjutor in the anti-slavery work of Gilliland, Williamson, Dyer Burgess, Dr. Campbell, and others, up to 1822, and after that date of those named and of Messrs. Rankin and Gilmer. Under the pro-slavery violence of Jackson's Administration he faced several mobs with courage.

In 1810 the four McCoys (John, William, George, and James) were added to the Brown County list of heroes, and in 1811 Robert Miller came in from Kentucky with the Menaughs, John and William.

At the very time Mr. Birney was opposing the Kentucky Assembly joint resolutions for recaption of slaves, Samuel Grist, of Virginia, was purchasing two large tracts of land in Brown County, Ohio, with a view to making homes there for one thousand slaves. He brought them on a few months afterward, gave them farms, farming implements, and stock, superintended their settlement, and remained ever after their fast friend. He became poor for conscience' sake. (See Harrison's "History of Ohio," page 100.)

It would give me pleasure to add accounts of the Hopkinses, Salsburys, Snedigers, Dickeys, and Kirkpatricks, who belonged to this band of Christian workers, but my space and plan will not permit. All whose names I have mentioned were immediate abolitionists—unmitigated, pure, zealous, and efficient. They were ever ready to give food, shelter, and aid to fugitive slaves, and before 1817 they had forwarded to Canada, through trustworthy friends, more than one thousand of this wretched class, besides finding elsewhere safe homes and work for many others. They were all Presbyterians and nearly all emigrants from slave States, and the record of their disinterested benevolence is one of the noblest that belongs to the history of Southern society.

APPENDIX F.

THE chief writings of Mr. Birney were as follows :

1. *Ten letters on Slavery and Colonization*, addressed to R. R. Gurley, the first dated July 12, 1832, the last December 11, 1833.

2. *Six essays on same*, published in the Huntsville, Ala., *Advocate* in May, June, and July, 1833.

3. *Letter on Colonization*, resigning vice-presidency of Kentucky Colonization Society, July 15, 1834.

4. *Letters to Presbyterian Church*, 1834.

5. *Addresses and Speeches*, 1835.

6. *Vindication of the Abolitionists*, 1835.

7. *The Philanthropist*, a weekly newspaper, 1836, and to September, 1837.

8. *Letter to Colonel Stone*, May, 1836.

9. *Address to Slave-holders*, October, 1836.

10. *Argument on Fugitive Slave Case*, 1837.

11. *Letter to F. H. Elmore*, of South Carolina, 1838.

12. *Political Obligations of Abolitionists*, 1839.

13. *Report on the Duty of Political Action*, for Executive Committee of the American Anti-Slavery Society, May, 1839.

14. *American Churches the Bulwarks of American Slavery*, 1840.

15. *Speeches in England*, 1840.

16. *Letter of Acceptance.*

17. *Articles in Quarterly Anti-Slavery Magazine and in the Emancipator*, 1837-1844.

18. *Examination of the Decision of the United States Supreme Court* in the case of Strader *et al.*, *vs.* Graham, 1850.

INDEX.

THE END.